Dimitrios Buhalis
Walter Schertler (eds.)

Information and Communication Technologies in Tourism 1999

Proceedings of the International Conference
in Innsbruck, Austria,
1999

SpringerWienNewYork

Dr. Dimitrios Buhalis
Department of Tourism
University of Westminster, London, U.K.

Univ.-Prof. Dr. Walter Schertler
Europäisches Tourismus Institut GmbH
Universität Trier, Trier, Federal Republic of Germany

Printed in Austria

Printed by Novographic, Ing. Wolfgang Schmid, A-1230 Wien
Graphic design: Ecke Bonk
Printed on acid-free and chlorine-free bleached paper
SPIN 10710584

With 66 Figures

ISBN 3-211-83258-0 Springer-Verlag Wien New York

Preface

During the last couple of years we learned that information and communication technologies have to be seen as key factors for the success in various industries. Especially in tourism it became evident, that missing the developments in this sector could not only be fatal for the unfolding of the businesses, but also unrenouncable in order to withstand in competition.

The objective of ENTER is to show the chance that information technology offers for all participants in the touristic competition to act successfully in permanently changing information environments. It reflects the important role of information technologies in this field.

Within the last six years ENTER united various experts – practitioners as well as researchers – to exchange their experiences, ideas and visions in the sector of tourism and information technology. The conferences scope is to provide an international platform to discuss the topical situation and future trends, and the possibilities to shape the own strategies. The various points of view of all the participants in workshops, reports and discussions always lead to most interesting perceptions.

As a result and to follow up the last years analyses there are almost 40 papers featured in the proceedings for ENTER 1999. For this year there are the following eight main topics on which discussions, workshops and reports concentrate:

- *Knowledge management in tourism:* which are the strategic opportunities the internet provides for the travel industry?;
- *changing consumer behaviour through information technology:* how can the consumer participate on the touristic supply?;
- *using IT to support consumer choice and skills:* what are the advantages in the use of IT to support consumer demands?;
- *engineering tourism applications*: the technical components of consumer support;
- *the empowerment of small and medium enterprises through IT:* how does IT influence the competition of small and medium sized enterprises in tourism?;
- *using IT for hospitality management:* effects of the IT implementation in the hospitality industry;
- *using IT to redesign travel distributions and destination marketing systems and IT developments:* new paradigms in the marketing of destinations because of IT.

All articles in this book refer to one or the other theme. The emphasis in this year's discussions lies on the strategic components more than on the technical issues.

We'd like to thank all authors and all the colleagues who helped us to audit the abstracts and to evaluate the final papers for their participation. We additionally want to express our thanks to Silvia Schilgerius's of Springer-Verlag and last not least we want to thank Arne Schulke for his support and Eva-Britt Schulz for her patience and for the great job she has done helping us to edit the proceedings in a form which helps the ENTER conference to be an attractive platform for science.

Dimitrios Buhalis
Walter Schertler

Contents

6 Using IT for Hospitality Management

7 Using IT to Redesign Travel Distribution

8 Destination Marketing Systems and IT Developments

Index of Authors

Program Committee and Chairs

6th International Conference on
Information and Communication Technologies in Tourism

Applied Track Chairs

DENNIS, Peter	The Time Communications Group
CARTER, Roger	Napier University
RAFFERTY, John	Irish Tourist Board

Scientific Track Chairs

BUHALIS, Dimitrios	University of Westminster, UK
SCHERTLER, Walter	University of Trier, Germany

Local Host Committee

LAMP, Georg	Congress Innsbruck GmbH, Austria
MARGREITER, Josef	Tyrolean Tourist Board

Members

AANONSEN, Kari	Braathens Airlines, Norway
ARCHDALE, Gilbert	ASW Consulting, UK
BECHEREL, Lionel	Tourism Consultant, UK
BEDARD, Francois	Université du Quèbec, Montreal, Canada
BENTLEY, Robert	Travel Tech, Spain
DANIELE, Roberto	RMIT, Australia
EBNER, Arno	TIS, Austria
FESENMAIER, Daniel	University of Illinois, USA
FRANK, Klaus	University of Worms, Germany
FREW, Andrew	Napier University, UK
GO, Frank	Erasmus University, The Netherlands
JAFARI, Jafar	University of Wisconsin, USA
KÄRCHER, Karsten	Imminus, UK
KLEIN, Stefan	Muenster University, Germany
KUBICEK, Herbert	University of Bremen, Germany
LANFRANCO, Sam	York University, Canada
LIPMAN, Geoffrey	World Travel & Tourism Council, UK
MAIN, Hilary	Swansea Institute, UK
MATA-MONTERO, Erick	Instituto Tecnologico de Costa Rica
MINGHETTI, Valeria	CISET-University of Venice, Italy
MEIJS, Chris	Wageningen Agricultural University, The Netherlands

O'CONNOR, Peter	Institut de Management Hotelier Intern., France
POLLOCK, Anna	The Pembridge Group, UK
PRESS, Larry	University of California, USA
REVELL, Norman	Middlesex University, UK
SHELDON, Pailine	University of Hawaii, USA
STOCK, Oliviero	Istituto per la Ricerca Scientifica e Tecnologica, Italy
TJOA, A Min	Vienna University of Technology, Austria
VAN DER PIJL, John	Tilburg University, The Netherlands
VAN HOOF, Hubert	Northern Arizona University, USA
VENEMA, Magiel	NHTV, The Netherlands
WAGNER, Roland	University of Linz, Austria
WERTHNER, Hannes	University of Vienna, Austria
WOEBER, Karl	Vienna University of Economics, Austria

Using Data Mining in Analysing Local Tourism Patterns

G.Tichler, W.Grossmann, H.Werthner
Dept. of Statistic, Operations Research and Computer Methods
University of Vienna
g.tichler@gmx.net

Abstract

Data Mining is a growing discipline in data analysis, linking data management with statistical methods. Discovering new patterns or assuring behaviour that has been observed over the years is a central information for a company or an organisation. This is especially true for the field of tourism, where great volumes of data are collected, but not often analysed in depth. The paper presents an application of several techniques used in the field of Data Mining on the "Tux-database" of the tourism resort Tux in Tyrol, Austria. This database is based on the entities of the registration sheets in this tourism resort. Times series models of seasonal decomposition as well as simple descriptive procedures were used to detect primary pattern. In a second step explorative multivariate statistical techniques such as clustering, log-linear models and decision trees were applied to underline the primary results and to discover new ones.

Keywords: Data Mining, Knowledge Discovery, Arrival patterns

1 Introduction

Many different works concentrate on the behaviour of tourists in Austria in order to identify find some specific pattern [1]. Nevertheless only few papers deal with the analysis of registration sheets (Meldezettel), which are collected by every overnight facility for every incoming tourist. A summary report for all regions, federal states and the entire Austria deriving from these data are presented every month by the „central statistical office“ in Vienna [2]. These summaries only contain the volume of arrivals and length of stay, differentiated with respect to categories of accommodations and countries of origin, but not an in-depth analysis of all data, which are collected in a registration sheet. This paper focuses on an analysis, which subsumes techniques under the name Data Mining, of all variables, which are available in the registration sheets for the community of Tux in Tyrol. The resort of Tux consists of three main zones, which are also identified separately: the village, the glacier region and the area between those two.

Data Mining is an overall term for the procedure of the selection, transformation and analysis of data to discover hidden information. It is described as a procedure, which is often also called knowledge discovery in Databases, as the "non-trivial process of identifying valid, novel, potentially useful and ultimately understandable patterns in data" [3]. Since its early beginnings many companies have developed special software packages to cover the whole process. This paper will not refer to any of these packages, but go through all required steps, beginning with the data collection and ending with the final analysis. In the next section the approach how data were collected, transformed and grouped into a single datasheet, is necessary for an effective analysis, is described. This is followed by the descriptive and explorative data analysis in order to discover new patterns. The final conclusion will sum up the obtained results and give an outlook to further work.

2 Data Preparation

2.1 Datasheet Construction

The data were collected using a software product based on the relational database Informix. All data were locally managed, and periodically stored in different back-up files. Data in the form of records were related by primary keys consisting of the registration sheet number and the date of arrival. The static information about the different accommodations such as location or accommodation category were stored in static files. In order to analyse these data they had to be transformed using a single relational database. Its Entity-Relationship diagram corresponds to the relationships between the different back-up files.

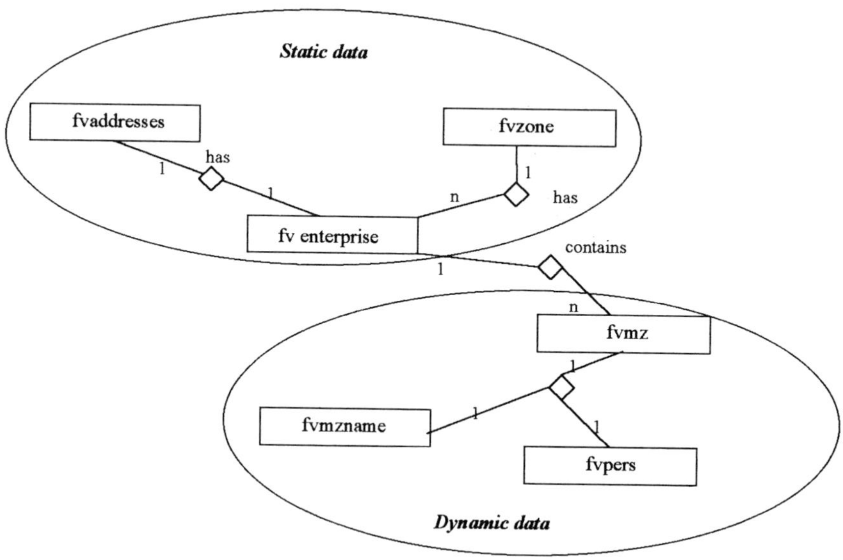

Fig. 1: Entity-Relationship diagram describing the back-up files

In order to insure date privacy - in agreement with the tourism office of Tux - information such as tourist names or bank accounts of accommodations was deleted. This resulted into 267.000 records, describing the registration sheets.

A screening of the data showed that only approx. 30 % of the tuples contained information regarding the sex, number of arriving adults or/and number children. The variable postal code was just available in 62 % of the entities and the variable age in 80 %. All the other important variables related to tourists like arrival and departure date or provenience country had more than 99 % coverage. In a following step the different relations of the database were mapped onto a single datasheet, relating dynamic data about tourist arrivals with static data describing accommodations. It included the variables: arrival and departure date, age of person filling out the registration, amount of person arriving, country of origin, postal code, accommodation code, accommodation category and zone code.

2.2 Cleaning and Transforming the Datasheet

The obtained datasheet was used for further transformation steps. The variable arriving date was split up into four variables: the day, the week, the month and the year. Then by subtracting the birthday from the arrival day the age of the incoming tourist was calculated. Subtracting the arrival date from the departure date created the variable "stays". These new variables were then analysed on input failures. Surprisingly there was just three registration sheets that had wrong arriving date inputs. After cleaning these input failures a second transformation of variables was done to group some special variables like the county of origin into six groups or the year and month variables into seasonal groups, as it was discussed with the tourism office of Tux. The final datasheet, used for the subsequent descriptive and explorative analysis, contained 218.000 tuples (80%). Table 1 shows all variables from the datasheet and their domain.

datasheet

variable name	*intervall*
year	Nov.1992-Okt1997
month	1-12
week	1-52
day	1-7
country	1-6
postal code	only for germany
age	1-100
group-size	1-100
zone	1-3
accomod-cat.	1-3
# of overnights	1-1000

Table 1: Variables of the datasheet

3 Descriptive Analysis

The first analysis concentrated on a time series analysis of arrival patterns, covering five years. Therefore a seasonal decomposition procedure as written in equation 3.1 was used to separate the existing seasonal factor of every year from the time series [4].

$$\text{Variable} = \text{trend component} * \text{seasonal component} * \text{error component} \tag{3.1}$$

Plotting the seasonal adjusted variable over the observation period and calculating a linear regression with gives a slope of 0,03 and a correlation coefficient 0,015. These two index numbers underline the assumption that no general trend can be observed over the five years. Nevertheless this result is not valid for all the other variables of the datasheet. An analysis of the other transformed arrival variables brings no further information. There are more arrivals in the autumn (Oct. - Dec.) and less in the winter (Feb. - Apr). Figure 2 shows the yearly behaviour for the variable arrival day. It demonstrates the different performance of weekdays (Mon-Fri) and weekend arrivals. The arrival distribution during the week is slightly higher in autumn; and the one of the weekends is centred in the winter period.

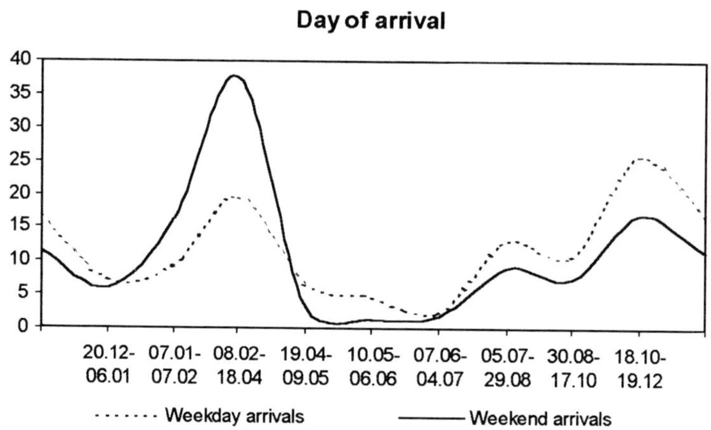

Fig. 2: Distribution of the grouped variable day over the five years

Of importance is the variable season, which divides the year into nine periods. These periods represent the different price levels and give a better overview of the arrival distribution. Comparing the grouped day variable with the seasonal factor over the five years results into a change in the arrival patterns of tourists: it shifts from weekends to arrivals during the week.

As first variable, specific for an individual tourist, the country of origin was analysed. It was divided into six groups: Austria; Germany; Switzerland and the Netherlands; eastern European countries; other European countries; and the other countries. Germany represents 80% of all arrivals. This would imply a further decomposition of Germany, e.g., into four regions. However, since postal codes were not widely available, this couldn't be done. The other groups show a contradictory behaviour. All eastern European countries have a growing tendency, with a correlation coefficient of 35% over the five years. The other countries - apart from Austria, which shows a slight increase of arrivals in the autumn and decrease in the winter - have a highly declining trend. An important result is that tourists from Switzerland and the Netherlands visit Tux in the winter period (more than 70%). The group "other European countries" is responsible for the small peak in and around august. All the other countries have two peaks in autumn and winter.

The second tourist specific variable refers to his age. The variable was divided into four and five age classes. The "best" result could be obtained with a five-class grouping: under 26, between 26 and 35, 36 to 45, 46 to 55 and over 55 years. Plotting these five groups over the observation period shows a contradictory behaviour. The younger groups are declining and the older ones are growing. Especially important is the result of the group with the tourists over 55 and fewer than 26 years. In the first case the correlation coefficient is 0,42 and has a slope of 2,4, in the second one there is a negative correlation with a negative slope. These estimators are the results from the seasonal adjusted time series age over time.

As next variable the group size was analysed. All groups which are bigger than 2 persons represent a minority. In total they represent only 15% of all entities. Due to that a division of the variables into three groups was done. They represent 1, 2 and >2 persons arriving. A cross tabulation of the variable age and group size shows that most of the younger tourist come on their own, tourists between 36 and 55 years arrive in bigger groups and the elderly with more than 55 years arrive in pairs. This is shown in the following table.

Distribution of age of arriving tourists - over one year

	<26	26-35	36-45	46-55	>55
1 Pers	57	39	26	23	31
2 Pers	34	45	40	53	51
More than 2 Pers	9	16	35	25	19

Table 2: Cross-tabulation between age and group size

The cross-tabulation between country groups and age shows that the majority of tourists from eastern European countries are in the age group of 36 - 45 years.

The two location variables, the resort zone and the accommodation category, show no mayor changes over the five years of observation. Just the high segment accommodations, such as four and five star hotels, grow in their volume of incoming tourist, but at the losses of the second category class, which subsumes the middle class accommodations. But these two accommodation variables are nearly independent from the three tourists specific ones, except of age and zone. The following cross-validation between the age and the zone shows that the growing elderly class prefers the zone village, with its specific character. This result is shown in the table 3.

Distribution of age in the different zones -over one year

Zone	*<26*	*26-35*	*36-45*	*46-55*	*>55*
glacier region	8	30	26	10	26
area between	12	34	20	10	24
village	10	31	23	10	27

Table 3: Cross-validation between resort zone and age in percent over one year

As last variable the length of stay was looked at. It was subdivided into four classes: < 4, 4 to 6, 7 and >7 days. The time series analysis of these four groups, with a seasonal decomposition, brought no significant trend. Just the group of short vacations, which are those with a duration below 4 days, could gain a little bit. In statistical terms the correlation coefficient is 0,341. A cross-tabulation with the variable arrival day shows some significant arrival behaviour. In 80% of all the cases the arrival day plus the variable stays equals Saturday or Sunday. So either tourists come for a whole week or for a longer weekend but they all go back on Saturdays or Sundays. Table 4 shows this behaviour.

days	Mon	Tue	Wed	Thu	Fri	Sat	Sun
<4	6,2	5,7	10,1	20,0	30,7	18,1	9,2
4-6	12,4	8,7	16,1	8,3	9,7	18,8	26,1
7	2,0	1,5	2,3	1,7	4,2	75,5	12,8
>7	7,2	5,0	7,8	8,5	14,0	39,5	17,9

Table 4: Validation of the variable length of stay and arrival day

The analysis of the country groups in relationship to duration shows that the eastern European country group is mainly staying less than seven days, mainly for a longer weekend. A further discussion of the different country groups depending on several other variables will be made in section 3.2.2. The comparison of the four "stays" classes in the different zones and accommodation categories brings an intuitively logical behaviour. All those tourists, who just stay for a maximum of three days or between 4 and 6 days, like to be in an accommodation, which is near the skiing area, the glacier zone. The others prefer the zone village where they have more possibilities.

4 Explorative Analysis

The descriptive analysis of the previous chapter, though uncovering interesting information, only contained relationships between two variables. In contrast, multivariate statistical techniques enable the analysis of more than two variables at the same time. This paper concentrates on the use of grouping and classification techniques and linear relationships with one dependent and several independent variables.

4.1 Pattern Searching

One of the fastest and most popular applications of multivariate analysis is the use of factor- and cluster-analysis to group variables into factors. A four-group classification can be obtained by taking all variables of the datasheet (table 1), excluding the two variables month and week, standardising them between -1 and 1 and applying the principle component analysis. These four factors are represented in the Table 5 with a possible factor-name for each of them.

Factor 1	Age, number of overnights, arrival day
Factor 2	Country of origin, group size
Factor 3	Zone
Factor 4	Season

Table 5: Four factors obtained from the factor analysis

Calculating with the same variables using a hierarchical cluster algorithm with the nearest neighbour method reveals nearly the same result. The only difference is that the season-factor does not represent a group.

4.2 Dependence Relationships

After grouping the variables it is important to obtain dependency models for a better target segmentation of the incoming tourists. The first approach uses decision trees, followed by a discriminant and a log-linear model, and finishes with a neural network.

4.2.1 Tree Models

All results are the outcome of the CART-procedure, which is implemented in S+ [5]. The decision, which variable should be the dependent in the model, is based on the descriptive analysis and the hypothesis formulated by the local tourist office. There are three important variables to consider. The first is the season, the second the country of origin and the third the length of stay. Let us consider the variable season first. The most important variable in this context is "length of stay", which divides the tree into two branches: short stays (<7) and long stays (>6 days). For the latter a further partition exists, the zone within Tux. Looking at the zone "village", the variable age (<45, > 44) produces two additional subgroups.

The second variable, the country of origin is mainly dependent on the season in which tourists arrive. This was already shown by the descriptive analysis. However, the result obtained from the cluster analysis could not be confirmed where countries are grouped within one factor containing also the number of arriving tourists.

As the last dependent variable the length of stay was taken. According to the result of the descriptive analysis as well as intuition, it depends firstly on the arrival day, which was shown in Table 3. For those who stay longer the season is of importance as is the age. For tourist groups with shorter duration, a division into the respective age classes can be observed. For younger people the season, whereas for older tourists the zone is more important.

4.2.2 Discriminant and Log-linear Models

Discriminant analysis and log-linear model represents another possibility for the analysis of dependent variables. Following the request of the tourist board an analysis the number of overnights had to be considered. Therefore equation (2) was used for the log-linear model as well as for the discriminant analysis.

$$\text{Log(length of stay)} = \text{daygr*season*agegr*kat} \tag{2}$$

The discriminant analysis showed the variable "length of stay" is grouped into 4 classes, mainly depend on the arrival day and on the season. The two other variables are less important. Figure 3 shows the graphic result of the discriminant analysis. But it has to be mentioned that the overall classification was only 45%. A better result would be generated if we divide the variable "length of stay" into only 2 groups. In this case a classification of more than 70% could be obtained. The log-linear model was calculated by dividing the dependent variable into two groups with more than six days and equal or less than 6 days of overnights. This produced the best results. This result can be compared with table 4 where it can be seen that weekend arrivals fit much better with the higher longer overnight numbers than the shorter overnights with arrivals during the week.

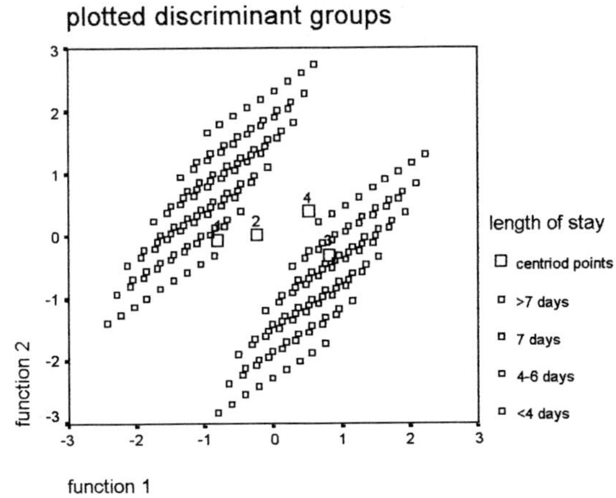

Fig. 3: Discriminant groups

4.2.3 Neural Networks

The last procedure used was a feed-forward neural network. It is a flexible way to generalise linear regression functions. The algorithm was proposed by Ripley as a "fit feed-forward neural network with a single hidden layer but allowing skip-layer connections" [6]. In this specific context the neural network was used to compare its results with those obtained by classic statistical procedures.

The model for the neural network was chosen with two hidden units, a weight decay of 1e-3 in order to avoid overfitting [6], and a maximum of 1000 iterations. The following figure shows the network.

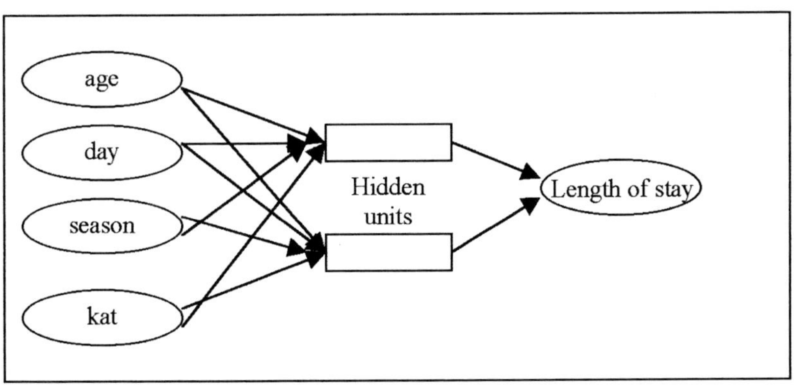

Fig. 4: The neural network model

This analysis showed that the neural network produced better results in 5% of the cases compared with the results obtained by the discriminant analysis.

5 Conclusion

The most important result for the tourist board of Tux could already be obtained by applying rather simple descriptive analysis methods. But also the multivariate methods produced valuable information for the tourist board. Especially the decision tree approach produced - in a fast way - useful results, which could also be confirmed by the other multivariate procedures.

The tourists of Tux are becoming older. Germany holds the dominant position with 80% of all arrivals. Although the eastern European countries hold just 3%, it is the fastest growing customer segment. The general trend shows that tourists stay for a shorter period, with a rising autumn season. The summer season represents the biggest challenge for the resort, especially to loosen its dependency from winter tourism. The region itself is a sport-"paradise" for younger tourist, and for the older one a place to relax. However, it is not a place where families will go.

On a methodological level several improvements could be envisaged:

- number of recurring tourist, e.g., by appropriate coding of the names of tourists,
- inclusion of information about the sex, by completely filling out the registration forms.

References:

1. Weiermair, K.: Austria's Tourism Development from 1992-1995: Cyclical or Sructural Changes?, in Vellas, F. (eds.): An Encyclopedia of International Tourism, I. Tourism Trends in Western, Europe, Paris (1995).
2. Tourismus in Österreich, Österreichisches Statistisches Zentralamt (ÖSTAT), Wien (1997).
3. Fayyad, U., Piatetsky-Shapiro, G.: Advances in Knowledge Discovery and Data Mining. MIT Press (1996).
4. Chatfield, C.: The analysis of time series, an introduction. Fifth Edition. Chapmann & Hall (1996).
5. Chambers, J.M., Hasty, T.J.: Statistical Modeling in S. Chapmann & Hall (1991).
6. Ripley, B.D., Venables, W.N.: Modern applied statistics with S-PLUS. Springer (1996).

Towards interactive tourism: capitalising on virtual and physical value chains

Frank M. Go
Professor and chairman of the Centre for Tourism Management,
Rotterdam School of Management,
Erasmus University, Netherlands.

Robert Govers
Consultant / project manager contract research with the Centre for Tourism Management of the Rotterdam School of management,
Erasmus University, Netherlands.

Mark van den Heuvel
Lecturer at the Department of Leisure Sciences,
Tilburg University, Netherlands.

Abstract

The global development of recreation has lead to global brands and standardised products. Standardised recreation products neither capitalise on the uniqueness of place, nor the 'mass-customisation' market trend.

This paper analyses the peculiarities of the recreation and tourism sector. It suggests the value- chain/network approach as a means of regional co-operation and investment in innovation in order to achieve three objectives: product differentiation, integrated quality and chain optimisation. And proposes that for the theoretical design to be realised, various critical success factors must be met at the aforementioned three levels.

The present paper examines the potential application of the recreation chain approach in rural regions. Specifically, the focus will be on Brabant, one of the provinces in the Netherlands. It concludes with the observation that the implementation of the design is only feasible if one possesses the required knowledge about chains and knowledge in chains.

Key words: innovation, recreation, tourism, sustainable development, value chain, network, competition, and co-operation.

1 Introduction

Recreation and tourism represent an increasingly important economic sector in many nations. At the same time the sector may be classified as problematic in nature. In particular, the recreation and tourism sector comprises of a small number of large enterprises and a large number of small businesses. Put differently, the sector is highly fragmented and most entrepreneurs in the sector find it very difficult to cope with issues such as 'mass-customisation', increasing competition, the rise in rules and regulations imposed by government, for example with regard to the physical environment, and, paradoxically, the 'retreating' role of government, for instance in connection with subsidies. Competition, especially through the influence of international market penetration, increases the number of suppliers and reduces profitability margins. It also offers consumers more choice and allows consumers to assess goods and services against the benchmarks set in other industries that have been able to successfully apply advanced technology to achieve important improvements in quality.

During the post-war period significant branches of the recreation and tourism industry, such as parks, museums, and cultural festivals and events evolved with the support of government subsidies. This approach resulted in a product-based orientation amongst institutions and entrepreneurs alike. Presently, governments across Europe are 'in retreat', which implies that subsidies are in decline and entrepreneurs have to deal with the market forces. During the product-based era, institutions built on the notion that consumers would beat a path to their door and seize each opportunity as it came. Today, however, it is essential to shift operation to a value-based approach of operation. Last but not least, there is mounting public pressure to preserve the physical environment in many jurisdictions around the world. For example, in the Netherlands there is pressure on the government to strictly maintain the quota of the number of passenger arrivals and departures at Schiphol International Airport.

It is essential to observe and explain the potential impact of the aforementioned issues on the recreation and tourism sector. From a managerial perspective one might refer to such approach as "outside-inside" or an "Porterian" orientation, based on the work of Porter (1990), who places a premium on how macro forces and particularly the competitive environment influences the business strategy of institutions on the meso-level. The next step would be to consider what steps the recreation and tourism sector might take to capitalise on the aforementioned issues. Put differently, the question arises how an institution might transform potential threats into opportunities? Such management orientation could be coined "Peterian", because Peters' (1987) analytical perspective typically flows from the "inside-out" and from meso to macro-level. Traditionally, industrialists have increased productivity and profitability, largely through economies of scale. While the advancement of management thought greatly influenced both the thinking and practice in manufacturing, the theories espoused by a 'mixed bag' of social scientists seemed irrelevant to the recreation and tourism sector.

The recreation and tourism sector is presently in a period of transition. The twin forces of globalisation and technological innovation have put considerable pressure on institutions in the recreation and tourism sector to achieve advances by moving to new products and new processes (Go and Govers, 1997). As a consequence of these developments, the trend toward more concentration is gathering momentum in the recreation and tourism sector through mergers, acquisitions and joint ventures, both nationally and internationally. The growing concentration of corporate power in the hands of fewer companies has lead to more capital intensity and caused intense competition.

In response, most entrepreneurs have adopted a militaristic perspective on competition. However, such perspective is inappropriate for competing in today's marketplace, where flexibility is at a premium, and potentially restricts the performance of firms as well as the sector in which they operate. (Park and Smith, 1986) In particular, a militaristic perspective on competition fails to address one of the important issues: How can all players in the sector co-operate so that customers get the sum of good ideas that producers and intermediaries generate? Under an alternative perspective, which is based on inter-as well as intra-industry learning, a growing number of competitors in the sector have begun to co-operate in networks to ensure their individual survival.

The driving force behind organisational adjustments to new approaches, methods and orientations to fit the needs of the task environment is survival in the market through competitive differentiation. The opportunities for achieving competitiveness diminish as corporations exhaust the alternatives or duplicate the work of rivals, resulting in heightened competition and less opportunities for differentiation. In either case, an individual entrepreneur seeking a competitive differentiation has to make a major, risky and expensive change (Hickman and Silva, 1987:7).

Another challenge for the industry is the growing individualisation and market power of the consumer. Consumers are being increasingly demanding and versatile. Consumer needs and wants change over time and place, and therefore consumer behaviours are altering fast. It seems almost impossible to retain consumers in the straightjackets of segmentations based on sex, age or social class. Therefore the standardised product lines of rigid packaged holidays offered by most tour operators are no longer a basis for creating competitive strength, not even when offered at rock bottom prices. As Bloch et al (1996: 2) state: "Consumers wish more frequent, but shorter travel, last minute reservations, global advice, service quality, market transparency, and a certain self-service mentality – e.g. 'modern' travellers begin to gather recreational micro-services on their own and form their customised holiday package. This leads to an elimination of non value-adding stages (...but particularly non value-adding players...) in the tourist service systems".

What is needed is tailor-made travel, customisation and modular design of travel services. Transforming toward more flexible structures and strategies is therefore a profound urgency for the travel and tourism industry. Such flexibilisation is the best approach in the struggle to attract and retain the individualised customer. Dutch consumer surveys show that the percentage of travellers that book either their transport or accommodation or both through a travel agency or tour operator is still growing (NIPO, 1996). This means that the market share of DIY (do-it-yourself)-travellers is decreasing. However, research also shows that this decrease in self-reliance is accompanied by an increase in the flexibility of the composition of travel services and packages. More and more modular products are being offered, in which micro-services are combined in a flexible way, to create the possibility for consumers to assemble their own package according to their individual preferences. The travellers themselves decide on when they want to travel, by which means of transport, when they want to undertake only those activities that they are interested in and which parts of their holiday they will organise themselves. All these challenges call for dramatic changes in the tourism value chain

2 Mass customisation

What is needed in the travel and tourism industry is an evolution (or revolution if you like) towards mass customisation. This concept, with Pine (1993) of the Harvard Business School as the spiritual father, recognises that in today's turbulent business environment mass production no longer works. As Joseph Pine makes clear, the most innovative companies are rapidly embracing a new paradigm of management - mass customisation - which allows them the freedom to create greater variety and individuality in their products and services at desirable prices. In the automotive industry this concept has been very successful for years now. Some of the characteristics discussed by Boynton, Victor and Pine (1993: 49) are easily applicable to the travel and tourism industry. First of all, mass customisation creates the opportunity to deal with constant, unpredictable changes in market demand. As travellers wish more frequent, but shorter travel, last minute reservations, and ever changing individualised holiday experiences, one would conclude that the so-called market turbulence in this industry is ever increasing. Second, mass customisation utilises a wide variety of specific value chains tailored to the individual product or customer. This means that mass production and stockpiles of standardised package deals are no longer sufficient. What is needed is the ability to react fast to changing consumer demands. Therefore the product should be assembled only after the customers have expressed their preferences and demands. As a result of that, another bedrock for mass customisation, is the use of loosely linked dynamic networks of players involved in the production and assembly of the product or service on offer. This creates the possibility to construct modular products in a flexible way, by dynamically linking various players in the network to create customised value chains. Different players or nodes in the network are specialised in just one or few of the micro-services (accommodation, transport, entertainment, insurance, etc.) that collectively comprise the total holiday experience. Lastly, the use of contemporary ICT is vital in all of this. Communication has to be impeccable and fully integrated with the dynamic network. Integration and flexible assembly of travel services that are tailored to the consumer can only be realised with the use of innovative technologies, computerisation and telecommunication. At the moment tour operators and travel agents are offering only few modular tour packages, because they are assessed as being too expensive. Communication costs are relatively high, because with every booking and change in package structure, service providers at the destination have to be contacted by phone, leading to a significant increase in billing by the Telephone Company. However, with the introduction of the electronic highway and new ICT-applications such as e-mail, this should be history.

Looking at individualisation, the more demanding and versatile consumer, the ever-changing needs and preferences of customers, the tourism industry often replies with more choices and thicker brochures. But as Pine et al (1995: 103) state: "customers...do not want more choices. They know exactly what they want – when, where, and how they want it – and technology now makes it possible for companies to give it to them". Travellers want the tourism industry to offer the exact product they want to satisfy their specific needs. The system or value chain should be capable of adapting to the specific needs of the individual customer. Then products and services on offer are tailored to the consumer. Mass customisation is a concept that with the use of ICT and dynamic networks deals with the aforementioned issues.

3 Dynamic networks

One of the characteristics of dynamic networks is the broad availability of open information systems. All the members in the network have access to computerised systems that handle the communication and information flows within the network. At the moment the travel and tourism industry with its GDS's is moving in this direction. As explained by Bentley (1996): "technologies first penetrated sector by sector – airlines, hotels, car rentals, travel agencies, now destinations. The second stage is integration of the sectors, which is ongoing...The third stage is delivery of these technologies to the retail trade, also under way. The fourth is integrating the individual consumer into the use of information technology." With the wide availability of Internet into the people's homes in the near future, and the connection of GDS's onto the Internet, this last stage will also be accomplished. These changes in the travel and tourism system will have far reaching effects on some of the players and stages in the value chain. For instance in the presence and roles of intermediaries, which are basic parts of the dynamic network.

Intermediaries have different functions, such as: exploiting economies of scale; marketing of products; matching supply and demand; bearing risk; and reducing the number of communication channels. Van der Heijden (1995) explains this last role of intermediaries, through the application of the network theory. Suppose there were no travel agents nor tour operators in the present tourism value chain. The number of communication channels in that case would be countless. Every consumer would have to communicate with a wide range of travel principles (for instance, hotels, motels, airlines or coach companies), in order to find out what the possibilities are to satisfy their specific needs. This would inevitably lead to an information overload. Such an information overload can be avoided by increasing the information handling capacity of the network. This can be done in two ways. Either by increasing the data handling capacity of the individual players through the use of ICT. Or by changing the structure of the network in a way that intermediaries are largely responsible for taking over most of the information gathering and processing activities of the consumer. Clearly, by constructing tour packages and holiday brochures and by matching the consumer's demand with the wide range of travel services available, most tour operators and travel agents are currently fulfilling this function of information crossway in a still traditional way. But with the introduction of high capacity ICT, the electronic highway and new interactive media, things are rapidly changing. The information handling capacity of the network is increased and therefore new structures arise and new opportunities for alternative product assembly are created. Many of these challenges and opportunities are addressed by relatively new applications of the value chain approach as discussed in the remainder of this paper.

4 Value-chain approach

The Dutch National Council for Agricultural Research report (NRLO, 1997: 4-5) states that the central idea of the value chain approach is that horizontal and vertical harmonisation and co-operation are essential when one seeks to provide the consumer with the demanded quality and desirable assortment of products in an efficient way, and to keep doing so in future. This train of thoughts comes down to:

- Identifying consumer groups, including their needs and wants;
- Reflecting upon the products and services that should be delivered, in which consumer preferences on the one hand and production opportunities on the other, are taken into account;
- Verifying how to yield the products with the largest possible value added;
- Identifying what types of co-operation would be most profitable. This would include co-operation with suppliers and buyers (vertical), as well as co-operation with producers of similar or related products or services (horizontal).

As a result of this process, newly formed value chains and their strategies, could position themselves according to three generic objectives (NRLO, 1997: 28-29):

- Chain differentiation: the uniqueness of the product or service delivered. Chain differentiation is characterised by three key words: innovation-strength, flexibility, and responsiveness, all essential qualities that are needed in order to be able to respond to the highly versatile and superior consumer demands.
- Integrated quality: in the today's competitive arena, reliability is an ever increasingly important issue. In order to satisfy consumer demands for high quality, healthy, safe, durable and environmentally friendly products and services, it is essential to co-operate within the value-chain.
- Chain optimisation: strategic chain objectives could also be formulated in relation to the efficiency and effectiveness of the production process. This involves the optimisation of the mutual coherence of the nodes within the network.

4.1. Toward process innovation

Rising consumer expectations and global competition are pressuring the recreation and tourism sector to manage all activities in the value chain. Such activities may be of a virtual nature (electronic commerce) and of a physical nature (logistics).Based on the lessons learned from manufacturing, the recreation and tourism sector needs to explore process innovation as a means to gain new approaches to old routines. Though product innovations should be added wherever feasible and capital expenditures made wherever a cost/benefit study supports the introduction of a new product, new products, alone, are unlikely to make the recreation and tourism sector a winner in the 21st century. In future, success shall be "owned" by entrepreneurial networks which perform services most effectively and efficiently. Put differently, what used to be secondary - process technology - becomes primary. That change has implications for everything from the educational and training infrastructure to how people are 'fast tracked' in the sector.

The need to apply process innovation in the sector will be driven in particular by the growing problem all over the world in securing competent labour. Since the travel and tourism industry may be classified as a "people-based" as opposed to an "equipment based" sector, it relies heavily on people for its innate abilities. But the shrinking labour pool presents both a challenge and opportunity to explore alternative processes of service delivery to enhance both service quality and productivity improvement. The creation of 'value-added' products requires the intense listening to the 'voice of the customer' to identify market opportunities. To respond to market opportunities effectively requires the mobilisation of the "talent of teams" 'around' the sources of competitive differential that is most likely to propel regional networks ahead of their rivals.

4.2. Value chain

The recreation and tourism sector has been generally slow to adapt to the changing customers needs and expectations and gain a better understanding of other firms as part of the "value chain" (Porter, 1990). The value chain is introduced here because of its merits in recognising that the various recreation and tourism 'vendors' are not neatly separated into hotel firms, transportation carriers, travel agents, and tour operators. Instead they function increasingly within a chain of economic transactions or as a "chain of customers", both internal and external, (Schonberger, 1990) ranging from buyers, to intermediaries and suppliers. This paper introduces the value-chain' paradigm as a means for greater co-operation between entrepreneurs and institutions in the recreation and tourism sector (Borgstein et al 1997; Van Roekel 1997). Such application of the 'value chain approach' in the recreation and tourism sector is based on a number of arguments. In general, it should be observed that the issues which impact the recreation and tourism sector, also affect other sectors and industries, including the agro-business. The latter sector has opted for the application of the value-chain and has been able to successfully implement the value chain model.

First, the application of the value chain allows producers to reverse business processes by thinking and acting with the needs of customers first and foremost in mind. Clearly, such system is customer-driven. Second, co-operation between producers and intermediaries is based on the need to serve the well being of customers. It promotes the cohesion of products and offers the opportunity to design an assortment of products, from which customers select the desired elements. Third, the chain approach enables small enterprises to build 'critical mass', which they require to achieve the required 'market power' and an increase in efficiency, where possible.

Within this context the scale economies with regard to joint purchasing and a joint reservation system for an entire region come to mind. Last but not least may co-operation within chains lead to facilitate the design of possible solutions to problems or the prevention thereof. For example, the successful implementation of the chain approach may attract more visitors and therefore additional traffic, which could lead to traffic congestion. In anticipation of the traffic increases the producers and intermediaries within a chain could jointly design a 'transportation plan', which is used on 'nature transferia'. The latter afford the public to park their vehicles near areas of natural beauty, but sufficiently away from them so as to avoid the desecration and destruction of nature. The nature transferia design includes public transportation to move visitors to the area, which attracted them in the first place. In summary, the value chain model appears to be an appropriate strategy for application in the recreation and tourism sector. But the question arises how to apply such chains' in the recreation and tourism sector. We shall return to this question later.

5 Benchmarking the agro-business

Wierenga (1997) analysed the major changes that are taking place throughout the agribusiness, both on the demand and the supply side. The agro-business complex has opted to pursue 'Value-Adding Partnerships' so as to increase competitiveness and capitalise on 'opportunity share' rather than market share (Hamel and Prahalad 1994:32). Accordingly, from a strategic perspective, the agro-business may provide an appropriate benchmark for the recreation and tourism sector. And from a structural perspective, it is important to observe that the agro-business comprises many small enterprises.

Whilst, such small enterprises have been successfully integrated in chains, it is not the intention of the authors to raise the impression that the example of the agro-business could be copied on a one-on-one basis. There are two major arguments that reason against copying agro-business practices outright. These are first the differences between agro-businesses and tourism and recreation businesses, and second the need to preserve uniqueness of place as an attraction in cultural tourism and the visitation of heritage sites.

5.1. Benchmarking

Benchmarking has been defined as 'a continuous search for and the application of significantly better practices that leads to superior competitive performance (Watson 1993:2). It is possible and desirable to apply the 'benchmarking' technique to help improve the performance and competitiveness of enterprises in the recreation and tourism sector. A quick benchmark review identifies three significant differences between the agro-business and the recreation and tourism sector, namely:
The agro-business aims to transport its products in an efficient manner to customers. Due to the nature of recreation and tourism, which have to be consumed 'in situ', there is a structural difference. Within this framework, the issue of 'mobility' and 'parking' has reached problematic proportions in many European cities and regions and impedes the efficient and pleasant access of attractions, special events and festivals. A second point of comparison that should be addressed concerns the 'combination possibilities' of products. Whereas in the agro-business chain it is full well possible to offer most products in one and the same place, it is more difficult to do so in the recreation and tourism sector, due to the 'touring' or dynamic element of the business. A final point is that, in general, the market offerings that are produced within the recreation and tourism sector are based on two foundations, namely nature and culture. Both nature and culture are classified as 'public goods' and are 'magnets' that 'pull' visitors to specific destinations. Therefore, many times, the heart of the tourism and recreation product consists of public goods, while agricultural products are fully tradable objects.
There may be many other differences between the agro-business and the recreation and tourism sector that could be cited. However, the intention of the authors is to note that one should not imitate, without any reflection, ideas from the agro-business environment for application in the recreation and tourism sector, rather than offer an exhaustive list of examples.

5.2. Preserving uniqueness of place

Attractions in destinations are at the core of most tourist products because they draw visitors. Recreational developments in the past three decades have been characterised by patterns of capacity expansion of supply, followed by market expansion, followed again by capacity expansion and so on. The resulting mass recreation and the transformation and standardisation of host communities and regions caused Bosselman (1974) to ask: " Can places maintain their attractiveness despite increasing crowds of visitors? Or does tourism gradually destroy what the tourists seek?"

Few parts of Europe are unaffected by developments of all sorts, including leisure and recreation. In non-urban areas where the ecology is most fragile the design of recreational developments should be appropriate to a region's eco-system. Unfortunately, this is often not the case. There is a great need in Europe to differentiate recreational products based on natural and cultural heritage. Regional recreation networks could in this regard make a significant contribution to identify and preserve the qualities of a place that are unique and special. Traditionally, the government has played a major role in the preservation of nature and culture in most European countries. It is anticipated that governments shall continue to play a considerable role with regard to such public goods. If so, it may lead to special formats of 'Public-Private Partnerships' (PPP's). It is difficult, at this point in time to articulate such PPP's, more precisely. In contrast, the role of the government in the agro-business has been on the decline and it is anticipated that it will decline even more in the future.

6 Case study: Brabant

In light of the impact of recent market developments, it is advisable for entrepreneurs and institutions in the recreation and tourism sector to pool their individual energies through the applications of networks and chains. Co-operation through networking in the recreation and tourism sector will be the key to enhance future performance and competitiveness. The following case examines the Province of Brabant initiative to test the feasibility of the co-operative chain application in its recreation and tourism sector with the aims of improving quality, productivity and competitiveness.

6.1. Demand

The importance of a customer orientation has been eloquently discussed by Levitt (1960) who traced the chronic problems of the railroads to top management's belief that it was in the railroad not in transportation. Gaining a solid comprehension of the customer, the central theme in recreation and tourism, is made all the more urgent by international competition. Among the more salient trends on the demand side are: the trend toward 'mass-customisation'; a rise in the demand of eco-travel; the trend from 'certainty' to 'safe adventure', the rise of active, nature and health oriented types of tourism; the co-existence of both mega-size and mini-size facilities and services; the trend towards more 'short-breaks'. Consumers are in search for regions that match their touristic needs best.

Consumer research shows that the holiday market (at least 1 overnight stay) in Brabant mounts up to two million visits a year. In comparison to the total domestic holiday market, children up to the age of fourteen are over-represented, as is the age bracket 40-49. Compared to the national average distribution, the higher social classes are under-represented amongst the holidaymakers in Brabant. Not surprisingly, because of the many attraction parks in the area, it appears that visiting fun and recreation parks is a relatively popular activity among visitors to Brabant. Hiking is the most favourite active pursuit of holidaymakers in Brabant, as it is for the whole of the Netherlands. But also eating out, shopping and swimming are popular activities. For most of these day trips people use their private car as a means of transport.

6.2. Supply

The Province of Brabant has a varied supply of existing and potential recreation products. But besides these commercial entrepreneurs it appears both reasonable and desirable to involve other institutions, such as nature-organisations, farmers, and retailers. Currently, the Province of Brabant has many farmers, both with large and small farms, who have to make difficult choices concerning their future. A number of these farmers shall search for the alternative use of their land and facilities. It is anticipated that many farmers will prefer to live in a rural region, and may use recreation to generate part of their income. Similarly, recreation represents an important source of income for other groups, but first and foremost, of course, entrepreneurs in the recreation and tourism sector.
Based on interviews with entrepreneurs in the region, the holiday market in Brabant could generally be described as a market with various opportunities, but at same time many changes are taking place that could be threatening. A notable change is the stabilisation or decrease in the number of permanent residents in holiday accommodations. This has much to do with the changing holiday pattern of elderly amongst who these facilities are most popular. These senior holidaymakers are being increasingly mobile and therefore more often opt for a holiday abroad. This shift will only intensify in future, making the importance of the (non-residential) tourism market even more prominent. In order to better serve this tourism market, additional efforts will have to be made. Offering quality is essential in this, which means that higher demands will be expressed towards the tourist accommodations, the recreation facilities, organised activities on campsites, arrangements, etc. Besides that, the communication with the customer is increasingly important. Providing relevant and accurate information and making sure that the customer is satisfied is essential, according to the present businesses in Brabant. Therefore, tourist accommodations in Brabant are extending their co-operation with providers of day-recreation facilities. These are associations with for instance catering services, restaurants, bars, nature reserves, and the main attraction parks.

6.3. The Challenge

The present heterogeneous market is unified by only one factor: customers who demand quality and value for their money. As the delivery of quality service in individual companies depends on employees, one can deduct that a company's ability to meet its buyers' needs (external customers) depends directly on how well it satisfies the needs of its employees (its internal customers). The emergence of the idea of the "internal customer" has led Schonberger (1990) to suggest that companies depend for their success on a "chain of customers", both within and outside the company. The reconfiguration of the market logic is especially relevant to the recreation and tourism sector in that its reason for existence consists of linking buyers, producers and intermediaries and maintaining satisfying relationships with them. Additional concerns are mentioned underneath.

Table I. Brabant's value chain concerns

Concerning the content	Organisational concerns
♦ Nature ♦ Peaceful and spacious ♦ Nostalgia ♦ Small scale ♦ Brabant's vibes and culture ♦ Hospitality ♦ Authenticity ♦ Adventurous smuggler routes	♦ Customised products and services ♦ Flexible, responsive tour packages ♦ Consumers assembles their own day-activities ♦ Intense communication with the consumer at location, and before and after the visit ♦ Customer information system with the use of databases ♦ Intense co-operation between tourist accommodations and day-recreation facilities and attractions

7 Conclusion

The common goals of the recreation and tourism sector, may frequently differ from the goals of the individual entrepreneurs, representing different industries such as transportation, accommodation, catering, recreation, cultural and travel service activities. It is important to note that practitioners in each industry understand that their participation in a co-operative network shall enable the network to achieve synergistic results that strengthens the performance of both collective- and individual actors.

It can be argued that the recreation and tourism sector has focused on increasing visitor volume rather than adding value for its stakeholders, including the host community, visitors and the industry. To be competitive, the recreation and tourism sector must develop productivity and quality gains that flow from value-adding chains, i.e. and networks that provide actors access to skills, knowledge, means and ends, which they require as a basis for distinguishing their product and enterprise from that of competitors.

The chain approach that has been detailed in this paper can help shape effective partnership designed: to raise the quality product standards and performance; to foster the ability among entrepreneurs to learn within a support system in a dynamic and pragmatic manner, and to turn learners ultimately into leaders who will have the ability and desire to move the recreation and tourism sector from its present orientation towards 'volume', i.e. the notion that 'bigger is better', toward the provision of more 'value' for the money., i.e. integrated quality.

It should be clear from the analysis that the potential application of touristic-recreational chain designs would only be feasible if one possesses the required knowledge about chains and knowledge in chains. The present study in which the authors are involved aims to gather such knowledge in the context of the Province of Brabant, prior to testing it in other settings.

References

Bentley, R.B. (1996), "Information Technology and Tourism: An Update".

Bloch, Michael, Yves Pigneur & Thomas Steiner (April 1996): "The IT-enabled extended enterprise: Applications in the tourism industry", http://www.hec.unil.ch/mbloch/docs/enter96.htm, p. 2.

Borgstein, M.H., Graaff, R.P.M, Hillebrand, J.H.A., Scherpenzeel, J.F., Sijtsma, F.J., Strijker, D. (1997): *Ketens en plattelandsontwikkeling markt-, keten- en netwerkkennis toegepast op het landelijk gebied: een programmeringstudie*, Den Haag: Nationale Raad voor landbouwkundig Onderzoek/ Netwerk voor Onderzoek en Ontwikkeling Ruimtelijk Beleid.

Bosselman, Fred P. (1978): *In the Wake of the Tourist: Managing Special Places in Eight Countries*, Washington D.C.: The Conservation Foundation.

Boynton, A.C., Victor B. & Pine B.J. II (1993): "New Competitive Strategies: Challenges to Organisation and Information Technology", *IBM Systems Journal*, (32:1), p. 49.

Go, Frank M. en Govers (1997): *Ondernemen in Toerisme*, Den Haag: Stichting Maatschappij en Onderneming.

Hamel, G., and Prahalad , C.K. (1994): *Competing for the future*, Boston: Harvard Business School Press.

Heijden, J.G.M. van der (November 1995): *The Changing Value of Travel Agents in Tourism Networks: Towards a Network Design Perspective*, Rotterdam: Erasmus Institute for Advanced Studies in Management, Erasmus University (Management Report Series No. 234).

Hickman, C.R. and Silva, M.A. (1987): *The Future 500: Creating Tomorrow's Organisation Today*.

Levitt, Theodore (1960): "Marketing Myopia", *Harvard Business Review*, (July-August), pp.45-56.

NIPO (December 1996): *Vakantie-onderzoek 1996*, Amsterdam.

NRLO, M.H. Borgstein, R.P.M. de Graaff, J.H.A. Hillebrand, J.F. Scherpenzeel, F.J. Sijtsma, D. Strijker (1997): Ketens en Plattelandsontwikkeling: Markt-, keten- en netwerkkennis toegepast op het landelijk gebied: een programmeringsstudie, Den Haag: National Council for Agricultural Research and the Network for Spatial Policy Research and Development (NRLO-Rapport nr. 97/34).

Park, C. Whan and Daniel C. Smith (1986): *Competitors of Innovative Marketing Strategies, Cambridge*, Massachusetts: Marketing Science Institute (Report No 86-109).

Peters, Tom (1987): *Thriving on Chaos: Handbook for a management revolution*, New York: Alfred A. Knopf.

Pine, B.J. II (1993): *Mass Customization: The New Frontier in Business Competition*, Boston: Harvard Business School Press.

Pine, B.J. II, Peppers D. & Rogers M. (1995): "Do you want to keep your customer forever?", *Harvard Business Review*, (73:2), p. 103.

Porter, Michael E. (1980): *Competitive Strategy Techniques for Analyzing Industries and Competitors*, New York: The Free Press.

Roekel, Jan van, (1997): *Ketens en Ruimte, springt het licht op groen? De zin van een consumentgerichte ketenbenadering*, Klv Studiëdag "Ketens en Ruimte: Staat het licht op groen?", 5 juni, Wageningen: Stichting Agro Keten Kennis, Rosmalen; LEI-DLO, 's-Gravenhage.

Schonberger, Richard J. (1990): *Building a Chain of Customers Linking Business Functions to Create the World Class Company*, New York: The Free Press.

Watson, G.H (1993): *Strategic Benchmarking: How to rate your company's performance against the world's best*, New York: Wiley.
Wierenga, Berend (1997): "Competing for the Future in the Agricultural and Food Channel", *Agricultural marketing and Consumer Behaviour in a Changing World*, Wierenga, Berend , Tilburg, A, van, Grunert, K., Steenkamp, J-B. E.M., Wedel, M. (eds), Boston: Kluwer, pp. 31- 55.

Tourism as an information business: The Strategic Consequences of e-Commerce for Business Travel

Univ. Prof. Dr. Walter Schertler, Universität Trier, Germany
Dkff. Claudia Berger-Koch, Universität Trier, Germany

1 Introduction

For good reasons, the catchword of "the Mediatization of Society" is often found in literature, both scientific and popular. While in the beginning of the 1990's everyone talked about the "Information Age", today "Virtual Organization", "Mobile Office", "Electronic Commerce" or "Electronic Markets" are the predominant buzzwords. The preoccupation with the topic "Mediatization of Society" is not surprising given the fact that a great many ideas which were still visions few years ago, have been transformed into reality by today. Often only the speed of data transmission is to blame for the fact that technically feasible applications are not being marketed. Not yet, one must say.

An example out of the life of a consultant may elucidate this, an example which most readers will probably judge from their experience to be well within the range of possibility. The consultant in this example represents employees of any other travel intensive business function: Sales, Distribution, Purchasing etc.. Frequent travel, frequent and often unexpected changes in bookings as well as an extensive use of the whole service range in business travel (Flight, Hotel, Rental Cars, Credit Cards etc) is typical for this type of business traveler. Ideally, such an employee will log onto a computerized reservation system directly from his PC with Internet connection to take care of all his individual travel arrangements. His distinct customer profile within the mediator's system, available after entering user name and password, ensures that all entered data is in line with the applicable travel guidelines. Even the mediator's system with its waiting list, seat reservation or best buy functions can be integrated and used. Sudden changes of a reservation, late hotel or rental car bookings can be performed by the employee without making use of a travel agent, the firm's own travel office or a secretary. The ticketing is done via ETIX or the issue of reservation numbers (for hotels and rental cars). Besides the flexibility of the system and the on-line check of all arrangements, a major bonus for the traveler is the access to the reservation system 24 hours a day, 7 days a week. The opening hours of travel agencies or call-centers become irrelevant. For employees with a PC and a fast Internet access, this is already a feasible and well-working alternative to the traditional travel agency or implant.

The idea of "seam- and paperless travel" as introduced by Lufthansa early this year may seem a bit more visionary. There, all reservations via the Internet are stored on a multi-functional Smart Card which is then charged with the ordered services during the different stages of travel. But even this idea is no longer utopia, but already being prepared by Lufthansa's system engineers. Today, even the problem of needing a phone plug in order to log onto the Internet is practically not a problem anymore. Using a notebook PC, a cellular phone and a data-card, the frequent traveler can log

on and arrange his travel without the use of a telephone plug by using the GSM mobile communications system.
Even though bandwidth remains a bottleneck in many cases, this problem is bound to disappear for traditional telephony as for mobile communications within the next few years.
At this point, we should contemplate the strategic consequences of the Internet for business travel. The following paragraphs will provide a few hints about this topic:
Strategies are developed in order to ensure and increase long term business success. This applies to tourism as well as to any other industry, to suppliers as well as to mediators. At the level of business unit strategy – and business travel is at this level for most of the suppliers in the area of tourism – the question is raised how sustainable competitive advantage can be created on the basis of a value oriented company management. Taking pattern from PORTER, we can identify cost- or price-oriented measures (improvements of the cost situation) as well as performance-oriented measures (increases in the attractiveness of the services offered). The increased use of the Internet allows for achieving competitive advantage on both of these levels.
To underline this statement, we shall refer to the Structure-Conduct-Performance Paradigm. This normative causal model assumes that the profitability (Performance) of a firm in a given market situation depends directly on its actions (Conduct). The firm's conduct again depends on the conditions (Structure) within the market environment (cf. Hanker 1990, pp. 86). Due to the one-sided causality market structure is the actual critical factor, so it can be viewed as the starting point of a strategic business logic. For this reason, the following summarizes the major trends in business travel of the past years.

2 Business Travel – Trends and Facts

Since 1990, business travel has been rapidly expanding. Due to the opening of the Eastern European markets and a trend towards professionalization on the supply side of business travel, the mediators were able to see an annual increase of around 10 percent in sales volume. Increased outsourcing of travel arrangements in medium and large companies contributed to this development. Only in the most recent years has the growth slowed down to an annual 3 percent (cf. FVW International 1993-1996). Besides the restricted nature of the market's potential, a number of changes in the market's structural framework caused this slow-down:

- The introduction of information- and communication-technology in tourism led to an increasing product differentiation, resulting in a wide range of often confusing price structures. This coincided with an increased price competition on the side of the suppliers, and increased internal attempts to cut costs. The focus of cost saving attempts were sales costs, an area where Lufthansa cut its commission from 9% to 5% last year. This automatically decreased the already small margins of mediators further, leading to a situation where the commission often is insufficient to cover the costs of issuing a ticket. Furthermore,
- the suppliers expanded their direct marketing activities. Many business clients nowadays keep direct business relationships on a net basis with the suppliers. In air travel, this becomes most obvious through the frequent attempts to bypass the

traditional travel agency by direct booking via Internet (e.g. Lufthansa Infoflyway) or corporate implant offices.

- From the mediators' view, customer demands have changed dramatically. Instead of the mere issuing of tickets, customers now demand a professional travel and billing management. The traditional kick-back contract is increasingly replaced by new and performance oriented arrangements (e.g. settlement of accounts on a net basis and compensation via management fee). Due to an extending internationalization of the economy, the international orientation of all services becomes critical. This especially applies to the adequate attendance on travelers abroad as well as to the possibility of international consolidation of billing data.

In order to deal with the cost and performance pressure in international business travel, a great many mediators recently relied on growth and concentration through mergers and acquisitions (M&A) strategies, with the goal of being able to hold their ground against the supplier´s market power. While in 1993, 30 percent of all business travel was done via chains, this share had risen to over 60 percent by 1995. Furthermore, an increased professionalization can be witnessed today as well as the frequent establishment of business travel as an independent business unit. Because of the cost pressures and the fact that for many companies, price is a critical factor when choosing a partner for business travel, operative cost savings are important for the mediator. Setting up call-centers, which can often be operated cheaply even in the most rural locations, is thus a frequently chosen strategic option in business travel.

In fact, the nature of the tourism business and business travel in particular allows for transacting bookings simply over the telephone. It is no coincidence that literature on tourism management regards tourism as a prototypical information business (Schertler 1994).

"Purchasing [in tourism] means the acquisition of factual information concerning services and objects, prices and quantities. Selling means the presentation of this information in an adequate format, for example in a CRS, a catalogue, during customer communications or as a travel document" (Huber 1997, translation by author). In the area of business travel, this type of information is largely standardized and free of emotional involvement, so that the desired travel products can be completely described by the attributes destination, travel dates and times, quality classification and price. Assuming that mediators or suppliers keep customer profiles, fulfilling booking orders becomes a relatively easy task to be fulfilled through the use of an information system (in this special case through CRS). Personally visiting a travel office becomes obsolete and in most cases is already, with the possible exception of picking up tickets. And even ticketing is obsolete in the era of electronic ticketing (ETIX).

Management literature talks about "search goods" in this context, i.e. goods that can be entirely judged *before* purchase (after collecting the adequate information) and after consumption. Goods with a high share of search qualities generally offer a high potential for disintermediation. Disintermediation means the bypassing of traditional mediators in trade, as this is the case for example with the booking of business travel via a central call-center: The traditional travel office is bypassed and instead, the order is transmitted from the call-center through electronic media. Generally, call-centers today are directly connected to the organization of a mediator or supplier. The operation of telephone centers is in most cases out-sourced to a professional service supplier who works according to the specific regulations of the responsible business travel unit. While key account management remains in the hands of the mediators, the operative business in this area is long in the hands of industry outsiders. But, how will the trend evolve in the future?

3 Forces driving the Internet towards becoming a travel market – Explanations for, Consequences of and Obstacles to the Mediatization Trend

3.1. Definitions

What do we mean when we talk about electronic markets? Basically, the Internet is a network technology that, based on the TCP/IP transmission protocol family, allows for a platform-independent communication between different types of computer networks.

Electronic markets can be defined as markets or market mechanisms which can be realized using information and communication technologies (ICT) (cf. Bakos 1991, p. 286, Schmid 1993, S. 3). Probing deeper, we see that electronic markets consist primarily of communication and interaction between the actors in the market, technologically supported or integrated or automated respectively (cf. Krähenmann 1994, pp. 12-16)[1]. It is a case only very rarely to be found that *all* phases of a market transaction – from the information phase (e.g. the search for a convenient flight) to the contracting phase (e.g. price bargaining) to the transactional phase (e.g. payment) and to the delivering phase (e.g. geting the ticket) – can be automated through the use of electronic systems. For this reason we even talk about electronic markets if only single phases of the transaction are executed electronically.

Concerning access authorization, the Internet technology – independent of the concrete organization of system access – is generally designed as an open system, one which any interested member of the "Internet community" may use at his disposition at very low cost (technical and legal openness). Yet system access can be restricted for economic reasons: *Intranets* for example connect the resources within a given organization, but are protected from outside access through the use of a so-called "fire-wall". *Extranets* on the other hand serve to connect a clearly defined clientele to the organization, e.g. suppliers, customers or other partners (financial institutions, insurance companies etc.). Extranets, like Intranets, are internal networks protected by security mechanisms, but access is granted to outside business partners by issuing access authorizations. Finally, the *Internet* is usually defined as a completely open communication platform that allows communication with existing or potential customers, suppliers, financial institutions and other sources of information. Despite the deliberate restriction of access in the case of Intra- and Extranets, all three forms of communication make use of and will hence be summarized under the term "Internet technology".

Even though popular scientific literature often deals with the increasing use of Internet technology in the business-to-consumer segment and drafts visionary

---

[1] Even when market transactions are largely automated (e.g. from machine to machine), the regulatory framework for the transactions is provided by humans, so that in this case, too, we can speak of communication between market actors (cf. Krähenmann 1993, p. 14, Zbornik 1996, p. 56).

scenarios about the consumer business landscape of the future, experts are unanimous that over 70% of electronic business is located in the business-to-business segment (cf. Jupiter Communications 1997). For the year 2000, a sales volume of $ 90 to 160 billions is predicted (cf. BDZV 1997). Due to intensified competition and increasing economic globalization, transaction efficiency and flexibility are key factors in business-to-business management. If this applies to the industrial sector and trade industry in general, it is even more true and important in business travel. Business travel, being the interface between trading or business partners, enabels personal contact and direct communication. Yet travel itself is not at the heart of the traveler's business, and is thus to be minimized in cost and expenditure. The constant efforts of industry and trade to lower travel costs have indeed dominated the discussion in recent years. In this discussion, not only direct travel expenses (e.g. flight, hotel, car rentals) are central, but also the internal costs of organization and transaction which can, according to travel agencies, add up to 15-20 percent of direct costs (cf. Wirtschaftswoche 1997). The Internet offers an interesting alternative to all involved in business travel (supply and demand side) as a means of lowering transaction and communication costs.

3.2. Attempts to explain the rise of electronic markets

We can identify different explanatory patterns in literature for the rise of electronic markets that we will elaborate on in the following. In all patterns, the anticipated or actual consequences of the mediatization of society constitute a major force accelerating or, in the opposite case, obstructing the diffusion of electronic markets.

"The formation of electronic markets is based primarily on the evolution of existing information systems" (cf. Picot e.a. 1998, p. 327). These systems can be single-source sales channels (for example the early CRS operated by one single airline), closed electronic trading systems (most current CRS belong to this category, with access being restricted until not long ago to mediators and suppliers), or existing value added services, with extended functionalities to accommodate electronic transactions (e.g. the operation of Expedia Travel World by Microsoft Corp.). By opening existing systems to a bigger group of users or by integrating additional functions, electronic markets evolve. Past experience has shown that electronic transactions often emerge parallel to the conventional forms of transaction, and then develop a more and more substitutional character. Furthermore, electronic markets can either emerge as complements to traditional markets (e.g. CRS that support the work of travel agencies), or constitute new and innovative solutions that are impossible in conventional arrangements.

Primary motivators for an increased use of IT on the supply-side so far are possibilities to cut coordination and communication costs. In business travel, these are first of all expenditures for sales personnel, which applies to travel agencies as well as to suppliers. Strategic implications that reach beyond cost cutting seem to play a minor role so far. Aspects like

- Building market power
- Realizing competitive advantage
- Improving the quality of services offered
- Preventing the breach of business relationships
- Building new business relationships

are rather seldom to be found when analyzing the rationales of companies for setting up electronic market structures.

On the demand side, price advantages are also of primary importance. Nonetheless, there are a number of other potential advantages to be named which, if realized, can speed up the process of electronic markets diffusion. These are:

- Convenience, e.g. through
  - Independence of opening hours
  - Independence of location
- Establishment of value added partnerships between supply and demand side of business travel, e.g. through joint realization of cost and efficiency advantages. This is most likely feasible for the transaction of all standardized booking requests via Internet, while complex request can still be processed the conventional way.
- Increased depth of available information and speed of transmission
- Reduction of complexity through specialized search engines
- Integration of different products (flights, hotels, car rentals via the same system).

An indispensable condition for the acceptance of electronic markets is that a number of knock-out-criteria be met (cf. Maier 1998, to be published). Among these are primarily issues concerning transmission speed, user friendlyness, system stability, security and data protection.

While technical problems most probably will not be an obstacle to the diffusion of electronic markets in the long run, there are strong indications that in the present situation, a lack of speed of data transmission is a major obstacle to the spread of the use of Internet technologies in business travel. Yet the rapid diffusion of powerful ICT leaves no doubt that the users' needs have been recognized and that the necessary infrastructure will be available in the medium term.

These statements must not divert from the fact that the diffusion of electronic markets involves a number of effects which will have a deep impact on the travel industry's structure. Especially because of the already identified potentials of disintermediation, travel agencies fear to be driven out of (parts of the) business travel segment. Sales personnel reacts understandably sensitive to any increase in Internet involvement of a supplier. An increased use of the Internet poses a threat to CRS operators as well. Questions of market power play a crucial role in this context. A structural change in the value chain might cause an extensive reorganization of the whole travel industry, where the tasks performed by travel agencies and CRS operators as well as a number of new task would have to be redistributed. For example, responsibility for system operation and maintenance, customer consulting services, trust-building measures and quality management within such a future model would have to be negotiated. Possibly increased market transparency also spurs new questions, as the possible degree of differentiation on the supply side (special conditions, complex price structures) might become substantially restricted. In extreme cases, the supplier would face severe profit losses that could only be recovered through the use of decoy strategies.

As long as the above questions remain unanswered, profound structural changes in the market mean an incalculable risk to all market actors. This risk has to be minimized by adequately planned organizational strategic conduct.

4 Strategic Implications for the Tourism Industry (Conduct and Performance)

How can long-term business success be assured in business travel given the situation described above? Which conduct on the supply side is apt to create sustainable competitive advantage (hard to imitate for competitors, recognized by customers and an important performance criterion for them)?
Usually for "volatile markets", i.e. markets with intensive competition, continually changing customer demands, frequent technology changes and short product life-cycles, modern management literature demands

- Being close to market
- Being flexible and
- Being innovative.

As shown above, the business travel market can well be categorized as a volatile market. So what conduct of business travel suppliers is suitable to ensure being close to market, flexible and innovative? And what role can the Internet play?
Industrial economics define supplier conduct as all strategic and tactical patterns of behavior that are used to adapt to changes in the market. We will exemplify supplier conduct using three typical classes of conduct patterns and analyze the Internet technology's potential to support conduct for mediators as well as for suppliers. In a market with largely standardized basic services, price is a major competitive instrument. As a consequence, questions of competition on price are at the center of our interest. For traders of flight services, the Internet poses a certain threat, as it makes prices directly comparable for customers and thus raises the probability of an extensive competition on price. In practice, certain patterns of cooperation and collusive tendencies are observable independent of the Internet technology. For that

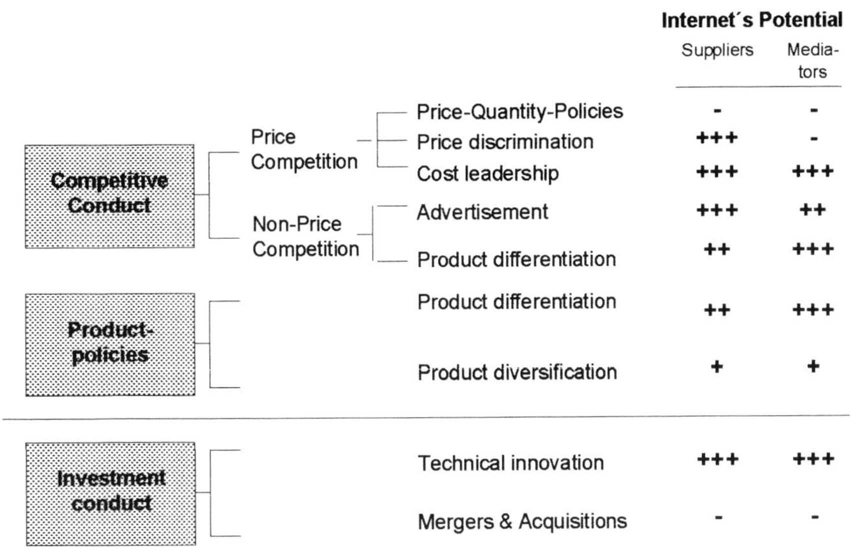

Fig. 1: Classes of Strategic and Tactical Conduct Patterns

reason, it is unlikely that increased market transparency alone will lead to more price competition.
On the other hand, the Internet even offers improved possibilities for price differentiation: With its high potential of individualization, companies can very accurately identify and serve specific market segments of homogenous customer groups. This means that charging different prices based on the need structures and financial situation of the customers can be applied to maximize profits. Modern yield management can be used as an example of this. Consistent use of the Internet in business travel allows for collecting, saving and flexibly updating individual customer preferences. Special conditions can be negotiated directly with the customer and stored in his personal profile, price discounts or special privileges concerning scarce seat contingents. Administration of customer profiles can be transferred away from the mediators to the company travel offices or the business travelers themselves.
Besides aspects of the pricing strategy, the Internet technology offers significant advantages for internal cost savings for both mediators and supplier. Savings can be realized through lower communication costs and minimized customer consulting. Especially standardized activities can thus be cost efficiently transacted via Internet, while more complex transactions (travel abroad, complex flight arrangements) remain within the responsibility of the mediator's direct and personal counsel. From the supplier´s point of view, the more efficient and quicker the management of, which leads to opportunity cost savings, is of primary importance. Due to the fact that services cannot be stored like goods (which means that unused seats or hotel beds immediately lower sales and profits), capacity utilization is of primary importance to business travel and unused capacity management represents a critical success factor. Especially for searching hotels, the Internet offers more transparency to the business traveler about the supply side and adds flexibility by being independent of time and location, resulting in better hotel capacity utilization. Ideally, the realized cost savings can be transferred to the customer through lower prices.
The Internet also proves to be an ideal vehicle for advertisement. Creating a professional Internet-Homepage can serve to convey the image of an innovative, technology-oriented company. As the services of supplier and mediators are classic examples of "experience-" goods whose quality cannot be judged before using the service (only after), this kind of advertisement can create advantages by generating trust on the customer side. For the hotel business, the opportunity of a multimedia-based presentation is especially promising, so that potential customers can acquire a clear picture about a hotel's quality, location and service range. By using data-based marketing methods, companies can gain direct access to customers in order to inform about incentive offers, conferences and conventions, business travel news or new service offerings. Statistical analyses, conducted by mediators for their business travel customers to ensure a professional travel cost management, can be sent via Internet to the customer in a convenient pre-determined format.
Furthermore, the Internet offers a wide array of possibilities to differentiate the original (travel) service. This applies to mediators and their task of informing and booking in particular. Thus, mediators expand their business travel offerings without extensive additional expenses by providing

- Individuality through stored customer profiles
- Neutrality through access to a neutral reservation system

- Convenience through independence of time and location (this way, even late at night vacancies can be found and reservations processed)
- Attractive management fees through realized cost savings for standard services
- High quality customer consulting for speciality services through the effective use of human resources that become available.

After collecting sufficient experience on sales via the Internet, it is quite possible that the know-how and the data-base acquired will serve to enable product diversification. One possible application might be the transfer of specific knowledge into the area of insurance services.

Investment conduct also accounts to the strategic and tactical options of companies in tourism. While – as mentioned initially – the industry recently held a tendency towards M&A, the following will focus on the increasing impact of innovations on competition.

The question if the use of the Internet in business travel is more technology-driven (push) or induced by demand (pull) is very important to be answered in this context. According to the latter possibility, it would be primarily market powers, a demand pull in particular, that drives companies towards increased research and development (R&D) activities around the Internet technology. This assumption complies with the Structure-Conduct-Performance-Paradigm at the basis of this analysis, which defines the market actors' conduct as a direct reaction to the market structure. Abstracting from the current technical obstacles caused by data transmission speed restrictions, we can securely anticipate the Internet to have a major impact on our society. The number of users and companies increasing as rapidly as transmission speed may serve to emphasize this statement. Given this background, the travel industry in general and the market for business travel in particular seem to hold a special potential for innovation.

Another aspect seems to be of importance: Every technological innovation, every leap to another learning-curve first demands a step back before a progressive increase in

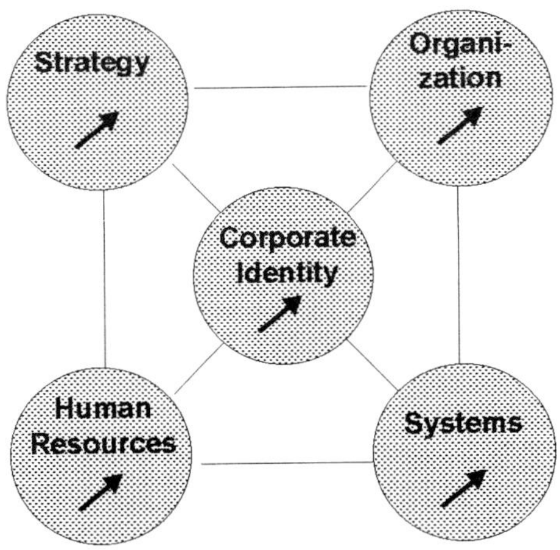

Fig. 2: Components of the Management System

marginal utility can be realized. This may be the reason why many innovations are recognized late and tend to be realized only hesitatingly.
A third aspect should be discussed before the background of the diffusion model of technological innovations. Typically, *innovators* initiate technological innovations, which are then taken over by *imitators*. While the first phase of the evolution is dominated by uncoordinated R&D- and testing activities, a strong trend towards specialization and standardization can be witnessed in the following phase. Concerning the Internet technology, the 1970s are viewed as the test phase, while the initiation of the TCP/IP protocols in the mid-80´s started an "up-scaling" phase which was followed by the status of a "global information and communication medium" after the introduction of the WWW in the early 1990s. Only recently, the term "global transaction medium" has emerged. While there is a certain apparent standardization of the Internet on a technological level, the processes associated with the use of the Internet as a transaction medium are still changing. Functioning business models are the exception, competitive structures unclear, customer structures and user acceptance also. Yet there are strong indications that standardization and specialization will soon appear on the process level as well. A timely positioning in this area may be the basis for creating future strategic competitive advantage.
It is essential for the conduct of the supply side in tourism that the enormous potential of the medium be recognized and strategically implemented. Successful companies exhibit a well-balanced management system where Strategy, Organization, Corporate Identity, Human Resources and Systems are working in the same direction.

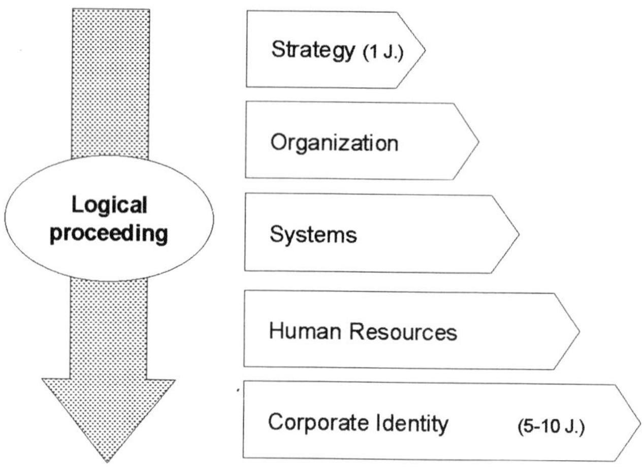

Fig. 3: Timeframe for Strategic Redirection

Using reverse logic, this means that companies in the tourism industry cannot expect to be successful if their Internet activities are implemented without dedication, with unattractive product portfolios, inadequate budgets and no underlying strategic logic. The starting point of an innovative orientation is the development of a consistent long-term business strategy which includes all the above mentioned aspects. Only when the commitment to the Internet technology is sufficient, implementation can begin at the level of the Organization, Human Resources, Systems and Corporate Identity in order to create an adequate business model for the Internet trade. This whole process takes its time. While strategy formulation can be realized within a few months' time, the implementation may take several years. Therefore it is advisable to initiate the process early.

Not surprising, the possibilities of the Internet technology are most widely used by small enterprises, as these firms are more apt to risk and master the task of a complete strategic redirection. One reason for this is that both the pressures on and the relative opportunities for small firms are greater. On the other hand, the threat of competitors' sanctions as a reaction to attempts to change the rules of the game is significantly lower for small enterprises. Yet we have to keep in mind that these exact positive conditions for an intensive Internet orientation apply to new entrants and entrants from other industries as well, who might be able to establish a presence in this new market at relatively low risk.

The integration of Internet technology into the strategic sales concept of a company is hence advisable in any case, and already constitutes a valuable investment into tomorrows competitiveness and profitability.

References

- Bakos, Y. (1991): A Strategic Analysis of Electronic Marketplaces, in: MIS Quarterly, #15, pp. 295-309.
- BDZV (1997): Digitaler Handel vor allem zwischen Unternehmen, in: BDZV report Multimedia, # 4, p.7.
- FVW International (1993-1997): Reisebüroketten und Kooperationen, documentation 1993-1996, addition to FVW International.
- Hanker, J (1990): Die strategische Bedeutung der Informatik für Organisationen, Zürich.
- Huber, R. (1997): Daten, Informationen und der Mensch, in: FVW, Jubiläumsausgabe 5/1997, p. 138.
- Jupiter Communications (1997): European Online Markets, http://www.jup.com.
- Krähenmann, N. (1994): Ökonomische Gestaltungsanforderungen für die Entwicklung elektronischer Märkte, Dissertation, Bamberg.
- Maier, M. (1998): Charakteristika von Electronic Commerce Anwendungen, Düsseldorf.
- Malone, T. W./ Yates, J./ Benjamin, R. I. (1989): The Logic of Electronic Markets, in: Harvard Business Review, May-June, pp. 166-170.
- Picot, A./ Reichwald, R./ Wigand, R.T. (1998): Die grenzenlose Unternehmung, 3rd edition, Wiesbaden.
- S. & K. und Partner (1995): Idealtypische Neuausrichtung von Unternehmen, unveröffentlichtes Manuskript, Düsseldorf.
- Schertler, W.: Dienstleistungseigenschaften begründen Informationsgeschäfte – dargestellt an Tourismusdienstleistungen, in: Schertler, W. (ed.) Tourismus als Informationsgeschäft, Wien, 1994
- Schertler, W.: Informationssystemtechnologie und strategisches Tourismusmanagement, in: Schertler, W. (ed.) Tourismus als Informationsgeschäft, Wien, 1994
- Schmid, B. (1993): Elektronische Märkte, in: Wirtschaftsinformatik, Vol. 35, # 5, pp. 465-480.
- Wirtschaftswoche (1997): #11, 6.1.1997.
- Zbornik, S. (1996): Elektronische Märkte, elektronische Hierachien und elektronische Netzwerke, Konstanz.

DBM as a Source of Competitive Advantage for the Hotel Industry

Dr. Marco Antonio Robledo.
Lecturer in the School of Tourism of the Balearic Islands-UIB.
Titular Professor in the Business and Economics Dept. of the University of the Balearic Islands (UIB)

Abstract

In the decade of the individual, mass marketing is no longer valid; relationship marketing is the key to success. The purpose of relationship marketing is to build long-term relationships with customers. In order to achieve this objective many actions can be undertaken but in nearly all of them, DBM will play a central role.This paper examines the applicability of Database Marketing (DBM) and its current use in the hotel industry. Research was undertaken to answer those questions. DBM is a customer-orientated approach to marketing that builds a continuous relationship with the customer. DBM is measurable, targeted, personalized, it builds loyalty and it involves adopting a customer focus. Typically, a hotel marketing database will contain personal data, planning data and global sales information about every customer or prospect. The hotel industry (an industry where the Pareto rule is particularly true) is considered very suitable for the adoption of DBM since the presence of the customer in the facility makes easier the process of gathering the information. The applications of DBM that the hotels examined are using include customer loyalty programmes (e.g. frequent-stay programmes), personal attention and recognition (noting preferences, rewarding repeat business and building long-term relationships), programmes for catching new customers, direct marketing used as a sales promotion tool, as a means of targeting specific customers or as a means of selling directly, cross selling and line extensions programmes to identify customers who could be interested in other products of the company, control tool for the reservation desk, opening up new channel possibilities, strengthening relationships with the sales channels and becoming list vendors of their own databases. There are different levels of usage of DBM within the hotel industry ranging from the mere uncomputerized guest-history system to sophisticated networks. The data gathering process uses sources such as the current guests, financial databases, list vendors or directories plus census data. The paper concludes that DBM is crucial for achieving a competitive edge in the hotel industry and all hotels should implement it regardless of size or target market.

1 Objectives

This paper examines the topic of DBM as a source of competitive advantage for the hotel industry. Both desk research and ad-hoc field research were carried out in order to achieve the following objectives:

1. To provide a full insight of the concept of database marketing and its link with relationship marketing.

2. To review the current strategic and operational use of database marketing in the hotel industry.
3. To assess the applications of database marketing in the hotel industry.
4. To recognise the opportunities and benefits of database marketing for the hotel industry.

2 Relationship Marketing and Database Marketing

Relationship Marketing is *"the business process of establishing and maintainig mutual benefit relationships with customers on a long-term basis."* (Robledo, 1998:23). The objective of relationship marketing is to come back to the roots of traditional hospitality: knowing every single customer intimately and developing a continous relation that does not expires at the end of the customer´s stay.
Database Marketing (from here referred to as DBM) is an essential part of a relationship marketing strategy. Building on the seminal definition of Shaw and Stone (1988) we can define DBM as follows:

> *"Database Marketing is an interactive approach to marketing which uses a computerised, relational database system in real time of comprehensive up-to-date relevant data on our target market, and addressable communications media (such as mail, telephone, and the sales force) for the purpose of developing customer-orientated programmes in a personalised, articulated and cost-effective manner, stimulating demand and winning customer loyalty, and send the desired message at the right time, in the right form, to the right people."* (Robledo, 1998:51)

From the above definition we can infer that DBM is a fundamental element to build a continuous relationship between principal and customer.
As Shaw and Stone (1988) pinpoint, a key tool of DBM is a marketing database. A marketing database is marketing speak for a relational database, i.e. one in which various tables or files are linked together trough key expressions. A relational database enables anything in it to be matched with anything else.
Kottler (1991) defines a marketing database as:

> *"an organized collection of data about individual customers, prospects, or suspects that is accessible and actionable for such marketing purposes as lead generation, lead qualification, sale of a product or service, or maintenance of customer relationships".*

The organised set of files of all historic customer data that is the marketing database allows to develop an enhanced picture of the customers and their buying behaviour and increases its value every time is used (Alet, 1994:68).

3 Characteristics of a DBM system

According to Shaw and Stone (1988), the characteristics of a fully fledged DBM are:

1. Each actual or potential customer is identified as a record on the database. The implication of this fact is that markets and market segments are not identified primarily through aggregate data, which cannot be broken down into individual customers, but as agglomerations of individual customers, this process has been labeled as *supersegmentation* (Robledo: 1998, 69).
2. The database maintains on-line details of guest's previous visits to the establishment. The files are created automatically after a guest's check-out and includes such information as personal data -name and address, marital status, age, date of birth, children etc.-, planning data -geodemographics, comments concerning behaviour and preferences, etc-, global sales information -number of visits, most recent visit, method of payment, room number, to-date nights stayed, to-date revenue, average expenditure per stay, credit information etc.- and about campaign communications -whether the customer has been exposed to particular marketing communications campaigns-.
3. The information is available to the company during each transaction with the customer, to enable it to decide how to respond to the customer's needs.
4. The database is used to record responses of customers to company initiatives. This is especially relevant for hotels, since they are in a market where a substantial number of customers make frequent repeat purchases. Each such purchase represents an opportunity to learn more about their customers.
5. The information is also available to enable them to decide such point as which target markets of segments are appropriate for each product or service and what marketing mix is appropriate for each product in each target market.
6. In large corporations, the database is used to ensure that the approach to the customer is coordinated, and a consistent approach developed.
7. The database eventually replaces market research. Marketing campaigns are devised such that the response of customers to the campaign provides information which the company is looking for.
8. Marketing management automation is developed to handle the vast volume of information generated by DBM.

4 Advantages of DBM

- It is measurable: Response to campaigns are measured enabling to identify the effectiveness of different approaches. By knowing precisely what worked and what did not ,the marketer can allocate the marketing budget much more effectively.

- It is testable: It is possible to test the effectiveness of different elements of the approach used -the product, the medium, the offer, the target market, etc. Tests can be carried out quickly so quick action on the results may be taken.
- It is targeted and accurate because it communicates with specific customers. This reduces the waste inherent in many other types of communication.
- It is personalized: Communication to each customer is personalized by including details relevant to them and not to others.
- It is flexible
- It frees marketers from the task of generating market data. It give them time to concentrate on creative and competitive data.
- It builds the loyalty of existing customers.
- It expands the market share of the company through identification and acquisition of potential customers, through "conquest sales" or through the discovery of new, untapped markets.
- It provides a basis for revenue-stream analysis, as well as helping generate incremental revenues.
- It involves adopting customer focus and becoming customer driven.

5 Current use of DBM in the Hotel Industry

The research tried to identify the current level of usage of DBM in the hotel industry. The research methodology consisted on personal interviews with marketing managers (or equivalent) of hotel companies with a presence in Spain (including hotel chains, marketing consortia and individual hotels). In particular, the interviews tried to shed some light upon the following areas:

- Users of DBM
- Sources of data
- Uses of DBM
- Level of usage

5.1 Users of DBM

The research revealed that mostly the big hotel chains are the ones taking advantage of this technology. Smaller chains and independently-owned hotels either use it very limitedly or do not use it at all. However, there is a growing awareness among them of the tool and its possibilities and many of the interviewees are considering the implementation of a DBM system.

There was some confusion between DBM and Frequent-Stay Programmes. Almost all of the interviewees knew first about Frequent-Stay Programmes than DBM. Actually, many of them did not know what DBM was but knew about loyalty programmes. Others, thought that both things were just the same.

The extent of use of DBM depends as well on the target market of the hotel. In luxury hotels, hotels targeted to executives or big chain of hotels where there is a big amount of repeat guests, DBM was was regarded as a very important weapon and is used extensively to support frequent-stay programmes and customer loyalty and care programmes. In smaller hotels and hotels targeting vacational segments DBM is either not used or used for the current guests or for occasional direct marketing campaigns. However, a growing trend initiated by Riu Hotels and rapidly followed by other companies such as Sol Meliá is to create databases of travel intermediaries and use DBM to improve the relationship and to foster the loyalty of travel agents.

5.2 Sources of Data

Information is the raw material of DBM. The marketeer can use a huge variety of sources of information to feed his database. The more important ones used in the hotel industry are the following:

1. Data gathered in the moment of the customer's purchase or during his stay. This was by far the source most widely used. Unlike other businesses, the hotel business can easily gather most of the information they need about their guests for marketing and service purposes while they stay at the resort. Companies like Ritz-Carlton incentivate their employees to gather as much information as possible about guests.
2. List acquisition from external sources: This source of data was used mainly when there was a need to expand the business to untapped new segments that were not present in the database or at the moment of starting up the database.
3. Data gathered through direct communication with the customers or prospects (questionnaires, coupons, telemarketing, etc.).
4. Financial information about customers kept in accounting databases. This was used for a few companies to feed the first data into the database, but is a very limited source.

Therefore, data sources differentiate essentially the DBM practice in hotels since they do not have to rely as much in direct marketing tools (mailings, telephone etc.) and in list brokers as other industries do to stay close to the customer.

5.3 Uses of DBM

Possibilities of DBM are numberfold. The ones cited by the interviewees as used by their companies include among others the following:

- Market and buyer research.
- Testing.
- New product launches.
- Direct marketing.
- New market development.
- Generating and quantifying sales leads.

- Demographic market data.
- Customer loyalty and care programmes.
- Expansion of customer base.
- Distribution communication and incentive programmes.
- New income source through list vending.
- Price Testing.
- Qualification of customer's lifetime value.
- Control mechanism at the front desk

  Of all these possibilities the most commonly used are the following ones.

Customer loyalty and care programmes.

DBM is used to reinforce loyalty, through three factors noted by Francese and Renaghan (1991) - namely, incentives, individual attention and recognition.

Incentives: DBM supports such marketing strategies as Frequent-stay programs, a very popular tool in the hotel industry to foster loyalty. With a marketing database in place, even small properties were offering such programmes without incurring extraordinary expenses. Moreover, DBM was used as a merchandising tool: Thank-you notes, greeting cards, goodies, special offers on the customer's birthday and promotional material mailed to past guests are some of the most common applications.

Personal Attention: Many hotels analyzed were very concerned about personalizing the guest experience to build customer's loyalty and create repeat business. The challenge is to make service as tangible as possible. To accomplish this, hotel operators have to note, remember, and automatically accommodate guests' individual preferences. As DBM is actually market segmentation in computerized form, was regarded as a powerful tool to achieve this purpose.

Recognition: Most of the DBM systems studied were linked to reservations to increase the usefulness and accuracy of the guest-history files. With this link, the reservationist can determine whether a customer is a repeat guest at the time the reservation is made. Scanning the guest history, the reservationist can confirm previous stay information such as room type, credit card number, and special request and preferences. When the guest's preferences are verified at the time the reservation is made, not only does the guest feel surprised and flattered because the hotel personnel "remembered" his preferences, but front-desk personnel can ensure that a room with the desired amenities is reserved for that guest. Any additional information obtained during repeat stays is entered in the database to provide more personalised service in the future.

In the case of group of hotels, they were trying to give this kind of VIP treatment to its customers by sharing guest history information by means of a centralized system or a network. With this system, the group can give the same services to a repeat guest in any of the hotels of the group.

Catching new customers

The focus of attention for a hotel must be not only establishing a better and more resilient relationship with our existing customers, but also on refining a formula for building new and lasting relationships with customers whose cultures, lifestyles and language are yet largely unknown to the hotel. Originally catching new customers was possible solely by broadcast advertising. Now this can be done by getting a list of potential new customers, and using the data base to identify prospects and to narrowcast by tailoring messages and incentives to individuals.

Direct marketing

Over the past few years the cost of above-the-line advertising has soared, therefore, below-the-line advertising such as direct marketing is becoming increasingly popular in the hotel industry with the perpetual support of DBM .The database of a DBM system is the information source required for direct marketing campaigns. Direct marketing is used in the hotel industry as a sales promotion tool to give a short-term sales boost, to target specific customers who cannot be reached by the usual media, to obtain leads for the sales force, or to sell directly.

Cross Selling and line extensions

In the case of companies offering a number of different products and/or services it is common to use their combined databases to introduce a customer who for example has stayed in one of its hotels to the other activities of the company. Since all customer contacts are recorded in the marketing database, opportunities for cross-selling other hotels or even other products or services are maximised. In this way customer loyalty is built up over time.

In the same way the customer database is used by some companies in line extension by using direct mail and telemarketing to existing customers inviting them to visit a new hotel of the company or to promote a new service.

The Control Link

Hotels make guest histories accessible to the reservationist, and the reservation desk becomes an additional control point. Guests who have created difficulties for the hotel through credit problems or unacceptable behaviour can be flagged in the system so the reservationist can be alerted to undesirable guests. Hotels can save a great deal of money by avoiding guests with a past history of bad credit or destroying hotel rooms.

Guest-history databases that maintain guests' credit-card numbers also serve as a backup for credit transactions. If a credit voucher is lost or illegible, accounts receivable can obtain the necessary information from the guest history to process the transaction.

Sales Channels

Many hotels (specially vacational hotels) find difficult to reach their customers directly because of cost and overdependence on Tour Operators. DBM is opening up

new channel possibilities, for some hotels in which the sole initial marketing assets are brand image and customer base. The opportunity to deal directly with the clients without the hassle of intermediaries was considered extremely interesting by all the interviewees. Direct marketing is the key starting point to this new approach to hotel sales. The measurability of the direct marketing campaigns run with the support of DBM makes it moreover a very cost-effective method.
On the other hand, DBM is helping building up relationships with the travel organizers sector, typically by improving information flows, sharing lists of customers so that the quality of supply can be improved and cost reduced. These benefits can be passed down the value chain in the form of improved value or benefits to the ultimate customer.

New products and services
Information is increasingly being regarded as a product to be sold in its own right. DBM is thus by itself creating new products and services.
Hotels are continually collecting data about their guests. The sale of these customers lists to other firms is a major retail opportunity that is already being tapped by some operators.

During my research I have been able to identify the following phases of development of DBM in the hotel industry:

6 Levels of usage

There are many different levels of usage of DBM in the companies researched. The below clasification represents an attempt to group them into categories ranging from the less sophisticated approachs to DBM to the more sohisticated ones. Obviously, the smallest operations are the ones that showed the less sophisticated developments whereas the big chains with international presence are the ones in the cutting edge.

6.1 Uncomputerized Guest Histories

Guest histories are kept by hand, recording repeat customer's special preferences and peculiarities on index cards or rolodex files. The files are used prior to check-in to anticipate guest's needs and updated and check-out with any new insights.
Although these methods are cumbersome and time consuming, some hotels still use them.

6.2 Database Of Current Guests

A simple database of the guests staying at the hotel is kept and used for some marketing purposes. These databases are hard to analyze for marketing purposes.
Thanks to the database they can get:

- Daily lists of guests' birthdays, name days, anniversaries in order to offer them a gift or compliment (e.g. a birthday cake).
- Guests profile
- List of repeat guests staying at the hotel.

Hotels in this phase usually keep a less detailed database for long periods of time to identify repeat guests but the lack of information contained in the database makes sometimes difficult this identification.

6.3 Decentralised DBM

In this phase, sales and marketing databases are well organized, but there may be many databases. Each hotel of the chain has its own database. Each DBM campaign is well planned and executed in itself, but many overlap with other campaigns (e.g. different, even conflicting hotels to the same market). This may be because the customer appear on different databases. In very large hotel companies, different originators of campaigns may simply not know what their colleagues are planning.

6.4 Tactical DBM

DBM is used at corporate level as a tactical tool.It is not an integral part of marketing strategy. There may be no mention of DBM when marketing strategies for a hotel or target market are under consideration. DBM is brought into play specially to foster loyalty by sending Christmas cards or birthday cards to guests who stayed over a certain length of time or who spent over a certain amount. Also they can be sent promotions of new hotels or services or details of special events locally (a golf tournament, perhaps, or an art festival) to potentially interested guests.
Loyal guests are usually rewarded with loyalty cards at this stage.
In this phase the importance of customer information is recognized and even lists of potential customers are occasionally bought in but they are not integrated with the database. They may be used once to identify potential customers and then discarded.

6.5 Co-Ordinated Customer Communication

In this phase, the emphasis is not on the database, though it is the power which makes it all possible. The emphasis is on customers, that is the starting point is the customer and works inward. The first questions are: Who are the hotel's customers; What are their needs and how shall be planned and co-ordinated all the communication efforts to meet them.
If there are databases available to all hotels in the company, there may be too many campaigns overlapping and ineffective. A co-ordination system is needed to ensure that all potential conflicts are removed and all resources available.

6.6 Integrated DBM

Individual hotel systems join into a network to share guest information. One database drives all customer information and management. The central marketing database connects all the hotels of the company allowing the Barcelona property to give a French guest the same recognition he or she receives at the Paris hotel. Moreover both strategic and tactical capabilities of DBM are fully recognised in this phase.

References

- Alet, Josep, "*Marketing Directo Integrado- Como crear y fidelizar clientes creciendo con rentabilidad.*" Barcelona, Ediciones Gestion 2000. 1991
- Francese, Paula A. and Renaghan, Leo M. 'Finding the Customer'. American Demographics. Vol 13, pp 48-51. January 1991
- Kotler, Philip. *Marketing Management.* 7th edition. London, Prentice-Hall. 1991
- Robledo, Marco Antonio. *Marketing Relacional Hotelero: El Camino Hacia la Lealtad del Cliente.* Madrid. Ediciones Profesionales y Empresariales. 1998
- Shaw, Bob and Stone, Merlin. " *Database Marketing: Strategy and Implementation*". Nueva York, John Wiley & Sons. 1988
- Shaw, Bob and Stone, Merlin. 'Competitive Superiority through Database Marketing'. *Long Range Planning (UK).* Vol 21, Octubre, pp 24-40. 1988

Printing-on-demand as a channel for tourist information

G.J. van der Pijl,
Tilburg University, the Netherlands

H. Bartelink,
Foliquest Internationl N.V., the Netherlands
vdrpijl@tref.nl

1 Introduction

This paper describes Instant Response as a new way of distributing pre-sales documentation. It provides dealers of internationally operating organisations with the possiblility to log in on a WWW-site to order sales documentation for their prospects. This documentation is then printed (on demand) in a print centre near the prospect and sent to the client within one day. Out-of-stock and out-of-date will never occur again with Instant Response and prospects receive personalised (one-to-one) and up-to-date information. The Instant Response concept is presently tested by several major international companies (Philips, Husqvarna). We argue that the concept is also applicable in the tourist industry.

In the paper, we first elaborate on the Instant Response concept. Next, we will argue why we think the concept is applicable in tourism. Finally, we give some hints regarding the practical implementation of printing on demand, using the building stones model for virtual organisations.

2 The Concept

In the old days, sales brochures of big, internationally operating companies were often produced and printed centrally. Then they were distributed among decentral selling points and stored locally. Local salesman supplied their clients with brochures from these local stocks. An important disadvantage of this approach is that expensive stocks of glossy brochures had to be held. Quite often, these brochures were outdated before the stock was empty.

Instant Response is a new way of distributing sales materials making use of the possibilities of the Internet and of electronic publishing, to support the sales force and marketing department of internationally operating organisations.
The core of this Instant Response concept is a Web-based application to support corporate user's sales force in delivering pre-sales documentation to their prospects. Dealers/sales representatives log in on the Instant Response WWW-server [http://www.foliquest.com], through an Internet connection on their laptop or desktop. Here, they select the sales documentation they need from the (object-oriented) Catalogue Database. A request is then sent, in the form of an EPC (Electronic Print

Command), to a local print centre (called fulfilment centre). Here, a software component called FoliMerge assembles the incoming information (out of the EPC) with the stored standard cover letter. Eventually, the total request (which consists thus of a personalised cover letter and requested enclosures) is printed. The documentation is printed on an interfaced high-quality colour copier, packed in the fulfilment centre and delivered on the prospect's desk by mail the next day [see Figure 1].
In co-operation between the corporate user, the IR-server operator and the print centre, the documentation stock is "stored" on the Web. There is no actual stock of documentation, but the sales representative can still "order" (in fact: give the print command) the documentation from the virtualised stock. The dealer logs in on the Web and orders his documentation via the actual look-and-feel of the corporate user. Thus, because of the possibilities of IT, organisational parts of this co-operation are being virtualised

An extra benefit is the availability of real-time market feedback. Statistics on requests are gathered, which thus provide marketing departments with very useful information for further one-to-one-maketing strategies.

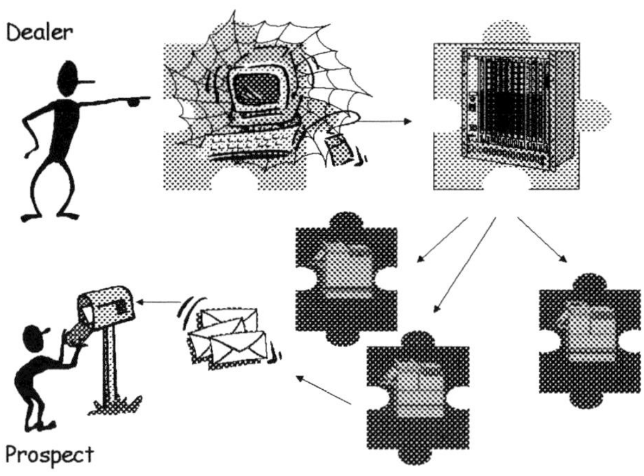

figure 1: full Instant Response cycle

3 Instant response and the tourism market

3.1 Market characteristics

A customer characterisation was developed for the Instant Response service in order to position the service. The Instant Response service is applicable to the following characterisation:

- distributor or manufacturer selling through indirect channels (dealers)
- short product life cycles
- many products
- unknown prospects now
- not an impulse buying decision
- in several countries with different languages
- with a reasonable margin

Especially the short life cycle and the reasonable margin are prerequisites in order to make Instant Response feasible for a corporate user. The benefits of Instant Response are fully exploited with often changing leaflets/brochures available in several languages.

Many actors in the tourism sector seem to be candidates for using the Instant Response concept. Let us take a look at some of them:

Hotels and other accommodation

Especially hotel chains seem to have a high potential for using instant response. The only two points on which there could be doubts are the "short product life cycles" and the "not an impulse bying" requirements. For the former, though, most chains do have special offers that can be seen as ever changing product varieties with short product life cycles. Discussions with travel agents show that holiday decisions in the lower end of the market are indeed quite often impulse bying decisions. In the upper end of the market and in the bussiness sector, this is less clear. Small individual hotels and other acommodation could make use of the Instant Response concept using the intermediation of local, regional or national tourist boards.

Tourist Boards

Tourist boards also seem to fit the requirements for the use of instant response, especially in the upper end of the market. Using the concept, tourists can be provided with up-to-date, high-quality destination information that is tailored to their needs. By bringing together the supply of local accomodation, attractions and entertainment, they certainly market the wide and rapidly changing product environment that can benefit from Instant Response.

Airline industry and surface transportation

Airlines too, sell many different products, have unknown prospects, and sell their products through indirect channels. The purchase of an airline chair does not seem to be an impulse decision. Because of the fact that product changes can easily be incorporated in the electronic pre-sales documentation, the system could also handle last-minute offers.

Tour operators

Tour operators seem to be another group that can make use of the Instant Response concept. As Sheldon indicates, brochures represent a significant expense for agents, which could be cut back through electronic distribution of brochures to the travel agents' screens (Sheldon, P.J., 1997). Instant response would be a possibility to maintain the paper brochures that consumers like so much, while at the same time achieving the cost reductions and flexibility of electronic distribution.

Travel agents

Travel agents will have the role of the dealers in the instant response concept. Interviews with a major Dutch travel agent indicate that, in the lower end of the market, tourists often make impulse buying decisions that do not fit in very well with the Instant Response concept. This type of consumer wants to carry home a set of brochures at the moment they visit the travel agent. In the upper end of the market, however, the travel agent recognizes, however, the possibilities of Instant Response.

3.2 Goals/benefits

The intended benefits or goals of implementing Instant Response are different for the various stakeholders:

Corporate user

For corporate users, like hotels, destinations and possibly also the airline industry and surface transportation, implementing Instant Response means a decrease of their documental waste (documentation is printed on demand and not in advance). Not only will there be a reduction in printed material, but there will also be a decrease in distribution costs compared to the old "stock-and-forward"-situation. The Instant Response concept means a shift from a Just-In-Case concept to a Just-In-Time service, and thus decreased obsolescence.

Not only will Instant Response save distribution costs, it can improve revenues as well. Due to Instant Response, faster promotion and more special actions are possible. Mass customisation will lead to higher customer satisfaction and hence to better financial perspectives.

- Finally, market feedback (for the marketing department) and insight into its own selling channels can be obtained through statistics. This insight will lead to faster product changes and a wider assortment, due to better market understanding.

Dealer/Sales representative

The dealer or sales representative, in our case the travel operator, will never be out of sales documentation. He is always able to send up-to-date information to his prospect, fitted to the client's needs, and, due to the Internet, sales documentation will be accessible 24 hours a day.

Prospect

The prospect, that is, the tourist or bussiness traveller, will obtain customised documentation. This will increase customer satisfaction because he receives what he wants. Less waste will be produced because the prospect only gets what he asked for through the sales representatives. So the information overload for the prospects will diminish. However, it is not clear yet to what extend an overload of brochures is part of the fun of tourism. This needs to be researched before engaging in large-scale application of the concept in the lower end of the tourist market.

Fulfilment Centre

- Print centres are operating in an intensely competitive and changeable market (Hayes, J., 1997; CAP Ventures 1997). Implementing Instant Response will give them an opportunity for differentiation and a closer link with their (Instant Response) customers. They will be able to offer corporate users complete outsourcing of sales document distribution instead of the regular printactivities of today. This means a shift from price-based competition in the present to quality-based competition in the future.

4 Implementing instant response in a virtual organisation

The companies that take care of the distribution of pre-sales information through the IR-server together form a virtual corporation. From the literature (Martin, J., 1996; Venkatraman, N. and Henderson, C., 1996) we derived eight areas of attention or 'building blocks" which the virtual organisation needs to pay attention to in order to serve its clients effectively and efficiently.

Building block 1: Alliance of organisations

It may be hard to determine the borders of a virtual organisation. In our definition, only those companies belong to the virtual organisation that really have to adapt their business processes to cooperation in the new networks (Hoffman, W., Hirschmann, P., and Scheer, A.W., 1996). Other parties involved have roles as suppliers and customers of the virtual organisation. The core of the virtual organisation in the case of IR implementation in the tourism environment would be the parties from the different travel and tourism branches, the IR-server operator, and the fulfilment centres where the sales information is printed. These printshops have to change their printing procedures from bulk production to on demand printing of single copies. Companies in tourism will have to change the process of producing of sales information from one in which new brochures are produced once a month, season, or year to a process in which sales information is continuously updated and translated into printable documents.

Building block 2: Core competencies.

In the virtual organisation, every party involved limits itself to those activities, it performs best (Lucas,, H., 1996; Martin, J., 1996). Thus, in the case of Instant Response, the tourism organisation limits itself to the production of sales documentation. Document handling, printing and distribution are done by other parties that are experts in their own fields.

Building block 3: IT-infrastructure

Virtual organisations need a good IT infrastructure (Enterprise one to one, 1998) in order to replace the physical handling of materials and the personal exchange of information in classic organisations. Instant Response makes use of the public IT infrastructure of the Internet for distributing its products. Only at the central point, where supply and demand of sales information are brought together, is some additional IT capacity required. In this case this is provided by the IR-server operator, whose core comptency is to provide the required IT infrastructure and facilities. Since Instant Response is only in its initial stages, experience has yet to be gained in coordinating the distribution activities and using IT support for this coordination.

Building block 4: Knowledge infrastructure

Using the Instant Response concept in tourism requires several types of knowledge:

- classic knowledge of the tourism markets and their salesinfornation needs, which will be provided by the tourism partners; this type of knowledge can be enhanced by the IR systems because it makes it very easy to keep track of the pattern of distribution of the material and to analyse these data statistically;
- knowledge of the semi-electronic distribution of sales documentation and its effects on sales. This type of knowledge can be accumulated by the IR-server operator organisation and distributed to the tourism partners;
- knowledge of the technical aspects of the system. This knowledge will be incorporated into the IR-server operators organisation and the network of fulfilment centres.

Building block 5:People

A Virtual Organisation can offer people truly independent jobs in a lifely environment. On one hand people are pleased with the freedom this involves; on the other hand their sense of belonging to an organisation is in danger. How do you work together with people every day, when you have never met them in person? Virtual linkage to an organisation is definitely looser than "normal" workrelationships. There is less social control, and motivation problems are not clearly visible. So, additional measures have to be taken in order for people in the Virtual organisation to feel comfortable. First, reward structures have to be higher than normal to compensate looser work relationships. Second, work conditions should be motivating to virtual workers: they need to be intellectually challenged. A Virtual Worker doing the administration is probably not a good idea. Third and finally, inter-personal contact remains important. Face-to-face meetings are also important in virtual organisations, not only for economic motives but also for social reasons. They are recommended for people in a CyberCorp in order to get to know each other and to re-build a team spirit (Finnley, M. and Robbins, H., 1996).

Building block 6: Management

In the virtual organisation, the overall management will be in the hands of the IR-server operator. Because of the widedistribution of people over different organisations and countries, management of the IR-server operator will have to focus on "relationmanagement". But technology should not be neglected. Although management should not improve technology itself, insight into the possibilities and impact of IT should be present within management. This technology should always be aimed at improving the marketapproach and the knowledge infrastructure.

Building block 7: Teams

The following three sorts of teams will generally be present within the virtual organisation:

- *Implementation team.* These teams will be formed – in a flexible way- when a new corporate user joins the virtual organisation. Employees of the corporate user and employees of the IR-server operator will have to work together in order to adjust the service to the needs of the corporate user (or its dealers) and implement it within the dealer organisation and the corporate user's organisation itself.
- *Technical team.* In order to improve the technical specifications of the system, technical specialists from both within the IR-server operator and within the fulfilment centres will need to work together, possibly backed by technologists from outside the virtual organisation for specific tasks. This team has to provide technical support for the corporate user and its dealers as well.
- *Sales team.* Gathering knowledge from the market is essential for virtual organisations [see *Building block 4: Knowledge infrastructure*]. A so-called "island" strategy, where sales people only have to deal with their own region (which is normal for selling regular products) is out of the question. Within the sales team, there must be co-operation and communication in order to get new customers (or in this case new partners: corporate users) and to satisfy their needs. Control over the total sales team will be in the hands of the IR-server operator management again.

Other teams (for specific tasks) will have to be formed on an ad-hoc basis and quickly in order to tackle problems.

A lot of this teamwork will be scattered across time and place. But face-to-face meetings should not be neglected because of the added value of inter-personal contact. It is recommended for teams to meet in person at least twice a year (Finnley, M. and Robbins, H., 1996).

Building block 8: Control/monitoring systems
Control over the total process has to focus on two main issues:

- *Quality of documentation delivered at prospect.* Certified print centres will have to be monitored continuously in order to check the quality of the printed and packed documentation. To check every package after it has been pre-packed by the FFC is too time- and effort consuming. Therefore, fulfilment centres should be randomly tested in order to remain certified. The IR-server operator should prepare regular quality reports to the tourism organisations based on these checks.
- *Time-to-deliver.* The speed of getting the right documentation at the prospect's desk is the major asset of Instant Response. Therefore, because of the multiple parts of a delivery chain, the whole cycle has to be closely monitored. At present, the construction of a graphical monitoring system is being considered.

5 Conclusion

In this paper, we argue that Instant Response, as a new means of distributing of pre-sales information, could also be useful for organisations in the tourism branch. Making use of Instant Response actually means taking part in a virtual organisation. Therefore, some areas for attention or building blocks are described that could help companies to make full use of the Instant Response concept.
Instant Response may prove to be an attractive way for information technology to support the tourism industry.

References

- CAP ventures press release 617-837-7200, 1997, *CAP ventures projects continued strong growth for printing on demand*;
- *Enterprise one to one*, 1998, proceedings of Don Peppers Top Seminar, Amsterdam;
- Finnley, M. and Robbins, H., 1996, *Why teams don't work: what went wrong and how to make it right*, Petersons Guides, 1996;
- Hayes, J, 1997, *The future of document and digital printing*, CAP ventures;
- Hoffman, W., Hirschmann, P., and Scheer, A.W., 1996,Die Imitierung Virtueller Unternehemen: leisten cooperationsbursen unterstuetzung?, *CIM management 6*, 10-14;
- Lucas,, H., 1996, The T-form organisation: using technology to design organisations for the 21st century, Josey-Bass publishers, San Francisco;
- Martin, J., 1996, Cybercorp, the new business revolution, Amacom, New York.
- Sheldon, P.J., 1997, *tourism information technology*, CAB international, New York;
- Venkatraman, N. and Henderson, C., 1996

The Internet as a Marketspace – The Percepton of the Consumers

Ph.D. Peter Björk
M.Sc. Thomas Guss
Swedish School of Economics and Business Administration, Vasa/Finland

Abstract

Marketing people are facing a new challenge - being successful in the marketspace. Technical development and unprejudiced consumers have created new marketing opportunities, leaving no industries unaffected. According to many researchers tourism and the Internet are a fruitful combination, but no matter how much potential marketing people see in the new channel, the core concept of marketing must not be forgotten, i.e. to satisfy consumers' needs and wants. In this study we are interested in the consumers' perception of the marketspace created on the Internet. The marketspace has its own characteristics, advantages and disadvantages, but the final success is determined by the users. The consumers of today use the Internet mainly as an information source or for fun, not for buying. We asked potential consumers about their use of the Internet as a marketspace and *elicited the perceived barriers of consumers for not using the Internet as a channel for commerce*. We used a hermeneutic approach in this exploratory study and the results presented originate from three different studies. The results of our first, pre-study show that consumers demonstrate an obvious cautiousness towards using the Internet as a marketspace and that the barriers are of the cognitive, affective and behavioural type. The weak structure of barriers found in our first study was extended in the main study. A categorisation of the reasons for not using the Internet as a marketspace show that there are four main types of barriers: scepticism, perceived uncertainty, security and personal service. The elicited structure was supported in the follow-up study. Our results can easily be translated into tactical marketing operations. Companies should confirm bookings not only by e-mail, but also by letter. The structure of the site and the booking page must be logical, and tactics to get the consumers to use the booking page for the first time should be introduced.

Keywords: Marketspace, Internet, purchase barriers, tourist behaviour

Introduction

Our purpose in this study was to elucidate the perceived barriers of consumers for not using the Internet as a marketspace. The new trade possibilities offered by the Internet are a result of technology development, changing consumer behaviour and a growing interest among companies to find new markets and marketing channels. The Internet can be used for different purposes, and data based on on-line surveys show that most Internet "surfers" use the Internet for entertainment purposes [35]. The share of respondents who say that they purchase products over the Internet varies considerably from 21 percent [35 (Internet User Survey #2)] to 76.2 percent [33]. These figures can hardly be generalised to the whole population due to the research method used. Internet literate people (especially frequent users) have a much higher probability of purchasing via the Internet compared to "ordinary" people. There are for example in Finland about 150.000 shoppers who regularly purchase over the Internet, which can be considered a low rate (3 percent (150.000/5.000.000)) considering the fact that using the Internet as a marketspace has been possible since the beginning of the 1990s [22] and the density of Internet users per capita is among the highest in the world [19]. Most researchers are convinced that the share of "surfers" on the Internet who will use it for shopping will increase, but there are barriers [8, 30].

The new market channel the Internet creates will leave no industry unaffected. The combination of tourism and the Internet seems promising and in an American survey travel had the second highest mean sales per company (real estate companies had the highest mean sales) [22]. The faster computer processors of today and better links (ISDN) make the Internet more user-friendly, and we can see that more and more computer owners choose to connect their computers to a network [30].

The content of the literature related to the Internet is often very technical or marketing oriented. The amount of books and articles describing how to construct homesites is huge, and the same goes for books and articles related to the Internet as a marketing channel [14, 12, 3]. A less studied area is the consumers found in the marketspace, if we do not include all those studies focusing on the characteristics of Internet users [22, 30]. If we want to understand Internet users and marketspace consumers we have to broaden the research area to also include a consumer perspective.

Barriers for using a new market channel, in this case the Internet, can be of different kinds. The fear of not doing the right thing, i.e. to fill in wrong information, is always present when the consumer has to deal with new technology. Another barrier, also related to fear, is the willingness to reveal secret data such as, for example, account numbers and social security numbers [30, 28]. A third barrier can be of a more affective kind, a feeling that new technology is nothing for me, or "I can live without using the Internet as a market channel". Finally, we have barriers due to access problems and we can find at least two types. Before a consumer can use the Internet as a market channel, s/he must have access to an Internet connected computer[1]. The second type of access problem is related to the speed at which the Internet operates. Sometimes it is impossible to get through to the Net and in these situations a consumer may get frustrated and use another market channel instead (if it is possible).

Companies have to develop interfaces consumers find attractive, and we are not only talking about an audio-visual dimension but a user friendly dimension too. Theoretically, we are in an challenging situation where existing consumer behaviour

---

[1] There are also some attempts to develop techniques to make TV:s Internet connected.

theories and models have been developed for market situations where the consumer is passive and collect information that companies are distributing [6]. The activity pattern of the buyer and the seller (company) can be completely different in Internet based markets [8]. The possibility of the consumers to collect information about products available on the markets increases tremendously and Schultz [29, p. 145] says "the buyer has become the advertiser, and the sellers have become the respondents or consumers". The changing marketing structures and consumer behaviour indicate a need to at least adapt existing consumer behaviour theories, if not completely develop new ones.

Marketspace, possibilities, threats and barriers

The Internet, the platform for marketspace, is for many people around the world a tool used daily for different purposes and marketing people have not been late recognising the markets and marketing potential the Internet entails[2]. The development of the Internet and the fields of applications is very fast and Levin [20] believes that all companies, independent of size and industry, will in the future have a Web site of their own (see also Cronin, [4]).

We define marketspace in this paper as a channel of commerce in a virtual environment[3]. Marketspace is one area found in cyberspace, an area where business activities take place. We do not think that the marketspace will replace traditional marketplaces but complement them. The new technology and changing consumer behaviour will create new and different marketing concepts [12]. The basic marketing philosophy found in a traditional market will be the same in a marketspace, but there are also some differences worth discussing [17].

In a *traditional marketplace* goods are exchanged for money and the face-to-face environment entails a multidimensional communication. We can, for example, hear different intonations and see facial expressions alongside verbal communication. The communication in a traditional market is, from the perspective of a consumer, limited in two ways due mainly to time constraints. The number of outlets visited is limited and contacts to actors not immediately relevant for the purchase is kept to a minimum. The warranty, for example, is not checked with the importer, or the producing company is not contacted on spare part issues. [12, 17]

---

[2] Cyberspace could be defined as:
a) a total world, where we can move around in search of different kind of information without leaving it, b) a world to live in, c) an easy world, d) an objective world that it is there though I'm not, e) a common world, is open for everyone, f) an active and interactive world through the presence of users, g) a world with a history, meaning that it is continuing from older kinds of information.[18]

[3] Virtual means that something seems to exist when it only appears through a network. A company might seem to have facilities though it doesn't. It just uses them as it owns them. [23].

The interaction in *the marketspace* is mainly built on electronic information, which can be multidirectional from customer to intermediaries to producing companies and their partners, but all physical contact with the company in the purchase situation is at a minimum. The physical walls of companies are at a minimum and the companies can at one extreme be classified as imaginary [23]. The visual part of a company can in a purchase situation be the interface on the computer screen or a print-out.

The difference between marketplace and marketspace can be seen in content, context and infrastructure [9, 12] (Table 1). Gummesson [12] gives an example of an car auction on the net, where the cars are presented as information, text and pictures (content). The auction takes place on-screen instead of face-to-face (context). The actual car lot is replaced by computers, telecommunication and TV screen (infrastructure).

The content of a marketplace is mainly goods which are traded against money. Information is the main content in a marketspace.

Table 1: The main differences between marketplaces and marketspaces

	Marketplace	Marketspace
Content	Goods (+services that need the physical presence of a provider)	Information (+services not in need of the physical presence of a provider)
Context	Dynamic environment	Static environments
Infrastructure	The physical store, opening hours how to get to the store	Address, phone number, what kind of system, where to keep information

The contexts surrounding the consumer can either be dynamic or static with a respect to the possibility of integrating the decision and purchase context. The two separate contexts model characteristic for cybershopping, the Internet context found on the web-site and the place where the consumer is physically present (at home or at work), can also be found in a marketplace.

The contexts surrounding the consumer can either be dynamic or static when considering the possibility of integrating the decision and purchase context. In cybershopping there are two different contexts, the Internet context found on the web-site and the place where the consumer is physically present (at home or at work). You can see a corresponding situation in the marketplace where the decision is made at home and carried out in a store. But we can also find a situation in a marketplace when the two contexts are integrated. Take, for example, a consumer who makes an unplanned purchase decision in a store.

The infrastructure is where the business place is located. In the marketplace it is the geographical location and in the marketspace a web-site. The common dimension is the address, which can be a street address or an Internet address. New technology creates both possibilities and threats. Consumers differ in their readiness to accept innovations and marketspace is no exception. The reason for not using the Internet as a marketspace can be of different type, which we call barriers. A literature review [2, 7, 21, 28, 31] and a review of the results based on on-line surveys [34, 32, 33] show that these barriers are of two main types, psychological and technical.

Psychological barrier. One category of barriers consists of felt insecurity as a result of lack of experience. This situation can be compared to the situation when credit cards were introduced. People had no experience of using them and therefore felt insecure using them. These barriers will probably vanish as more and more people buy and their own experience increases. To state such personal information as, for example, social security number may become a barrier for shopping [10].

Technical barriers. A second category of barriers is technology and safety. Access, payment and identification are three dimensions related to technical barriers. Slow, non access and unreliable systems may frustrate the consumer and force him to make another choice [10]. A question many consumers on marketspace consider is the security of the system [2]. Is it safe to give away the credit card number and/or information about oneself? This barrier might be dealt with through the SET system (Secure Electronic Transaction). SET is a specification using technology for authenticating the parties that are involved in card purchases over the net. SET will hopefully make cyberspace a safer place to do electronic business [36].

Support. Consumers buying complex products, products purchased infrequently, and products which are purchased only once may need additional assistance in their decision process [11]. Charter tours ought to be a good example. The customers want to know about the weather and details about the hotels, updated information not found in any brochure. A non interactive site not offering the buyer the possibility to ask questions or endearments might make him turn to other markets [3]. A company can of course put out all information details thought to be needed. But there is a risk that the system will become very slow.

Customer preferences. Consumers use the Internet as a marketspace for different reasons. The consumer may save time, money and/or get a unique product. The learning capacity of the computers can be used to tailor different offers and also store information about the customers [5]. Computers taking my order can be taught to store my preferences and to start offering me only the goods that I seem to prefer, which will save me time. Customers will also gain bargaining power through more information. Today the seller is the one having more information and using it to make a profit. When the customer is able to collect information through the Internet, the information can be used to give the customer the best bargain [13].

Research process and results

Due to the fairly new research area a Hermeneutic research approach was applied in this study [15, 1]. We started the research process by doing a pre-study where 13 potential marketspace users had to answer questions related to their probability of using a company's website when booking a hotel room and a trip by ship, and their perceived barriers for using it. We did also ask the respondents what they thought of the booking page visited. Finally, they had to fill in background information, how many hours they use the Internet weekly, if they had bought a product from the marketspace and their age and sex.

The four companies the respondents had to contact represented two different industries, the lodging industry and the transportation industry. The hotel chains used were Sheraton and Radisson, and the home-site visited was the Swedish one. The task of the respondents was to book a room at these two hotels, first at the Sheraton hotel and then at the Radisson Hotel in Stockholm, for two persons and one night. The ferry companies used in our study were Scandlines and TTline, and the respondents were asked to book a trip by these two ferry companies for four persons and a car. The journey had to start in Trelleborg and the destination was Travemünde.

The result of the pre-study shows two things. Firstly, there are *safety* and *security* dimensions the marketspace users perceive as barriers and that these barriers can be elicited in an empirical study. The sample size used in the pre-study was small and the results have to be interpreted with some caution. Secondly, the data collecting method used in our pre-study could be improved. The data was collected using an introspective approach and the respondents were put in front of a Internet connected computer and were then asked to complete an open-ended questionnaire. We encouraged the students to visit one site at a time and to write down, in their own words, how they perceived the booking pages and possible barriers for not using it.

Data for the second study was collected using personal interviews [24]. Fourteen users and potential users of Internet as a marketspace were studied. To use two hotels and two ferry-lines seemed to be too cumbersome for the respondents. The respondents in our main study had therefore to discuss only two sites with the interviewers. The companies selected were Sheraton and TTline, because they represented two different industries and have an international booking system. A highly structured approach was used in the data collecting phase and the data was analysed by two researchers [25]. The two researchers' interpretations of the data were compared in order to check for the researcher effects. Only small interpretation differences occurred and the similarities in the categorisations indicate a high common understanding. The structure found in the pre-study was extended and strengthened in our main study and the perceived barriers elicited were of four types; perceived uncertainty, personal service, scepticism and system security.

A follow-up study was undertaken three weeks after the main study was completed with a new set of respondents in order to replicate the findings [25]. The booking-pages of Sheraton and TTline were also used in this study and the results of the personal interviews show that the four dimensions found in our main study are also found in the follow-up study. The number of respondents interviewed in the follow-up study was twelve.

Results of Study 1, pre-study

We collected data in our pre-study using an unobtrusive procedure. The respondents were put in front of an Internet connected computer. We handed out our questionnaires, provided the respondents with some basic information after which the respondents were allowed to proceed at their own pace. This procedure was chosen due to its unobtrusive character, which is an advantage in a pre-study. We studied 13 potential users of the marketspace and the results will be presented hereafter.

Would you use the Internet as a marketspace?

Our results show that 62 percent (8) of the respondents would not today book a hotel room or a ferry ticket using the Internet, and the probability of using it among those respondents who did not definitely say no varies considerably. No respondent claimed that they for certain would book a trip or a room using the Internet, but the probability varies between 50 and 90 percent. An interesting result is that if one thinks booking a room is too risky, the booking of a ferry ticket is also perceived as unsafe.

We also asked the respondents to state their opinions about the booking page and a weak connection between the perception of clear structure and the probability of using it for booking could be noticed.

Barriers for using the Internet as a marketspace.

Our purpose was to study the barriers for not using the Internet as a marketspace. Although we have a small sample size in this pre-study, the homogeneity of the answers makes the results interesting. What the respondents want is some kind of confirmation of their booking. This is not an unexpected result, and the form in which they want the confirmation was somewhat unexpected. Most respondents wanted a confirmation by letter. A confirmation by e-mail was not enough, but has to be complemented by a more "concrete" confirmation. A confirmation by telephone could also be accepted.

The interesting results found in this study and the somewhat shallowness of the answers made us continue with our second study. We used personal interviews to collect data from the 14 respondents selected through a convenience sampling method [27]. The booking pages of Sheraton and TTline were visited and analysed by the respondents.

Results of study 2, main study.
We used the structure qualitative analyse technique that Miles and Huberman [25] advocate and four main categories of barriers for using the Internet as a marketspace could be elicited.

1) Perceived uncertainty
Consumers are afraid of doing something wrong when booking and a summary of the interviews clearly shows that one category can be labelled *perceived uncertainty*. One respondent for example said "that it is easy to do something wrong" and another "it seems so easy to type in the wrong date, for example". It is obvious that the technical layout must support the user and show the decisions that s/he has made. The simplicity of changing wrong decisions, misspellings and typing errors must be enhanced.

2) Personal service
Doing business on the Internet was not supported by everyone, but about one third of the respondents claimed that they prefer doing business in a face-to-face situation, a common answer was "I like the personal service" received, for example, at the front desk of a travel agency. Developing the Internet to become more personal in a affective dimension is stressed. We also have another dimension in the face-to-face category. The respondents also wanted to discuss different options with the seller, which should be no problem with the technology of today. You can have an interactive communication on the marketspace, voices, text, pictures and sounds.

3) Scepticism
The most common answer we received as to why respondents would not use the Internet was scepticism of the system. This category of barriers seems to have two dimensions: does it really work and bad experiences. Our results show the importance of a reliable system. Although the respondents see a booking page and are allowed to use it, this does not convince them. A common result was "does it really work". The second dimension is a result of bad experiences of the Internet in general. One com-mon comment was "what will happen if the system is out of order when it is needed".

4) Security
This category consists of two dimensions, security of personal information and financial transaction security. All of the respondents were afraid to write down their personal data and their credit card number. Our results also show that this barrier will probably diminish in the future when the system becomes more trustworthy and the respondents more experienced.

The four categories of barriers found in our data are all related and a suitable model consisting of four overlapping circles can be presented as a general summary (Model 1).

Model 1. Barriers for not using Internet as a marketspace

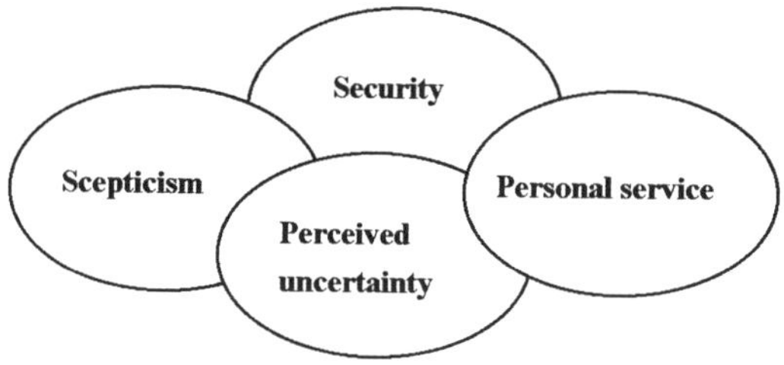

We also asked the respondents what they thought a company must do and how the system must be developed in order to receive them as customers. A categorisation of the results show that there are four categories and Model 1 can also in this respect be used as a framework. Most respondents want some kind of feedback from the company, and the confirmation must not only be electronic, but also in a more manifest form. These results are related to the category perceived uncertainty. Security on the Internet must be improved, and we are not only talking about the technical part but also the perceived security. The system must be user-friendly and reliable. The personal service dimension was not mentioned when we asked the respondents what must change so that their probability of using the Internet as a marketspace will increase, but another dimension was included, perceived value. The customer must receive some advantage from using the Internet as a marketspace. Some of the respondents mentioned that the product must be cheaper on the Internet compared to those sold in a traditional store. Convenience was also mentioned as one aspect contributing to perceived value. When fully developed, the Internet will, according to Ghosh [8], include all these benefits.

Results of study 3, follow-up study.
Twelve respondents were interviewed in our follow-up study in the same manner as in the main study. The results of this study show that the reasons why the respondents are not completely convinced and the Internet not used as a marketspace are percei-ved lack of the possibility of immediate feedback about the current

booking situation, the reliability of the system, lack of personal service and feeling of insecurity.

We also asked what should be done to increase the probability of using the Internet as a marketspace. Most respondents said that they would like to receive a confirmation, and if possible a confirmation by letter. The booking pages of the two companies used in this study (Sheraton and TTline) were considered easy to use, but the structure of the Sheraton site was not that clear. The perceived reliability and security of the system must be convincing (read improved)[4].

Conclusions

The marketspace on the Internet is already today an important market and marketing channel. The number of web users is increasing very fast in most parts of the world, and the number of buyers on the Net is accumulating, although the speed is not that dizzy if we look at absolute figures [30, 16]. All industries are in one way or another influenced by the new channel and the tourism industry is no exception.

Smith and Jenner [30, p. 77] state "Technology is always in advance of the vast majority of the human race and most people just take a longer time to adjust to new ideas". We studied perceived barriers for not using the Internet as a marketspace in this study, applying a hermenutic approach. Four categories of barriers could be elicited and they are: consumers feel uncertain about the system, do not completely believe in the security of the Internet, want personal service and are sceptical towards their own behaviour. The first barrier is very much related to personal experiences and is a result of behaviour. The second and third barriers are more related to personal feelings and are of an affective type. Finally, we have the "sceptical" category, which is on a cognitive dimension.

We also asked the respondents how the system must be improved in order to increase the probability of becoming "Internet shoppers". The answers we got show that the customer must get feedback from the company about what has been purchased (or ordered), security must be improved and experience increased. Consumers trade benefits to costs and the Internet must provide the user with value [26], which is not impossible according to Ghosh [8]. Two aspects were mentioned in our study: price and convenience. It must be convenient to do business on the Internet and the price must be competitive.

---

[4] We also asked the respondents in all three studies what kind of products they have or would consider buying using the Internet. Products, whose quality can be assessed or specified prior to purchase have the largest probability of being purchased on the marketspace. Some examples are books and CD:s. Products the respondents would not buy are more expensive ones, for example technical products. Even unknown brands were mentioned as product types which would not be bought on the Internet.

Our literature review shows that most researchers have focused on the technical dimensions of the Internet or the functions of the Internet in companies and organisations. Less studied is the Internet from the perspective of customers. We focused in this study on how respondents perceive the booking page of only two companies (one hotel chain and one ferry company) (four companies were used in the pre-study). The presented results must therefore be interpreted with some caution and our exploratory study would benefit by studies of other industries. We would like to see studies where booking pages of other companies are included and especially studies comparing the perceived barriers of using booking pages of service companies to companies selling physical goods.

The new technology and the changing interactions between sellers and buyers in consumer markets in general and the tourism market in particular make us wonder how applicable the established consumer behaviour models and theories are. Already a shallow mental exercise shows a potential for an immense research area, and tourism can without doubt be a fruitful area for empirical studies due to its world wide importance.

References

1. Andersson, S.: Positivism kontra hermeneutik. Bokförlaget Korpen. Göteborg (1982).
2. Burke, R.: Do You See What I See? The Future of Virtual Shopping. *Journal of the Academy of Marketing Science*. Vol. 25, No. 4, p. 352-360 (1997).
3. Cano, V. & Prentice, R.: Opportunities for endearment to place through electronic "visiting": WWW homepages and the tourism promotion of Scotland. *Tourism Management*. Vol. 19, p. 67-73 (1998).
4. Cronin, M.: The Internet Strategy Handbook. Harvard Business School Press. Boston (1996).
5. Davies, J.M.: The Essential Guide to Database Marketing. McGraw-Hill. London (1992).
6. Engel, J., Blackwell, R. & Miniard, P.: Consumer Behavior. The Dryden Press (1995).
7. Fredholm, P.: Elektroniska affärer. Studentlitteratur. Lund (1997).
8. Ghosh, S.: Making Business Sense of the Internet. *Harvard Business Review*. March-April, p. 126-135 (1998).
9. Gill, P.: Creating Virtual Value. *Canadian Business Review*. Autumn, p. 15-17 (1996).
10. Green 69 J. & Johansson S.: Cyberworld. Høst & Søns forlag, Copenhagen (1993).
11. Gonyea, J.C. & Gonyea W.M.: Selling on the internet. McGraw-Hill, New York (1996).
12. Gummesson, E.: Relationship Marketing: From 4Ps to 30Rs. Stockholm University, Stockholm (1997).
13. Hagel, J. & Armstrong, A.: Net Gain. Harvard Business School Press, Boston (1997).
14. Hedman, A. & Pappinen, L.: Affärer och marknadsföring på Intenet. Pagina Förlags Ab, Stockholm (1996).
15. Helenius, R.: Förstå och bättre veta. Om hermeneutiken i samhällsvetenskaperna. Carlsson Bokförlag. Stockholm (1990).
16. Jaakkola, A.: Laamanen rakentaa virtuaaliverkosta. Kehittyvä Kauppa, p. 26-28 (1998).
17. Jakobsson P.: Internet i marknadsföringen och marknadskommunikationen. Stud.litt.(1995).
18. Janlert, L-E.: Hemma i Cyberspace. Scandinavian University Press, Lund (1995).

19. Landquist, Å.: Internet fortsätter att leva sitt eget liv. Huvudstadsbladet, 8.9 (1997).
20. Levin, M.: A corporate Web site is different from a marketing Web site. *Harvard Business Review*. November-December, p. 154-156 (1996).
21. Lombardi, R.: Shopping in cyberspace. *CAmagazine*. April, p. 35-36 (1998).
22. Marcussen, C.: Marketing European Tourism Products via Internet/WWW. *Geography and Tourism Marketing*, p. 23-34 (1997).
23. Martin, J: Cybercorp, the new business revolution. AMACOM. New York (1996).
24. Maxwell, J.: Qualitative Reserach Design. An Interactive Approach. Sage Publ. CA (1996).
25. Miles, M. & Huberman, M.: Qualitative Data Analysisi, A Sourcebook of New Methods. Sage Publications. London (1984).
26. Monroe, K.: Pricing, Making Profitable Decisions. McGraw-Hill. New York (1990).
27. Patton, M.: How to Use qualitative Methods in Evaluation. Sage Publ. London (1987).
28. Reinders, J. & Baker, M.: The Future for Direct Retailing of Travel and Tourism Products: The Influence of Information Technology. *Progress in Tourism and Hospitality Research*. Vol. 4, p. 1-15 (1998).
29. Schultz, D.: The Inevitability of Integrated Communications. *Journal of Business Research*. Vol. 37, p. 139-146 (1996).
30. Smith, C. & Jenner, P.: Tourism and the Internet. *Travel & Tourism Analyst*, p. 62-81(1998).
31. Spar, D. & Bussgang, J.: Ruling the Net. *Harvard Business Review*. May-June, p. 125-133 (1996).

Internet References

32. http://www.forrester.com
33. http//www.gvu.gatech.edu/user_sur…y-1998-04/reports/1998.04Use.html
34. http://www.navidec.com/cybershopper/summary.html
35. http//www.survey.net/inet2r.html
36. http//www.visa.com

The Tourist as Value Creator on the Internet

Benedict G.C. Dellaert
CentER, Tilburg University,
The Netherlands

1 Introduction

The rapid increase in capacity and usage of the Internet in recent years provides exciting opportunities for structural change in the design, marketing and creation of tourism services. Many businesses, government agencies, and researchers have recognized this potential impact of the Internet. For example, in the domain of marketing research, Hoffman and Novak (1996) highlight the opportunity of the Internet to provide many-to-many communication by offering an efficient platform through which individuals and organizations can send and receive communications. This possibility could greatly affect marketing communications and branding strategies because it allows individual tourists to influence destination images directly by sharing detailed tourism experience information with other tourists. Alba et al. (1997), in addition, discuss the opportunities the Internet to provides as an electronic marketplace through which increasingly interactive consumer-supplier relationships can develop. For example, the Internet may allow tourists to bypass traditional travel agents and communicate with accommodation and transportation providers directly.

These examples illustrate how the Internet may cause traditional roles in the tourism value creation process to shift in important ways. This study focuses on the fact that tourists may become much more actively involved in various stages of the supply chain, making market players more dependent on individual tourists' contributions to provide maximum value added to their customers. For example, tourists may need to become involved in travel package design by using Internet communication platforms that are accessible to destination, accommodation and transportation marketers; they may need to play a role in branding and image-building by providing user feed-back about tourism experiences, e.g., by participating in on-line discussion groups; and they may need to initiate (just-in-time) transactions and service delivery processes by ordering electronically through the Internet.

The aim of this study is to begin to analyze the underlying structure of these tourist directed interaction processes that may evolve in Internet-based design, marketing and production processes, and more specifically, to analyze the tourist choice to contribute time and labor to Internet-based value creation processes. Specifically, the paper addresses the following two questions:

- When and why will tourists choose to interact with suppliers on the Internet?; and

- Which elements in the interaction process open up opportunities for additional tourist-based value creation?

2 The tourist choice process

It is assumed that various functions need to be performed for a tourism experience to take place and that these functions may be undertaken partly by suppliers (both commercial and non-commercial) and partly by tourists themselves. Tourists select the mix of services and activities that provide the highest utility within their budget. For example, in a one week holiday a tourist may wish to allocate an amount M and a time period T to dining, and will decide how to allocate this budget over various options such as fast-food restaurants, à la carte restaurants, and preparing ones own meal.

Furthermore, it is assumed that, over time, tourism service suppliers and tourists interact in such a way that their market relationships tend towards a Pareto optimal combination of (c.f. Wernerfelt 1994, 1996):

- Channel structures (e.g., a combination of Internet-based transaction mechanisms, and real-world travel agents), and
- Labor division within channels (e.g., tourists driving their own car to the airport vs. using a transportation provider's services to fly to their destination).

Generally speaking, the outcome of this process is maximized if the total of value-added minus costs is maximized. This implies a tendency both to maximize tourist utility, and to minimize overall costs. Price determines the surplus split between tourists and suppliers.

The focus in this study is on the so-called total tourism product (Middleton 1988), which encompasses all components that make up a tourist's travel experience. These components include transportation, accommodation, destination attractions, and destination facilities and services (e.g., Jansen-Verbeke 1988). Although it is recognized that tourists' evaluations of total tourism products may involve a number separate trade-offs for each of the components (e.g., Dellaert, Ettema and Lindh 1998) in the current study they are analyzed jointly. The perspective that is taken is that of an abstraction of the separate components into an overall tourism value creation process. Still, the total tourism product value creation process also requires several functions to be performed for which working definitions are given below. These definitions are based in part on Middleton (1988) and on three more general references from the manufacturing and retailing literature: Anderson (1997) who provides an overview of manufacturing cost-components as a basis for developing flexible production processes, Biglaiser and Friedman (1994) who give a review of generic cost-components in the marketing channel when middlemen are present, and Alba et al. (1997) who define the dimensions that affect the relative attractiveness of different retail formats to consumers.

Figure 1 summarizes schematically the functions applied in the framework. It also illustrates two other relevant aspects: First, each function can be performed through different channels, one of which is the Internet (e.g., Internet-based information search vs. travel agent assistance with search), and secondly, preferences for functions and channels may vary between individuals. On an abstract level, the value creation process embedded in these functions represents an iterative cycle in which the output of each function provides input to the subsequent function. Note that not all functions necessarily require extensive time and money allocations in each value creation cycle (e.g., routine trips may not require much search), and that feedback loops between functions may exist (e.g., travel consumption may provide input for evaluations, but may also trigger a need for additional supply of travel services). The functions are:

- *Research* The research function incorporates activities such as tourists' searches for services and destinations of a desired quality and price. The function also includes research in the sense of studying possibilities for valuable travel experiences and effective allocation of resources. These activities may involve tourist contributions, for example when drawing on experiences of innovative travelers looking for new experiences, destinations and activities.
- *Composition* The travel composition function requires a mental integration of different (physical and non-physical) components into a new unity that can address certain unresolved consumption needs. Communication of this solution is part of the composition function also. For example, Dietvorst (1993) discusses the planning process involved in creating demand oriented tourism complexes. The composition function differs from the research function in that it is directed more towards problems solving and creativity and is more communication oriented. For example, a library search for possible travel itineraries would be classified as research, whereas an integration of components from different suppliers to create a new travel package would be classified as composition.

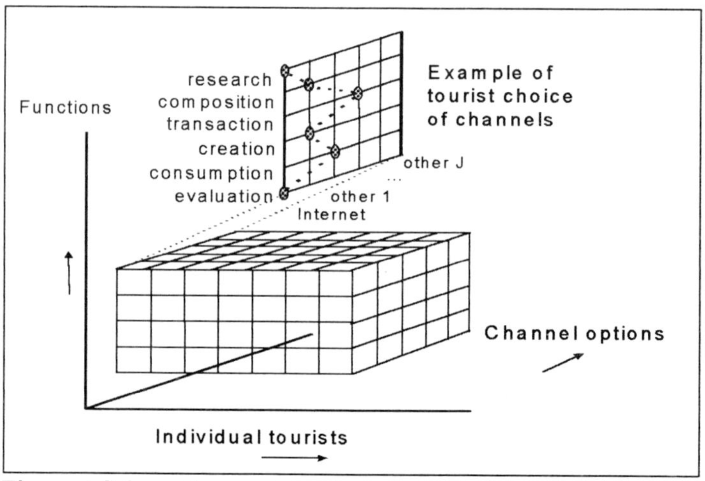

Figure 1 Schematic representation of tourist channel choice

- *Transaction* The transaction function covers all activities that relate to the process of transferring information, products and services from suppliers to tourists. These activities range from monetary and informational transactions, to accommodation and transportation of people and products. The traditional role of the travel agent falls mostly within this function area (e.g., see Betancourt and Gautchi's (1990) discussion of retailers and Biglaiser and Friedman's (1994) analysis of the functionality of middlemen).
- *Creation* This function includes all activities that have as outcome facilities or services that can be applied by tourists to generate a tourism experience. Thus, it is similar to the production function in most managerial models but differs from the notion of production in the traditional household production model (Becker 1965) in that not all household activities are classified as creation. For example, writing a travel guide would be classified as creation, while a household's 'production' of a travel experience is classified as consumption. Sometimes, creation, transaction and consumption may be difficult to separate, especially in the case of tourists creating services jointly with other consumers, and for their own direct consumption. For example, in the case of two people playing a game of tennis, each player more or less simultaneously creates, distributes and consumes the game that they are playing together.
- *Consumption* This function is the only activity that can be performed solely by the tourist him or herself. It constitutes the core of the value creation process in the sense that, most, if not all tourist utility is derived from this function. Multiple simultaneous consumption functions can be performed, e.g., eating popcorn while watching a movie. Furthermore, consumption may create positive and negative externalities that affect other tourists' utilities. For example, tourists in a café create a positive utility for each other, up to a certain critical level, when the negative effects of crowding outweigh the positive ones.
- *Evaluation* Often, tourists derive value both from a tourism experience itself, and from reflecting on the experience. For example, tourists may gain social benefits from discussing their experiences with others. In part, evaluation provides positive utility to tourists (e.g., a feeling of satisfaction) and thus, could be regarded as postponed consumption, in part also evaluation provides a feedback mechanism from the consumption function to the research function and as such could be included in a definition of search cost. The reason that evaluation is classified as a separate function is the unique character of the activities that it involves.

3 Formal model

To facilitate analysis of the role of the Internet in the different stages of the value creation process, the process is modeled from the perspective of the tourist's choice of activities. The notion of tourist activity includes both the traditional consumption and the production types of activities (e.g., both eating and preparing a meal, and both searching for destinations and providing travel advice). This approach allows one to generate a model along the lines of household production theory, in which tourists' decisions to allocate time and money to Internet-based channel options are modeled (c.f., Becker 1965, Gronau 1980, Kooreman and Wunderink 1997).

The value creation process for a given tourism experience is described in N different functions that need to be performed. It is assumed that each function $n \varepsilon N$ is offered as a separate module, and that no loss of efficiency occurs if functions are combined from several suppliers and/or channels. For example, it is assumed that using the Internet for travel information search purposes, does not affect a tourist's efficiency in placing an order with a traditional travel agent. For the sake of simplicity, it is assumed also that all functions are priced separately. Given that the focus of the current study is on the demand side of the tourist-supplier interaction, the analysis of the impact of bundling of facilities and services is left for future research.

In formal notation, let U_{ie} be the utility of a tourism experience e to tourist i, let N be the total of functions n that need to be performed for a tourist to be able to experience consumption utility U_{ie}, and let K_n be the total of channel options k that is available to perform function n. Functions can be performed either by tourist i or by a supplier p. Tourists maximize their utility by allocating time and money amongst functions, and channels within those functions.

Given the time and money budgets T and M, tourist i maximizes the following utility function (subscripts for i and c are suppressed for readability):

$$\textbf{\textit{Maximize}}\ U = Z(m, t) + \Sigma_N Z_n(X_{nk}, H_{nk}, C_{nk}) \tag{1}$$

subject to constraints:

$$\Sigma_N\, p_{nk} X_{nk} + m = M \tag{1a}$$

$$\Sigma_N\, (H_{nk} + C_{nk}) + t = T \tag{1b}$$

where, $Z(m,t)$ is the utility that can be generated by spending m units of time and an amount t of money in other consumption areas, with m and t being the remaining money and time after providing for tourism experience C_{nk}, Z_n is the (dis)utility of generating function n, by using X_{nk}, the vector of goods and services purchased for function n through channel k at price p_{nk}, H_{nk} is time allocated by the tourist to home production and C_{nk} is time allocated for consumption, both in relation to function n performed through channel k.

For example, if the tourism experience under study is '*a trip to Paris*', examples of elements of X_{nk} could include the travel guide, the train that brings one to Paris, and the bar in the hotel, H_{nk} could include the time spend riding the train, booking the trip, and discussing the trip with friends, and C_{nk} could be time spent sightseeing in Paris.

Note that in the household production approach, goods and services do not provide utility per se, they provide utility only by facilitating consumption experiences (i.e., $U(X_{nk}) = 0, \forall n \in N, \forall k \in K$). If it is assumed that the fixed costs of durables (e.g., buying a car to drive on the weekends) are distributed over all current and future consumption experiences, the following consumer utility applies:

$$U_{\{1k,\dots,Nk\}} = Z(m, t) + \Sigma_N Z_n(X_{nk}, H_{nk}, C_{nk}) \qquad (2)$$
$$= Z(M, T) - Z(\Sigma_N p_{nk} X_{nk}, \Sigma_N(H_{nk} + C_{nk})) + \Sigma_N Z_n(X_{nk}, H_{nk}, C_{nk})$$

where $Z(M, T)$ is the total utility that can be generated with the household's time and money budget (which is an unknown constant value), $Z(\Sigma_N p_{nk} X_{nk}, \Sigma_N(H_{nk} + C_{nk}))$ is the utility that can be generated by spending an amount $\Sigma_N p_{nk} X_{nk}$ of money, and $\Sigma_N(H_{nk} + C_{nk})$ of time elsewhere.

4 The role of the Internet

The impact of the Internet can be analyzed in how it may affect tourist and service supplier roles in terms of the division of labor required to facilitate tourism experiences. In principle, many functions in the marketing and service supply channel can be performed either by tourists themselves or by commercial and non-commercial service suppliers, and there is no ex-ante reason why one structure should be more beneficial than the other. Many of the expected shifts in tourist-supplier relationships that the Internet may bring about should therefore become apparent from the structure of activities in the tourism value creation channel.

For the purpose of the current analysis each one-on-one relationship between a tourist and service supplier is regarded as a two party game in which the players reach a certain division of labor that is optimal in terms of channel efficiency (Wernerfelt 1994). Side payments are assumed to take place in cases of local sub-optima's, so that joint pay-offs can be maximized. Note that this implies that suppliers might pay tourists if this can improve overall channel efficiency. For example, a travel agent can offer commission to tourists wanting to recommend the trips that the agent offers to other tourist and refer those other tourists to the travel agent's web site. The ultimate value that is created in the tourism channel is determined largely by the choices that individual tourists make; both by tourists' choices to purchase certain travel services and by their choices to conduct certain types of non-priced activities.

When analyzing how the Internet may influence such structures, the most general starting point one can take is arguably to regard the Internet as a general-purpose communication facilitator. For example, see the discussions in Hoffman and Novak (1996), and Alba et al. (1997), who emphasize the changes that the Internet may bring about in the way in which consumers and producers, and consumers amongst themselves communicate.

Three main information flows can be distinguished with respect to the role of the Internet:

- Tourists can signal their utility and search costs for certain goods and services to service suppliers. These communications may involve activities such as participating in user-discussion groups, requesting certain types of services and/or offering suggestions for improvements.
- Service suppliers can signal their capability to provide services and facilities at certain levels of quality and at certain costs. These communications may

involve activities such as advertising, direct mail, and specific types of signaling that may increase the credibility of the offerings that suppliers are aiming to sell.

- Tourists can communicate directly with other tourists about the quality and price of the services, facilities and destinations that they have experienced. Tourists may also provide general destination information and suggestions tot facilitate other tourists' search processes.

Table 1 reviews how the six functions in the proposed tourism value creation framework might be affected. In the proposed framework, the set of functions *N* consists of the components: {*Research (Re), Composition (Cm), Transaction (Tr), Creation (Cr), Consumption (Co),* and *Evaluation (Ev)*}.

Table 1 Possible tourist contributions in Internet-based value creation processes

	Beneficiary		
Function	*Self*	*Other Consumers*	*Producer*
Research (*Re*)	Search for destination and services	Provide information on travel experiences	Provide information on travel needs
Composition (*Cm*)	Provide individual specifications	Generate new ideas for trips	Provide specifications; generate new ideas
Transaction (*Tr*)	Conduct transactions, arrange distribution	N/A	Reduce costs of transactions
Creation (*Cr*)	Arrange made to order travel experiences	Communicate desirable destination image; provide social recognition	
Consumption (*Co*)	Go through travel experience	Possible externalities, such as congestion	Increase social attraction of destination
Evaluation (*Ev*)	Provide feedback on travel experience; participate in social networks; provide information on destinations and future travel needs.		

The observations in Table 1 can be summarized in four major effects that may determine which Internet web sites can be most effective:

- Increased opportunities to reduce communication costs between tourists and service suppliers (e.g., more efficient information searches, ordering, or evaluations),
- Increased opportunities to enhance tourist-based value by providing opportunities for individualized travel experiences (e.g., individually tailored trip composition, or unique purchase history-based interaction mechanisms),
- Lower costs to signal quality of the service supplier (e.g., services with external quality control mechanisms, markets with middlemen, or markets with options for non-Internet signaling),

- Increased possibilities of valuing tourist contributions explicitly (e.g., by providing social recognition, or making explicit payments to tourists).

5 Selective empirical analysis

This section illustrates some implications of the proposed framework and the previous analysis on the basis of a survey of consumer preferences and expectations for Internet-based travel services. Consumer preference data was gathered in April 1998 from 1792 consumers who regularly participated in an ongoing consumer panel in the Netherlands. Of these consumers, only those were selected that used the Internet regularly. This group consisted of 345 consumers. The results of the questionnaire illustrate the following elements of the proposed framework:

- Tourists' time use across various functions in the value creation process, and their expectations of how this time use may be affected by the Internet. These expectations were measured by asking respondents to allocate time to the following activities representing different functions in the household production process for travel consumption: information search before the trip (i.e., research function), planning and booking their trip (i.e., design and distribution function), information search during their trip (i.e., production function), and evaluation and information exchange after their trip (i.e., evaluation function).
- Tourists' expectations with regard to the possible utility gains that the Internet can provide. These expectations were measured by asking respondents to rate the likelihood that using the Internet would provide them with each of the following four possible benefits: finding lower prices, finding more attractive travel options, being able to search more quickly, and going through a more pleasant search process.
- Tourists' preferences for some Internet-based information services. For this purpose, respondents were presented with 8 profiles of Internet-based travel services that were constructed on the basis of a $4*2^3$ fractional factorial design. In these profiles, the following variables were varied systematically: type of organization (at four levels), type of information provided, information source, and price (all at two levels). Respondents were asked to rate each profile in terms of the probability that they would use the service if it were available to them on the Internet. Differences between the levels of each variable were compared on significance.

Table 2 presents the questionnaire results for the first element It shows that, in general, respondents expected to be able to reduce their information search time whilst traveling by using the Internet. Most likely, this gain in information search costs is achieved by performing more in depth information searches before the trip is made. Furthermore, respondents regarded the Internet as a means to reduce the time they spent planning and booking a trip. Respondents did not expect to spend more time sharing information with others after they had made their trips when having access to the Internet. This finding implies that tourism services suppliers operating on the Internet may need to compensate tourists if they would like them to share their experiences with others.

Table 2 Tourists' time-use expectation functions with and without Internet usage

	Expected time use (in minutes, n = 345, Internet users, s.d. in brackets)			
	Traditional channels only		*Internet freely available*	
Function		*Relative size*	*Internet*	*Traditional*
Information search before trip	222.9 (427.3)	<	118.7 (246.5)	134.0 (268.4)
Planning and booking of trip	112.1 (358.0)	>	40.0 (138.4)	56.4 (134.3)
Information search during trip	151.2 (269.0)	>	20.6 (90.1)	121.6 (223.6)
Evaluation and information exchange after trip	192.3 (363.8)	=	24.8 (89.8)	163.5 (384.4)

Table 3 Tourist preferences for Internet information components

Information component		*probability-of-use rating**
Type of organization	Airline business	5.00 (2.46)
	Hotel business	4.92 (2.38)
	Independent travel agent	5.25** (2.40)
	Internet-based intermediary	4.95 (2.34)
Level of information	Extensive, as in travel guides	5.10** (2.37)
	Limited, as in travel brochures	4.96 (2.42)
Information source	Information from other travelers and company itself	5.35** (2.43)
	Information provided by the company only	4.71 (2.35)
Price	$25 reduced price	5.87** (2.27)
	$25 more expensive	4.19 (2.52)

* *s.d. in brackets, 10 pnt scale, 0 =would never use, 9 = would certainly use*

** *difference between option levels significant at 95% level confidence interval*

On average, tourists had fairly neutral expectations of the benefits that the Internet provides (none of the scores was significantly different from neutral). Respondents had the highest expectations with regard to being able to find more attractive travel options through the Internet (an average score of 5.8 out of 10, with a s.d. of 2.26). This indicates that a relatively stronger focus existed on the potential gains in consumption utility that the Internet can provide than on potential reductions in search costs. Respondents also regarded the Internet as a relatively pleasant way to search for information for their trips (a score of 5.35, s.d. 2.32).

Table 3 shows that the relative preference for having access to information from other tourists is a strong benefit that tourists can see in the Internet. For example, the size of this effect is stronger than the effects of organization type and type of information. This finding supports the notion that there is a need for obtaining credible signals about service quality. As expected, tourists preferred more extensive information to less information. Furthermore, respondents preferred web sites of independent travel agents for booking their trips to web sites of hotels and airline businesses. However, in comparison to hotel and airline businesses, Internet-based intermediaries did not do well, possibly because their lack of expertise outweighed the possible benefit of being independent. Finally, respondents were relatively price sensitive as was apparent from the fact that a relatively small discount ($50) had a strong impact on preference.

6 Discussion

The impact of the Internet on interactions between tourists and service suppliers may be far reaching. However, there is still considerable doubt as to how exactly the Internet will affect existing marketing and supply channel structures. This article has attempted to shed some light on some of the effects that may influence tourists' choices of how to interact with tourism service suppliers through the Internet.

A utility framework was proposed to describe the functions that need to be performed in the tourism value creation process. This framework was based in household production theory. On the basis of empirical data from an exploratory tourist survey some of the main elements in the proposed framework were illustrated and some empirical support was provided for the relevance of the various components.

A further step in this line of research could be to fully estimate the proposed model and/or to integrate the current tourist choice model in a market mechanism structure that also captures (part of) the dynamics in the supply side of the market. Issues that could be addressed might include the supplier decision to introduce Internet-based services, and market mechanism design of Internet transactions between tourists and suppliers as well as from one tourist to another. An exploration of the impact of various mechanisms on Internet based tourism value creation would be worthwhile also (e.g., by comparing one-on-one transaction structures with auctioning mechanisms that sell tourism services).

Acknowledgments

The author's research is funded by the Dutch Science Foundation (NWO). CentER*data*'s grant for data collection through the CentER*data*-panel is gratefully acknowledged. The author thanks Corrie Vis for questionnaire programming and suggestions.

References

1. Alba, Joseph, John Lynch, Barton Weitz, Chris Janiszewski, Richard Lutz, Alan Sawyer and Stacy Wood (1997), 'Interactive Home Shopping: Consumer, Retailer and Manufacturer Incentives to Participate in Electronic Commerce', *Journal of Marketing* 61 (July), 38-53
2. Anderson, David M. (1997), *Agile Product Development for Mass Customization*, Chicago: Irwin.
3. Becker, Gary S. (1965), 'A Theory of the Allocation of Time', *Economic Journal* 75 (September), 493-517.
4. Betancourt, Roger R. and David Gautchi (1990), 'Demand Complementarities, Household Production and Retail Assortments', *Marketing Science* 9(2), 146-161.
5. Biglaiser, Gary and James W. Friedman (1994), 'Middlemen as Guarantors of Quality', *International Journal of Industrial Organization* 12, 509-531.
6. Dellaert, Benedict G.C, Dick F. Ettema and Christer Lindh (1998), 'Multi-faceted Tourist Travel Decisions: A Constraint-Based Conceptual Framework to Describe Tourists' Sequential Choices of Travel Components', *Tourism Management* 19, 313-320.
7. Dietvorst, Adri (1993), 'Planning for Tourism and Recreation: A Market-Oriented Approach', in; H.N. van Lier and P.D. Taylor, *New Challenges in Recreation and Tourism Planning*, Amsterdam: Elsevier, 87-124.
8. Gronau, Reuben (1980), 'Home Production - A Forgotten Industry', *The Review of Economics and Statistics* 62, 408-416.
9. Hoffman, Donna L. and Thomas P. Novak (1996), 'Marketing in Hypermedia Computer-Mediated Environments: Conceptual Foundations', *Journal of Marketing* 60 (July), 50-68.
10. Jansen-Verbeke, Myriam (1988*), Leisure, Recreation and Tourism in Inner Cities: Explorative Case-Studies,* Nederlandse geografische studies 58. Amsterdam/Nijmegen: KNAG/ geografisch en planologisch instituut KUN.
11. Kooreman, Peter and Sophia Wunderink (1997), *The Economics of Household Behavior*, London: Macmillan Press.
12. Middleton, Victor C. (1988), *Marketing in Travel and Tourism*, Oxford: Heinemann Professional Publishing.
13. Wernerfelt, Birger (1994), 'An Efficiency Criterion for Marketing Design', *Journal of Marketing Research* 31 (November), 462-470.
14. Wernerfelt, Birger (1996), 'Efficient Marketing Communication: Helping the Customer to Learn', *Journal of Marketing Research* 33 (May), 239-246.

The Impact of the Internet on Consideration Sets - the case of International Tourist Destinations

Philip Curry and Frank Alpert,
Department of Marketing, Monash University, Australia
philip.curry@buseco.monash.edu.au

Abstract

The tourism industry is experiencing rapid adoption of Internet technology. The nature and characteristics of the industry expose potential tourists to an array of destinations (brands) to visit, together with places to stay and things to see at each destination. Tourists now have the ability to efficiently access and evaluate more competitive offers about brands at the aggregate level of destination(s) or disaggregated to discrete components (accommodation, etc) within the tourism system supporting each destination.

This work in progress report reviews this interactive environment for globalised hypercompetitive offers, and expects to establish that the size of the Awareness sets and the shape of the overall Consideration Sets of brands for tourists significantly increases as Internet usage increases. The implications of this are that individual domestic economies will reduce if they cannot control the balance between inbound and outbound tourism.

1 Introduction

Given that international tourism is vital to global and national economies, this study is to focus on the area of assessing the impact of the Internet on consumers choice of destinations internationally. Destination selection is the outcome of some decision making process described by Lumsdon (1997:47) in the six stages below:

1) Need, 2) Search, 3) Attitude formation, 4) Evaluate alternatives, 5) Purchase,
6) Post-purchase.

The concept of consideration sets is an effective method of tracking the progress of brands (destinations) through the decision stages.

This study examines consideration sets, comprising brands at various stages of the decision process, and how the size and shape of sets is impacted by integrating Internet communications, including E-commerce and Electronic Word of Mouth, with traditional marketing communications, including traditional Word of Mouth.

It is expected that three factors will combine to drive significantly different size and shape of consideration sets. As tourists increase their use of the Internet, compared to current practice, it is expected that these three factors are the three currently topical areas: 1) globalisation, 2) hypercompetition, and 3) Intermediation.

This study is particularly important because of the driving forces of globalisation and the resultant hypercompetition. Globalisation increases the universal set of brands that consumers have available for processing their choice.

Globalisation

Globalisation effects are in two directions, as a natural consequence of the global platform of the Internet. The first effect is that the potential customer base increases from the traditional sphere of operations (either local, regional, national or a small incidence of global) prior to the Internet, to an immediate global sphere for everyone (buyers, sellers and information providers, etc) once they have access to the Internet. The ultimate positive effect of this is that more international tourists have awareness of destinations within your specific nation, and may consider visitation. The second effect has the opposite impact, where tourists from your nation become aware of international destinations, and may consider visitation. This visitation could be a substitute for specific domestic tourism, or increasing the frequency or range of international destinations.
In 1995, the World Tourism Organisation reported that international tourist *arrivals* exceeded 521 million globally. The data is logged as tourists cross national boundaries, and the below regional spread gives some insight into movements:

- 16 million in Africa
- 102 million in Americas
- 81 million in East Asia/Pacific
- 306 million in Europe
- 11 million in Middle East
- 4 million in South Asia

There are over two hundred countries in the world, and the choice of each international vacation involves a selection of destination(s) within one or more foreign country(s). All countries comprise multiple destinations, for example northern, central and southern regions, or east and west coasts. *Therefore the total number of available destinations globally numbers many thousands, at many varied stages of infrastructure development.*

1.2 Communications

The range of destination information available comprises the traditional marketing communications mix (advertising, promotions, personal selling, public relations and publicity) delivered in the traditional media (television, radio, newspapers, magazines, etc) and emerging non traditional electronic marketing interactive television, Internet, etc, Also of relevance are the Word of Mouth mechanisms of other public and private data, often gleaned from amongst circles of family and friends. The marketing communications uses a mix of traditional and non-traditional media and channels of distribution. The Internet and its WWW browser is most common non-traditional media and is forecast to rapidly grow in both the number of web page and the portion of the population browsing (surfing the Internet).

1.3 The opportunity or threat

It is the combination of four factors; the large potential number of international destinations, the structure of the tourism system, the increasing adoption of the Internet by portions of the global population and the information processing in the decision making process that creates the significance of this research project.
The focus is on identifying the major relationships that influence the size and shape of these consideration sets as they change as a consequence of the small but ever increasing portion of the worlds consumers using the Internet to choose international travel destinations. Nua (1998) report that the Internet currently has about 115 million users worldwide, from a global population of almost 6 billion, and they forecast that there will be 329 million users by 2002, with 80 million based in Europe.
Lumsdon (1997:70) describes an application of Rogers (1962, 1995) diffusion theory where the innovations are various evolving delivery technologies to access the channels of distribution for booking tourism offerings. He currently suggests that Internet and email technology is used by today's innovator consumer category to book such tourism offerings. In the future, such Internet technology is expected to be diffused through to the early adopter category then eventually laggard category. The speed of transition through these different categories will depend on many factors including ease of access together with the utility and value of the destination marketing process to tourists.

1.4 Current status

Evidence exists for USA households and their increasing use of the Internet for travel. It is expected that adoption by other countries will occur over the short term future. The TIA (1996) in their survey of American households report that people "would consider using online services/Internet for travel plans or reservations next year"

Total adult population	25%
Travellers	28%
Frequent pleasure travellers	42%
Frequent Business travellers	45%
Current online/Internet users	58%

Travellers are defined as "1 or more trips of 100+ miles one way in the past year".

Furthermore, the TIA (1997a) report finds that the "source preferred for type of travel information" is as follows:

	Booking inquiry	Price	Type of Vacation	Schedule	Where to go	Things to do	Maps
Online/ Internet	17%	23%	24%	27%	27%	31%	30%
Travel Agent	62%	58%	57%	53%	50%	43%	44%
Other	13%	11%	9%	11%	14%	16%	17%
Internet Growth 96 to 97	+19%	+23%	+27%	+26%	+20%	+32%	+31%

Finally, this TIA (1997a) survey of American households report that usage of Online services/Internet has grown since last year and more markedly for travellers:

	1996	1997
Total adult population	16%	26%
Travellers	19%	29%
Frequent travellers	23%	38%

There are three notable conclusions from this data. Firstly, the portion of adult population using the Internet is still less than 20% (but evidence suggests that this is rapidly increasing). Secondly, travellers usage of the Internet is significantly above the average population. Thirdly, all types of information is showing significant growth via a preference for the Internet

1.5 E-commerce

Nua (1998) report an Activmedia forecast for E-commerce revenues in 1998 to be US$75 billion, double the 1997 revenues; therefore at this level they equate to about 0.35% of Global GNP. Negroponte (1998) confirms this magnitude and trend by projecting E-commerce (will grow exponentially) to be around US$1,200 Billion by the year 2001, with 70% being business to business transactions. Interestingly, Nua (1998) also report that the portion for consumers buying online is forecast by Price Waterhouse to increase by 1800% between 1997 and 2002 to reach US$94 billion.
In another TIA report (1997b) the five year outlook for online travel revenues are forecast to grow substantially from the actual 1996/97 data, as follows:

	US$ Million
1996	US$ 276
1997	US$ 827
2000	US$ 4,700
2002	US$ 8,900

Endicott (1998) reports that there are now 3,183,975 web pages containing the keyword travel. The breakdown by publication date is:

More than two years old	200,817
Between 1 and 2 years old	391,867
Between 6 and 12 months old	607,409
Between 1 and 6 months old	1,536,604
Less than 1 month old	447,278

This distribution indicates the quantum of web pages activated by the travel keyword; therefore confirming the substantial recent growth for Internet tourism and travel.

This establishes the contextual background as to why the destination marketing of individual nations needs to consider augmenting their marketing by combining traditional methods (via intermediaries) and integrating this with the emerging acceptance of Internet marketing to consumers. It is anticipated that nations that do not integrate the Internet into their marketing programs will be exposed to two threats:

1) tourists within their home nation may see global destinations and be influenced to travel internationally, thus increasing the component for outbound tourism flow and reducing the component for internal domestic tourism..

2) inbound tourism flows are less than maximum because international tourists may be influenced by Internet communications that determine the destination. Ultimately there is some potential for inbound volumes to even reduce below current levels.

There is a scarcity of research literature directly relevant to this domain; in fact none can be found. Indirect and peripheral literature exists in Jung and Baker (1998) reviewing market effectiveness of the WWW for National Tourism Offices.

2 Research Issues

2.1 Internet and channel functions

Peterson et al (1997) identify and discuss the fact that the Internet is but one possible distribution, transaction and communication channel in a world dominated by conventional retailing channels. Discussing the role of the intermediary for each of these three channel functions; they suggest that transaction and communication functions are likely to have the Internet as a substitute channel that may dominate in the future. The tourism sector is one such industry that suits the Peterson scenario.

2.2 Risk

Within the context of risk perceptions associated with pleasure travel, Roehl and Fesenmaier (1992) remind us that choice involves risk when the consequences associated with the decision are uncertain and some outcomes are more desirable than others. They remind us that in consumer behaviour, seven different types of risk have been identified, each of these can relate to tourism activities:

1. Equipment risk: possibility of equipment or organisational problems on vacation.
2. Financial risk: possibility that vacation will not provide value for the money spent.
3. Physical risk: possibility of physical danger, injury or sickness on vacation.
4. Psychological risk: possibility of vacation not suiting personality and self-image.
5. Satisfaction risk: possibility that a vacation will not provide personal satisfaction.
6. Social risk: possibility that vacation will affect others' opinion of me.
7. Time risk: possibility that vacation will take too much time or waste time.

The Internet is ideally suited as a transaction and communication forum to validate whether these seven dimension of risk are relevant and justified to each tourist.

2.3 Hypercompetition

Given over 250 countries globally, thousands of destinations exist, and these become the "universal set" of brands in the choice process. All destinations compete for patronage by tourists.
Given that the expected outcome is that the below four factors contribute to increasing hypercompetitive (D'Aveni 1994) rivalry between destinations:

1) the large number of international destinations available globally,
2) the complex role and structure of information processing in deciding the choice of destination,
3) the interdependency of the tourism system for each destination: travel, accommodation and content,
4) the increasing global adoption of the Internet,
   the purpose is to gain knowledge and understanding into the combined effect of the Internet on the decision making process, and consequently identify factors that influence patronage of each unique destination.

3 Method

The proposal is to conduct an international survey, recruiting three different groups of Internet users, selected because they have participated in international tourism sometime in the last three years.

The three respondents groupings will be:

a) users who completed bookings and paid "on-line" for any tourism activity, or
b) users who completed bookings but paid "off-line", or
c) users who gathered information, without progressing to bookings and payment. Respondents will be asked questions relating to three phases of their tourism activity:
a) recall details about their last international trip, prior to them using the Internet.
b) recall details about their last international trip, since using the Internet.
c) project their current knowledge and behaviour to planning their next international trip, using the Internet.

International travel experiences are relatively infrequent and considered to be in the high involvement category of decision making; therefore "recall" reliability errors are expected to be minimised.
These respondents will be probed for their consideration sets and their exposure to destination marketing communications.
It is proposed to develop and test a model based on Roberts and Lattin (1991), Shocker et.al (1991) and the following:

a) Dependent variables: stages of consideration sets, as developed by Pearce (1998),
b) Independent variables: exposure to traditional and Internet communications,
c) Moderating variables: i) communications "contents", ii) Internet communications issues, and iii) personal and situational factors.

3.1 Dependent variables: Stages of the Consideration Set

Pearce (1998: 87) offers a travel decision making framework, based on choice sets. This cascading and rejection model has eight stages, the major components are:
Stage 1: The "total awareness set" which comprises:

a) the "recall set" is unprompted, immediately recalled from memory
b) the "prompted set" is recalled from memory, after exposure to cues,
c) the "unaware set" is that part of the "universal set" that remains unaware, even after prompting.

Stage 6: The "late consideration set"; requiring extensive processing to screen choice; typically 2 to 5 destinations are included in this phase (Brown and Wildt 1992).
Stage 8: The "decision set", is the successful outcome of destinations in favour; this is either one or multiple destinations.

3.2 Independent Variables: Traditional and Internet communications exposure

Given the nature of this decision category as high involvement and infrequent purchase, it is expected that people will have reliable recall of their past behaviour. The mix of media that respondents were consciously exposed to in progressing their decision will be monitored and it is expected that a background quasi-experimental manipulation of these groupings will demonstrate significant influence on the size and shape of consideration set stages.

3.3 Moderating variables:

Marketing communication moderating factors include the following:

a) the integration and consistency of a destination's traditional communications,
b) the degree of interconnection of Internet communications relating to a destination,
c) the confusion of consumers, caused by the inherent local customisation of traditional target marketing techniques, contrasting to the Internet which typically contains minimal customisation.

Internet communication moderating factors include the following:

a) the degree of expertise with the Internet, comprising:
    i) skills in search, navigation and information processing
    ii) knowledge and use of the various Internet platforms.
b) accessibility issues related to time and cost, that constrain usage.
c) language communication issues.

Personal and situational moderating factors include the following:

a) prior travel history,
b) frame of reference and cross-culture differences between origins and destinations,
c) accessibility between origins and destinations,
d) lifestyle and psychological factors such as personality and motivation.

Given the recent literature on Internet survey methodology (Sackmary 1998), it is proposed to intercept potential respondents over the Internet; and invite them to participate by completing the instrument in one of a variety of forms, namely:

a) An online web survey: a homepage with a questionnaire form online for immediate completion.
b) An optional email method: the same form emailed to respondent at their initiation. After offline completion the form could be returned via email, fax or post.
c) An optional download web page method: for offline completion and fax return. This should maximise response rates, but the latter two methods are relatively inefficient for collection time and data entry.

The interception will be done by a variety of methods, namely:

a) Post to Listmasters of Newsgroups and Bulletin Board Services (BBS) specifically related to tourism and travel,
b) Post to Listmaster, Postmaster and Webmaster addresses of forums relevant to critical cells within the sample frame,

Intermediation and Disintermediation issues will not be included in this current study sample, although respondents are generally expected to have a case history including the use of traditional intermediaries such as travel agents in past transactions.

4 Expected results

The proposed study of Internet users is expected to observe significant positive effects, for most user groups, in both the size and shape of the consideration set model.

4.1 Size of the Total Awareness sets

The size of the "total awareness set" is expected to be significantly larger as Internet usage increases, and that the major portion of the increase will be in the "prompted" sub set. The primary causes of this are expected to be the effect of:

1. *Memory recall*, from browsing a global information platform such as the Internet,
2. Linking of Internet information, that has *greater accessibility enabling convenient looping in the decision process*, to add updates to previous stages,
3. *Increased experience* causing increased awareness (Johnson and Lehman 1997),
4. It is also expected that *pioneer brands* (Kardes et.al 1993) *and proto-typical brands* will comprise significant portions of both the "recall" and "prompted" awareness sub-sets.

4.2 Shape of Consideration Sets

The overall shape of the Pearce (1998) model, is expected to have significantly more retention and significantly later rejection, as Internet usage increases. The primary causes of more retention and later rejection are expected to be:

1. Recall of global pioneer and prototypical brands with their positive associations.
2. Linking of Internet information, that has *greater accessibility enabling convenient looping in the decision process*, to add updates to previous stages.

3. Linking of Internet information, that has *greater accessibility enabling convenient and more thorough review before rejection.*

Also of fundamental importance, it is expected that users who integrate traditional information with Internet communications, will also have both larger sized and deeper shaped consideration sets because of the pre-conditioning created by the combined effect of prior exposure from traditional communications leveraging positive response from Internet communications.

5 Conclusions

Substantial management implications for the tourism sector within each nation are expected.

1) Market size of international tourism has the potential to increase because of substituting domestic destinations with international. This is caused as a consequence of tourists including more international destinations in the processing of their consideration sets.
2) Each nation's market share of international tourism has the potential to change due to this inclusion of more international destinations. Some nations will have a net out-flow that reduces share, whilst other nations will have a net in-flow that increases share.

This research project is expected to add to academic knowledge in the areas of understanding the impact of the Internet on behaviour. It is also expected to have practical relevance and insight into the management of national tourism industries within the global market, now and into the future.

6 References

- Brown, J. J. and Wildt, A. (1992). Consideration Set measurement, Journal of the Academy of Marketing Science, 20(3), pp235-243.
- D' Aveni, Richard (1994). Hypercompetition: Managing the Dynamics of Strategic Maneuvering. Free Press, New York.
- Endicott, Marcus (1998). Internet "travel" site statistics; Hotbot search statistics, as reported on a moderated discussion group INFOTEC-TRAVEL@PEACH.EASE. LSOFT.COM on 19 May 1998. http://www.infotec-travel.com.
- Johnson, M and Lehman, D. (1997). Consumer experience and consideration sets for brands and product categories, Advances in Consumer Research, Vol. 24, pp295-300.
- Jung, Hyung-Soo and Baker, Michael (1998). Assessing the market effectiveness of the World Wide Web in National Tourism Offices, ENTER 98 Conference proceedings, Springer Wien New York, pp 95-102.
- Kardes, Frank R, Kalanaram G, Chandrashekaran M, Dornoff R. (1993). Brand retrieval, Consideration set composition, consumer choice and the pioneering advantage, Journal of Consumer Research, Vol. 20, pp62-75.

- Lumsden, L (1997). Tourism Marketing, International Thomson Business Press.
- Negroponte, N (1998). NUA Survey, V3-11, 14 April 1998, http://www.nua.ie/surveys
- Nua, (1998). NUA Survey, Vol 3 No. 14, 20 May 1998, http://www.nua.ie/surveys/
- Pearce, Philip. L, Morrison A. M, Rutledge J. (1998). Tourism: bridge across continents, Mc Graw Hill, Sydney Australia.
- Peterson Robert, Balasubramanian S, and Bronnenburg B (1997). Exploring the Internet for Consumer Marketing, Journal of the Academy of Marketing Science, V25-4, pp329-346.
- Plog, S (1991). Leisure travel: making it a growth market again! Wiley, New York.
- Roberts, John, and Lattin, J. (1991). Development and testing of a model of Consideration set composition, Journal of Market Research, Nov 1991, pp429-440.
- Roehl, Wesley and Fesenmaier Daniel (1992). Risk perceptions and pleasure travel: An exploratory analysis, Journal of Travel research, Spring 1992, pp17-26.
- Sackmary, Benjamin (1998). Internet Survey Research: Practices, problems and prospects, AMA Educators Proceedings, American Marketing Association, Summer 1998, Volume 9, pp41-49.
- Shocker Allan D, Ben-Akiva M, Boccara B, Nedungadi P, (1991). Consideration set influences on consumer decision making and choice: issues, models and suggestions, Marketing Letters 2:3, pp181-.
- TIA (1996) Travel Industry Association of America, "Technology and Travel report".
- TIA (1997a) Travel Industry Association report on "Travellers use of the Internet"
- TIA (1997b) Travel Industry Association of America report on "Travel & Interactive Technology: a five year outlook"

The Impact of the Internet on the Information Search Process and Tourism Decision Making

Elizabeth Beirne, Honors Student,
Department of Marketing, Monash University, Australia

Philip Curry, Lecturer,
Department of Marketing, Monash University, Australia
philip.curry@buseco.monash.edu.au

1 Purpose:

The purpose of this report is to explore how users of the Internet utilize the medium to gather information in the context of tourism decision making. It seeks to assess how users of different skill levels navigate their way through travel related web sites. The focus of this study is on communication issues on the Internet, in the tourism domain. It does not seek to examine the usability of individual web pages. Although such insights may arise incidentally, it seeks predominantly to explore consumer attitudes towards the effectiveness of the Internet in communicating travel-related information, and its impact on the tourism decision. A qualitative mode of research was considered most appropriate given the exploratory nature of the investigation, and to gain a rich understanding of Internet users.

2 Literature Review:

Tourism and information technology, are two of the largest and most dynamic industries in the world today. Separately and together they are changing the way society operates (Sheldon, 1997). The nature of the tourism product renders it highly suitable to Internet advertising. In the tourism industry, the consumer is often located far from the product or service of purchase. Additionally, tourism is a search product as opposed to being an experience product, thus enabling its features to be objectively assessed by perusing product-related information (Peterson et al. 1997). Typically, purchase of a tourism product is based solely on such information as well as knowledge, word of mouth (WOM) and perceptions. For these reasons, communication tools and information transmission, are indispensable to the tourism industry.

It seems inevitable then, that tourism will be increasingly influenced by, and has already been transformed by the new business environment created by the technical revolution.

Information technology will be instrumental in the industry's ability to enhance its future efficiency and competitiveness (Buhalis, 1997).

2.1 Communication in Computer Mediated Environments

Effective communication is of vital importance to tourism marketing activities. The advent of radio, television and now the Internet have accelerated communication activities and put increased pressure on the importance of understanding the nature of the communication process (Targowski and Bowman, 1988). Hoffman and Novak, (1996) have made pioneering efforts to try and understand hypermedia, computer mediated environments (CME's) in terms of their communication style and their potential impact on marketing communications. They have presented various models of the communication process, which reflect different media environments including the new computer mediated environment typical of the Internet.

Their model illustrating the communication process typical in mass media, is consistent with the traditional models of the communication process (Targowski and Bowman, 1988), which imply that in mass media, information flows in one direction, from the firm to the medium, then on to the consumer. In contrast to this, their model representing communication in a computer-mediated environment is a many-to-many communication model. It indicates interactivity with the firm, with the medium itself, and with other consumers. The primary relationship is not between the sender and the receiver, but rather with the mediated environment in which they interact. Hoffman and Novak (1996) likened the Internet to an international trade hall, stating that consumers can enter passively and browse, or they can become vigorously interactive in their search for information. This potential for interactivity greatly increases the communication potential for marketers.

2.2 The Information Search Process:

Ironically, in spite of the many studies focusing on the information search process, there is substantial evidence throughout the literature that consumers have little enthusiasm for the pursuit and exhibit very limited prepurchase information search activity, even for high priced, durable goods (Morothy, Ratchford and Talukdar, 1997; Bloch, Sherrell and Ridgway, 1986; Midgley, 1983).

However Bloch, Sherrell and Ridgway, (1986) contend that the focus solely on prepurchase search typical of many studies, is deficient because it does not account for search activity that is recreational or that occurs without a recognised consumption need. The Internet provides the perfect environment for ongoing search due to its entertainment value and its interactive nature. Maignan and Lukas (1997) add credence to this, asserting

that the Internet is no longer just a consumption environment, but an object of consumption.
The first step in the consumers information search process is an internal search, which is a mental process of retrieving and reviewing information about alternatives stored in memory, that may relate to the purchase situation (Moutinho, 1987). Typically in travel and tourism, the amount of internal information is not sufficient to allow the tourist to select a destination. The external information available to a potential tourist emanates from two sources, the formal or commercial environment and the informal or social environment. (Raitz and Dakhil, 1989; Etzel and Wahlers, 1985; Moutinho, 1987). Informal information sources include oral communication and recommendations, or WOM from friends, relatives, and social groups. Formal information sources may be divided into three subgroups: print media, electronic media and the professional consultant.

In the numerous studies that center on the information search process, there is no agreement among authors as to the relevance and validity of formal versus informal sources of information. But there are two consistent themes. The first is that consumers rarely rely on one information source. Information acquisition is a cumulative process with consumers using a combination of both sources (Gitelson and Crompton, 1983). Destination specific literature and the media generally perform an informing function while friends, relatives and consultants assume a legitimizing or evaluating function. The second consistency is that the usage, popularity and efficaciousness of different information sources varies according to variables such as education, gender, age, purpose of the vacation, income, family status, destination location and previous experience (Gitelson and Crompton, 1983; Etzel and Wahlers, 1985).

2.3 Tourism Decision Making and Destination Selection:

Selection of a vacation destination, at its broadest dissection, is conceptualized as a three-stage sequential decision. It includes the development of an initial awareness set of possible destinations, discard of some of those destinations to form an evoked set and a final single choice from the remaining alternatives (Woodside and Sherrell, 1977; Woodside and Lysonski, 1989; Crompton and Seoho, 1992; Crompton, 1977).

The theory of choice sets and decision rules is well documented and supported throughout the literature. Their support in terms of the tourism decision is almost unanimous and they will not be discussed in greater detail here. Throughout the literature, one alternative way to conceptualize a destination decision has been introduced. Crompton, (1992) proposed a two-stage model to describe a consumers destination choice process. In his study, destination choice behavior was characterized as being a function of the interaction between a consumer's constraints and the destination image or perceived benefits. This is

a theory based in economics. It contends that consumers will behave rationally, making decisions that best suit their goals, budget constraints and earning power.
There is relatively little understanding of how internal processes and external influences interact and effect the information search process and tourism decision making, particularly when the Internet is incorporated. It is crucial to understand that these processes do not operate in a vacuum. They are in fact, influenced by a multitude of variables, both internal and external to the individual. These include promotional activity, destination attributes and facilities, cognitive and actual distance, time available, motivation, destination image, stage in the family lifecycle, previous experience, perceived risk, attitude and socioeconomic level. Destination image and attitude are greatly influenced by marketing activities. They are explored in more detail, below.

2.4 Destination Image and Attitude

Destination image is of paramount importance in tourism because images transpose representation of an area into a potential tourist's mind, thus giving them an overall view of a destination. Additionally, all places have an image, whether it be good, bad or indifferent (Moutinho, 1987). Some authors consider image an impression; others place image into a broader context equating it to knowledge. Similarly, an attitude is a favorable, indifferent or unfavorable predisposition created by learning and experience to respond in a certain way toward an object (Moutinho, 1987).

Potential travelers generally have limited knowledge about the attributes of a destination that they have not previously visited. Consequently, image and attitude dimensions of a place are likely to be critical elements in the choice process, irrespective of whether or not they are true representations (Um and Crompton, 1990). Image and attitude are closely linked but attitude is more rational and more firmly grounded in fact than image as it is based on experience and information.

3 Methodology

The research completed consisted of an observational experiment in which respondents were given a search task to complete on the Internet. Subjects were advised that they had $5000 to spend on a four-week holiday to either Hawaii, Nepal or Ibiza. Subjects had one hour in which to search for information on the destinations, after which time they were required to select one of the three, to visit. The task aimed to give subjects a situation that would prompt search activity not atypical to their usual style. Due to the focus on communication and behavioral issues, the respondents were required to complete an exit survey after completing the task.

The subjects used in this research, were students from the Caulfield campus of Monash University, Australia. A judgement sample was used to select the students, because one of the aims of the research was to explore differences in search style and overall satisfaction between Internet users of different skill levels. The sample size of twenty-five subjects was considered adequate for qualitative research, but its selection was also constrained by the capacity and availability of the facility at which the research was conducted.

Recruitment surveys were used to ensure that the most suitable group of available subjects were selected. Approximately five hundred students were surveyed. Fifty-nine individuals who met the criteria of the target population, expressed interest in participating in further research. The target population consisted of students who had previous Internet experience. Individuals who had little or no experience were not targeted because the focus of the research was on the tourism decision making and information search processes and novices may have been baffled by the task, thus limiting the insight gained. Internet experience was classified as being either 'low' or 'high'.

The respondent's nationality, the country of their birth and their level of international travel experience was also considered. Twenty-five subjects were selected from the group of fifty-nine who agreed to participate in the experiment. They were selected according to their level of Internet experience and their level of international travel experience, which was also classified as being either 'high' or 'low'.

4 The Research

The task given to respondents in this research yielded preliminary answers to a number of research questions, which are discussed below. However this honors project is a work in progress which has been constrained by tight time limitations. More comprehensive analysis and conclusions will be appended at the conference.

4.1 How do subjects of different skill levels find travel related web pages? Do subjects search for information randomly or do they have a plan of action?

It was overwhelmingly clear from the research that regardless of Internet skill level, search engines were used as tools to find information on the Internet. For all three searches, 88% of subjects used a search engine. Although for each search, the 12% of subjects not using a search engine was comprised of different individuals, no one indicated that their change in method was related to dissatisfaction with their results. Rather it was motivated by a desire to experiment with different methods.

Generally, it appeared that with a task in mind, irrespective again, of skill level, users planned either the sequence in which they searched for information, the method they used to find it, or both. 76% of the subjects agreed that they initiated their first search with an action plan in mind.

4.2 What type of web pages do subjects seek, process and find effective when trying to decide what destination to visit?

The most frequently used pages were those sponsored by hotels with 80% of subjects using them to aid their decision. Of those, 20% considered them to be ineffective communicators of travel-related information giving reasons such as, "prices were too hard to access", "they contained too much advertising" and "they contained information on the hotel, but not the destination". However, pages sponsored by airlines fared much worse, with 58% of those who accessed them concluding that they were ineffective. One subject said, "they are too busy promoting themselves rather than giving information such as prices and time tables", and this reflected the general theme.

The most effective web pages, according to the research were those sponsored by publications, specifically Lonely Planet, originally a travel guide handbook. Of those who accessed the site, 85% agreed that it was very effective. "It is an excellent reference site with relevant information provided. Excellent, direct links to other related sites". Pages sponsored by national governments, private business and other travelers were also accessed by a number of subjects.

4.3 What methods of communicating information do subjects use and find effective whilst inside travel related web pages?

Pictures were clearly considered the most effective means by which to convey the attributes of a destination. Of the 23 respondents who commented on their effectiveness, 91% agreed that they were very effective. The following comments were typical of those made by many subjects after their search: "Pictures are very effective as they are able to convey what the traveler would actually see instead of imagining the sights through words". Text also fared well with 52% of subjects considering it to be an effective way to communicate information. Those who found text ineffective made comments such as, "text is only effective when it is related to your specific area of interest, otherwise it gets in the way". 56% of those who sought price lists agreed that they were effective, stating that such information "lets the traveler see at a glance whether the tour is suitable to their budget". The 22% of subjects who considered such information to be communicated ineffectively, had trouble accessing it or felt they couldn't rely on it, since prices were subject to such frequent change.

4.4 Did a subject's perception of a destination change as a result of the information they viewed on the Internet?

It was revealed that the information viewed, positively changed the perceptions of many subjects. Even for Hawaii, 20% of subjects experienced a change in their perceptions, despite the fact that it is a well know tourist destination. With Nepal, a destination that is possibly not as well known, the number was much higher with fifteen of the respondents indicating that they now consider the destination in a different light. "I didn't think there was much to do in Nepal, now I see it is filled with historical sights, you can go white water rafting, trekking and on scenic flights."

4.5 Was a subject's selection of a destination related more to their satisfaction with the information or to the attractiveness of the destination?

The subjects clearly encountered difficulty finding information on Ibiza, with only three respondents indicating that they were able to access a sufficient amount of relevant information, compared to thirteen for Hawaii and seventeen for Nepal. Twelve subjects rejected the destination, solely because they were dissatisfied with the information. Two subjects indicated that they selected Ibiza, despite a lack of information, because what they did see was overwhelmingly appealing. Twelve of the thirteen subjects who selected Nepal expressed a desire to consult additional sources of information, as did six of the seven who selected Hawaii and all five of those who selected Ibiza. Despite this 64% of subjects expressed satisfaction with the information yielded by the searches, for their selected destination. Only two subjects indicated that they were confident enough with the information yielded on their selected destination to book immediately, either on line or off line. Both were 'high skill' and both had previously visited the destination.

4.6 Did the subjects consider the Internet to be an effective medium for communicating travel related information and would they would use it again in future?

Fifteen out of twenty-five respondents agreed that the Internet effectively communicated travel related information, and nineteen indicted that they would use it for a similar purpose in future. The main reasons in favour of using the Internet were that it was 'easy',' cheap', 'convenient', it 'saved time' and there was 'no pressure to book anything after reviewing information'. "Using the Internet is a major time saving operation. Information can be gathered at your convenience and offers just as extensive background information as a travel agent. It gives you greater flexibility to look into multiple locations through links, that you may not have previously thought of."

Interestingly, those subjects who said that they would use travel agents over the Internet in future stated similar reasons. "I would go to a travel agent. It's easier, faster and saves time." Another argument presented against the Internet was the reliability of the information. "I am a skeptic and would be reluctant to believe anything on the Internet. I would prefer to speak to a travel agent face-to-face." Seven subjects were undecided.

The three subjects that did not consider the Internet an effective medium for communicating travel related information, were all 'low skill'. Additionally, four 'low skill' subjects compared to two 'high skill' subjects said they would not use the Internet in future or were undecided as to whether or not they would use it.

5 Analysis and Conclusions

The research completed has provided many useful insights and raised significant implications for tourism marketers with an Internet presence and for those desiring an Internet presence in the future.

The overwhelming use of a search engine to find travel related web sites, highlights the importance for marketers to ensure that their web pages have a commanding presence in the list of results produced by a search engine when a key word search is utilized. Ideally in combination with this, sites should be connected to search engine home pages such as yahoo.com via the travel hot links that exist on such pages. Given that consumers have little enthusiasm for the pursuit of pre-purchase information search, if information is not easily accessible, they may abandon their Internet search in favor of other methods. This is likely to have negative connotations for their future use of the medium.

Regardless of the types of web pages accessed by subjects and the methods of communicating information employed within, a few common themes arose from which the following suggestions have been developed. As much as possible advertising should be unobtrusive and should not impede communication of the main messages. Pricing and timetable information, if available should be easily accessible and up to date. The absence of such information should be clearly communicated so that consumers do not waste time searching for information that is not contained within a site and become frustrated. Pictures should be used wherever possible and blocks of text should be avoided. Rather, home pages should contain an index of the information to allow subjects to enter only the pages that interest them. Text should be kept brief and relevant.

The fact that the information viewed on the Internet changed many of the subjects perceptions of a destination, in some cases, an exceedingly well known one, infers that generally, the subjects believed the information communicated. This is significant for tourism marketers because purchase is frequently based on the destination's image and the consumer's attitude. Whether subjects are participating in a recreational search or a pre-purchase search, images of destinations may be cemented, to form attitudes as a result of exposure to destination specific information. This will have a bearing on a consumer's consideration set and choice criteria if a future purchase situation arises. Thus, it is crucial that the destination is represented as accurately and attractively as possible.

In addition to this it was apparent from the research that for a destination such as Ibiza where not much internal information is available, there seemed to be a relationship between the quality of information and the selection of the destination. With the two destinations where the quality of information yielded was generally more satisfactory, it seemed that destination choice was based on the attributes of the destination. This may suggest that if an insufficient amount of information is available, consumers may eliminate a destination from their consideration set, particularly if they are able to find information on other destinations in the evoked set.

Twenty-three out of twenty-five subjects felt the need to seek additional information on their selected destination, even though sixteen of those indicated satisfaction with their search. This indicates that at the moment, the Internet is affecting the media consumption patterns of users, but is not replacing traditional media and methods of gathering information. Subjects generally considered it a good starting point for gathering background information. It appears to be considered in the same vein as traditional print or television advertising, but subjects still desire the personal contact with friends and/or professional consultants, who apparently do, assume the legitimizing function mentioned in the literature. Perhaps in the future, marketers will exploit the interactive nature of the Internet more. It does have the potential, through chat lines and email loops to perform the functions of both informal and formal information sources.

The relationship between the skill level of Internet users and their satisfaction with the medium's capacity to communicate travel related information, indicates that the more consumers use the medium, the more competent they become and the more confidence they place in the information they access. The potential of the Internet as a marketing tool will continue to grow, particularly if users gain confidence in its performance and feel they can rely the Internet as a source of both formal and informal information.

6 References

- Bloch, P., Sherrell, D., Ridgway, N.: Consumer Search: An Extended Framework. Journal of Consumer Research 13: 119-126 June (1986)
- Crompton, J.: Structure of Vacation Destination Choice Sets. Annals of Tourism Research 19: 435-449, (19 77)
- Crompton, J.: The Roles of Perceived Inhibitors and Facilitators in Pleasure Travel Destination Decisions. Journal of Travel Research 30 (3): 18-25 (1992)

- Etzel, M., Wahlers, R.: The Use of Requested Promotional Material by Pleasure Travelers. Journal of Travel Research 23 (4): 2-6 Spring (1985)
- Gitelson, R., Crompton, J.: The Planning Horizons and Sources of Information Used by Pleasure Vacationers. Journal of Travel Research 21 (3): 2-7 Winter (1983)
- Hoffman, N., Novak, T.: Marketing in Hypermedia Computer-Mediated Environments: Conceptual Foundations. Journal of Marketing 60: 50-68 July (1996)
- Maignan, I., Lukas, B.: The Nature and Social Uses of the Internet: A Qualitative Investigation. Journal of Consumer Affairs 31 (12): 346-347 Winter (1997)
- Midgley, D.: Patterns of Interpersonal Information Seeking for the Purchase of a Symbolic Product. Journal of Marketing Research 10: 74-83 February (1983)
- Morothy, S., Ratchford, B., Talukdar, D.: Consumer Information Search Revisited: Theory and Empirical Analysis. Journal of Consumer Research 23: 263-277 March (1997)
- Moutinho, L.: Consumer Behavior in Tourism. European Journal of Marketing 21 (10): 5-44 (1987)
- Peterson, R., Balasubramanian, S., Bronnenberg, B.: Exploring the Implications of the Internet for Consumer Marketing. Journal of the Academy of Marketing Science 25 (4): 329-346 (1997)
- Raitz, K., Dakhil, M.: A Note About Information Sources for Preferred Recreational Environments. Journal of Travel Research 27 (4): 45-49 Spring (1989)
- Seoho, U., Crompton, J.: The Roles of Perceived Inhibitors and Facilitators in Pleasure Travel

The Analysis of Demographic Profiles and Prospects of Internet Users in National Tourism Organisations
Case study : Korea National Tourism Organisation (KNTO)

Hyung-Soo Jung
School of Management Studies for the Service Sector,
University of Surrey
H.Jung@surrey.ac.uk

Introduction

The tourism industry has been highly influenced by the Information Technology over the last few years. The advent and the growth of the Internet technology have led to the appearance of a new marketing and distribution channel. As a new medium, Internet technology has allowed tourism organisations to communicate information and also to reach enormous prospective customers easily and cost effectively. As the number of National Tourism Organisations (NTOs) adopt the Internet as a marketing tool continues to grow rapidly, the analysis and apprehension of Internet users is important for NTOs to use the Internet as an effective marketing tool.

The purpose of this research is twofold. Firstly, this study seeks to identify the potential market segment which the Korea National Tourism Organisation (KNTO) can reach through the Internet. In order to accomplish this, the analysis of the demographic profiles of the KNTO Website visitors was conducted. Secondly, this study investigates the tourism intentions of the KNTO Website visitors. The result from an e-mail survey of visitors to the Korea National Tourism Organisation (KNTO) is reported.

Demographic Profiles of Internet User

Internet is one of the most exciting recent developments in communications and information transfer. Gray (1997) reports that the number of Internet hosts increased from 1.3 million in 1993 to 16.2 million in 1997 and the number of World Wide Web (WWW) increased from 130 in 1993 to 650,000 in 1997. ActivMedia (1997) forecasts that overall movement to online commerce may well swell Internet-generated revenues to $ 1 trillion by the year 2001. Estate (1998) projects that global Internet user growth will quadruple over the next five years, from 36 million in 1997 to 142 million by the year 2002.
The following Internet user profile has been generated from GVU Survey, one of the best and most often quoted Internet survey, by Georgia Technology Research

Corporations' (1998). The Ninth GVU Survey was conducted from April 10, 1998 through May 15, 1998 and around 10,000 web users participated in the survey.

Gender

Females represent 38.7% of the respondents to the ninth survey which is virtually unchanged since the eighth survey (38.5%). Europe is considerably less gender-balanced with females accounting for only 16.3% of respondents. For the rest of the world (mostly Canada & Australia), female account for 30.5% of respondents. Younger respondents are more likely to be female: 43.8% of those age 11-20 compared to 33.9% of those ages 50 and over.

Educational Attainment

Although the average education level of web users has been declining to be more representative of the general population, respondents are still quite highly educated with 80.9% having at least some college experience and 50.1% having obtained at least one degree. Respondents who have been on the Internet for 4 years or more are much more likely to have advanced degrees (Masters & Ph.D.) than newer user.

Marital Status

The largest category of respondents is married (41.1%) and the next largest is single (38.7%). European respondents are much more likely to be single as they are younger respondents.

Age

The average age for all respondents was 35.1 years. 36.4% of respondents are over 40 years old and European respondents continue to have a dramatically different age profile with many more in the 21-30 age range. The respondents with the most online experience tend to be in the 21-30 age range.

Geographic Location

The majority of respondents are currently in the US (84.4%) and the next most common locations are Europe (5%), Canada (4.9%), and Oceania (2.3%). The Other (excluding US) category consists mainly of respondents from Canada (49.9%), Oceania (23.5%) and Asia (11.1%).

Occupation

The largest category of respondents for this survey work in education-related fields (26.2%), followed by those in computer (22.3%) and professional (21.7%) fields. European respondents are much more likely to be in computer-related jobs than other respondents. Females are more likely to be in education or other fields while males are most likely to be in computer positions.

Marketing on the Internet

The definition of cybermarketing was described as "The use of actions, tools and techniques implemented by an organisation to promote the growth of its commercial activities using Internet (both the global network and its tools, such as the Web or e-mail) or on-line services"(Dufour 1997). According to Tetzeli (1994), the business use of the Internet includes electronic mail for communication and collaboration with business counterparts, information gathering, advertising, and direct marketing. Sullivan (1997) suggests that the import aspects of the Internet include low-cost communication, searching and gathering information, and conducting test marketing for new products. Internet marketing is usually conducted through hypermedia WWW pages and electronic mail. Traditional marketing on the WWW employs the WWW as an alternative marketing communication channel.

There are several comparisons between marketing on the Internet and traditional marketing. Compared with traditional marketing communication channels, the WWW is faster, less expensive, round the clock and global (Ellsworth & Ellsworth 1996). It also allows bi-directional marketing and offers wider and deeper material and richer advertisement content. Several ways in which the Internet marketing differs from traditional marketing. These are mostly to do with cost savings, setting up, delivering information, providing information to additional prospects (Emery 1995). Cronin (1994) asserts that the WWW is usually portrayed as being superior to alternative traditional marketing channels, and will therefore eventually replace traditional channels altogether.

The benefits to the customers and firms are mentioned by various researchers. There are several reasons for buying on the Internet. Customers buy the product on the Internet due to the lower cost, convenience and uniqueness (Kohli 1996). Hoffmann and Novak (1995) mention that the recreational uses of the medium, manifested in the form of nondirected search behaviour, can be an important benefit to consumers intrinsically motivated to use the medium. Kohli (1996) mentions the benefits to the firm. He suggests that there are six reasons for selling on the Internet, such as cost savings, access to new customer, access to remote or niche markets, alternative access for traditional customers, only feasible on the Internet and testing new products before market launch.

Internet Technology and Tourism

Many researchers have commented that the Internet is ideally suited to the tourism industry. Shertler (1994) mentions that the evolving technologies in telecommunications and particularly the WWW have created the opportunity for tourist sites and intermediaries to present themselves in a completely different and customer-oriented way. The Internet is a perfect platform for the tourism industry to bring information about products to customers all over the world and that the hypertext feature might have been perfectly designed for the tourism industry (Burger 1997). Clyde and Landfried (1995) comment on the potential of the WWW's hypermedia functionality for product distribution. Frew and Dorren (1997) comment that developments in electronic communication are significant for tourism service providers who sell a perishable, intangible, heterogeneous and high-risk product. Hanna and Miller (1997) mention that the continuing growth of the Internet and, in particular, the World Wide Web gives rise to a new marketing potential for tourist regions. According to Smith and Jenner (1998), travel products are perfectly suited to online selling. Kasavana *et al*(1997) comment that the Internet is a new communication tool offering unparalleled opportunities for advertising and promotion to the tourism industry.

The Examples of the Internet Marketing by NTOs

The growing influence and the use of the Internet have introduced a new form of competition and opportunity for the tourism industry and many NTOs are using the Internet for destination marketing.

In Europe, The British Tourist Authority (BTA) offers information through the BTA Website about the image of Britain; British destination, activities & attractions; and travel; as well as giving facts and figures and providing a shop. The Danish Tourist Board (DTB) has established a Website for potential customers. DTB offers a range of facilities including the option to make bookings. The Finnish Tourist Board (FTB) provides country information, suppliers' profiles and contact persons, package tours and excursions, accommodation, transportation, conference & meeting facilities, events and attractions, and equipment hire through Professional Marketing Information System (PROMIS).

In Asia, The Singapore Tourist Promotion Board (STBP) was amongst the early adopters of the WWW to use it to market a tourist destination. STBP provides information on attractions, hotels, restaurants etc. through Singapore Online Guide. The Korea National Tourism Organisaion (KNTO) provides bilingual information through the Korean Tour Homepage. This information includes KNTO Service, useful information, Korea at a glance, planning a trip, getting in and out of Korea, travel within Korea, tourist attractions, accommodation, travel destinations, tour programs, convention destination etc. The Japanese National Tourism Organisation (JNTO) provides information on regional travel, travel hints & budget travel, reasonable accommodation, leading hotels & ryokans, conventions, events & museums and theme parks & amusement parks etc.

Minneapolis Convention & Visitors Association offers tourism information: 24-hour international access for information; multilingual information possibilities; an information request from that enables tourism area to determine where the request are coming from and the type of information being requested; individual housing service; complete tourist service including purchase options for theatre tickets, hotelrooms, restaurant reservations, rent a car etc. The Australian Tourist Commission (ATC) provides news, marketing opportunities, products & services, research, intelligence & advice, ATC contacts, media resources, and external links and contacts.

Methodology

Data Collection

The sample of this study included those Internet users who were visiting Korea National Tourism Organisation (KNTO) Website. A sample of 246 respondents was collected through the on-line questionnaire which was attached to the KNTO Website. The period of this survey was from 20 May in 1997 to 31 October 1997. In order to get a larger sample for the analysis of demographic profiles, another 776 samples were collected from the Korea Quiz questionnaire from Korea Tour Homepage from 1 January 1998 to 30 June 1998. Therefore, 1022 samples were used for the demographic analysis and 246 samples were used for the investigation of views about Korean tourism by Internet users.

Questionnaire Design

The questionnaire was designed to identify the demographic profiles of the KNTO visitors and their general view about Korea as a tourist destination. The questionnaire consisted of three main sections. The first section contained five questions to extract KNTO visitors' demographic characteristics including age, nationality, gender, marital status and occupation. The second section contained two questions asking for the overseas travel such as the number of trips to foreign country and the country which want to visit in Asia. The third section contained questions asking for travel information on respondents such as the purpose of visit, the experience of visit, attractiveness of Korea as a tourist destination and plans to visit to Korea.

Results

Jung (1998) reported the results of research on a comparison of demographic profiles,such as age, gender, nationality and occupation between Seventh GVU survey and KNTO Website Survey. According to Jung (1998), there is little difference in the profiles between them with one exception-geographic distribution. This research reports on a comparison of demographic profiles, such as geographic, gender, age distribution between KNTO Website Survey and KNTO Statistics in 1997. This results of this research also reports the views about Korea as a tourist destination by KNTO Website visitors.

Demographic Profiles

The majority of respondents were from USA although responses were generated from 34 different countries. The next largest group was Canada (6.8%) and then Singapore (4.0%). Table 1 shows a comparison of the top 10 countries between KNTO Website Survey and KNTO Statistics. There were big difference between the two sets. First of all, Japan, the largest visitor-generating market, represented only 2.3% in KNTO Website Survey. The ohter countries, such as Canada, Singapore and Australia and USA, reflected the possibility of potential online market in KNTO Website Survey.

Table1 Geographical Distribution

Country	KNTO Website Survey	Country	KNTO Statistics
USA	56.2%	Japan	42.9%
Canada	6.9%	USA	10.8%
Singapore	4.7%	China	5.5%
Australia	4.0%	Philippines	4.8%
Japan	2.3%	Russia	3.5%
Brazil	2.3%	Taiwan	2.7%
Malaysia	2.3%	Hong Kong	2.5%
Germany	2.2%	Thailand	1.6%
Indonesia	1.7%	UK	1.5%
UK	1.5%	Singapore	1.4%
Other	16.9%	Other	22.8%
Total	100.0%	Total	100.0%

Table 2 shows that the gender distribution of KNTO Website Survey and KNTO Statistics. 65% of the respondents were male and 32% of the respondents were female. There is little difference between two survey.

Table 2 Gender Distribution

Gender	KNTO Website Survey	KNTO Statistics
Male	65%	64.7%
Female	32%	35.3%
No Response	3%	0.0%
Total	100%	100.0%

Table 3 shows the distribution of age group. 79% of the KNTO respondents were between age of 21 to 50, with highest proportion (51.7%) being between 21-30. Compared with KNTO Statistics, the group between age of 21 to 30 represented the highest proportion. This indicates that the young age group is an attractive market segment for KNTO.

Table 3 Age Distribution

Age	KNTO Website Survey	KNTO Statistics
Under 20	6.8%	9.3%
21-30	51.7%	22.4%
31-40	16.6%	22.6%
41-50	10.7%	23.3%
51-60	8.2%	15.3%%
61 and Over	3.6%	7.1%
No response	3.4%	0.0%
Total	100.0%	100.0%

With regard to marital status, 45.1% of the respondents were married and 40.2% of respondents were single. The main characteristic of the distribution of occupation is the proportion of student group increased from 18.6% to 39.7%. This reveals that the number of students who are visiting the KNTO Website has been growing and this student group is also an attractive market for KNTO.

The first question asked about the number of trips to foreign country in the last year. The following question asked. " How many trips to foreign countries have you taken in the last year?". Table 4 shows that 27.2% of respondents had no experiences of trips to foreign countries in the last year, while 26.4% of respondents travelled abroad once and 13.8% of respondents travelled two times and 10.6% travelled abroad more than five times. A total of 63.5% of respondents travelled abroad at least once and this fact indicates that there is a close correlation between those types of people who subscribe to and use the Internet and those people who have a high propensity to travel.

Table 4 The number of trips to foreign countries

Number of trips	Frequency	Percent
One	65	26.4 %
Two	34	13.8 %
Three	22	8.9 %
Four	14	5.7 %
Five or more	26	10.6 %
None	67	27.2 %
Do not remember	2	0.8 %
Other(Missing)	16	6.5 %
Total	246	100.0 %

A second question was asked about the country which Internet users want to visit, "Which of the following Asia/Pacific countries do you want to visit for pleasure travel?" Table 5 shows that a total of 60 (22.4%) out of 246 respondents answered that they wanted to visit Korea for pleasure travel, 20.7% of respondents wanted to visit China, and 16.3% of respondents wanted to visit Japan respectively.

Table 5 The Country which Want to Visit in Asia

Country	Frequency	Percent
Korea	60	24.4 %
China	51	20.7 %
Japan	40	16.3 %
Australia	18	7.3 %
Thailand	18	7.3 %
New Zealand	16	6.5 %
Taiwan	9	3.7 %
Hong Kong	8	3.3 %
Philippines	8	3.3 %
Malaysia	5	2.0 %
Indonesia	5	2.0 %
Vietnam	5	2.0 %
Singapore	3	1.2 %
Total	246	100.0 %

The following questions were also asked. " Have you ever visited Korea?" and " Do you have a plan to visit Korea within 3 years?" Table 6 shows that 50.8% of respondents had already visited Korea and 76% of respondents have a plan to do so. This indicates that people who had already visited Korea visited the Korea Tour Homepage and that the majority of visitors to KNTO's Website had already decided to travel to Korea.

Table 6 Visit to Korea

Answer	Already visited Korea		Plan to visit Korea	
Yes	125	50.8%	187	76.0%
No	103	41.9%	12	4.9%
Other	18	7.3%	47	19.1%
Total	246	100.0%	246	100.0%

Table 7 shows the results of the next question, which asked "Do you think Korea is attractive as an attractive tourist destination?" Table 7 shows that majority of respondent (63%) answered 'very much' and 'much' to the question. This indicates that KNTO Website visitors regarded Korea as an attractive tourist destination.

Table 7 Attractiveness of Korea

Attractiveness	Frequency	Percent
Very much	102	41.5 %
Much	53	21.5 %
Some what	38	15.4 %
A little	17	6.9 %
Not at all	4	1.6 %
Other	32	13.0 %
Total	246	100.0 %

The next question asked about the information about Korea which KNTO Website visitors wanted to get through the KNTO Website. Table 8 shows that 32.9% of respondents wanted to know about tourism attractions, and 11.8% of respondents wanted to know about the Korean people.

Table 8 Information through the Internet

Information	Frequency	Percent
Tourism attraction	81	32.9%
People	29	11.8%
History	12	4.9%
Nature	12	4.9%
Economy	5	2.0%
No response	107	43.5%
Total	246	100.0%

Conclusion and Implications

The objective of this paper was to identify the potential market segment. In order to accomplish this objective, the analysis of demographic profiles and tourism intentions of KNTO Website visitors was conducted. The results of the Ninth GVU Survey shows that the Internet user is a very attractive target market, including educated professionals with high incomes. The demographic profiles of KNTO Website visitors are similar to those of the GVU Survey, and KNTO Website visitors also represent a very attractive market.

The comparison of demographic profiles between the KNTO Website Survey and KNTO Statistics showed that there is new poential market on the Internet. The characteristics of this market included new geographical locations (Canada, Singapore, Australia), a young age group between the ages of 21-30 and a student group. In addition, most of the KNTO Website visitors had made a trip to foreign countries at least once and wanted to visit Korea, China and Japan. The majority of them have already visited Korea or plan to visit Korea and also regard Korea as an attractive destination, and they wanted information about tourism attractions through the Internet.

There are some implications of this case study of KNTO Website visitors. The Internet users, especailly visitors to NTO's Websites, represent a very attractive market segment. This market has different features from the existing market segment and NTOs can use this information to identify a new potential market segment to develop their own Internet based marketing.

References

- ActivMedia The 1997 Real Numbers behind 'Net Profit' http://www.activmedia.com (1997)
- Burger, F., TIS@WEB-Database Supported Tourist Information on the Web, in Tjoa, A.M. (ed) Information and Communication Technologies in Tourism, 1997, Proceedings of the International Conference in Edinburgh, Scotland, Springer-Wien, NY, 39-46 (1997).
- Clyde, S. and Landfried, T. Our Town: A Distributed, Multi-media System for Travel and Tourism, in: Schertler et al. (eds): Information and Communication Technologies in Tourism, 1995, Proceedings of the International Conference in Innsbruck, Springer-Wien, NY (1995).
- Cronin, M.J. Doing More Business on the Internet, New York, Van Nostrand Reinhold, (1994).
- Dufour (1997) http://www.alphis.com
- Ellsworth, J.H. and Ellsworth, M.V. Marketing on the Internet-Multimedia Strategies for the WWW. New York, John Wiley, (1996).
- Emarketer, NET Geography, http:// emarketer.com. (1998).
- Emery, V. How to Grow Your Business on the Internet. Coriolis Group Books. (1995).
- Frew, A.J. and Dorren, C. Intelligent Agents and the UK Hotel Sector, Proceedings for the Hospitality Information Technology Association World-Wide Conference, Edinburgh, May 18-20, (1996).
- Georgia Technology Research Corporation, Ninth WWW Survey, http://www.cc.gatech.edu/gvu/user_surveys/. (1998).
- Gray, M. Internet Statistics Growth and Usage of the Web and the Internet, http://www.umich.edu/~sgupta/herms/. (1997).
- Hanna, J.R.P. and Millar, R.J. Promoting Tourism on the Internet, Tourism Management, 18(7), 469-470, (1997).
- Hoffmann , D.L. and Novak, T.P, " Marketing in Computer-Meditated Environments", Journal of Computer Mediated Communication. 1 (3), (1995).
- Jung, H. and Baker, M. Assessing the Marketing Effectiveness of World Wide Web in National Tourism Offices, in Tjoa, A.M. (ed) Information and Communication Technologies in Tourism, 1998, Proceedings of the International Conference on Information and Communication Technologies in Tourism, Springer-Wien, NY, 94-102, (1998).
- Jung, H. The Use of the Internet as a Marketing Tool by National Tourism Organisations, Proceedings of Asia Pacific Tourism Conference, 1998, in Tanyang, Korea, 249-255, (1998).
- Kasavana, M.L., Knuston, B.J. and Polonowski, S.J. Netlurking: The Future of Hospitality Internet Marketing, Journal of Hospitality and Leisure Marketing, 5 (1), (1997).
- Kohli, R., Information Technology in Marketing, Graduate School of Business, Columbia University, (1996).
- KNTO Annual Statistical Report on Tourism (1997).
- Sheldon, P.J. Tourism Information Technology, CAB International. (1998).
- Schertler, W. Tourismus als Informationsgecheft-Strategische Bedeutung neuer Informations-und Kommunications technolgies im Tourismun, Wien, (1994).
- Smith, C. and Jenner, P. Tourism and the Internet, Travel & Tourism Anayst, No. 1. (1998).
- Sullivan, R. Design Tips for Your Webpage.
- http://frontpage.inet-images.com/progressive/autjors/sullivan/designtips.htmm. (1997).
- Tetzeli, R. The Internet and Your Business, Fourtune International, March, 129(5), 56-61. (1994).

Holiday Packages on the Web

B. Pröll†, W. Retschitzegger‡, R.R. Wagner†
† Institute for Applied Knowledge Processing (FAW)
University of Linz, AUSTRIA
{bproell, rwagner}@faw.uni-linz.ac.at

‡ Institute of Applied Computer Science,
Department of Information Systems (IFS)
University of Linz, AUSTRIA
werner@ifs.uni-linz.ac.at

Abstract

The tourism industry has reported dramatic changes in its structure over the last few years, not least due to the emerge of the Internet. Among others, tourists want to find products which are tailored to their personal needs in a minimum of time, without having to navigate through all the products offered by the tourism information system. Thus, from the tourism information supplier's point of view, one major requirement for effective tourism information systems is to support both, the production and distribution of individually tailored holiday packages. This paper focuses on the holiday package facility as realized in TIScover [TISc98a], the largest Austrian Web-based tourism information system. In TIScover, holiday packages can not only be assembled and maintained directly by tourism information suppliers but also easily retrieved, further customized and finally booked online by the tourist.

1 Introduction

For many years, tourists have had access to computerized tourism information and reservation systems through travel agencies only. Today, however, more and more tourists get tourism information directly through the Internet in an efficient way. This new technology provides advantages for the tourism information suppliers too, in that, e.g., the offer time for tourism products can be extended towards the time of consumption. This increases the likelihood that a buyer is found and herewith reduces the costs for committed but not consumed resources [Kärc97].

Besides, the structure of the tourist's demand is altered towards more frequent, but shorter travel, last-minute reservations, global advice, service quality, market transparency and individual holidays [Bloc96], [Kärc97]. Tourists want to find and book products online, which are tailored to their personal needs in a minimum of time, without having to navigate through all the products offered by the system. Therefore, the type of services offered by intermediaries such as tour operators and travel agents must be adapted to today's electronic markets.

To cope with this trend, tourism information systems must support the flexible *production* and *distribution* of *individually tailored holidays* in form of *packages*. By means of this new types of added values, the effect of disintermediation caused by the growth of individual holidays and late bookings can be turned around into some kind of reintermediation [Kärc97].

This paper focuses on the holiday package facility of TIScover, the largest Austrian Web-based tourism information system. With this facility, holiday packages can not only be assembled and maintained directly by tourism information suppliers but also easily retrieved, further customized and finally booked online by the tourist.

In what follows, Section 2 summarizes the requirements for holiday packages in web-based tourism information systems before giving a brief overview about TIScover in Section 3. Section 4 goes into detail concerning the functionality of TIScover's holiday package facility concerning both, tourism information suppliers and tourists. Section 5 is dedicated to related work and finally Section 6 concludes the paper with a short summary.

2 Requirements for Holiday Packages

The requirements for holiday packages can be best described when looking at the complexity of tourism products. As illustrated in Figure 1, the continuum of complexity concerning tourism products which should be supported by a tourism information system can be partitioned into four levels, ranging from pure information to consumer-defined holiday packages (HPs).

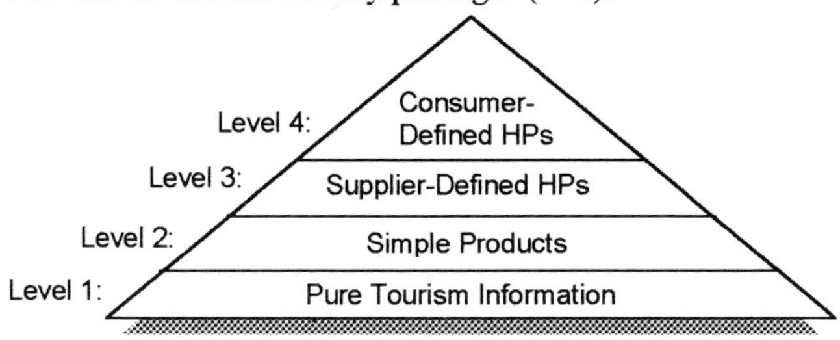

Fig. 1. Levels of Product Complexity

Pure Tourism Information. At the lowest level of complexity, pure information about destination facilities is presented.

Simple Products. At the second level, a destination facility can be transformed into a tourism product by making it bookable. For this, two additional attributes are necessary, namely the *price* of the product and the *allotment*, expressing the number of times a product can be booked.

Supplier-Defined Holiday Packages. Holiday packages are a more sophisticated type of bookable product, especially concerning their *granularity*. According to Kärcher, holiday packages can be seen as abstract products or information packages specifying the individual components of a holiday in terms of *simple products* or *pure tourism information* such as *transportation*, *accommodation*, *catering*, *entertainment*, *destination* and *additional service* [Kärc97]. In this respect, it is required that a holiday package can be predefined and maintained by a tourism information supplier by *assembling* possibly *heterogeneous simple products* offered by himself or by another third party. This means that any combination of these products which is oriented at a certain *target group* and feasible according to a set of underlying *business rules* should be possible.

From the tourist's point of view, as already mentioned, appropriate packages should be found in a minimum of time, without having to navigate through all the products offered by the system. The tourist has to be supported by means of sophisticated *navigation* and *search facilities* allowing to narrow or expand the offer of packages in an efficient way or by tracking the tourist to more restricted sets of offers which will most probably meet his requirements according to a certain profile.

Consumer-Defined Holiday Packages. Although, supplier-defined holiday packages are already tailored to target groups, tourists often require to adapt a pre-defined package even further to their personal needs, thus constituting the first step towards consumer-defined holiday packages. This conforms to the claim of Kärcher, that a move from a "supplier market", with the supply mainly determining the production of holidays, to a "consumer market", with the demand mainly determining the production of holidays, is taking place. *Customization possibilities* are especially required concerning aspects like *price*, *departure time*, *length of stay*, and the *pre-defined combination of products*. With this, the creation of *individualized* as well as *itinerary-built or multi-centered holidays*, i.e., holiday packages consisting of any feasible combination of components is possible [Kärc97]. After having customized a package to individual needs, the system should allow to book the package online.

Another even more visionary approach would be to allow the tourist to assemble a whole holiday package from scratch by means of a *product basket*, thus leading to fully consumer-defined holiday packages. However, from a technical point of view, online booking of fully customer-defined packages is much more complicated than that of simple products, especially due to their non-atomic nature, requiring some kind of nested transaction [Kapp96, Proe98a].

3 Overview of TIScover

The functionality provided by the Web-based destination information and booking system TIScover can roughly be categorized into three different components according to the different user groups which are able to work with the system. These components are all located around the central TIScover database [Proe98c].

Public Internet. The *public Internet* component comprises those functionality of the system which is accessible by every tourist all over the world and can be further divided into four modules. First, the module *Atlas* allows the tourist to browse through all kinds of destination information by following a geographical hierarchy. Second, the module *Scout* allows for a direct search of every kind of tourism information, like villages, hotels, available rooms, events and camping as well as online booking of tourism products. Third, the module *Reports* is used to provide actual and frequently changing tourism information like snow and avalanche conditions, water temperatures, weather forecast, traffic news and flight schedules. Fourth, the module *Trailer* represents a tourism magazine, featuring articles and videos about highlights or special events in a certain region.

Extranet. The *Extranet* component is only accessible with proper authorization from all tourism information suppliers being partners of TIScover. The major functionality of the Extranet is the *decentralized maintenance and customization* of tourism information and products. Besides that, the tourism information supplier is able to access a professional tourism journal called *Insider*, and information about, e.g., statistics concerning overnight stays as well as access statistics concerning TIScover itself by making use of the *Manager*. The tourism information supplier is also able to get information about the current booking status of his products by using the *booking reports module* [Proe98b].

Intranet. Finally, the *Intranet* component of TIScover is accessible at the system supplier's side only. With this, the whole system can be configured in various ways, e.g., by extending the geographical hierarchy, defining expiration dates for reports, specifying the default language for Intranet, Extranet and public Internet and constructing layout templates for the individual presentation of tourism products.

Originally, TIScover was realized to market the facilities of a certain region of Austria, namely Tyrol, only. Meanwhile, four additional Austrian federal states, although partly different in their destination characteristics use TIScover as official tourism information system. Currently, TIScover manages more than 100.000 Web pages covering among others 1.500 villages and 55.000 accommodations, originating from more than 4.500 tourism information suppliers, ranging from hotels to local tourist offices. The extensive customization possibilities of TIScover constituted a major prerequisite that the system is also employed in Asia, presenting tourism information about Thailand [TISc98b] and used by the German company START Media Plus to present tourism information about Germany [TISc98c]. For more detailed information about the other parts of TIScover it is referred to [Proe98a].

4 Holiday Packages in TIScover

In the following, the holiday package facility of TIScover is described in more detail, mainly from a functional point of view, ranging from the definition and maintenance of packages by tourism information suppliers to search, customization and online booking possibilities provided for tourists.

4.1 Assembling and Maintaining Holiday Packages in TIScover

TIScover fully supports the first three levels of product complexity as described in Section 2. Consumer-defined packaging is supported by TIScover in that the tourist is able to customize supplier-defined packages in different ways (cf. Section 4.4). In general, a holiday package in TIScover is defined as an accommodation with some kind of boarding "enriched" by some additional (entertainment) services like a skiing ticket or a visit of a museum. A simplified version of the data model used for realizing the holiday package facility is depicted in Figure 2. Note, that the syntax used follows UML, the new standard in object-oriented modeling [Fowl97].

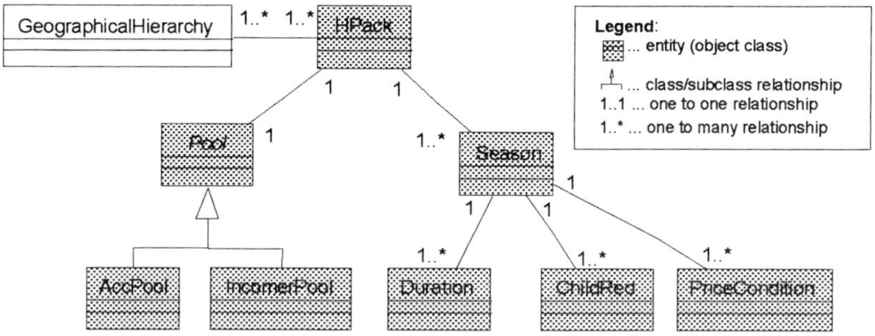

Fig. 2. Simplified Data Model of Holiday Packages in TIScover

According to the decentralized maintenance approach supported by TIScover's Extranet, holiday packages are assembled and maintained by authorized tourism information suppliers via Internet basically in the same way as other tourism information and products. Holiday Packages can be created, modified and deleted by accommodation managers, town/village managers and tour operators. Figure 3 shows one form of the Extranet used for defining a holiday package in TIScover.

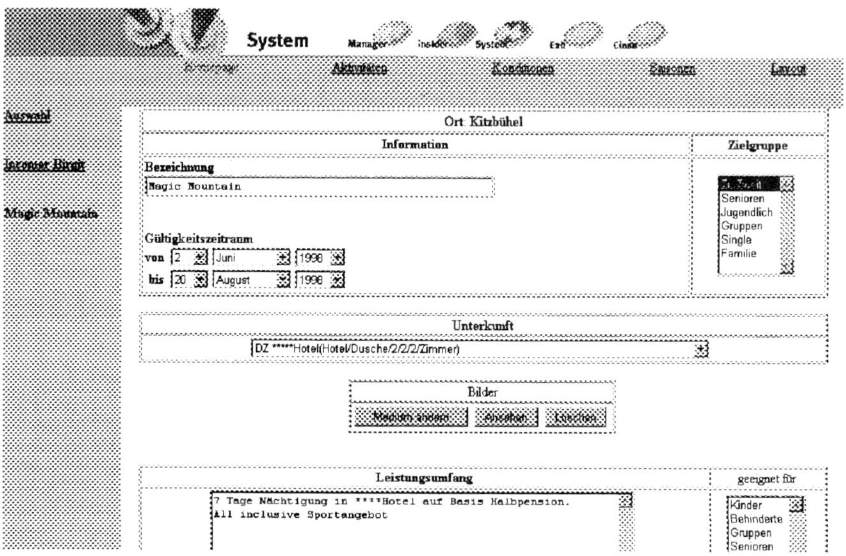

Fig. 3. Form of the Extranet for Defining of a Holiday Package by a Supplier

The most important attributes the supplier has to define when creating a holiday package are explained in the following.

Geographical Hierarchy. TIScover requires that a holiday package (cf. `HPack` in Figure 2) is integrated into a geographical hierarchy (`GeographicalHierarchy`) on the town/village level. Usually, a holiday package will be assigned to a single town or village. However, since TIScover also allows to configure packages offering a round trip, these packages can be assigned to all the locations being part of the round trip, with the effect that the package is automatically presented to the tourist on the Web-pages of each of these locations.

Pool. In TIScover, the allotment of a holiday package is dependent on the availability of the associated accommodation. To cope with this, a holiday package is assigned to an accommodation pool (`Pool`) through which a type of accommodation (e.g. a hotel) and its category (e.g. a three star hotel), a type of room (e.g. a double room) and a type of board is defined. A pool can be a specific accommodation (`AccPool`) in case that a hotelier is offering the holiday package or a virtual accommodation (`IncomerPool`) in case that the supplier is a tour operator. A tour operator usually does not own an accommodation by himself but rather uses accommodation allotments he gets from hoteliers for defining a package. For this reason, he defines *virtual accommodation pools*, each consisting of accommodation allotments of the *same type and category*, but possibly received from different hoteliers. Consequently, the accommodation property within a package offered by a tour operator does not contain a specific hotel, but only a certain hotel category and room type. At the time a tourist books a certain package, a definite accommodation is allocated and the number of allotments available within the pool is reduced accordingly.

Price and Time Conditions. Price conditions (`PriceCondition`), child reductions (`ChildRed`), different durations, as well as arrival/departure conditions of holiday packages are defined for unrestricted time-intervals (`Season`). TIScover allows that one and the same holiday package can be sold for different conditions and different prices. For example, different types of board or different seasons imply price reductions or an increase of the price. By means of this approach sophisticated price tables, customized for different groups of tourists can be constructed. Through time conditions it can be specified that a holiday package is available during a certain season and starts on defined weekdays only. In addition, a package can be defined to be a unique offer, being bookable for a certain date only.

Additional Service(s). Additional services are described in a text field and therefore cannot be searched further by means of the Scout.

4.2 Entry Points for Searching Holiday Packages

TIScover provides three entry points for the tourist to effectively find appropriate holiday packages.

Geographical Hierarchy. Analogous to pure tourism information or simple products, holiday packages can be retrieved by the tourist by browsing through the geographical hierarchy represented by the module Atlas. This kind of search can be regarded as browsing or leafing through a catalogue and is supported by many other systems too. However, the interesting point is, that the Atlas representing the destination information module of TIScover and the searching module Scout are seamlessly integrated in a manner that a tourist can arbitrarily switch between these modules while preserving all necessary context information. On the one hand, when, e.g., browsing on the Tyrolean level of Atlas a switch to Scout implies that the following search is done automatically in the context of Tyrol only. On the other hand, the tourist is able to navigate from the result list of a previous search for holiday packages to the Atlas and to browse through the whole destination information of the village the holiday package is related to. This seamless integration of searching facilities and destination information distinguishes TIScover from many other Web-based tourism information systems.

Life Style Types. By means of TIScover's Intranet, a system administrator is allowed to define arbitrary so called *life style types* used for categorizing holiday packages according to certain target groups (e.g. holiday packages for singles, family packages or senior packages). Within TIScover's Extranet, suppliers can subsequently assign their holiday packages to one of these life style types herewith constructing target group oriented products. A tourist in turn can decide on the basis of the available life style types located in the left menu bar (cf. (1) in Figure 4) which offers will meet his preferences to a high probability.

Campaignes. By means of the Extranet, tourist boards are allowed to announce so called *campaigns* which are characterized by a specific advertising motto (e.g. senior hiking in autumn) and by a certain price reduction. Holiday package suppliers can in turn assign appropriate holiday packages to the available campaigns, inferring that tourists are very much attracted by the campaign.

4.3 Searching Holiday Packages via Scout

The approach taken for searching holiday packages via Scout is different to the search of simple products (cf. Figure 4). Whereas for simple products, the tourist has to navigate to different pages in order to specify the required search criteria, for holiday packages this can be simply done on a single page. A tourist specifies holiday packages meeting his imaginations by selecting a certain criteria (cf. (2) in Figure 4) and setting the properties which are in turn displayed at the same page on the right side (cf. (3)). After each setting step the number of holiday packages matching the specified criteria is displayed below (cf. (3)). The tourist is allowed to redefine his settings further in order to either increase the number of matching packages by making the settings more general (the most general setting being "No selection") or reduce the result list by further restricting the settings. By means of this display/setting cycle which can be repeated an arbitrary number of times, the tourist is able to find those packages most closely meeting his needs. The criteria which can be set by the tourist are described in the following.

Interests. A tourist can specify a preferred interest, e.g. sports/skiing, to restrict the holiday package offers to those cohering with the activities he would like to undertake in his holidays.

Provinces. Holiday packages can be searched on each level of the geographical hierarchy. A search on a higher level than the town/village level, a holiday packages is assigned to, e.g. within a region, implies a search in all the towns/villages located within the specified region. By default, provinces is defined by the previous geographical level the tourist has been surfing in TIScover before entering the Scout. For example, if the tourist has been navigating to Tyrol, the default province for searching holiday packages will also be Tyrol. However, the tourist can restrict the number of offered holiday packages by choosing a certain town/village or broaden it by choosing Austria and by this implying a search on the state level.

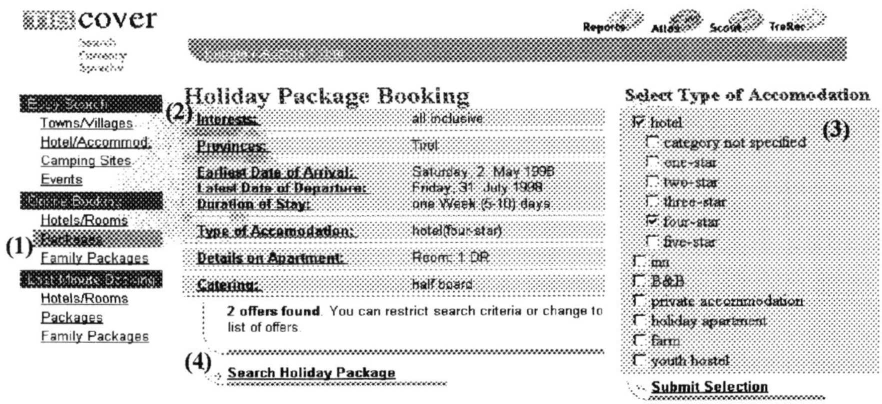

Fig. 4. Specifying a Desired Holiday Package

Date. *Earliest Date of Arrival* and *Latest Date of Departure* specify the time interval within which the holiday packages of the result list must be available, while *Duration of Stay* represents the length of the holiday.

Type of Accommodation. The accommodation's type (e.g., hotel) and its category (e.g., three star hotel) can be chosen.

Details on Apartment specify the type of the room and the number of persons in the room (e.g., double room or apartment for four persons).

Catering means the type of board (e.g. breakfast or full board) the tourist prefers.

4.4 Customizing and Booking Holiday Packages

After finishing the display/setting cycle and by this reducing or increasing the number of holiday packages matching the current settings, the tourist is able to view the result list. Concerning each holiday package, the tourist is not only able to request detailed information about its components and a detailed price list but can further customize the package to his personal needs by modifying the date of arrival, the duration of stay or the type of board (cf. Figure 5). Modifications to these settings can be made within the border settings as predefined by the supplier. Each modification to the settings implies an immediate recalculation of the price. Finally, the tourist can proceed with the online booking process by simply hitting the booking button.

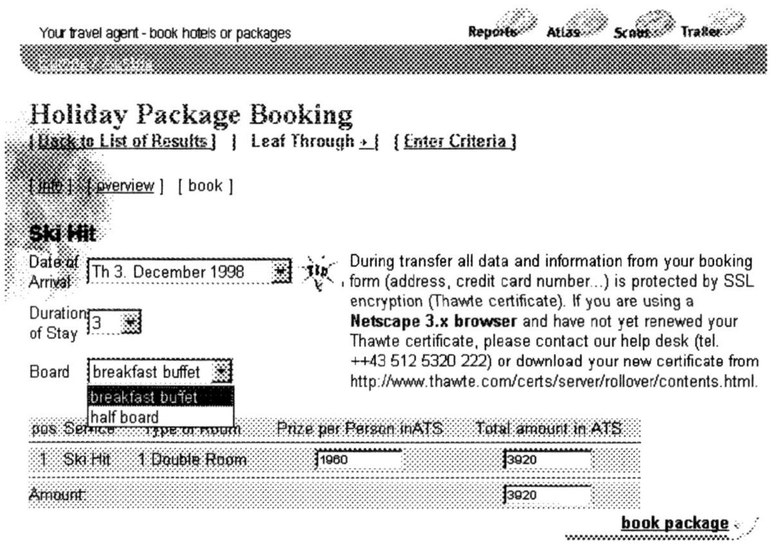

Fig. 5. Customizing a Holiday Package

5 Related Work

This section compares three of today's major Web-based tourism information systems with respect to the support of holiday packages.

Although one of the major players in the area, to the best of our knowledge, Expedia [Expe98] provides no support for holiday packages. So called wizards are provided by means of which a tourist is able to search for simple products such as a certain flight, a car, or a hotel, separately, in a convenient way.

Travelocity [Trlo98] in contrast, supports holiday packages to a certain degree. The tourist is provided with a list of all available holiday packages, sorted geographically on the basis of the name of the state or town wherein they are offered. However, there is neither a seamless integration of packages into destination information supported (cf. Section 4.2) nor is there a direct search facility for packages available. After selecting a holiday package, the tourist is provided with detailed information on the offer like included services, available add-ons, activities, and a detailed pricing chart showing the prices per season. These holiday packages cannot be further customized by the tourist. Furthermore, direct booking via Internet is not supported. Instead, he interested tourist is requested to call a phone.

Travelland [Trla98] supports holiday packages together with a sophisticated search agent. The tourist is able to specify his preferred departure airport, the destination country and further criteria on the room, the date and duration of travel, as well as a price limit. A clearly structured result list shows the available holiday packages including time, country and price per person. The tourist can proceed by booking the offer he decides for online. Selecting the search criteria as well as the indication of the result list and the booking process is similar to TIScover's approach. However, holiday packages are not seamlessly integrated into destination information. For example, browsing from a village to the holiday packages offered by this village is not possible.

6 Conclusion

This paper was dedicated to the holiday package facility of the Austrian Web-based tourism information system TIScover. TIScover's holiday packages can be assembled and maintained directly by tourism information suppliers and consist of various heterogeneous components possibly provided by third parties, ranging from accommodations to additional services. The tourist is able to search for packages out of three different entry points comprising the geographical hierarchy, life style types and campaigns which can again be arbitrarily configured by tourism information suppliers. By means of a display/setting cycle which can be performed comfortably on a single page, the criteria for a package can be (re)specified until the number of matching packages is acceptable for the tourist. Afterwards, a package can be selected, further customized if required and finally booked online by the tourist.

References

[Bloc96] M. Bloch, Y. Pigneur, T. Steiner, *The IT-enabled Extended Enterprise, Applications in the Tourism Industry*, Proc. of the Int. Conf. on Information and Communication Technologies in Tourism (ENTER'96), Springer, Innsbruck, Austria, 1996.

[Expe98] Homepage of Expedia, *http://www.expedia.com*, Microsoft, 1998.

[Fowl97] M. Fowler, *UML Distilled*, Addison Wesley, 1997.

[Kapp96] G. Kappel, S. Rausch-Schott, W. Retschitzegger, M. Sakkinen, *A Transaction Model For Handling Composite Events*, Proc. of the 3rd Int. Workshop of the ACM SIGMOD Chapter on Advances in Databases and Information Systems (ADBIS'96), Moscow, Sept. 1996.

[Kärc97] K. Kärcher, *Reinventing the Package Holiday Business*, DUV, Wiesbaden, Germany, 1997.

[Pass97] C. Passmann, W. Pipperger, W. Schertler, *How to assess WWW-applications for tourism information systems from the end-user perspective. Methodical design and empirical evidence*, Proc. of the International Conference on Information and Communication Technologies in Tourism (ENTER'98), A Min Tjoa (ed.) Springer, Istanbul, Turkey, 1997.

[Proe98a] B. Pröll, W. Retschitzegger, R.R. Wagner, A. Ebner, *Beyond Traditional Tourism Information Systems - TIScover*, Journal of Information Technology in Tourism, 1998.

[Proe98b] B. Pröll, P. Kroiss, W. Retschitzegger, R.R. Wagner, *Online Booking on the Net - Problems, Issues and Solutions*, Proc. of the Int. Conf. on Information and Communication Technologies in Tourism (ENTER'98), D. Buhalis et al. (eds.), Springer, Istanbul, 1998.

[Proe98c] B. Pröll, W. Retschitzegger, R.R. Wagner, *TIScover - A Tourism Information System Based on Extranet and Intranet Technology*, Proceeding of the Fourth Americas Conference on Information Systems (AIS'98), Baltimore, Maryland, 1998.

[TISc98a] Homepage of TIScover, *http://www.tiscover.com*, TIS Innsbruck, FAW Hagenberg, 1998.

[TISc98b] Homepage of TIScover ASIA, *http://www.tiscoverasia.com*, GoThailand, 1998.

[TISc98c] Homepage of TIScover, *http://www.deutschlandreise.de*, START Media Plus, 1998.

[Trla98] Homepage of Travelland, *http://www.travelland.com*, 1998.

[Trlo98] Homepage of Travelocity, *http://www.travelocity.com*, SABRE, 1998.

The Use of the Internet as a New Marketing Tool to Promote New Tourist Destinations in Asia

Case Study: Korea National Tourism Organisation (KNTO)

Hyung-Soo Jung and Abdulatif Twigeri
School of Management Studies for the Service Sector,
University of Surrey
H.Jung@surrey.ac.uk, A.Twigeri@surrey.ac.uk

Introduction

The development of the Internet during the 1990s has provided a new electronic infrastructure which facilitate new means of communication and information exchange, which was enhanced by the continuing rise of the number of Internet users world-wide. Speed, efficiency and cheapness are some of the many reasons that lead to the fast development of the Internet Technology.

The tourism industry is one of many industries that are highly dependent on information by means of promotion in different media. During the 1990s, the tourism industry has seen increasing demand for new tourist destinations (new products) which created an opportunity for new comers. Asia was one of the regions which responded to this new demand by combining the need for the new product and the use of information technology (Internet) to access global market.

National Tourism Organisations (NTOs) in Asian countries, such as Korea, Japan, Singapore and Malaysia have been adopting the Internet as a new marketing tool to promote and sell new products to a wide range of consumers on the Internet.

As a case study, the focus will be on the Web site of Korean National Tourism Organisation (KNTO). By covering the development of the Tourism Information Database which was developed during the early 1990s, the KNTO web site (Korea Tour Homepage) which was created September 1996 and look at KNTO plans for the next millennium.

The remainder of the paper is structured in three main parts. The first part presents the literature review on Destination Management Systems. The second part introduces the development of the Tourism Information System in the Korea National Tourism Organisation as a case study. Finally, the analysis of NTO's web site in Asia countries will be conducted.

Literature Review

Destination Management Systems (DMSs) is essentially a marketing tool promoting tourism products in particular destination, which might be a nation, region, town or other recognisable geographical entity. A DMS can have up to three components: a. A product database (of attractions, accommodation, travel information etc.); b. A customer database (or who have used, the database), and c. A booking and reservation system (Baker et al, 1996).

Destination Management Systems were introduced in the early 1990s through airline reservation system (CRS) known as the Global Destination System (GDS). It included a range of travel and leisure services and permitted reservations to be made for hotels, car rentals, cruises, railways, tours, theatres and sporting events such as Sabre. There are two main disadvantages of using CRS's as the backbone for GDS's are based on (outdated computer architecture that restrict information display and entail manipulation through complex codes and search commands) making it unsuitable for low-volume, leisure and rural tourism suppliers.

Several destinations around the world including New Zealand, Canada, Australia, Denmark, Austria have developed comprehensive DMSs that are available to a wide range of users, not just domestically but also internationally. Some of which are information only DMSs, like Canadian BOSS, Danish Dandata which developed by the Danish Tourist Board and in Austria the Tyrol Information System. Others such as Baden-wurrtemburg, the Caribbean and Queensland have developed reservation systems intended for professional use. Though some of those DMSs were successful, others failed, some with the loss of large sums of both public and private money.

On the other hand, the Internet technology provides a highly cost effective means of providing high quality information content in many formats (rich text, attractive images and live interesting video clips) to a global audience. Even more, web publishing enables the destination to customise its message to meet the needs of an ever-expanding number of market segments. Instead of having one feature, which suits many people, one can have many features, which suit one person. Interactivity allows that one person to explore products and services according to their own interests and find out what is important to them (Tapscott and MacGraw, 1995).

KOTOUR on the Net

1. Information System before INTERNET

Tourist Information DB

During the 1980s, KNTO did not have its own Tourist Information System (TIS). Korea National Tourism Organisation (KNTO) started to provide tourist information through different communication channels, such as public telecommunication networks (Chollian, Hitel), Korea Electric Power Corporation (KEPCO), Korean Airline and Asiana Airline etc. in the late 1980s. KNTO established Tourist Information Database on the host of that company and KNTO provides tourism-related data. The primary research on the building of Tourist Information Database was conducted by KNTO in the early 1990s and KOTOUR was established in 1995.

Table 1.1 shows the Tourist Information System and services. KOTOUR is an on-line accessible information database containing current information about Korea tourism, such as destination data (tourist attractions, accommodation, restaurants, events, shopping and sports and leisure facilities), tourism industry and market trends, tourism statistics, transportation and conference information. KNTO offers multi-lingual information (Korean, Japanese, and English) 24 hours per day for free through KOTOUR.

In addition to KOTOUR, KNOT has provided tourist information through Tourist Information Automatic Response System (ARS). This system has offered general information and transportation information on 600 major tourist destinations through the telephone since 1990. PC Information System also offered tourist destination information including photograph and map by using touch-screen PC to the visitors in the KNTO Tourist Information Center (TIC), TICs in international airports and Cheju Chungmun resort from 1987.

Table 1.2 shows when they began to provide each Tourist Information Service. Tour Information ARS Service started in October 1990, Tour Information DB Service in January 1996, Internet Service in September 1996 and May 1997 respectively. The number of Telephone ARS Service has increased from 121,352 in 1990 to 1,132,152 in 1992. However, the service has decreased to 470,052 in July 1998 since 1992. The number of Tour Information DB Service was similar to Telephone ARS Service. However, the number of Internet Service, both English and Korean, has increased on a large scale.

Table 1.1 Tourist Information System and Service ('98.8)

Service	Information	Access	Communication Channel
Korea Tour Homepage (Korean)	KNTO Tour Information Service Tour Information Center (TIC) Photo Gallery Tour Map Tourism Statistics Chungmun Golf Club Duty-free Shop Event Information	Internet Web Browser http://www.knto.or.kr	Internet
Korea Tour Homepage (English)	KNTO Service Korea at a glance Planning a trip Getting in & out of Korea Travel within Korea Accommodation Tourist attraction Travel destination Tour programs Korea shopping guide	Internet Web Browser http://www.knto.or.kr	Internet
Tour Information Database (KOTOUR, Korean, Japanese, English)	Destination Information Tourism industry Transportation Tourism Statistics International Conference Culture-tour news Tour Data	Internet (Telnet) telnet://kotour.knto.or.kr	Public Communication Networks Chollian Hitel Unitel Nownuri 01410
Tour Information ARS	Transportation Information on major travel destinations	Call 02) 134	Telephone
PC Information System	Tour destination, shopping, accommodation Information through PC	Time 09.00-18.00 place KNTO TIC Kimpo International Airport Kimhae Airport Cheju Airport Cheju Chungmun Resort	Visitor

Source (KNTO 1998)

Table 1.2 Tour Information Service

	Tour Information ARS Service	Tour Information DB Service	Internet Service (English)	Internet Service (Korean)
Time Started	'90. 10	'96. 1	'96. 9	'97. 5
1990	121,352			
1991	864,384			
1992	1,132,152			
1993	1,097,074			
1994	872,908			
1995	627,396			
1996	732,263	470,234	15,100	
1997	588,019	581,422	79,595	92,391
1998. July	470,052	243,423	52,839	127,544

Source (KNTO 1998)

2. Korea Tour Homepage on the NET

In the autumn of 1996, KNTO decided to establish its own web site on the Internet to provide Korean tourism information and promote tourism world-wide in order to attract potential tourists. This decision was due to the explosive growth of the Internet and its user and the increase of the tourists' need of various informations. This project was also linked with the Information Super Highway project by the government. KNTO has been offering multi-lingual service (English, Korean) through the Korea Tour Homepage. This information includes KNTO Service, Korea at a glance, planning a trip, getting in & out of Korea, travel within Korea, accommodation, tourist attractions, travel destination, tour programs, Korea shopping guide, etc.

3. KOTOUR on the INTERNET

3.1 Background

The "KOTOUR on the Internet" project started in July 1998 and it will be completed by the end of 1998. The background of the project of KOTOUR on the Internet is to provide information to meet the needs of potential tourists (Internet users) by the development of Information Technology (Internet related) and rapid growth of the Internet. This project is a part of "'98 Culture & Tour Information Network Plan" in tourism sector by the Culture and Tourism Ministry. As the number of potential customers continue to grow dramatically, KNTO recognises the needs of the integration of the Tourist Information Database into the multi-media Internet

Homepage to improve existing Information System and eventually to reach the Internet-related multimedia information and the establishment of the effective Tourist Information System.

3.2 Contents of the New Homepage

There are several characteristics of the new homepage. It includes modernisation of Korean and English Internet homepage, discovering and adding new information, and diversifying functions of the homepage.

Modernisation of Korea Tour Homepage contains the mixture of English Internet homepage and Tourist Information Database, adding hyper link function to key tourist information, selecting and providing more information on shopping, accommodation, restaurant etc., adding more photograph and map. With regard to discovering and adding new information, it involves the tourist information on theme tour, legend tour, travel essay and budget accommodation. It also contains marketing information on tour products and overseas travel agents. The information on tourism industry, such as tourism statistics, PATA homepage, and weekly tourism news are included. Diversification of homepage functions comprises a Bulletin Board Service (BBS), Frequent Answer & Question (FAQ), search engine, chatting room for several different user and a system for user statistics.

3.3 Architecture of the New Information System

Figure 1.1 shows the hardware architecture of the new Information System. KNTO has offered information through two main distribution channels. First, KNTO have provided tour information database through the public telecommunication networks to the customers. Second, KNTO also have offered information service through the Internet homepage. The Tour Information DB main server is linked with Internet homepage server with Local Area Network (LAN) in the new Information System. Therefore, customers (Internet users) access the information service via two different channels.

3.4 Future Plan

The future plans of KNTO include establishing Internet homepage for the overseas travellers by the overseas offices, creation of accommodation booking system to prepare for the 2002 world cup, and offering booking facility to the hotels, airlines, travel agents on the Korea Tour Homepage. Therefore, KNTO will offer a Total Destination Management System (DMS) to control the existing Tourist Information Database and customer information database, destination database, distribution of tourist information, reservation system and tourist information networks.

Figure 1.1 Hardware Architecture of the New Information System

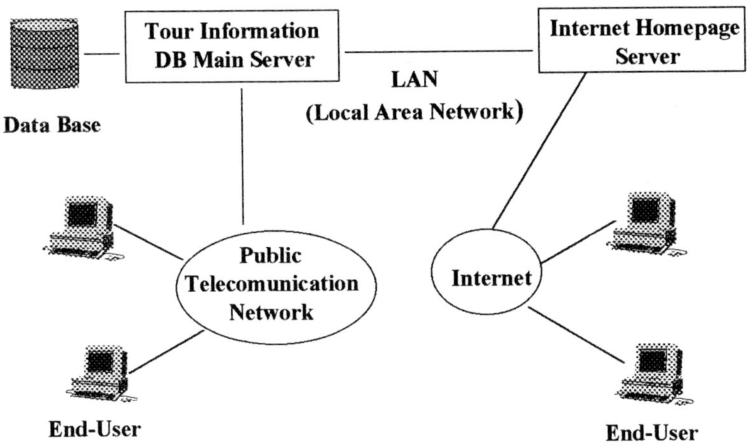

Methodology

The main approach taken by this paper is content analysis. Krippendorf (1980), defines content analysis as "A research technique for making replaceable and valid inferences from data to their context". Like any other research technique, content analysis is a tool whose purpose is to provide knowledge, facts and new insights.

Whenever a text is analysed, there is a process of creating identifying units. Rosenberg (1968), identifies five functional differences that most researchers use to identify units: (1) the word or symbol, (2) the theme, (3) the character, (4) the sentence or paragraph, and (5) the item. The unit that used in this study is the item. The item in the Internet is the web site, defined by its own URL address. The boundary of this paper is the Korean National Tourism Organisation web site. In addition to that, this paper looks at the web sites of three other NTOs in the same region, Japan, Singapore and Malaysia.

Korea National Tourism Organisation web site	http:// www.knto.or.kr
Japan National Tourism Organisation web site	http:// www.jnto.go.jp
Malaysia National Tourism Organisation web site	http:// www.tourism.gov.my
Singapore National Tourism Organisation web site	http:// www.travel.com.sg

Analysis of web site of other NTOs in Asia

National Tourism Organisations in many countries in Asia have also adopted the Internet technology as a medium for providing information and promoting destinations. In this part of the paper, we look at the web sites of Korea, Japan, Singapore and Malaysia to see how far is the web being used as a marketing tool in the promotion of destinations.

Korea National Tourism Organisation (KNTO) Web Site

The web site design is based on image and text format, although audio and video features are available by clicking on an icon. The site is targeted at both domestic and foreign travellers, as it is in both Korean and English. The information provided on the site range from planning your trip, getting in and out of Korea, travelling within to accommodation, tourist attraction and world heritage. It also provide contact details for hotels and tour operators. Transportation, shopping and food information is also available through the web site. Hotel reservation is only available through the World Hotel Center web site, which one can access from the KNTO web site. Bookings made by e-mail or fax, take 48 hours for confirmation.

Japan National Tourism Organisation (JNTO) Web Site

Designed mainly in text and images, Japan's NTO web site provides a wide range of information, varying from what's new, travel hints and budget travel to leading hotels, travel agents and convention sites. It also provides a large collection of maps, links to other sites and information about events, museums, theme and amusement parks.

Besides being a source of information, the JNTO web site promotes hotels and travel agents in the form of links or the display of contact information in its web pages. However, the main feature of the site is the accommodation reservation service provided by Welcome Inn Reservation Assistance, an affiliate of JNTO offering complimentary free assistance for reasonable accommodation to foreigners visiting Japan from abroad. By filling a form online three weeks in advance, one can made up to three booking arrangements for a single journey. This site is targeted at foreign travellers.

Singapore National Tourism Organisation Web Site

Heavy use of graphics and audio together with text make this site to load pages, yet the site is filled with very interesting information available contains food and entertainment, shopping, sports, exhibitions and conventions, festivals and events, accommodation, tours and traveller's essentials. Viewers can also find travel news, recipes, postcards, video clips, and photos of Singapore and even a screensaver for the PC.

Adverting is the main service offered on this web site, beside providing information on site and by mailing brochures to both travellers and traders. Hotel reservation can be made through a like to Hotlenet web site. This site is targeted at foreign visitors only.

Malaysia National Tourism Organisation Web Site

Designed in text and graphics, but one can also listen to some Malaysian music if designed to make it faster to move through pages. The site Map divides its content into ten categories. General information, activities, events, hotels, M.I.C.F (Convention Center Database), Historical, Nature, Regions, Services and others. Under each category you find a wide range of information. The region category provides links to each destination within that region. The hotel category holds the hotels database and a form for adding or updating the hotel list online. A travel agents database is under construction. This site aimed at the foreign visitor.

Table 4.1 shows the different format used in the design of the reviewed web sites, as web site design can affect the efficiency of the site. Heavy use of graphics, sound or video increases the loading time of the web pages, making it very slow. The web site of Korea and Malaysia contains text, image, audio and video. The web site of Malaysia contains text, image, audio and that of Japan contains text and image.

Table 4.1 Format Used for Designing Web Site

Design format	Korea	Japan	Singapore	Malaysia
Text	O	O	O	O
Image	O	O	O	O
Audio	O		O	O
Video	O		O	

Table 4.2 shows the different type of information offered by the reviewed web sites. While several categories are common among all web sites. Some categories are not offered by all of them. This could change, and one might find all off those categories covered by all NTO's web site. The reason being, as this medium is highly interactive, customers (visitors) will demand information if they think it is important. All four NTO's web site provides common information, such as accommodation, attractions, conventions, events & festivals, food & restaurant, shopping, tour programs etc. KNTO web site offers multimedia information and world heritage, JNTO web site offers F.A.Q., links and maps, Singapore NTO offers multimedia information, post cards and recipes, Malaysia NTO web site offers Electronic cards, links.

Table 4.3 shows the different type of services offered by the reviewed web sites. At this stage, all web sites are mainly providing information and promotion for destinations, hotels and travel agents. NTOs web sites are starting by linking to other reservation providers. JNTO web site offers information, advertising, reservation

Table 4.2 Information Offered by Web Site

Category	Korea	Japan	Singapore	Malaysia
Accommodation	O	O	O	O
Attractions	O	O	O	O
Conventions	O	O	O	O
E-cards				O
Events and Festivals	O	O	O	O
F.A.Q.		O		
Food and Restaurant	O	O	O	O
Links		O		O
Maps		O		
Multimedia	O		O	
Postcards			O	
Recipes			O	
Shopping	O	O	O	O
Tour Program	O	O	O	O
Weather				O
World Heritage	O			

Table 4.3 Services Offered by the Web Site

Service	Korea	Japan	Singapore	Malaysia
Information	O	O	O	O
Advertising	O	O	O	O
Reservation through the site		O		
Reservation through links	O	O	O	

through the site and reservation through links. Both of KNTO and Singapore NTO provide information, advertising and reservation through links. Malaysia NTO offers information and advertising.

Conclusion

Changing the backbone of the DMS form network technology to Internet technology is proving very effective in many ways. It is allowing information to be presented in powerful, interactive and visual forms. This can be very important to travellers. Being able to view a video about the destination for example can help in making much more informative decisions. In addition, having the DMS run on the Internet is not just cost effective, but it allows information to reach a global audience and can also be more customise at the same time, in order to meet the needs of larger market segment.

The reviewed Asian web sites are trying to take full advantage of the Internet technology. Though the net technology is still developing, NTOs are trying to be in front as they can see the opportunity of being the gateway for the tourism industry on the Internet.

Also, the KNTO development stages from providing tour information through different communication channels, such as Tour Information DB, Tour Information ARS, PC Information and Internet homepage. The KOTOUR on the Internet project, which started in July 1998, was designed to meet the needs of potential tourists, and is another examples of how the NTOs in Asia are endeavouring to secure their share of global travellers.

References

- Baker, M.G., Hayzelden, C. and Sussmann, S. : Can Destination Management Systems Give You Competitive Advantage? Progress in Tourism and Hospitality Research, 1 (3), 89-94. (1996).
- Krippendorf, K, : Content Analysis: An Introduction to It's Methodology, London, Sage Publications. (1990).
- Pollock. A. : Occasional Studies: The Impact of Information Technology on Marketing, EIU Travel & Tourism Analyst, No 3. (1995).
- Rosenberg, M. : The Logic of Survey Analysis, New York: Basic Books. (1968).
- Sussmann, S. and Baker, M. : Responding to the Electronic Marketplace: Lessons from Destination Management Systems, Hospitality Management, 15 (2), 99-112. (1996).
- Tapscott, D. and MacGraw, H. : The Digital Economy: Promise and Peril in the Age of Networked Intelligence. (1995).
- Korea National Tourism Organisation http://www.knto.or.kr
- Japan National Tourism Organisation http://www.jnto.go.jp
- Malaysia National Tourism Organisation http://www.tourism.gov.my
- Singapore National Tourism Organisation http://www.travel.com.sg

Matching traveller preferences to destination and product characteristics: It's all a matter of semantics.

Paul F. O'Brien
Information Systems Group
Business Faculty
Sunshine Coast University College
pobrien@scuc.edu.au

Abstract

The purchase of a very expensive, complex product or service such as an extended international holiday requires a great deal of information and reliable expert advice. The risks involved in such a purchase are substantial.

For this reason it is expected that travellers will continue to use retail travel agents to complete their travel arrangements provide they can continue to add value (O'Brien, 1998; AFTA, 1994; Bloch & Segev, 1996; Poon, 1993).

This paper discusses the implementation of systems that provide fast, easy access to reliable product and destinational information that closely matches the traveller's desired experience. An architecture for a World Wide Web based semantic matching system using formal ontologies is proposed.

KEYWORDS: Tourism, Technology, Semantic Mapping, Ontologies

1 Introduction

The travel industry is facing increasing competition through globalisation and de-regulation, changing customer demands for more specialised trips, increasing customer expectations, particularly in relation to customisation and increasing knowledge and sophistication of customers (Bloch & Segev, 1996). There is also a worldwide trend towards independent travel and away from packages, particularly with European, Canadian & American travellers (Queensland Tourist & Travel Corporation, 1997).

However, the purchase of a very expensive, complex product or service such as an extended international holiday requires a great deal of information and reliable expert advice. The risks involved in such a purchase are substantial. For this reason, opinion leaders in the Australian tourism and travel industry believe that, for the foreseeable future, consumers will continue to take advice from a human sales consultant before purchasing, with the exception of major corporate bookings and simple point to point bookings (O'Brien, 1998).

Poon (1993) argues that if travel agents adopt an appropriate strategic response to the changes that are occurring, there will be enormous prospects for increased income generation. „It is to ensuring the satisfaction of the travel consumers that agencies must give priority in order to ensure their long-term survival and competitiveness. *The ability of travel agents to acquire, provide and transmit unbiased information in a courteous, efficient and timely manner will be the key to their competitive success.* "

O'Brien (1998) recommended five key strategic responses for retail travel agents to address the growing consumer preference for personalised packages to more exotic destinations and the accelerating pace of technological change, namely:

1. reduce dependence on transactions for income;
2. re-position as a consultant working for the customer;
3. develop close relationships with customers to gain a clear understanding of their preferences and desired holiday experience;
4. implement systems that provide fast, easy access to reliable product, destinational and personal experience information;
5. implement systems that enable cost-effective production of personalised packages that are tailored to customer preferences.

The Internet provides the travel consultant with a huge repository of travel product and destination information but they are still required to manually access the relevant web pages and assess the reliability, quality and appropriateness of the retrieved information. Retail Travel Agents must become proficient at using the internet, and their own personal experience and knowledge, to access, integrate, analyse, interpret and present information from distributed, heterogeneous sources. This is a difficult task when the consultant has personal knowledge of the activity, product or destination but it is almost impossible when he/she has no personal knowledge or experience. In these situations the software agent must be able to search *semantically* for relevant products or destinations to meet the new demands of the „new tourist" (Geyer et al, 1996).

Baker et al (1996) recognised that „there is clearly a need for an intelligent system that incorporates local knowledge, regularly updated, and interpretation of the customers' needs, into the mapping process. Intelligent agents, either obeying rules when they exist, or observing and recording in order to learn or infer the correspondence, seemed ideally suited."

The travel agent, assisted by such an intelligent software agent, would create a very powerful travel cybermediary that could dramatically improve the quality of advice provided to the customer, and ultimately, improve customer satisfaction.

This paper proposes an architecture for a World Wide Web based semantic matching system using formal ontologies.

2 Purpose

Most existing World Wide Web (WWW) search engines rely on keyword out of context, or free text searching for words or boolean combinations of words to identify matching sites and pages. This assumes that the meaning of the words or keywords (semantics) is the same in the mind of the searcher and the page creator. While this may be true in many cases, in the vast majority of cases it is not so. For example an Australian searcher who is looking for recipes for the first course of a dinner party would use the word entrée for a search. This is likely to result in hits on main courses from US sites (as main courses are called entrees in the US), lobbying sites related to gaining access (entrée) to decision makers, not to mention the large number of French language sites that would contain this word. To reduce the number of hits to a manageable number the search would need be narrowed to something like „entrée AND Australia AND food ". This is only possible if the searcher is aware of the different meaning of the word entrée in different countries, languages and domains, and that they understand, and can use boolean logic correctly. This problem could be overcome if each WWW page included some standardised semantic information about the content of the page and more information was obtained from the searcher about her/his meaning of the word. For example, if the US WWW entrée recipe pages indicated that they were „main courses", and the search word was converted to „first course" there would be no match.

In the travel domain a similar problem occurs with classification schemes for hotels, restaurants and attractions. There are no international standards and in many countries, no national standards for these. Consequently, an Australian traveller who asks for a three star hotel in Britain will be very surprised when he/she discovers on arrival that there is only a shared bathroom. Travel consultants who have travelled to Britain could advise their clients of the differences, if it is in their interest to do so. But what if the destination is very exotic and unusual? The travel consultant is unlikely to have been there and probably doesn't know how to get information on the destination, let alone the product. In this situation, an intelligent semantic mapping assistant would help the consultant to provide higher quality advice to the client.

The purpose of this research is to develop an architecture that will facilitate semantic mapping of customer preferences to product and destination characteristics by an intelligent travel consultant's *assistant*. This will allow travel consultants who are using the system to carry out the matching function faster, more reliably and more accurately, thereby providing higher quality information to their clients, and satisfying one of their key strategies for business survival.

To enable automated semantic mapping of search data to WWW pages, each page must carry with it some additional information (metadata) that identifies the meaning of the text, images, graphics, audio and video content of the page. The format of this semantic information must be standardised, or the specification of the format must be specified in the WWW page itself in a standardised format. MIME encoded email uses the latter method.

There are many ways to represent semantic information electronically. Most are, unfortunately, difficult to integrate into HTML. The use of ontologies has been shown to be simple, flexible and easily implemented using simple extensions to HTML (SHOE, 1997). The release of XML (DSTC, 1998) and OML (WAVE, 1998) will further simplify the use of ontologies in WWW pages.

3 Use of ontologies in information systems

Formal ontologies provide a means of representing, or at least approximating, a conceptualisation of the world. Guarino (1998) defines a conceptualisation as a set of conceptual relations on a domain space, where a domain space is a set of possible states of affairs within a specific domain.

By committing to an ontology, users of that ontology, either human or intelligent agents, agree to represent their conceptualisations of the world using a common language. Although each conceptualisation is language independent, ontologies are language dependent (Guarino, 1998). If the models of their conceptualisations overlap they share a common conceptualisation of the world and are able to communicate. This shared conceptualisation of the world is essential for shared understanding between users. Shared understanding allows semantic matching of concepts between users and agents. Semantic matching is the underlying process used in information retrieval, natural language translation, intelligent assistants and agents and many other areas of information systems.

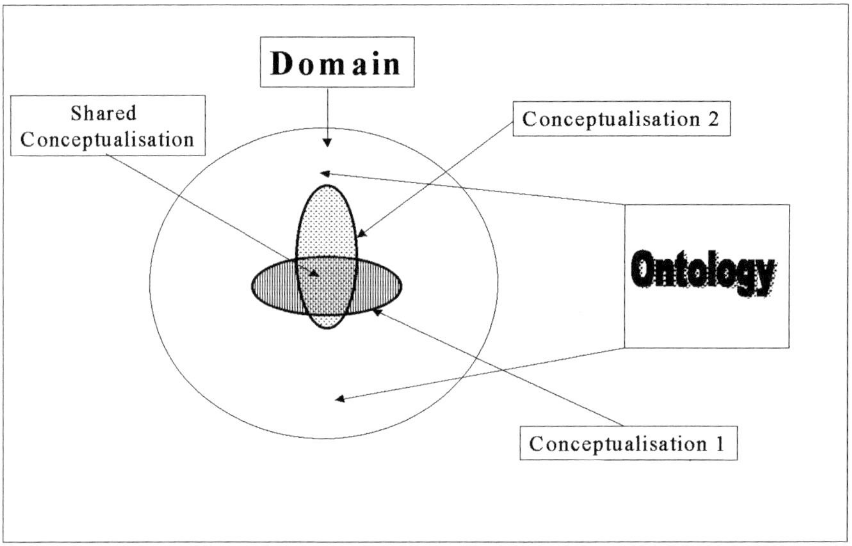

Fig. 1 Shared conceptualisation using an ontology

Formal ontologies are now being used in application areas such as knowledge engineering, natural language processing, natural language translation, electronic commerce, bills of materials, information extraction, standardised product knowledge, legal information systems and biological information systems (Guarino, 1998).

Information systems typically perform specific tasks in specific domains. For example, a travel reservation system is used to find and reserve transport and accommodation services. In other words, they operate in specialised areas doing specialised tasks. Guarino (1998) argues that an application ontology is required that 'describes concepts depending on a *particular domain and task* which are often specializations of both the related ontologies".

If communications between agents, either human or artificial, are formulated in terms of an ontology to which they have committed, the intended meaning of each message is clear. The ontology based sales consultant's assistant (OSCA) is based on this premise.

4 An ontology based sales consultant's assistant (OSCA)

The OSCA system is proposed as a solution to the problem of semantic mapping of customer preferences to product (and destination) characteristics.

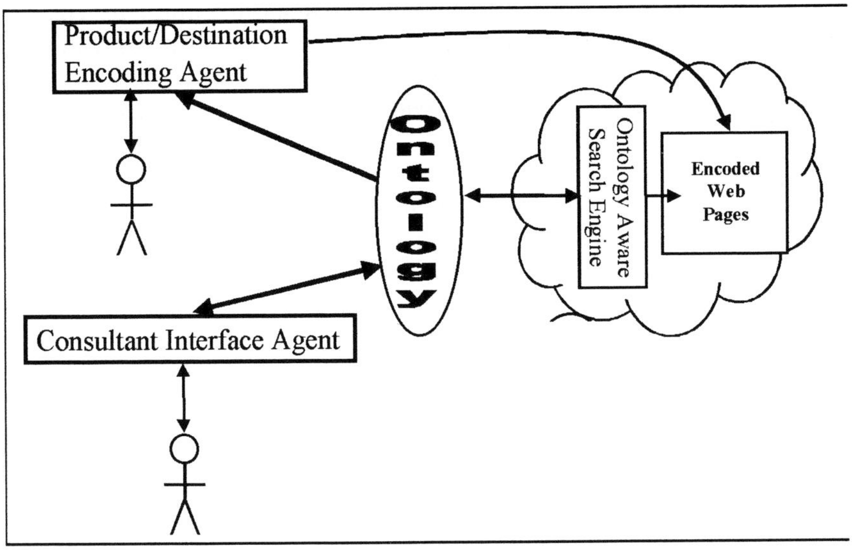

Fig. 2 OSCA Architecture

The system consists of a sales consultant's interface agent (CIA) and a product (and destination) encoding agent (PEA). Both agents use a shared domain ontology for encoding and retrieving web pages containing product and destinational information of any type.

When new product and destinational web pages are created, the PEA encodes the page with ontology information using the agreed ontology. Encoding of some information could be automated but in most cases human intervention is required during the encoding process. This is particularly true for non-textual information such as images, sound and video clips. Existing pages can be encoded in a similar way.

The CIA obtains the customer preference information from the consultant, converts it into a form that is consistent with the agreed domain ontology and initiates a search of web pages that have been encoded using the same ontology. An ontology aware search engine matches the encoded pages to the encoded request and returns them to the CIA that then presents them to the consultant in order of best match.

The CIA is responsible for requesting further information from the consultant until it is able to encode the request into a form that is consistent with the agreed ontology. For example, if the consultant requests a 3 star hotel, the CIA cannot determine what facilities are required without knowing the city and country of origin of the request.

If this cannot be obtained from the workstation environment settings, the consultant must be asked to enter this information. The responses are then recorded against that consultant's user identifier for future reference. To reduce ambiguities, similar requests for more information may be required by the PEA when encoding web pages.

No further information is required by the ontology aware search engine as both the web pages and consultant's requests have already been encoded into a consistent form.

OSCA is a system of co-operating intelligent agents that uses agreed and committed ontologies to minimise ambiguities thereby improving semantic matching of product and destination characteristics to customer preferences. The design of the system assumes that the intelligent encoding agent and consultant's assistant agents will require human intervention. As such, it is designed to *assist* consultants to efficiently access higher quality, more relevant information, not to replace them completely.

The OSCA architecture is very similar to the Ontoseek architecture (Borgo et al, 1997). The main difference is that OSCA relies upon the use of an ontology aware World Wide Web search engine. The query and classification encoding processes are also separated and distributed in the OSCA system.

5 Travel ontology

Ontologies in information systems are usually composed of a *taxonomy* of the domain (or application) and a set of *relations* between them. An example of a portion of a travel domain ontology is shown below.

5.1 Travel taxonomy

Travel Entity

- **Place**
- **Attraction**
  - Beach
  - EntertainmentVenue
- **Activity**
  - Fishing

Accommodation

  - Type
    - Hotel
  - Rating

- **Transport**
  - Aircraft
  - Train
  - Car
- **Organised Activity**
- **Person**
  - Traveller
  - TravelAgent
  - Operator
- **Reservation**
- **Itinerary**

5.2 Travel relations

Activity

"is available at"
↳"Activity"
↳"Place"

"participates in"
↳"Activity"
↳"Traveller"

Transport

"has a"
↳"Transport"
↳"Class"

"provides"
↳"Transport"
↳"Carrier"

5.3 Travel Ontology

An example of the encoding of the above ontology using OML, which is based on the new Internet markup language, XML is shown below.

```
<OML>
    <Ontology id="TravelActivity" version="1.0">
        <extends href=http://www.cg.org/CG_Ontology/" prefix="CG"/>
        <Object type="Place"/>
        <Object type="Activity"/>
        <Relation type="AvailableAt"/>
            <argument type="CG#Dest" valuetype="#Place"/>
            <argument type="CG#Thme" valuetype="#Activity"/>
        </Relation>
        <subtype specific="#AvailableAt" generic="#Relation "/>
        <subtype specific="#Place" generic="CG#Organization"/>
        <subtype specific="#Activity" generic="#Object"/>
    </Ontology>
</OML>
```

5.3 Example of semantically coded web page

```
<OML>
  <Collection type="TravelActivity#Object">
    <uses href=http://www.eg.org/examples/travelactivity/
    prefix="travelactivity"/>
    <TravelActivity#AvailableAt>
      <Dest><Place text=„Innsbruck“ /></Dest>
      <Thme><Activity text=„skiing“ /></Thme>
    </ TravelActivity#AvailableAt >
  </Collection>
</OML>
```

6 Lessons for industry and further research

The use of ontologies, implemented using HTML extensions, has potential for more effective and efficient matching of a traveller's desired travel experience to available products and destinations. Although there are only a few ontologies available at the present time, many research projects are currently in progress that are expected to yield ontologies for a number of new domains over the next few years.

Further research by the author will fully define an ontology for the travel domain. Intelligent encoding (PEA) and consultant's query (CIA) agents will then be developed to interface to these ontologies.

References

- Australian Federation of Travel Agents (1994) *Travel Industry Technology - Towards Information Highways*, Sydney, Australian Federation of Travel Agents.
- Brenner, W., Kolbe, L. & Hamm, V. (1997) The Net: Extinction or Renaissance for Intermediaries - An Analysis of Core Competencies in the Book Business, *Proceedings of the 1997 European Conference on Information Systems.*
- Bloch, M. & Segev, A. (1996) *The Impact of Electronic Commerce on the Travel Industry*, The Fisher Centre for Information Technology & Management, University of California, California.
- Borgo, S. and Guarino, N. (1997) An Ontology Theory of Physical Objects, *Proceedings of 1997 Workshop on Qualitative Reasoning* (QR 97), Cortona, Italy.
- DSTC (1998). Introduction to XML, Distributed Systems Technology Centre, University of Queensland, Australia.
- http://www.dstc.edu.au/aw3tc/slides/XML/index.htm
- Geyer, G., Kuhn, C. & Schmid, B. (1996) An Electronic Catalog for Distributed Environments, *Proceedings of the 3rd International Conference on Information and Communications Technologies in Tourism*, Springer-Verlag, Vienna.
- Guarino, N. (1995) Formal Ontology, Conceptual Analysis and Knowledge Representation, *International Journal of Human and Computer Studies*, Vol 43, No. 5/6.
- Guarino, N. (1998) Formal Ontology and Information Systems, *Proceedings of FOIS'98, Trento, Italy, 6-8 June 1998.* IOS Press, Amsterdam.
- Karcher, K. (1996) Re-engineering the Package Holiday Business, Proceedings of the 3rd International Conference on Information and Communications Technologies in Tourism, Springer-Verlag, Vienna.
- Milne, S. (1996) Tourism Marketing and Computer Reservations Systems in the Pacific, *Tourism in the Pacific: Issues and Cases*, International Thomson Business Press, London.
- O'Brien, P. (1998) Electronic Commerce, The Internet and Travel Cybermediaries, *Australian Journal of Information Systems*, Vol 6, No 1.
- Poli, R. and Simons, P. (eds.) (1996) *Formal Ontology*, Kluwer Academic Publishers, London.
- Poon, A. (1993) *Tourism, Technology and Competitive Strategies*, CAB International, Wallingford.
- Queensland Tourist & Travel Corporation (1997). International Marketing Briefs
- Sheldon, P. (1997) *Tourism Information Technology*, CAB International, New York.
- SHOE (1997). Simple HTML Ontology Extensions.
- http://www.cs.umd.edu/projects/plus/SHOE/

- Tschanz, N. & Klein, S. (1996) Internet Strategy Development in Tourism - Concept and Case Study, *SISnet Research Workshop 'Internet and Business'*, SISnet, Lisbon.
- Van der Heijden, J. (1996) The changing value of travel agents in tourism networks: towards a network design perspective, *Proceedings of the 3rd International Conference on Information and Communications Technologies in Tourism*, Springer-Verlag, Vienna.
- WAVE (1998). The WAVE Project, Washington State University.
- http://wave.eecs.wsu.edu/CKRMI/OML.html
- Werthner, H. (1996) Design Principles of Tourist Information Systems, Proceedings of the 3rd International Conference on Information and Communications Technologies in Tourism, Springer-Verlag, Vienna.

Acknowledgments

The author acknowledges the assistance provided by Dr. Robert Colomb, University of Queensland in clarifying and focussing the concepts in this paper.

The work reported in this paper has been funded in part by the Cooperative Research Centres Program through the Department of Prime Minister and Cabinet of the Commonwealth Government of Australia

Information technology and tourism education in Australia: an industry view of skills and qualities required in graduates

Roberto Daniele
Lecturer in tourism
Department of Hospitality, Tourism & Leisure, RMIT University
roberto.daniele@rmit.edu.au

Nina Mistilis
Coordinator undergraduate tourism courses
University of Western Sydney Macarthur
Department of Management & Marketing
n.mistilis@UWS.edu.au

Abstract

As technology increasingly becomes the driving engine for productivity improvement and business opportunities for enterprises in the 21st century, tourism and hospitality education and training must address these developments and aim at enhancing the ability of future managers to use a variety of IT tools and strategies to increase their organisation's efficiency and responsiveness in the global market place. Following an ENTER 98 workshop on IT curriculum development for tourism and hospitality courses, the authors of this paper undertook to examine the Australian tourism industry's needs and views in relation to information technology training and education. The findings suggest that operational IT skills take a greater priority over strategic management and marketing skills.

1 Introduction

Information technology (IT) is being recognised in government and industry circles in Australia as the dominant engine for productivity improvement and business opportunities for enterprises in the 21st Century and a key factor for generating future employment. Indeed the convergence of computing and communications as manifested in the Internet means that much commerce in the future will be carried out electronically (National Board of Employment, Education and Training:1997:xi). For Australia, in addition to this general global trend, there are other imperatives driving the use of technology in the business environment. This is a land of great distance, a long way from most of the world's markets. Participation in the information economy allows it to overcome the isolation of its remote areas and the disadvantages of national isolation from world markets. The extent to which the Australian economy will benefit from progress in information technology is associated with its readiness to adopt such innovations and exploit their strategic use (Ministerial Council for the Information Economy, 1998:3-6).

Indeed, growing Australian government recognition of this imperative led in 1998 to the development and release of a preliminary statement of its strategy for the information economy. Some attention is given to the question of education and training to fulfil the strategic objectives of the strategy. As part of its vision for Australia in the information economy, the Commonwealth Government envisages that the education and training system must be able to produce high quality information professionals with up-to-date skills (Ministerial Council for the Information Economy:1998:9).

Government has also made a strategic priority to train the workforce to harness opportunities in the information economy. This includes the notion of government, business and industry collaborating with education and training sectors in developing an enhanced information and communication technology culture (Ministerial Council for the Information Economy, 1998:12). However, the strategy is general and not industry specific. What is the situation for the tourism sector?

Tourism is essentially a collection of service industries and is also highly information intensive. It is true that there has, and to an extent still is, resistance by service sectors to adopt technology, in part associated with their misconception that this is not consistent with high service standards and quality consumer experience. Tourism managers often refer to this predicament as a choice of a high touch versus high tech approach to service delivery. However, increasingly in the 1990s, time gained through speedy, accelerated access and response has become an important component of service and competitive advantage (Sheldon:1997:7).

The impact of information technology on the business environment has been considered by the Office of National Tourism in the recent action plan for tourism in Australia. One component of the plan, undertakes to identify scope for technological innovation in tourism industry sectors, including addressing the factors which impede the use of technology development. It also recommends development, with industry, of a technology strategy for tourism (Department of Industry, Science & Tourism - Office of National Tourism:1998:2). One strategy listed is to take advantage of online technologies to enhance Australia's tourism marketing, distribution and settlement system. Another strategic action is to sponsor a national scoping study to identify deficiencies in Australia's tourism distribution and the scope for online innovation. Given its particular stage of tourism development, its vast geography and its relatively small population size, the development of appropriate online distribution strategies may well be critical to the delivery of competitive tourism and hospitality products in Australia.

The plan also notes the changing environment that can be expected to influence the direction of tourism development in the next few years. Key changes in the business environment include considerable advances in information technology and changes in distribution systems (Department of Industry, Science & Tourism - Office of National Tourism:1998:8). The plan recommends strategic action to make optimum use of new technologies for marketing purposes (Department of Industry, Science & Tourism Office of National Tourism:1998:11).

Some training issues are also examined in the report, including the need for new and specialised skills, particularly technology based skills (Department of Industry, Science & Tourism Office of National Tourism:1998:8). The government's commitment to the development of skills is also demonstrated by continuing support of Tourism Training Australia, the body responsible for advising the Australian National Training Authority (ANTA) on training priorities and developing training packages, including those for information technology skills (Department of Industry, Science & Tourism - Office of National Tourism:1998:23-24).

Tourism and hospitality education and training must aim to enhance the ability of managers to use a wide range of tools to increase their efficiency and responsiveness. Certainly, the effective use of information technology is increasingly regarded as an essential skill for competent managers. Indeed the competitiveness and profitability of tourism industry sectors will increasingly be associated with the ability of tourism professionals and managers to utilise emerging information technology in order to maintain a competitive advantage (Buhalis:1998:296).

In an environment of rapidly developing technological advances and increased competition in the Asia Pacific region, strategic use of information technology is imperative. There is also the need to research perspectives from the tourism and hospitality industry sectors regarding the skills and competencies in information technology they see as important for graduates to have.

2 Purpose

The general aim of this paper is to investigate a range of industry sectors' (such as airlines, accommodation establishments and attractions) views of major issues associated with teaching information technology in tourism and hospitality for graduates. Because most hospitality and tourism courses train graduates for employment in a wide range of industry sectors, this paper attempts to incorporate all industry sectors in an overview approach; the authors recognise that specific sectors might have differing educational needs or priorities and further research could address these more particular perspectives more in depth.

Following a workshop at ENTER 98 on IT curriculum development for tourism and hospitality courses, the authors undertook to examine the Australian tourism industry's training needs in relation to information technology and assess industry's views on the various models currently used for teaching IT.

Buhalis (1998:293) identified three key approaches to current information technology training and education: programming skills, operating skills and strategic management & marketing skills. These skills and competencies relate to both the internal organisation management (for example hotel property management systems) and external organisation management (for example computer reservation systems). The present research investigates industry's views and priorities in relation to these skills.

3 Methodology

The researchers conducted a series of fifteen structured personal interviews in Sydney and Melbourne with senior managers in a number of tourism and hospitality industry sectors. Main issues associated with tourism and hospitality education were identified and discussed. Using this information, the draft questionnaire, developed with reference to the existing literature, was then modified. The questionnaire was administered by fax in the form of a pilot study to ten senior managers selected again from different tourism and hospitality sectors in Sydney and Melbourne. Again modifications indicated from the pilot study were incorporated into the final questionnaire which was administered by post with an accompanying letter from the researchers. These are attached in Appendix 1.

A sample of four hundred and ten organisations was randomly selected from the Travel Trade Year Book, an annual publication listing tourism and hospitality operators in Australia. Sectors selected included transportation (airline and car rental firms), travel intermediaries (travel agencies and tour operators) accommodation establishments, MICE and government organisations.

It must be noted however that the sample selected is not representative of the spread of industry sectors in Australia because some are under represented, some over represented in the Travel Trade Year Book. For example, accommodation firms are unevenly represented in size (little or no representation of small to medium establishments) and in types of firms (no bed & breakfast establishments). None the less the listed firms are arguably representative of the most active tourism and hospitality firms.

Seventy two responses were received, constituting about a seventeen percent response rate. The proportion of these responses in each industry sector was similar to that of the sample, with the exception of an over representation in the government sector and an under representation in the tour operating sector. It is acknowledged that there maybe some response bias, with those more interested and active in IT more likely to respond.

4 Results

The results suggest that whilst there is some degree of disparity in the views of different tourism and hospitality industry sectors in relation to information technology skills and competencies necessary in graduates, for the most part, they tended to focus on operational rather than strategic management and marketing skills. Little or no importance was placed on programming skills.

4.1 Overall IT Needs:

The first question asked respondents to evaluate their overall level of information technology needs (see table 1). Not surprisingly for an information intensive industry such as tourism, 53% of respondents rated their IT needs as high with another 43% rating them as medium. The remaining 4% saw themselves as having low technology needs.

Table 1 Organisation's overall information technology needs

Value	%
High	53
Medium	43
Low	4
	100
	(72)

Despite their heavy reliance on IT, table 2 shows that most organisations still see customer service being enhanced by a combination of IT and personal services confirming the general recognition that technology by itself cannot create competitive advantage or satisfied customers.

Table 2 Factors enhancing consumer service.

Value	%
High Touch Personal Service	32
Hight Tech (IT)	0
Combination of both	68
No response	1
	100
	(72)

4.2 Skills required

Respondents were then asked to rank skills and competencies in relation to the three key areas previously discussed in this paper: programming, operational and strategic marketing and management.

It is clear from an analysis of table 3 that industry requirements seem to strongly emphasise operational skills with 65% of respondents ranking these as being of highest importance. These findings partly contradict the views of some authors (Buhalis:1998:294) who rightly argue that the need to train students in operational skills will gradually diminish as software applications become more and more consumer friendly.

Strategic and marketing skills are also being sought after but to a lesser degree than operational skills with 31% of respondents ranking them as highest importance. As IT is increasingly being used a tool for competitive advantage, it could be argued that there is an impelling need for graduates to be able to identify or develop creative uses of technology.

Programming skills were clearly not high on the agenda in terms of skills requirements with 72% of respondents ranking programming at the lowest level of importance: there seems to be a valid perception in the industry that programming needs increasingly specialised skills which cannot and perhaps should not be taught in a tourism or hospitality studies curriculum

Table 3 Skills rankings

Value	**% Programming**	**% Operating**	**% Strategic Mngt & Mkt**
1 (High importance)	0	65	31
2	7	28	53
3 (Low importance)	72	1	8
4 Other	6	0	0
No response	15	6	8
Total	100	100	100
	(72)	(72)	(72)

A series of questions were then asked to expand on the range of skills under the three main areas to further investigate industry requirements.

4.2.1 Programming requirements

At the programming level the ability to develop web pages (eg HTML authoring) was ranked as the most sought after skill by 43% of respondents reflecting the increasing penetration of Internet and Intranets in the industry. Knowledge of various computer languages was ranked very low with several respondents stating that they used in house or hired programmers for such tasks and that they did not see the need for tourism and hospitality graduates to have such skills.

4.2.2 Operational requirements

At the operational level, the majority of respondents (54%) expressed the need for graduates to have a good knowledge of basic business programs such as wordprocessing, spreadsheets, database and presentation applications.
Operational knowledge of CRS was the second most sought after skill with 36% of respondents ranking this competency at the highest level. This result is not surprising given the pervasiveness of CRS not only in the travel agency sector but in airlines and tour operators/wholesalers sector.
Internet usage skills were also ranked as highly valued by industry but mainly as second preference to either basic business programs and/or CRS skills.
Interestingly other sector specific applications (eg PMS, Conference Planning Software etc) accounting packages and specialist software such as GIS attracted relatively low ranking.

Table 4 Operational skills ranking

Skills	Rank % 1st	2nd	3rd	4th	5th	6th	No resp	Tot.
Business programs	54	26	12	1	0	1	4	100
Accounting	0	8	15	23	19	4	29	100
Sector Specific	6	4	17	11	12	17	33	100
CRS	36	14	15	8	7	1	17	100
GIS	0	3	4	7	18	32	36	100
Internet	3	40	21	21	4	4	7	100 (72)

4.2.3 Strategic management and marketing requirements

At the strategic management and marketing level the vast majority of respondents (62% of first rankings) clearly indicated that they were mainly interested in graduates being able to show general business/management skills in their approach to IT. The ability to deal with and manage information (eg information gathering, storage, analysis and dissemination) was also highly ranked.
Management information systems and decision support systems (eg loyalty systems, yield management systems etc) did not attract high rankings (6% of first preferences) perhaps reflecting the fact the in the majority of circumstances these systems tend only to be used by larger organisations.
Perhaps the most surprising finding in this section of our analysis was the relative low ranking given to electronic commerce skills (eg the ability to formulate Internet and/or Intranet enabled business strategies). Only 8% of respondents ranked electronic commerce as the most valuable strategic and marketing skill required in

graduates. This finding comes at a time were, according to many observers, the emerging online economy is turning the service industry on its head creating unprecedented opportunities for companies but also exposing them to a major threat of new and potentially devastating level of competition.
At the lower end of priorities were telecommunications skills (3% of first rankings) and systems planning and design (no first rankings).

Table 5 Strategic management and marketing skills rankings

Skills	Rank % 1st	2nd	3rd	4th	5th	6th	No resp.	Tot.
General business skills	62	15	10	3	1	1	7	100
Information mgmt	15	28	15	17	4	7	14	100
Management systems	6	20	20	17	11	4	24	100
Telecommunications	3	14	11	24	15	10	24	100
System planning & Design	0	1	11	7	21	31	29	100
Electronic commerce	8	15	21	8	14	10	24	100 (72)

4.3 Skills required by industry size:

A cross tabulation of first rankings in the three main skills areas by industry size (table 6) produced some predictable results: large organisations tend to require more strategic management and marketing skills in graduates they wish to employ whilst smaller companies still place a very strong emphasis on operational skills. This is most likely reflective of the different levels of sophistication present in the industry and is consistent with previous findings highlighting the lack of management and marketing expertise in small and medium sized tourism enterprises.

Table 6 First rankings of skills by organisation size

Organisation size	% 1st ranking in programming	% 1st ranking in operating	% 1st ranking in strategic mngt & mkt
Small	0	73	19
Medium	0	57	43
Large	0	53	47

5 Conclusion

It appears that most tourism and hospitality firms and organisations require graduates to have mainly operational IT skills. Clearly there is a gap between what students may learn in their undergraduate studies regarding information technology and the opportunity to apply it in their employment after graduation. This gap relates to graduates having managerial skills and competencies in information technology which are currently at least not widely utilised or indeed perceived by industry sectors to be important. The implications of the findings may also reflect the extent to which tourism industry sectors have embraced the use of information technology as a management tool to achieve and maintain a competitive edge rather than merely fulfilling operational requirements of management.

There are therefore important implications in these finding for future developments. Tourism in Australia has grown rapidly in the last decade and now makes a substantial contribution to export earnings. Given the increasingly competitive business environment, particularly in the Asia Pacific region, strategic use of technology becomes a tool of management. In a real sense it also may be a determinant of forecasted growth. It is therefore essential that future tourism and hospitality managers be equipped with the necessary IT skills and knowledge to survive and prosper both in their domestic and global markets.

References

- Buhalis, D., (1998) *Information Technology in tourism: Implications for the tourism curriculum*. Buhalis, D., Tjoa, A. and Jafari, J. (Eds). Information and Communication Technology in Tourism 1998. Proceedings of the International conference in Istanbul, Turkey, 1998. Springer-Verlag/Wien: New York, pp289-297.
- Department of Industry, Science & Tourism Office of National Tourism (1998) *Tourism A Ticket to the 21st Century National Action Plan for a competitive Australia.* Commonwealth of Australian: Canberra.
- Ministerial Council for the Information Economy, (1998) *Towards an Australian Strategy for the Information Economy*. National Office for the Information Economy (NOIE) Canberra. http://www.noie.gov.au.
- National Board of Employment, Education and Training, (1997) *Information Technology. Sink or Swim*, Report prepared by a working party appointed by the Australian Academy of Technological Sciences and Engineering.
- Sheldon P., (1997) *Tourism Information Technology*. CAB International: New York.

Appendix 1

A) Accompanying letter

Dear manager

RE: information technology and tourism education: an industry view of skills and qualities required in graduates

Good morning and greetings!
We would like a few minutes of your valuable time to assist us in a tourism and hospitality industry survey.
With Roberto Daniele of RMIT University, I am conducting a survey of tourism and hospitality managers. We are investigating your view of skills and knowledge in information technology you would like graduates you employ to have.
Please note that we a trying to obtain skill specifications for graduates of business, tourism and/or hospitality courses and not information technology courses. We would be therefore grateful if you could keep this perspective in mind when answering our questions.
Enclosed is a short questionnaire which we hope you can fill out and return in the enclosed pre paid envelope by 10 September; if you prefer you can fax it to me. Please do contact me or Roberto if you have any queries, or would like some more information about the survey (our details are on the cover page). Thank you so much for your time.

B) Questionnaire: information technology and tourism education: an industry view of skills and qualities required in graduates

Organisation, address & postcode, industry sector, name of respondent, contact phone number of respondent
Q1 How would you rate your organisation's overall information technology needs?
High, medium, low, none, Don't know
Q2 If you define personal service as high touch and information technology as high tech, which of the categories below do you think enhances customer service in your organisation?
high touch (personal service), high tech (information technology), some combination of both high touch & high tech
Q3 When you think of all your organisation's current and future information technology needs, you may assess some areas of competencies in new graduates to be more important than others. Programming (eg ability to develop computer software, knowledge of computer languages), operating (eg ability to use software packages and information systems such as back and front office systems), strategic management & marketing (eg ability to identify applications of information systems, electronic commerce and other technology related developments to create technology enabled business strategies), other (please specify), none
Q4 What skills and competencies in relation to programming would you like new graduates to have when starting a job in your organisation? computer languages, Web page development, other (please specify), none
Q5 What skills and competencies in relation to operating key information technology systems and/or software would you like new graduates to have when starting a job in your organisation? basic business programs eg word processing, spreadsheet, database, desktop publishing, accounting software package, sector specific software package eg PMS (property

management systems), conference module, transaction processing systems (point of sale), CRS (computer reservation systems) Eg airline reservation systems such as Sabre, hotel reservation systems, wholesaler/tour operator computer reservation systems such as Atlas, GIS geographic information systems, Internet usage Eg Web browser, email, Usenet and Newsgroups, other (please specify), none.

Q6 What skills and competencies in relation to strategic management and marketing would you like new graduates to have when starting a job in your organisation? general business/ management , information management (eg general knowledge of how information is collected, stored, analysed), management information systems and decision support systems (eg general knowledge of loyalty systems, yield management systems), telecommunication principles (eg general knowledge of telecommunication equipment, telecommunication media), management requirements for system design, implementation and maintenance, electronic commerce and/or marketing (eg general knowledge of development of Internet and Intranet business strategies), other (please specify), none

Q7 What is the size of your organisation/firm? small (1 to 19 FT employees), medium (20 to 199 FT employees), large (200 or more FT employees)

Q8 What is the position held by the respondent in organisation (eg general manager; manager human resources)

Q9 What is the year of birth of respondent?

Q10 What is the highest post school education level achieved by respondent? postgraduate degree, undergraduate degree, diploma, certificate, other (please specify), none

Q11 Any other comments you would like to make?

A General Datamodel for Tourism Information Systems

J. Küng, A. Dunzendorfer, R. R. Wagner
Institute for Applied Knowledge Processing (FAW)

Johannes Kepler University Linz

jkueng@faw.uni-linz.ac.at

Abstract

In the travel industry, information plays a very big role and throughout the properties of its products information is very important for this line of business. To process this information different information systems are developed and the information is stored system specific. When thinking of an universal interface to all tourism systems each system has to present its information in the same manner. That means a general data model, into that all specific data models can be transformed, is needed. In this paper we introduce such a model, discuss the transformation process, and show that it can also be used as a generic data model for new applications.

1 Introduction

In recent years Information Technology (IT) has become a very important factor in the travel industry. The extensive use of IT in tourism is a direct reflection of the high amount of information being produced, created and accessed within the tourist industry. The tourism product (or trip) has some unique features. Some of the characteristics that differentiate a tourist package from other are its heterogeneity, its intangibility and its perishability [7]. Information is one of the key factors of the travel industry. To manage this mass of information many different information systems have been developed. For example tourism information systems, destination systems, global reservation systems. Presenting products over the internet is another example of how the IT revolution has influenced the tourist industry, which can be compared with the introduction of jet engines. The development of closed and open networks, such as Wide Area Networks, Global Distribution Systems and the Internet, revolutionized the global tourism industry and enabled enterprises to enhance there operations and to expand geographically [1]. Especially the presentation of tourism in the World Wide Web is very successful. According to a recent survey this summer made by NPD Online Research, nearly 70% of Web surfers visited a travel-related Web site [9].
Behind most IT-systems a database system is placed to store all information. To create a database, data modeling is necessary. Every different system has its specific way of implementing the database and this is the reason why there is such a wide variety of data models in the field of tourism. Creating a data model requires

resources with strong technological background and knowledge about the processes in the field of tourism, which results in high costs for the development of such a model. Thinking of this, the idea for a general data model is born. Such a model should be the basis for developing a concrete data model of a specific application area of tourism.
On the other side, thinking on a universal interface to all existing tourist information systems each of these systems have to make its information available in the same manner. Due to that requirement of unified data presentation, one general data model into which the data of each different tourism information system can be transformed, would be used.

2 Basic Definitions

In this section we define some basic terminology concerning database and data modeling. Interested readers can find detailed explanations of these terms in [2],[4],[8].

In general the term *data model* is used for two different things. On the one hand it means a set of concepts that can be used to describe the structure of and operations on a database. Structure of a database means the data types, relationships, and constraints that define the "template" of a database and operations are retrievals, insertions, manipulations, and deletions. The "Hierarchical" and the "Relational Data Model" are examples for this kind of interpretation. On the other hand the term *data model* often is used for the description of data for a particular database. When we hear from a data model of a tourism information system we automatically imagine concrete object types, attributes, and relationships. As this paper is situated in an application oriented domain conference we use the second interpretation of the term "data model", as a synonym "application model" in the terminology of database theory.

One dimension data models can be classified is along the steps of the entire database design activity.

a) Conceptual design: This is the first step from the users perception of data towards a formal description of it. The result, the *conceptual data model* is at a very high nonsystem-specific level.
b) Logical design: After this step the data model, called the *logical data model*, is in an implementable form. All logical aspects such as object types, attributes, data types and relationships between object types are defined completely but, without considering physical details.
c) Physical design: Here the physical aspects in terms of indexing, clustering, partitioning and so on, are modeled and result in the *physical data model*.

3 Generic Data Model - General Data Model

Data modeling is one of the most important tasks in developing an Information System. It is the base on which the system is built. So the quality of the data model is in direct relation to the quality of the whole system. But, a good data model is very resourceful and needs personnel with a high standard of knowledge.

On the other hand data models are often made for similar application areas. For instance: Three hotels order a reservation system each of them from another software house. In this case each software house makes its own data model including all the tasks a data model needs (beginning with the analyzing phase, ending with building the physical model). From a more general point of view some tasks are done too often and reusability would be a big advantage. Figure 1 shows the situation using a general data model.

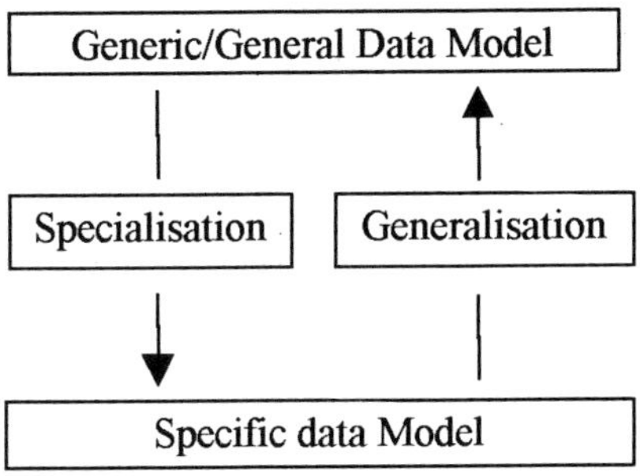

Fig. 1: The idea of a generic data model

A data model which can be used as a pattern for specific data models within one application area we call a *generic data model.* With respect to the transformation into a specific data model we suggest a distinction between three kinds of generic data models.

a) Reference Model on Paper
This is the oldest form of generic data models and they are often used intuitively. When application developers have to design a database for a specific application area normally they first look for some publications containing data models similar to their task. Then these models are often used as a pattern. In middle Europe one of the best known generic data models of that kind is Scheer's data model of an industrial company published in [6].

b) Offline Models
Also here the specialization process is done during application development, but computer based supported by special tools. After that, maintenance of the data model is the same as in a traditional application.

c) Online Models
In these kinds of models the transformation information is stored in extra meta data and is involved in every data access. So the specific data model can be seen as a view of the generic data model. Now most of later modification of the specific data model can be done by simple updates of the transformation information. Especially in the area of tourism information systems often modifications in the data model are necessary. New types of offers normally result in a modified data model.

A new aspect of generic data models is that also the other direction, the transformation of a specific data model into a general data model is important and brings advantages. As mentioned in the introduction a uniform view on each specific tourism information system is needed. This view can be seen as a *general data model* into that the specific data model of the underlying tourism information system is mapped. In our work the main motivation for building a general data model for tourism was to set up this universal view which on the other hand, can be used as a generic data model for new tourism applications.

4 A General Datamodel for Tourism Information Systems

The general datamodel was created through our experiences we made during developing the tourism information system "TIScover" (http://www.tiscover.com). It is a logical data model as described in chapter 2, independent from a specific database management system. The goal of the general data model was, to support a tourism information system which enables an interested tourist to find any information about a holiday destination. This could be information about the accommodation, the location, the infrastructure, sight seeing and activity possibilities and so on. But not only to be informed about this, also booking should be possible to be done over the system.
This needs a very important design phase including the development of a datamodel that represents all the information needed to be informed and to make booking of the wanted objects.

In this chapter the general datamodel will be developed stepwise with the object modeling technique [5]. In this technique classes are designed as squares and the meaning of the relationships are the following:

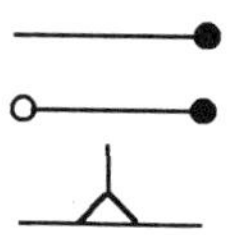

one TO zero, one or many
zero or one TO zero, one or many
generalization

The first thing to do was, to describe the central object of the system, the tourism object. During the attribute description of the objects, the different object types are defined. Such object types could be for example hotels, restaurants, sport gyms and sport places, campsites, sight seeing objects or alpine areas. Throughout this, the classes "Object Type" and "Tourism Object" are defined, where a object type has many specific tourism objects. Every specific object type has its own attributes, which will be described in the class "Attribute". An attribute belongs only to one object type.

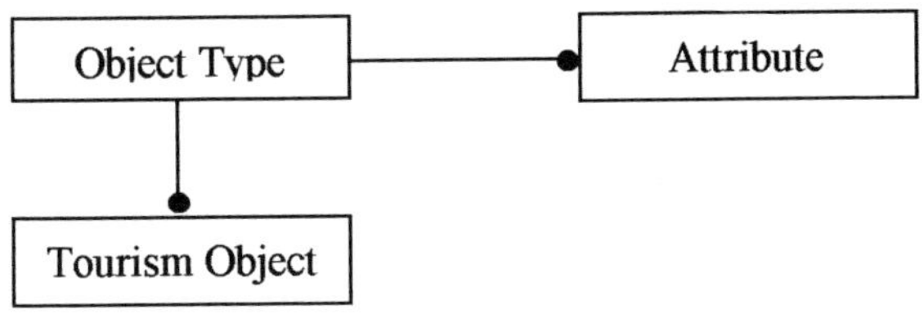

Fig. 2: creating a general datamodel step one

Object Type:
It contains, the different types of tourism objects, available in a tourism information system. For example these tourism objects could be a hotel, museum, event and so on.

Tourism Object:
This class identifies a specific tourism object.

Attribute:
The information which attribute belongs to which object type, is content of this class.

An attribute exists in different types and this leads to model the various possibilities of attributes in the way, that the class "Attribute" is the generalization of the various attribute types. But such an attribute type has not to be a simple one like integer for example, it is also possible that it is a much more complex one like needed for the storage of a picture or video, what needs special attention in the datamodel.

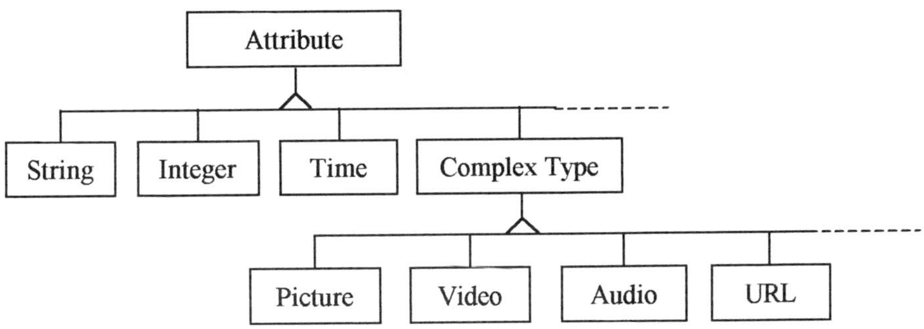

Fig. 3: creating a general datamodel step two

Now a tourism object knows, to which object type it belongs and so it is defined, which attributes are belonging to the tourism object. Till now the concrete values of the tourism object attributes are missing so a class for the values of the attributes should also be defined, that leads to the class "Value". It is used to store the values of the attributes of a tourism object.

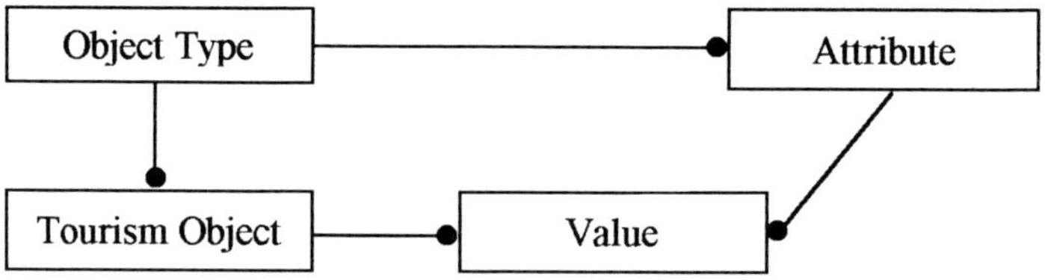

Fig. 4: creating a general datamodel step three

Value:
It presents the actual values of an attribute and also the information to which tourism object it belongs.

The next thing to do in developing the data model was to implement the geographical context. Every tourism object exists in a region. It should also be possible, that a tourism object is part of more than one region, thinking of the alpine tourism objects, for example in Austria the mountain called Großglockner is covering parts of three federal states. On the other hand, a region contains more than one tourism object.

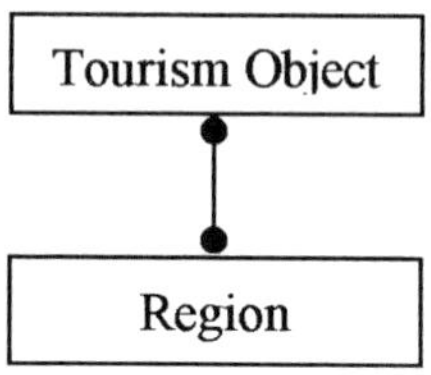

Fig. 5: creating a general datamodel step four

But not only tourism objects are belonging to regions, regions themselves could be divided into other ones. A region also belongs to one region or not, what this means is that on the top of the regional structure, there is the world and it makes sense to finish the modeling of the region structure at this point.

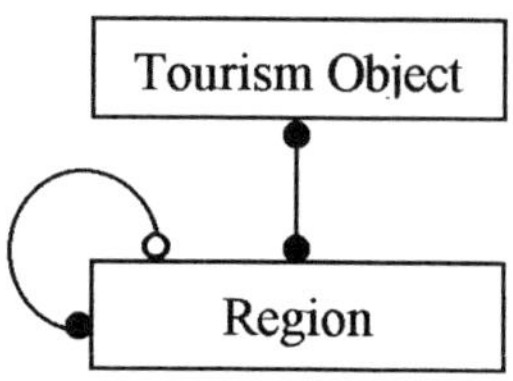

Fig. 6: creating a general datamodel step five

Region:
This class presents the regional structure of a tourism information system and contains on the one side the information which tourism objects are belonging to a specific region and on the other side, which region is part of or belongs to another region.

Very important information for the tourists will be about ability of booking, the opening time of a tourism object or some other information useful for the destination decision. A very complex part of information will be the booking information. At this point we are not looking in details to it, we just recognize that it is necessary and so we implement it in an abstract level using the class "Booking Info". But customers not only want to know if booking is possible and what the necessary conditions are, they also want to know if a special tourism object is available at the time they want to make their holidays. Information, about the seasons of tourism objects and their opening times will be content of the class "Opening Time". Now a potential tourist knows information about the conditions for making reservations and the opening times of tourism objects. Also important to know would be some additional general information for example a description about the location or possible activities of a tourism object. The class "Keyword" will be the pool for that information.

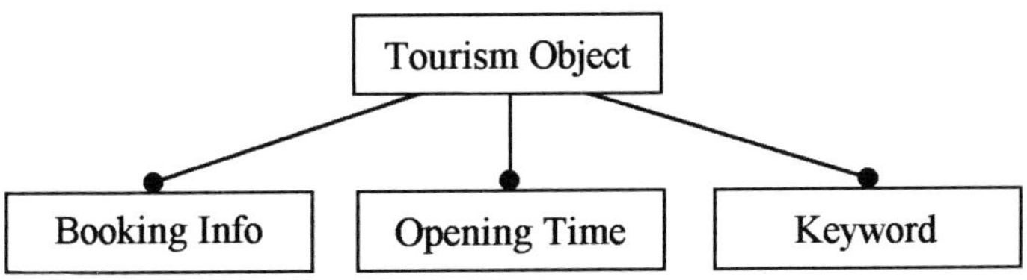

Fig. 7: creating a general datamodel step six

Booking Info:
This contains needed information for making reservations. This could be for example the information about the avaibility of products, different reductions, pay conditions, accepted credit cards and so on. The booking information is a very complex part and will be worked out more detailed in a later phase.

Opening Time:
Information about the availability of tourism objects, for example the seasons of a hotel or the opening times of a museum.

Keyword:
Some additional information to describe a tourism object. The keywords are similar to typical search words like snowboard, tennis, library or some words describing the location of the tourism object. It represents an additional possibility to present the

tourism objects and it offers an easy way to search for not so well maintained tourism information, only through adding some keywords.

To present the tourism objects to tourists of different countries it is necessary, to offer the information in the corresponding languages and currencies. Which languages and currencies are present in a tourism information system is content of the classes "Language" and "Currency". The currency effects the classes "Value" and "Booking Info". The language is important for the classes "Region", "Booking Info", "Opening Time", "Keyword", "Object Type" and "Value". Adding all classes together shows the whole general data model [3] and is shown in the figure below.

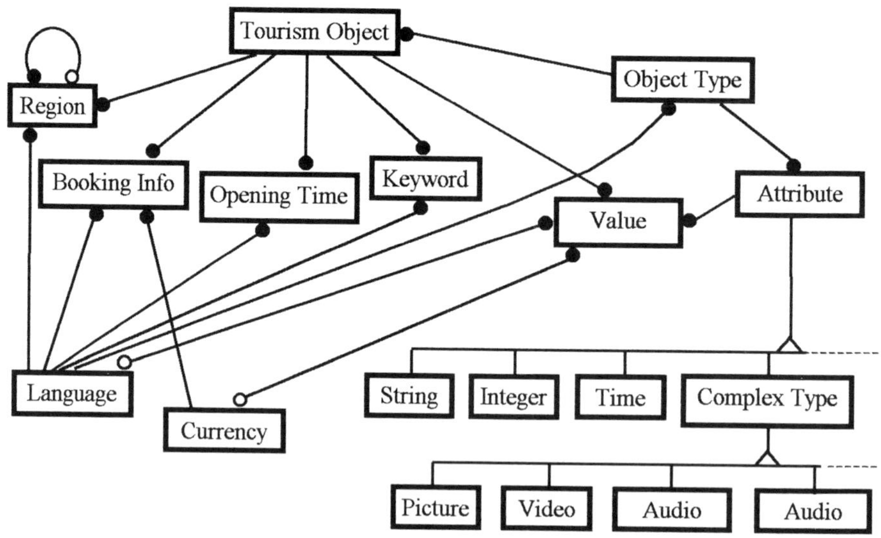

Fig. 8: The general datamodel

5 The Transforming Process

Through this general data model we have to deal with the transformation from and to a specific data model. Chapter 3 described the principle ways to do that. Our intention was to use this data model for a unified interface to heterogeneous tourism information systems. Each tourism information system should present its data in this model. Also the queries assume that the data is stored in that way. Therefore an online transformation of data is needed in both directions. In the one direction the queries from the general data model into the specific data model and in the opposite direction the result of the queries.

Out of a point of view of the data models, we have given specific data models of each existing specific tourism information system and all of these have to be generalized into the universal one. We decided to do this online via meta data.

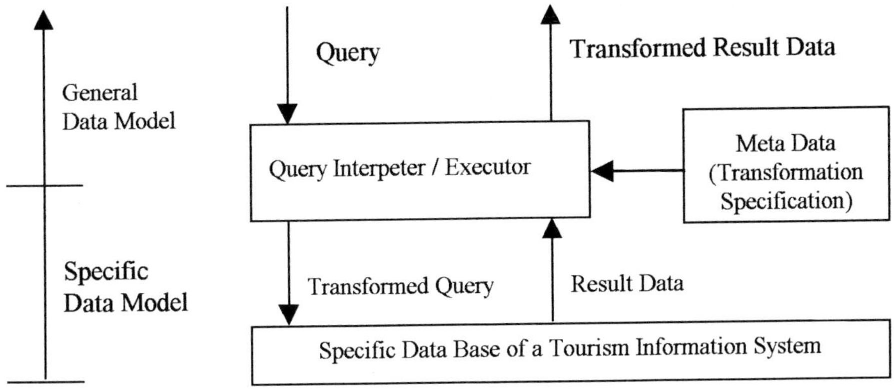

Fig. 9: Architecture of the transforming module

This architecture of the transformation module has two main advantages: First, when modifications are done in the data model of a specific tourism information system it normally results only in updates of the transformation specification. The software itself will not be affected. Second, a transformation module using this architecture can be adapted to another tourism information system much easier then a software module that does not use meta data.

6 Conclusion

A general datamodel was created through our experiences we made during developing the tourism information system "TIScover", a successful implemented tourism information system. This data model now can be used as a pattern for future applications in the sense of a generic data model. We take it as the universal data model for our work of building a uniform interface for heterogeneous tourism information systems like we presented at the ENTER'98 conference [3]. The query language TIS-QL (see also in [3]) and this general data model are the main concepts of that project.

References

[1] Buhalis D.: "Information Technologies in tourism: Implications for the tourism curriculum" in Buhalis D., Tjoa A.M., J. Jafari (eds): *Information and Communication Technologies in Tourism 1998*, Springer Computer Science, Wien, 1998, p. 289-297

[2] Elmasri R., Navathe, S.B.: *Fundamentals of database Systems*. Benjamin Cummings, Redwood City California, 1989

[3] Küng, J., Dunzendorfer A., Wagner R.: Data Access to Heterogeneous Tourism Information Systems; in Buhalis D., Tjoa A.M., Jafari J. (eds): *Information and Communication Technologies in Tourism 1998*, Springer Computer Science, Wien, 1998, pp. 46-54

[4] Navathe, S.B.: "Evolution of data modeling for databases" in:. *Communications of the ACM* 35, 9 (Sept. 1992), pp. 112-123

[5] Rumbaugh J., Blaha M., Premerlani W., F. Eddy, W. Lorensen: *Object-Oriented Modeling and Design*. Prentice Hall Inc., London, 1991, ISBN 3-446-17520-2
[6] Scheer A.-W.: *Wirtschaftsinformatik, Referenzmodelle für industrielle Geschäftsprozesse*, Springer Verlag Berlin, Heidelberg, 1994
[7] Sheldon P.J.: *Tourism Information Technology*. CAB International, UK, Wallingford, 1997, ISBN 0-85199-181-5
[8] Ullman, J.: *Priciples of Database and Knowledge-Base Systems*, Computer Science Press, 1988
[9] "NPD Online Research Shows Travel Sites Taking Off" http://www.npd.com/corp/press/press_980824.htm

Modelling of an electronic tourism market

Wolfram Höpken
START AMADEUS GmbH
Wolfram.Hoepken@start.de

Abstract

The present situation concerning the information-technological supply of tourism services is characterized by the coexistence of a multitude of service- and travel-type specific electronic markets (tourism markets). This results in the nonuniformity of information about tourism services and their access. In order to unify different electronic markets, this paper presents a reference model of an electronic tourism market. Tailored to meet particular requirements, specific models for components of an electronic market can be derived from this reference model.

In order to enable the customer the comfortable access to tourism services, customer-specific needs have to be considered. In spite of often only vague, inexact ideas about the required service, the customer expects a comfortable selection and composition process for tourism services. Therefore, to be taken into consideration as essential parts of the modelling are:

- selection hierarchies for the integration of fuzziness into the selection process and the support of the flexible derivation of specific models
- composition of elementary tourism services

1 Introduction

The present situation concerning the information-technological supply of tourism services is characterized by the coexistence of a multitude of service- and travel-type specific electronic markets (tourism markets) [4]. An electronic market is characterized by the set of offered services, the attributes, which describe the services, and the access to the offered services. Especially for the customer, the following problems result from the coexistence of heterogenous electronic markets:

- nonuniformity of the access to tourism services
- nonuniformity of the information available about tourism services
- restriction of the access to a specific part of the entire range of available tourism services (e.g. to the services of some service suppliers)

In order to enable the uniform access to the maximum number of tourism services, the objective is to unify the different electronic markets and, in the long term, to substitute the different markets by one electronic market, open to all participants of the present tourism markets (especially the customer) and containing all the tourism services.

The following requirements result from this objective:

- the information about tourism services has to be unified
- the possibilities of access to the tourism services have to be unified

However, the complete standardisation of tourism services is afflicted with the following problems:

- taking into consideration all specific details of tourism services, the different electronic markets show a large heterogeneity
- the suppliers of tourism services have no possibility to differentiate their offer

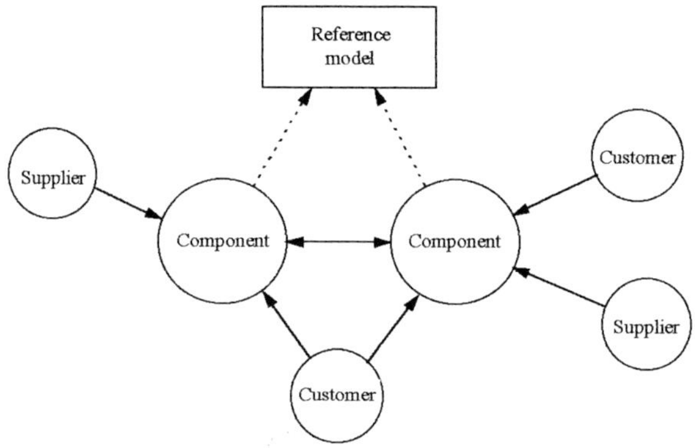

Fig. 1. Components of the electronic tourism market

The approach to avoid these problems is to supply a reference model of an electronic tourism market. Specific models for components of the electronic market, tailored to specific requirements, can be derived from this reference model. The common reference model enables the uniform access to and the interaction between components of the electronic market, which are based on different specific models (Fig. 1).

2 Objective

The objective of this project is the elaboration of a reference model of an electronic tourism market. The reference model specifies the common aspects of the different components of the electronic market and serves as a basis for the derivation of concrete models for components. The reference model specifies in particular:

- function points (services), which have to be provided by all components of the electronic market
- interface for the access to the function points of the electronic market
- objects (entities of the problem domain), which provide the function points (request, customer, booking,...)
- classification of tourism services on the basis of characteristics relevant to the selection (selection criteria)

In order to enable the customer comfortable access to tourism services, customer-specific needs have to be considered. In spite of often only vague, inexact ideas about the required service, the customer expects not only access to as many tourism services as possible, but also a comfortable selection and composition process for tourism services. The following requirements result from this and necessitate special consideration within the modelling:

- support of the selection process of tourism services by
  - integration of fuzziness in the form of fuzzy requests and similar results [1, 3, 6, 8]
  - formation of supplier- and customer-initiated compositions of tourism services [2, 9]
- support of the flexible derivation of specific models for components of the electronic market

The central approach to fulfil these requirements is the preparation of selection hierarchies for attributes (i.e. selection criteria) of tourism services. A selection hierarchy is build from the hierarchical arrangement of the values of a selection criterion on different levels of abstraction. Selection hierarchies enable the integration of fuzziness into the selection process by the definition of fuzzy requests and the search for similar results.

Selection hierarchies especially support the flexible derivation of specific models. The consideration of different levels of abstraction for the values of selection criteria enables the extension of the derivation mechanism. When deriving a more concrete class, i.e. changing the level of abstraction, not only classes are extended by selection criteria, but also the selection hierarchies of the selection criteria by more concrete levels of abstraction. In this way the integration of heterogenous information into the electronic market and the uniform access to heterogenous tourism services is made possible.

Implications on the tourism market

The use of such a reference model has the following implications on the tourism market:

- The reference model supports the suppliers in providing their services within the electronic market. Thus, especially for small and medium suppliers, the access to the electronic market is facilitated and the number of available services increased.
- The reference model enables the uniform access to heterogenous services of different suppliers. Thus, the services of different suppliers become comparable.
- The support of a comfortable selection process enables the direct access of the customer to the electronic market.
- The reference model enables the interaction between components of the electronic market. In this way, complex services can be constructed from elementary services, especially intermediary services such as complex requests (e.g. buying orders), aggregation of requests and creation of compositions.

The following changes result for the participants of the electronic market:

Customer/Supplier. As a result of the comfortable access for the customer to a large number of services (supported by intermediary services) and the comparability of the services of different suppliers, the market transparency for the customer and the power of demand of the customer over the supplier increases.

Intermediary. Due to the customer`s direct access to the electronic market, the intermediary will no longer be required in the present extent as an obligatory link between customer and supplier (only for special customer groups or advice intensive services). The field of activity of the intermediary will shift to the provision of additional mediation services within the electronic market.

3 Architecture of the electronic tourism market

The architecture of the electronic tourism market is a three-tier distributed architecture, consisting of the following tiers:

- user tier

The user tier contains the functionality concerning the interface to the user as well as the execution of requests from the user to the application tier.

- application tier

The application tier contains the functionality needed within the electronic market to deal with the available services. The application tier provides this functionality to the user tier.

- data tier

The data tier provides the data on all available tourism services as well as the elementary access mechanisms to this data. Concerning the structure of the database, a distribution of the data to several components (data server) has to be taken into account.

Fig. 2 shows the architecture of the electronic tourism market. This architecture is based on the following design decisions [7]:

- The application server makes its services available in the form of distributed objects.
- The access of the client to the services of the application server can be carried out in two ways:
    - A specific application on the client accesses the distributed objects of the application server.
    - A browser downloads special objects (applets) from the application server. These objects enable the interaction with the user and access the distributed objects of the application server.

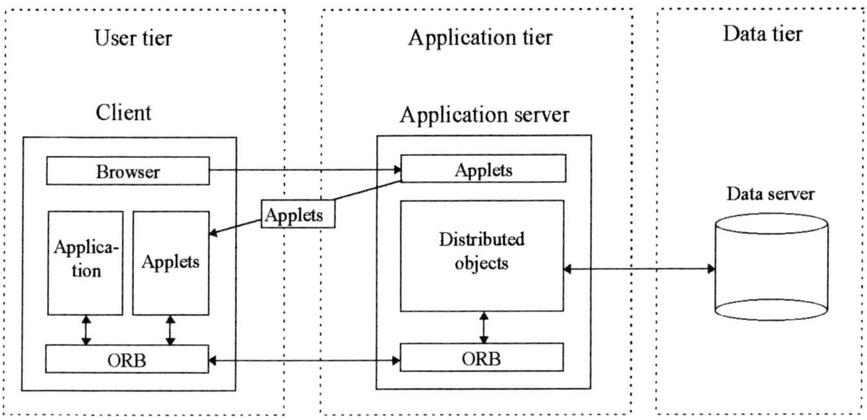

Fig. 2. Architecture of the electronic tourism market

The application tier is the central component of the three-tier architecture described above. Each component of the application tier provides a definite set of services (function points) in the form of distributed objects. These objects are available to user components (clients) as well as other application components. This modelling concentrates on the examination of the processes and objects within the application tier as well as the common interface, which provides the services within the electonic market.

4 Selection hierarchies

To support the selection process and the flexible derivation of specific models, *selection hierarchies* are introduced in the present model. The central approach is the consideration of different abstraction levels within the representation of selection-relevant characteristics (selection criteria) of a service. Then, the selection hierarchy for a characteristic results from the hierarchical arrangement of its values on different abstraction levels.

The use of selection hierarchies supports the following aspects:

- fuzzy requests

The use of values on higher abstraction levels enables the formulation of fuzzy requests. The hierarchical arrangement of the values supports the successive refinement of a request during an iterative selection process.

- similar results

Selection hierarchies enable the consideration of similar results on the basis of similarity relations between values of a selection criterion. As a similarity relation, which is obvious for the user, selection hierarchies provide the distance between two values.

- flexible derivation of specific models

Selection hierarchies enable the extension of the derivation mechanism by the possibility to add more concrete abstraction levels (Chapter 2). In this way, domains of selection criteria can be tailored to specific requirements and the flexible derivation of specific models is supported.

- selection by uncertain represented characteristics

A characteristic is called *uncertain represented*, if the corresponding selection criterion is not determined certainly. The extension of the derivation mechanism enables the use of uncertain represented characteristics within the selection of a service by identical definition of the higher abstraction levels of the selection hierarchies.

A selection hierarchy has the following structure:

- The lowest abstraction level consists of all values of the corresponding selection criterion (the *base set*).
- Elements of a higher abstraction level, named *generic terms*, are formed by collecting several elements of the underlying abstraction level as *subordinated terms* of this generic term. A generic term is a fuzzy set on the subordinated terms, i.e. a subordinated term has a gradual membership of a generic term.
- A selection hierarchy contains exactly one element (named *root*), containing all other elements directly or indirectly.

Two aspects are important for the construction of selection hierarchies:

- Selection hierarchies are polydimensional hierarchies, i.e. they can consist of orthogonal part-hierarchies. Two part-hierarchies are called orthogonal, if their root and their base set are identical and they have no more common elements.
- Selection hierarchies are extendable. An extension of a selection hierarchy is created by adding further elements and abstraction levels.

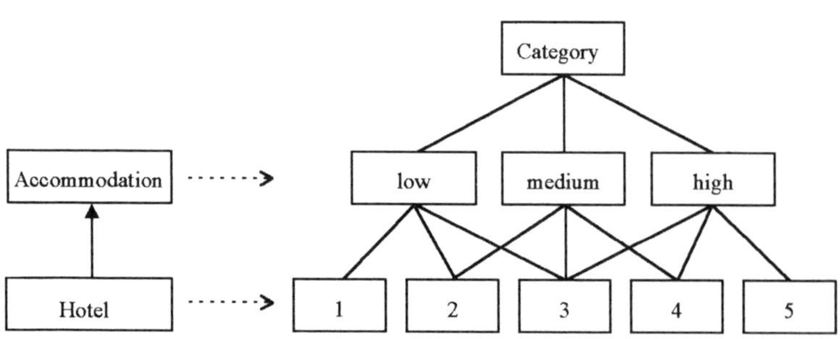

Fig. 3. Selection hierarchies of the selection criterion *Category*

Fig. 3 illustrates, for example, the selection hierarchies of the selection criterion *Category* of the tourism services *Accommodation* and *Hotel*. The selection hierarchy for the service *Hotel* is an extension of the selection hierarchy for the service *Accommodation* and is created by adding a further, more concrete abstraction level. Analogous, further subclasses with extended selection hierarchies can be created in specific models.

5 Composition

The composition of services denotes fitting together several elementary services (e.g. hotel and flight) to a service package. Compositions are formed either by suppliers to provide ready-made packages (possibly with choices), as well as by the customer to create individual packages. The objective of the composition mechanism is the comparability of customer- and supplier-initiated compositions.

5.1 Structure of a composition

The approach to provide comparable customer- and supplier-initiated compositions is the consideration of the degree of freedom of a composition. The degree of freedom is the number of combination possibilities existing within a composition. A supplier-initiated, ready-made combination of determined services is a composition without degree of freedom (e.g. the composition *travel*, consisting of a *flight* and a *hotel*). Combination possibilities within a supplier-initiated composition lead to a corresponding degree of freedom (e.g. the possibility to combine different hotels and flights of one tour operator). The combination of any services initiated by the customer is a composition with the maximum degree of freedem. If not all combination possibilities are allowed, the degree of freedom has to be restricted by combination constraints.

The following parts of a composition result from this approach:

- components: A component represents an elementary service being part of the composition. A component consists of:
  - a set of elementary services (to consider combination possibilities within the composition)
  - the role of the elementary service within the composition (e.g. *outward travel* as the role of a transportation service)
- selection criteria: Selection-relevant characteristics of a composition. Selection criteria of a composition are projected on the selection criteria of the contained components.
- evaluation instructions: Evaluation instructions enable the evaluation of the

value of a selection criterion from the selection criteria of the contained components.

- constraints: Constraints enable the restriction of the combination possibilities. Constraints refer to the selection criteria of the contained components.

To ensure the comparability of different compositions, a composition has to be dividable into any combination of subcompositions. The use of specific composition types for different combinations of elementary services (with specific selection criteria), leads to the necessity for any possible division of a composition into subcompositions being considered separately with regard to the projections, evaluation criteria and constraints. Thus, instead of specific composition types with specific interfaces, a common composition object has to be provided, whose selection criteria, evaluation instructions and constraints result from the contained components.

Example: A composition is created consisting of the components: outward flight (service: flight, role: outward journey), return flight (service: flight, role: return journey) and hotel (service: hotel, role: accommodation in the destination). The selection criteria, evaluation instructions and constraints result from the contained components as follows:

- selection criteria:

outward flight:	point of departure (= departure airport of the outward flight)
	destination (= destination airport of the outward flight)
return flight:	destination (= departure airport of the return flight)
	point of departure (= destination airport of the return flight)
hotel:	name of the accommodation (= hotel name)
	category of the accommodation (= hotel category)
	destination (= hotel place)

- evaluation instructions: price = sum of the prices of all components
- constraints:

outward flight + hotel:	destination airport of the outward flight = hotel place
	arrival date of the outward flight = hotel check-in date
return flight + hotel:	departure airport of the return flight = hotel place
	departure date of the return flight = hotel check-out date

5.2 Multiple person compositions

To support a comfortable selection process, the above composition mechanism has to be extended by the consideration of compositions for several persons travelling together. In doing so, each component of the composition has to be integrated into the composition in the required quantity.

The request for a multiple person composition is initiated by the specification of the travelling persons (by person-related data, such as name, age, person type,...). For each component of a multiple person composition, several parallel services for subsets of the specified persons can be defined.

A concrete composition contains the elementary services for each component in the required quantity. The projections, evaluation instructions and constraints of the composition are to be extended to the parallel services. Especially constraints between the parallel services of a component are to be added.

Example: A journey for three people (two adults, one child) is requested, consisting of an outward and return flight and an accommodation service. In addition to three outward and return flights, the accommodation services which come into question are: one apartment for at least three people, one double and one single room, or one double room with an extra bed. The request can be restricted by specifying a set combination of room types.

6 Components of the reference model

The reference model to be elaborated in this project will consist of the following components (Chapter 2):

Function points. Based on the requirements of the market participants, the function points of the electronic market have to be specified. Each function point has to be described by one or more scenarios. Taking into consideration the market participants *customer*, *customer application*, *supplier*, *supplier application* and *market application* the following function points mainly result:

- supply of tourism services (elementary services and compositions)
- selection of tourism services (formulation of requests, search for results, evaluation of the results)
- availability administration (request and modification)
- booking of tourism services (booking initiation, booking execution, state request, cancelling)

Electronic market interface (EMI). The common market interface defines the access to the function points of the electronic tourism market. The interface consists of the interfaces of a set of objects providing the function points within the electronic market.

Entities. The set of entities consists of all objects, which are necessary to provide the function points of the electronic market. Entities include both primary and secundary abstractions of the problem domain. Primary abstractions, i.e. actually existing objects of the problem domain tourism, represent the available tourism services (elementary services as well as compositions of elementary services). Secundary abstractions of the problem domain tourism represent conceptional objects (e.g. user requests) and mechanisms.

Classification of tourism services. The objective of the classification of tourism services is the uniform naming and description of tourism services. The description of tourism services concentrates on the available information and selection-relevant characteristics. One possible classification of tourism services by selection-relevant characteristics and the purpose of the tourism service results in the classes: Transportation, Accommodation, Event, Institution, Gastronomy, Shopping, Destination, Hired Vehicle and Cruise with further sub-classes.

7 Conclusion and future work

The basic concepts of a reference model of an electronic tourism market were presented in this paper. This reference model serves as a basis to derive specific models for components of the electronic tourism market. As fundamental aspects were discussed the use of selection hierarchies for the support of the selection process and the derivation of specific models as well as the composition of elementary tourism services.

A first version of the model is available at this current stage of the project. The future steps to be taken are:

- Committing a reference model of an electronic tourism market in cooperation with domain experts and participants of the tourism market. The objective of this process is the appointment of a common basis regarding the functionality and available information of tourism services, accepted by all participants of an electronic tourism market.
- Developing a prototypical framework, based on the above reference model, for components of the electronic tourism market. This framework enables the comfortable and flexible development of applications for components of the electronic market. To evaluate the usability of the framework (and the underlying reference model), prototypical component applications are to be developed by instanciating the framework.

References

1. Alagar, V.S., Bergler, S., Dong., F.Q. (eds.): Incompleteness and Uncertainty in Information Systems - Proceedings of the SOFTEKS Workshop on Incompleteness and Uncertainty in Information Systems, Montreal (1993).
2. Pröll, B., Retschitzegger, W., Kroiß, P., Wagner, R.R.: Online Booking On The Net - Problems, Issues and Solutions. In: Buhalis, D., Tjoa, A M., Jafari, J. (eds.): Information and Communication Technologies in Tourism, Istanbul, Springer, pp. 268-277 (1998).
3. Salton, G., Fox, E., Wu, H.: Extended Boolean Information Retrieval. Communications of the ACM 26, pp. 1022-1036 (1983).

4. Schmid, B.: Electronic Markets in Tourism. In: Schertler, W., Schmid, B., Tjoa, A.M., Werthner, H. (eds.): Information and Communications Technologies in Tourism, Innsbruck, Spinger, pp. 1-8 (1994).
5. Schroeder, G.: Lexikon der Tourismuswirtschaft. Hamburg, TourCon Hannelore Niedecken GmbH (1995).
6. Shen, S., Hu, J.: GFIRS: A Graphical Fuzzy Information Retrieval System. In: Schertler, W., Schmid, B., Tjoa, A M., Werthner, H. (eds.): Information and Communications Technologies in Tourism, Innsbruck, Springer, pp. 271-278 (1994).
7. Tenenbaum, J.M., Chowdhry, T.S., Hughes, K.: Eco System: An Internet Commerce Architecture. IEEE Computer 30 (5), pp. 48-55 (1997).
8. Tversky, A.: Features of similarity. In: Psychological Review, 84 (1977).
9. Weber, M.: Changes in the Leisure Travel Market Result in New Requirements for Tour Operator Systems. In: Schertler, W., Schmid, B., Tjoa, A M., Werthner, H. (eds.): Information and Communication Technologies in Tourism, Innsbruck, Springer, pp. 95-102 (1995).

An architecture for a distributed travel reservations system

Paul F. O'Brien
Information Systems Group
Business Faculty
Sunshine Coast University College
pobrien@scuc.edu.au

Abstract

Current travel reservations systems are based on either a centralised database of free-sale products (CRS) or private databases running on networked or standalone computer systems. There is typically no interconnection between the operator's in-house reservations system, CRS's and other operators' systems apart from simple gateway and switch services (Dombey, 1998). Consequently, CRS's must secure free-sale allotments of product from travel operators to enable them to provide an on-line, real-time availability and reservation confirmation service.

This paper discusses the architecture of a proposed distributed reservations system (DRS) that is targeted at small to medium tourism enterprises (SMTEs), including tour operators and accommodation establishments. The DRS architecture has been designed under the same principles as the Open Buying On the Internet (OBI) standard (OBI Consortium, 1997), namely, simplicity, use of existing industry standards, minimal customisation of existing systems and use of the internet as the transport backbone.

Keywords: Tourism, Technology, Central Reservations System

1 Introduction

It is not practical for most small to medium sized tourism enterprises (SMTEs), such as small tour operators and accommodation establishments, to allocate freesale allotments to CRSs because they may only have two or three seats, or rooms, in total. Even if an SMTE is prepared to offer freesale allotments, it is not usually cost effective for CRSs and wholesalers to deal with the small numbers available. As a result, the SMTEs' products are not typically available through CRSs and wholesale programs. Similarly, their small size generally precludes them from interfacing their in-house system to switch companies such as THISCO.

The emergence of the World Wide Web (WWW) has provided SMTEs with new opportunities to market their products worldwide. However, it does not provide a real-time availability or reservation service. Human intervention is still required to read incoming fax or electronic mail reservation requests, inquire into the in-house reservations system and reply to the requestor. The requestor may not receive a reply from the operator for hours (or even days). This delay is usually unacceptable to travel consultants who have a customer sitting across the counter from them waiting for confirmation. Consequently, travel consultants normally contact SMTEs by telephone to get an immediate response. The cost of sale of SMTE products is therefore significantly higher than that of products available through CRSs. This further disadvantages SMTEs in the marketplace.

2 Purpose

The purpose of this research is to develop an architecture that will facilitate interoperabilty of in-house reservations systems with those of other operators, accommodation establishments and CRSs. A distributed reservation system (DRS) is proposed.

Destination oriented information systems have begun to proliferate in recent years in response to the demand by travellers for more information about their proposed holiday. Recent advances in information and communications technology have facilitated the integration of a wide variety of information on destinations regardless of where it is located. This has resulted in the emergence of destination management systems (DMSs) (Buhalis, 1997). Although this is a step forward, it has focussed attention on the lack of a real-time reservations capability in SMTEs in these regions. Unlike product and destination information that is quite static in nature, availability and reservations information is very dynamic. The reservations functions of current and proposed DMSs (Proll et al, 1998; Gerdes, 1998) are based on the assumption that a central database of available product is maintained. This has most of the drawbacks of a CRS without providing any real benefit to the customer or the SMTE. Without the availability of free-sale allotments through a CRS, SMTEs require a distributed reservations system that is able to access and update their local hospitality management system (HMS). The availability of such a system would greatly enhance the power of DMSs to promote and sell the full range of products from the regions they represent.

The effectiveness of the distributed approach to reservations has been demonstrated by the success of the Imminus videotex system in the United Kingdom (Edwards et al, 1998). Unfortunately, this system is still not cost effective for SMTEs.

The system proposed is based on industry standard services and protocols that are currently available on the Internet together with a set of simple standardised reservations messages (SSRMs). The SSRMs are a simplified subset of the RESCON EDI standard reservation message. The protocols, services and message formats are specified in the DRS application-programming interface (DRSAPI). Keeping the messages simple and small in number simplifies the task of interfacing the existing in-house reservations systems to the DRSAPI, making it cost effective for SMTEs.

3 Methodology

This project follows a problem solving, engineering approach. It builds on existing theory and endeavours to provide a new technological solution based on existing theory and technology.

4 DRS architecture

The DRS architecture has been designed under the same principles as the Open Buying On the Internet standard (OBI Consortium, 1997):

- simplicity,
- use of existing industry standards,
- minimal customisation of existing systems and
- use of the internet as the transport backbone.

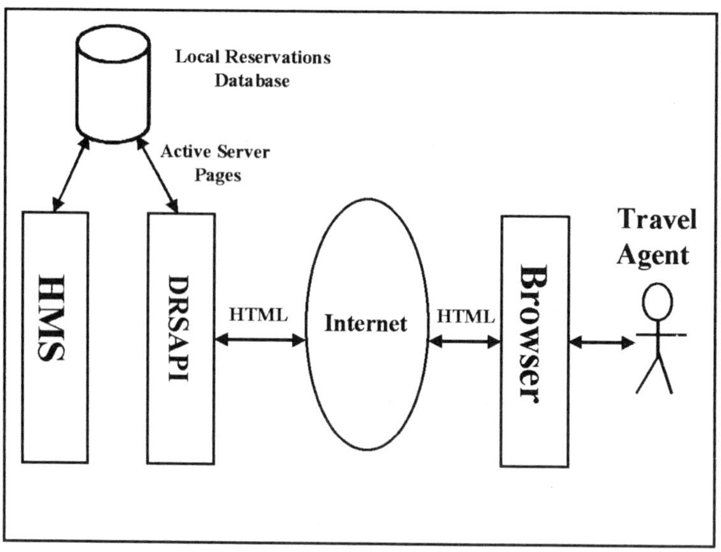

Fig. 1 DRS architecture using active web server pages

Availability and reservation requests are captured via a worldwide web interface. This can be provided using Java, HTML or XML (DSTC, 1997). The request is then transferred via the internet infrastructure to the SMTE's local system. The request is processed locally either automatically or manually. Automatic processing can be achieved by running web server software and active server pages, CGI scripting or JDBC on the local server (see Fig. 1).

Alternatively, requests can be transferred to the server using MIME encoded electronic mail. At the server, the message is converted and applied to the local hospitality management system (HMS) or reservations system by a standalone conversion and interfacing module (see Fig. 2).

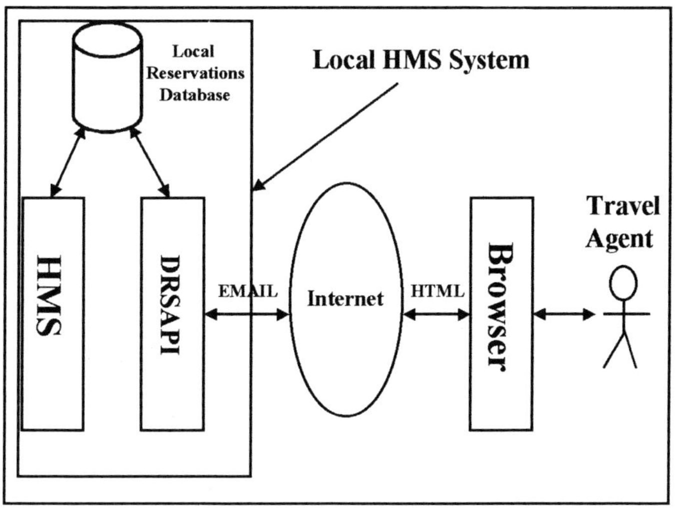

Fig. 2 DRS architecture using encoded email

Very small enterprises can continue to process incoming requests manually (see Fig. 3). Of course, the feasibility of manual processing depends on the reliability and speed with which the requests are processed.

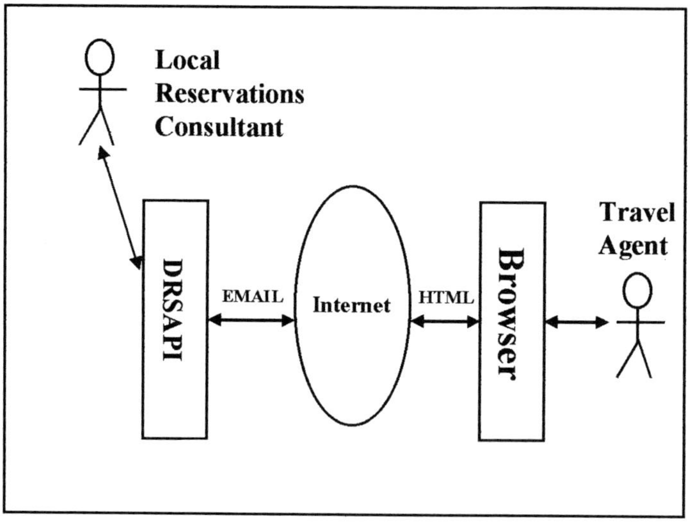

Fig. 3 DRS Architecture with manual confirmation

5 DRS Applications Programming Interface

The DRSAPI includes standard messages for availability, reservations, confirmations and cancellation. In the interests of simplification and security, no payment messages are included. It is assumed that sufficient time will be available between booking and use for alternative means of payment to be used.

The format of the messages will comply with the RESCON standard but will be a very restricted subset. In particular, a single option is specified for any optional format fields. While this does limit the applicability of the system to SMTEs it also significantly reduces complexity and hence cost of the HMS interface software.

6 Result

A small prototype is currently being designed and built to test the DRS concept with two different in-house reservations systems. Testing is expected to be completed within six months.

7 Conclusion and further research

The results of the prototype are expected to show that the DRS concept is effective, practical and easy to implement. Further research by the author will expand the DRSAPI to include all essential messages. Software will then be developed to map the DRSAPI to major in-house reservations systems.

References

- Australian Federation of Travel Agents (1994). *Travel Industry Technology - Towards Information Highways*, Australian Federation of Travel Agents, Sydney.
- Baker, M., Lockwood, A. & Sussman, S. (1996). Application Standards for Tourism Products. Proposals for a program of research, *Proceedings of the 3rd International Conference on Information and Communications Technologies in Tourism*, Springer-Verlag, Vienna.
- Bloch, M., Pigneur, Y. & Steiner, T. (1996). The IT-enabled extended enterprise, applications in the tourism industry, *Proceedings of the 3rd International Conference on Information and Communications Technologies in Tourism*, Springer-Verlag, Vienna.
- Bloch, M. & Segev, A. (1996). *The Impact of Electronic Commerce on the Travel Industry*, The Fisher Centre for Information Technology & Management, University of California, California.
- Buhalis, D. (1996). Information and telecommunication technologies as a strategic tool for tourism enhancement at destination regions. *Proceedings of the 3rd International Conference on Information and Communications Technologies in Tourism*, Springer-Verlag, Vienna.
- Buhalis, D. (1997) Information Technology as a Strategic Tool for Economic, Social, Cultural and Environmental Benefits Enhancement of Tourism at Destination Regions, *Progress in Tourism and Hospitality*, Vol. 3, 71-93, Wiley & Sons, Chichester
- Dombey, A. (1998). Separating the emotion from the fact – the effects of new intermediaries on electronic travel distribution, *Proceedings of the 5th International Conference on Information and Communications Technologies in Tourism*, Springer-Verlag, Vienna.
- DSTC (1998). Introduction to XML, Distributed Systems Technology Centre, University of Queensland, Australia.
- http://www.dstc.edu.au/aw3tc/slides/XML/index.htm
- Edwards, G., Dawes, C. and Karcher, K. (1998). The Imminus Travel and Tourism Intranet, *Proceedings of the 5th International Conference on Information and Communications Technologies in Tourism*, Springer-Verlag, Vienna.
- Gerdes, H. (1998). A National Destination Management System (DMS) based on examples of Germany and Switzerland, *Proceedings of the 5th International Conference on Information and Communications Technologies in Tourism*, Springer-Verlag, Vienna.
- Klein, S., Schmid, B., Tjoa, A. & Werthner, H. (Eds.). (1996). Information and Communications Technologies in Tourism, *Proceedings of the 3rd International Conference on Information and Communications Technologies in Tourism*, Springer-Verlag, Vienna.
- Lymer, A., Johnson R. & Baldwin A. (1997). The Internet and the Small Business: A Study of Impacts, *Proceedings of the 1997 European Conference on Information Systems*.

- Milne, S. (1996). Tourism Marketing and Computer Reservations Systems in the Pacific, *Tourism in the Pacific: Issues and Cases*, International Thomson Business Press, London.
- Near, D. (1997). Travelweek. (30 July, p 16).
- OBI Consortium. (1997). Open Buying on the Internet Standard, Release V1.0, The Open Buying on the Internet Consortium, USA.
- Paroz, D. (1997). Travelweek. (30 July, p 17)
- Poon, A. (1993). *Tourism, Technology and Competitive Strategies*, CAB International, Wallingford.
- Proll, B., Retschitzegger, W., Kroiss, P. and Wagner, R. (1998), On-line bookings on the net - problems, issues and solutions, *Proceedings of the 5th International Conference on Information and Communications Technologies in Tourism,* Springer-Verlag, Vienna.
- Queensland Tourist & Travel Corporation (1997), *International Marketing Briefs,* Brisbane.
- Smith, B. (1996). *The Impact of Electronic Data Interchange: An Australian Perspective.* Unpublished Master of Information Technology Thesis, University of Southern Queensland, Toowoomba.
- Tjoa, A., & Werthner, H. (1996). Interfacing WWW with Distributed Database Applications in the Field of Tourism, *Proceedings of the 3rd International Conference on Information and Communications Technologies in Tourism*, Springer-Verlag, Vienna.
- Werthner, H. (1996). Design Principles of Tourist Information Systems, *Proceedings of the 3rd International Conference on Information and Communications Technologies in Tourism*, Springer-Verlag, Vienna.

Measuring Tourism Consumer Behaviour Using ESCAPE: a Multimedia Interview Engine for Stated Choice and Preference Experiments

M.D. Klabbers, H.J.P Timmermans
Urban Planning Group,
Faculty of Architecture, Building and Planning,
Eindhoven University of Technology, The Netherlands

Abstract

In the few research cases that are available, conjoint or stated choice and preference (SCAP) experiments have proved to offer suitable models for tourism marketers [1-8]. These models give insight in the effect of particular characteristics of the tourism product on its desirability, utility, or market share. The experiments that feed these models involve hypothetical situations for which respondents have to state their preference and choice. These situations are constructed by varying the product's characteristics systematically according to an experimental design. However, these models, as well as the vast majority of models, have always been oriented on abstract dimensions, while the tourism consumer market is mainly visually oriented.

This paper, therefore, offers a tool to indulge *visual elements* in these conjoint experiments. It describes a multimedia engine that supports researchers in developing multimedia conjoint experiments and helps respondents to fill in these questionnaires more easily. The engine is called ESCAPE (Engine for Stated Choice and Preference Experiments) and is developed by the author dedicated to evaluate the effect of multimedia on conjoint or SCAP modelling. However, this engine also supports more 'normal' conjoint experiments. In addition this paper describes in what way this engine differs from other multimedia conjoint programs.

1 Introduction

Tourism marketing and management increasingly demands more insight in tourist's behaviour. Models to describe this behaviour have already been implemented in several decision support systems. The information and data needed for these models can be acquired in several ways.

One way to acquire these data is to analyse the decisions that experts have made, or to analyse their decision process (e.g. by the Analytic Hierarchy Process in [9]). This can be an unstructured and cumbersome process that requires several interview sessions with experts to validate the model at hand. For these reasons experts, if already available, are not always a preferable option.

Another way to acquire data is offered by revealed preference techniques. They enable the estimation of tourist behaviour models using observed choices [10]. These techniques, however, can lead to large biases under the following circumstances: (1) the number of observations is relatively small, (2) the characteristics of alternatives, which the tourists have chosen between, are highly correlated, (3) the choice sets, from which tourists have chosen, are unknown, or (4) the model is used to evaluate new not-yet-existing alternatives. This last point involves predictions of unobserved choices, which does not correspond with the basis of revealed preference, and forces researchers to rely on ad hoc extrapolations. Conversely, stated choice and preference (SCAP) techniques offer possibilities to avoid these problems [11].

SCAP techniques or conjoint techniques offer a method to acquire data from 'layman' experts. These experiments have proved to provide good data for modelling tourism consumer behaviour [4, 6]. SCAP experiments involve preferences and choices that people state for well described hypothetical situations. These situations usually convey a choice between or preference for one or more products. The products in these situations consist of combinations of systematically varied 'components' that are supposed to influence preferences of consumers for that particular product.

For reasons of simplicity, researchers traditionally have chosen to present these situations in a verbal presentation format. In rare occasions they described products in elaborate descriptions [12], but more often in a few keywords. Reality shows, however, that tourism products are more visually oriented and that, therefore, these experiments could be improved by the use of a visual presentation format. In our opinion, there are, until now, no (software) tools that support the process of conducting a multimedia SCAP experiment to a satisfactory level.

This paper proposes an engine for SCAP experiments (ESCAPE) that supports construction and execution of multimedia experiments. For that reason the requirements that the conjoint theory imposes are described in the necessary steps to conduct SCAP experiments. Subsequently the new demands are described, and with respect to these demands existing software is reviewed. Finally the specifications for the engine are formulated, which will focus on interactive interview methods and construction of multimedia SCAP experiments.

2 Conjoint theory

As described before, SCAP experiments offer a method for predicting consumer behaviour by measuring and analysing consumers' preferences in relation with a product's features. (The meaning of the word product must be seen in a broad context; product can also reflex a tourist recreation complex) By questioning respondents, conjoint analysists gather the data necessary for determining the important effects in consumer behaviour. After analysis, the resulting model predicts consumer behaviour.

Conjoint analysis involves studying the process of consumer behaviour in an experimental setting – first how alternative products are evaluated and then whether one particular alternative is eventually purchased. This process is described in the Information Integration Theory of Anderson [13], and it describes that purchase of a certain alternative is based on the fact that that product is deemed to be more useful then the other alternatives. The theory is based on the Random Utility Model that originates from Thurstone [14].

Anderson [13] states that consumers derive a utility V for a product i based on the usefulness of the product's characteristics, otherwise described as attribute evaluations or part-worths (β_j). Then an overall evaluation results in a product's utility V_i as presented in formula 1. In this formula X_{ij} denotes the presence of a characteristic or attribute level j in product i.

$$V_i = \Sigma_j \beta_j X_{ij} \quad (1)$$

Thurstone [14] claims that the observed or stated consumer's utility U consists of both a structural (V_i) and a random (ε_i) component (See formula 2).

$$U_i = V_i + \varepsilon_i \quad (2)$$

In short, SCAP experiments involve measuring choices or preferences for (sets of) products, which characteristics (attribute levels) are systematically varied. Only in this way independent measuring of attribute evaluations (part-worths) is ensured.

3 Steps in SCAP experiments

As stated before, ESCAPE should support the design and execution of SCAP experiments. The basic requirements for ESCAPE stem from the subsequent steps that are prescribed by conjoint theory. These steps, described by several authors [15, 16], also have proved to be effective in a number of tourism applications [2, 3, 5, 6, 17, 18]. The process involved in SCAP experiments can be divided in four stages: conceptualisation stage, task design stage, data collection stage, and data analysis stage.

3.1 Conceptualisation Stage

The conceptualisation stage involves formulation of the research goal. Generally, this goal is to predict the preference for a certain product, in this case a tourism product. This prediction could involve new product identification, optimal product pricing, market segmentation of products, or competitive analysis between products. The predictions will be based on the estimated part-worths (preferences for attributes) of the product.

3.2 Task Design Stage

After the conceptualisation stage the attributes and their levels are defined. For their definition a number of techniques can be applied (e.g. literature research, repertory grid, factor-listing approach, focus group interviews) that identify the product's characteristics relevant to the consumer. These characteristics comprise the eventual attributes and accompanying levels. Additional attributes may be defined to serve the research goal, for example managerial-oriented attributes [19].

The number of levels depends on: (1) the research goal, (2) assumptions and expectations about the linearity of effects of continuous attributes, (3) restrictions originating form the experimental design. Moreover, the levels should connect to the respondents' world of experience.

When the attribute levels are defined the task construction can start. First, if not already done, the data collection procedure (e.g., personal interview, mail interview, or interactive-computer interview) is selected. Subsequently, the response mode (e.g., rank order, rating, choice, allocation data, etc.) is chosen. These selections define the character of the SCAP tasks [20].

Next, the experimental design that creates the hypothetical product descriptions is selected or generated. The experimental design defines which combination of attribute levels will form a (hypothetical) product or profile, which combination of profiles will form a choice set (if required), and in which order the products or choice sets will be presented. Ultimately, these combinations determine which independent effects will be measured: effects of product attributes on consumer behaviour, effects of the task on respondent preferences, effects indicated by the investigated theories, etc.

The experimental design is restricted by the (maximum) size and number of SCAP tasks. As a consequence, the construction of the experimental design can be a tiresome process that forces researchers to retract to prior stages and simplify prior decisions in their research [21].

After construction of the experimental design the SCAP tasks can be finalised. These last steps involve the design of attribute levels and profiles, the formulation and design of both questions and directions, and the designing of the response items. For each level and every attribute a presentation format is selected (e.g. textual, verbal, pictorial, video, or even a real tangible copy) and designed. Finally, the SCAP tasks can be tested, evaluated, and revised until they are suitable for data collection.

3.3 Data collection Stage

The data collection stage involves measuring respondents' preferences by presenting them the constructed SCAP tasks. First the respondents are selected by (randomly) drawing a representative sample from the target consumer population stated in the research goal. Then the SCAP tasks are presented to them and their stated preferences or choices are collected. Finally, the data is coded and, if not already done, digitised.

3.4 Data analysis Stage

The data analysis stage involves estimating (quantifying) and testing the consumer behaviour model. Normally, the model estimation encompasses the estimation of part-worth utilities for the selected attribute levels. Subsequently, the model can be checked for validity and reliability [22]. Subsequently, the estimated model can be used to simulate future scenarios. Because existing data analysis software packages algorithms are abound and of high quality, data analysis will be represented only to some extent in the design of ESCAPE.

3.5 General SCAP process

As mentioned earlier, conducting SCAP experiments involves a highly iterative optimisation process. The iterations result from the fact that the consequences of early stage decisions appear in a later stage. The process can be compared with an optimisation process, where the researcher evaluates and steers the search to an optimal result. These process characteristics demand researchers to foresee later consequences of decisions in a very early stage. As we will discuss in section 0, the addition of multimedia will complicate this process even more. Therefore, a multimedia engine should support and alleviate researchers in this process and in these demands particularly.

3.6 Existing conjoint software

Computer programs that support SCAP experiments are already available. Several software manufacturers have introduced text-based conjoint analysis packages: Sawtooth Software has introduced Adaptive Conjoint Analysis System (ACA), Choice Based Conjoint System (CBC), and Conjoint Value Analysis System (CVA); Bretton-Clark has introduced Conjoint Designer, Conjoint Analyzer, Simgraf, Conjoint Linmap, and Conjoint Segmenter; Intelligent Marketing Systems has introduced Consurv; SPSS has introduced SPSS Categories; Hague Consulting Group has introduced Speed and Mint [23-25].

The latest software tools also support multimedia conjoint experiments: Sawtooth Software's Sensus Q&A (or to be more specific Sensus Multimedia) and Skim's Mixed Media for MS Windows, and the Interview Engine of Kozo Keikaku Engineering Inc. for the Macintosh. Of these multimedia engines, which are similar to each other, Sensus Q&A offers the most comprehensive package. It enables researchers to combine the different software packages of Sawtooth (Sensus Multimedia, ACA, CBC, CVA) to create interviews that encompass the presentation formats of Sensus Multimedia (text, pictures, sound) in combination with different interview techniques of the other packages.

All these conjoint software packages typically consist of modules that allow researchers to select an experimental design, create (and print) profile cards, enter response data, analyse this data, and predict consumer behaviour with these data [25]. Only one of these packages, i.e. ACA, supports a specific interactive interviewing technique. All these packages support the researcher in the task construction stage and data analysis stage. Although data analysis techniques are abound, support for task construction is very rigid; changes in decision of earlier stages would entail almost complete revision of decisions in later stages.

3.7 New demands: applying the visual presentation format

Applying the visual presentation format involves a reconsideration of the construction process of SCAP experiments. Visual presentations, if presented realistically, provide a lot of information to the respondent. In contrast to the construction process of a verbal oriented experiment, researchers now have to be careful which visual details they will present. Photographs of tourist places, for example, generally contain a lot of irrelevant details, like specific people, cars, animals, etc. These details can contribute to biased preference measurements, which endanger the quality of the eventual model.

Moreover, visual presentations force researchers to specify the product realistically, and, hence, in great detail. For example, a visual presentation of a remote fly-in fishing destination requires the definition of the tree types in the forest setting [26]. These details can have their specific influence on respondents' utilities and, hence, must be seen as an extra set of attribute levels. Of course, researchers could choose to fixate on only specific details (e.g. a specific tree type), but that would limit eventual predictions of the research to those details. These extra attributes not only enlarge the experimental design, which will result in more tasks and/or more respondents, they will also put a burden on the construction of tasks. The details in a visual presentation have to be attuned to each other, in size, colour, and position. If tasks are constructed individually by hand like in the research of Haider and colleagues, this will result in a long and expensive process, or, if tasks are generated and constructed automatically, an extensive face validation is required, with possibilities to alter the tasks separately.

Another option to tackle the problems arising from too many attributes and levels, is to apply interactive techniques. Either to select the most important attributes from a bigger pool, as in the ACA-method [27], or by selecting the most informative questions as described in the algorithm of Huber and Zwerina [28]. In our opinion, there are still a number of techniques that could be explored. Consequently, ESCAPE will comprise interview scripts, as a mean to support interactive and automatic adaptation of interviews.

4 The design of ESCAPE

A multimedia engine for designing SCAP experiments should support the steps in SCAP experiments. The addition of both this support and of multimedia itself will improve the consumer behaviour measurements. The engine should, therefore, guide the researcher through the design process and enable additions like pictures, sound, spoken words, and video. An engine that supports the addition of interaction in interviews provides the possibility to offer additional information to respondents when needed. Moreover, it enables researchers to adapt the interview on the basis of the respondent's prior actions in an intelligent way. Furthermore, the engine should record several measurements, not only the choices or the preferences, but also the actions and response times of the respondent, in order to check the measurements in a thorough way.

4.1 ESCAPE's Guidelines

Introduction

ESCAPE, a multimedia Engine for Stated Choice and Preference Experiments, is a tool that supports developing and conducting computer based SCAP experiments. The data flow between ESCAPE's interfaces, subprograms, and modules can be defined based on the process and steps in SCAP experiments. As stated before, the design emphasises both the task design stage (presentation format in particular) and the data collection stage. As a result, other stages are not or not extensively developed within ESCAPE.

Development Environment

ESCAPE has been implemented in Borland's Delphi on a MS-Windows based machine with multimedia facilities. Delphi is a Rapid Application Development Tool that supports graphical design of applications (visual programming) and translates this design into Pascal code, which offers a large flexibility. It is, therefore, a very suitable tool for developing very specific multimedia applications, like ESCAPE. The MS-Windows based machines are very popular; most software that supports SCAP experiments is written for these machines. For an optimal support, ESCAPE is developed on and for a general MS-Windows based machine.

ESCAPE's functions

ESCAPE's two major functions are task design and data collection. The former function aims to support the researcher designing the interview, the latter aims to support the respondent. Therefore ESCAPE entails two interfaces: the Designer-Interface and the Respondent-Interface (See figure 1).

The Designer-Interface uses a design-desk for questionnaires as its basic metaphor. The researcher builds the interview on this design-desk with objects that are common

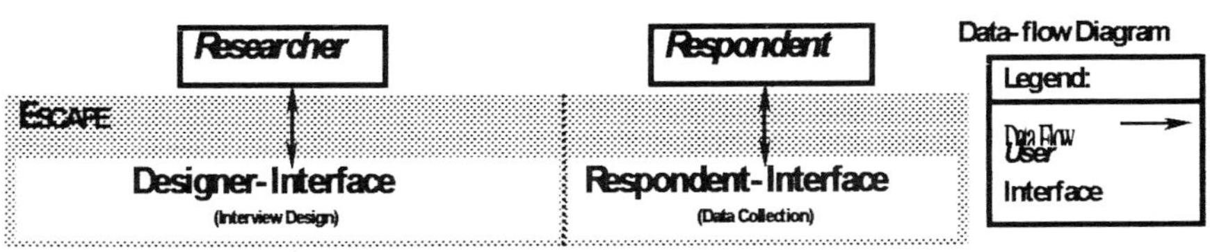

Figure 1: Course design of ESCAPE

in conjoint experiments (e.g. attributes and levels). Necessarily, he/she is also able to vary these objects systematically, by linking these objects to an experimental design. The design then controls the presence of these objects in a certain interview task.

The interface is based on direct-manipulation theory and a WYSIWYG-feedback (What you see is what you get-feedback). The applied direct manipulation theory enables the researcher to manipulate objects in the interview in such a way that he/she will see the consequences of these manipulations directly. The WYSIWYG-feedback enables the researcher to see the interview tasks exactly as the respondent will and, therefore, allows immediate evaluation and correction of the presentation of the designed tasks.

The Respondent-Interface uses a questionnaire-metaphor as basic concept. By manipulating ESCAPE's interview objects, the researcher can design this questionnaire metaphor. Additionally, ESCAPE supports this design by offering researchers several feedback mechanisms and response modes, which are commonly used in both SCAP- and ordinary questionnaires. ESCAPE also offers mechanisms that enable the respondent to browse through the questionnaire.

4.2 Task Design with the Designer-Interface

ESCAPE'S modules of the Designer Interface largely support the steps of the task design stage as described in section 3 (See figure 2). The most important one is the Task Design Module. To facilitate its support, the Task-Design module works with a task template that

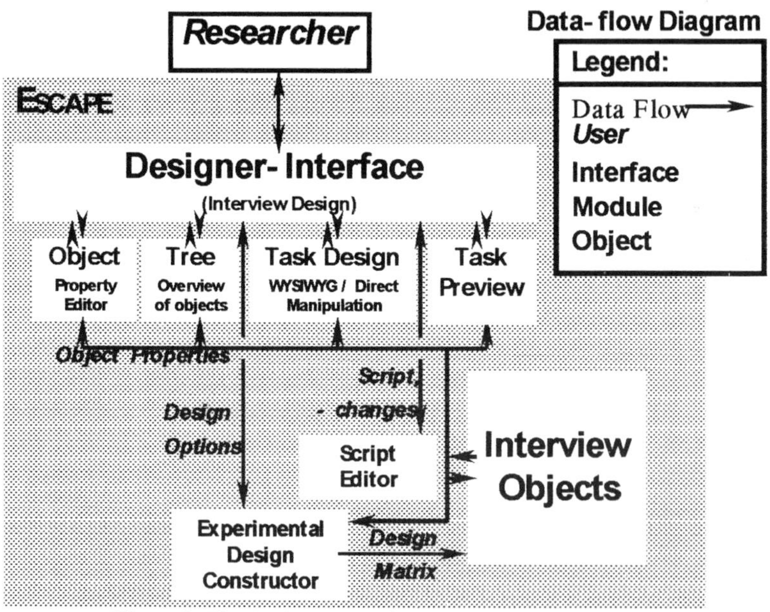

Figure 2: The Designer-Interface and underlying modules

contains all tasks and the elements within this task (like profiles, attributes, and levels). This concept helps to set up an interview without having to deal with the direct restrictions of the experimental design. At any time the researcher can evaluate the constructed task template by previewing its individual tasks. This function is handled by the Task Preview Module. The presence of the various interview objects in individual tasks is regulated by one or more experimental designs. The researcher can assign these objects to these designs. If elements are not assigned to a design, the Task Preview Module will generate and assign one to it, if necessary. ESCAPE's Task Design Module shows all objects used in the task template and offers a WYSIWYG-environment.

Another important module is the Object Module. Its function is to enable the researcher to specify precisely the properties of the various interview objects. These properties are a

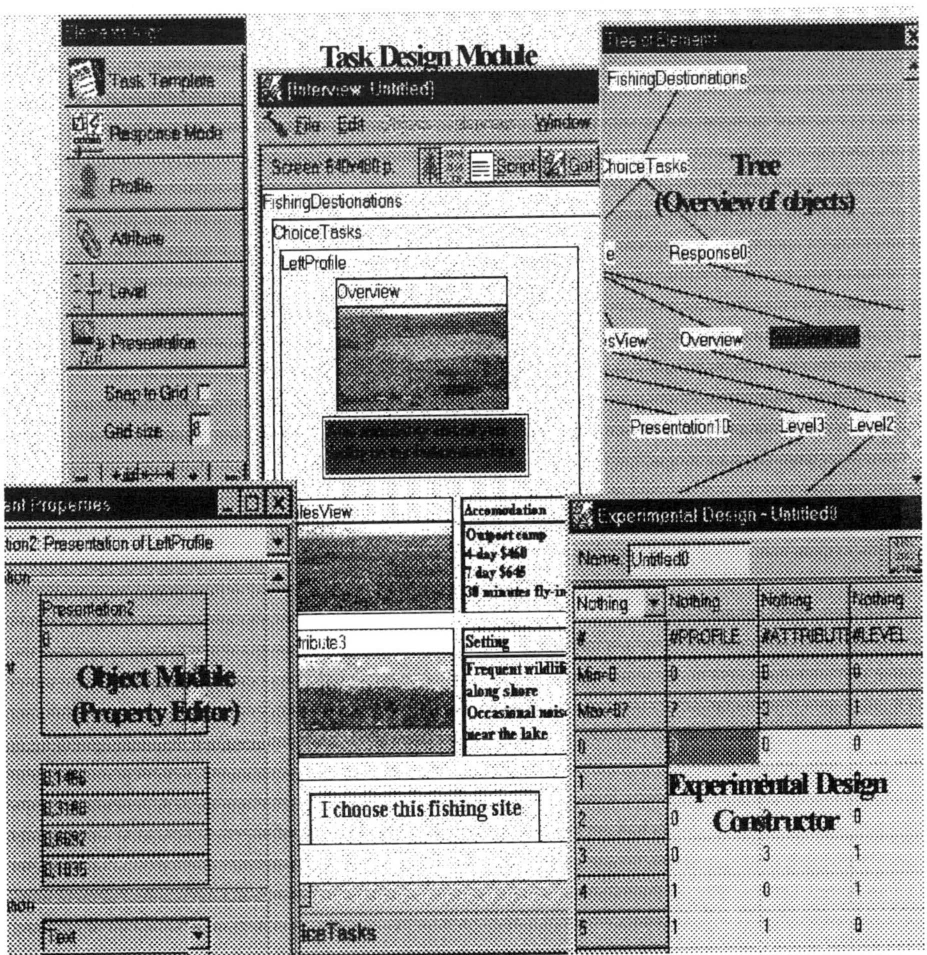

Fig. 3: Demonstration of Escape in a research on anglers' preferences for remote fly-in fishing destinations [24]

unique name, a number, exact position, extra comment, the experimental design this object is assigned to, and some more, dependent on the type of object. For example, the extra properties of a presentation object are: type of presentation (text, picture, and sound), content, and timing of presentation (at task presentation, at a user intervention, after a certain time period). Figure 3 presents the modules of ESCAPE in an example on how Haider and colleagues could have implemented their research on anglers' preferences for remote fly-in fishing destinations in ESCAPE.

Script Maker

The construction of the interview is stored in a script, created by the Script Maker. This module enables researchers to manipulate the script directly, however this should be discouraged, because of its rigid nature. The script defines the interview, that is, it enables the interview engine to execute the interview as described in this script. In this way even other programs can control the execution of interviews, which yields the use of interactive interview techniques.

4.3 Conducting an experiment using Data Collection

With The Interview Engine the researcher can complete the data collection stage by executing the script generated by the Script Maker. The script uses the data in the Experimental Design Data Base and the presentation data bases to present the SCAP tasks to the respondents, it records and stores the answers and possibly other actions of the respondent in a response data base. After the interviews, the data can be watched and coded for further analysis. Moreover, the Interview Engine will be available as a stand alone packet, so that it is smaller and easier to use when distributed.

5 Conclusions and Discussion

ESCAPE is an engine that integrates the several steps needed for constructing and execution of multimedia conjoint experiments. It not only adds the multimedia capabilities of modern computers to the presentation format of interviews, it also supports gradual and flexible development of these tasks and offers means to implement new interactive techniques to improve quality of the collected data. The precise impact of these improvements will be measured in a usability test of the engine. Moreover, ESCAPE will be used for research on the impact of presentation format on SCAP measurements.

References

[1] Louviere, J. J.,Timmermans, H. J. P.: Stated Preference and Choice Models Applied to Recreation Research: A Review, *Leisure Sciences*, vol. 12, pp. 9-32 (1990).

[2] Louviere, J. L.,Hensher, D. A.: Using Discrete Choice Models with Experimental Design Data to Forecast Consumer Demand for a Unique Cultural Event, *Journal of Consumer Research*, vol. 10, pp. 348-361 (1983).

[3] Lieber, S. R.,Fesenmaier, D. R.: Physical and Social Conditions Affecting Recreation Site Preferences, *Environment an Planning A*, vol. 17, pp. 1613-1625 (1985).

[4] Timmermans, H. J. P.: Hybrid and Non-Hybrid Evaluation Models for Predicting Outdoor Recreation Behavior: A Test of Predictive Ability, *Leisure Scienses*, vol. 9, pp. 67-76 (1987).

[5] Haider, W.,Ewing, G. O.: A Model of Tourist Choices of Hypothetical Caribbean Destinations, *Leisure Sciences*, vol. 12, pp. 33-47 (1990).

[6] Louviere, J. L.,Timmermans, H. J. P.: Testing the External Validity of Hierarchical Conjoint Analysis Models of Recreational Destination Choice, *Leisure Sciences*, vol. 14, pp. 179-194 (1992).

[7] Delleart, B. G. C.:Conjoint Choice Models for Urban Tourism Planning and Marketing, in *Urban Planning*. Eindhoven University of Technology (1995), pp. 130.

[8] Stemerding, M. P.:Modeling Constraints-Based Choices for Leisure Mobility Planning, Development and Test of a Constraints-Based Conjoint Choice Model for The Ex-Ante Evaluation of Leisure Mobility Policies, in *Urban Planning*. Eindhoven: Eindhoven University of Technology (1996), pp. 275.

[9] Moutinho, L., Rita, P.,Curry, B.:*Expert Systems inTourism Marketing*. London: Routledge (1996).

[10] Ben-Akiva, M.,Lerman, S. R.:*Discrete Choice Analysis*, 2 ed. Cambridge, Massachusetts: The MIT Press (1985).

[11] Ettema, D.:Activity Based Travel Demand Modeling, in *Urban Planning*. Eindhoven: Eindhoven University of Technology (1996), pp. 296.

[12] Louviere, J. J., Schroeder, H., Louviere, C. H.,Woodworth, G.: Do the Parameters of Choice Models Depend on Differences in Stimulus Presentation: Visual versus Verbal Presentations?, *Advances in Consumer Research*, vol. XIV, pp. 79-82 (1987).

[13] Anderson, N. H.:*Foundations of Information Integration Theory*. New York: Academic Press (1981).

[14] Thurstone, L. L.: A Law of Comparative Judgment, *Psychological Review*, vol. 34, pp. 273-286 (1927).

[15] Louviere, J. J.:*Analyzing Decision Making, metric conjoint analysis*, vol. 67. Newbury Park, CA: Sage Publications (1988).

[16] Green, P. E.,Srinivasan, V.: Conjoint Analysis in Consumer Research: Issues and Outlook, *Journal of Consumer Research*, vol. 5, pp. 103-123 (1978).

[17] Bojamic, D. C.,Calantone, R. J.: A Contribution Approach to Price Bundling in Tourism, *Anals of Tourism Research*, vol. 17, pp. 528-540 (1990).

[18] Kemperman, A. D. A. M., Borgers, A.,Timmermans, H. J. P.: Consumer Choice of Theme Parks: A Conjoint Choice Model of Seasonality Effects and Variety Seeking Behavior, *Leisure Sciences* (1998 (Submitted)).

[19] Oppewal, H.:Conjoint Experiments and Retail Planning: Modelling Consumer Choice of Shopping Centre and Retailer Reactive Behaviour, in *Urban Planning*. Eindhoven: Eindhoven Universtiy of Technology (1995), pp. 254.

[20] Vriens, M.:Conjoint Analysis in Marketing: Developments in Stimulus Representaton and Segmentation Methods, in *SOM (Systems, Organisations and Management)*. Groningen, The Netherlands: University of Groningen (1995), pp. 257.

[21] Steenkamp, J. E. B. M.: De Constructie van Profielensets voor het schatten van hoofdeffecten en interacties bij conjunct meten, (1985).

[22] Bateson, J. E. G., Reibstein, D.,Boulding, W.: Conjoint Analysis Reliability and Validity: A Framework for Future Research, , pp. 451-481 (1987).

[23] Carmone Jr., F. J.,Schaffer, C. M.: Conjoint Designer, Conjoint Analyzer, Simgraf, Conjoint Linmap, Conjoint Segmenter, Bridger; Consurv; Adaptive Conjoint Analysis

System, Choice Based Conjoint System, Conjoint Value Analysis System, *Journal of Marketing Research*, vol. 32, pp. 113-120 (1995).
[24] Oppewal, H.: A Review of Choice-Based Conjoint Software: CBC and MINT, *Journalof Retailing and Consumer Services*, vol. 2 (1995).
[25] Oppewal, H.: Software Review: A Review Of Conjoint Software, *Journal of Retailing and Consumer Services*, vol. 2, pp. 55-61 (1995).
[26] Haider, W., Anderson, D. A., Daniel, T. C., Louviere, J. J., Orland, B.,Williams, M.: Combining Calibrated Digital Imagery and Discrete Choice Experiments: An Application to Remote Tourism in Northern Ontario, Conference on Forestry and the Environment: Economic Perspectives II, Banff, Alberta, Canada, Paper Oct 12-15, 1994 1994.
[27] Johnson, R. M.: Adaptive Conjoint Analysis, presented at Conjoint Analysis and Computer Interviewing, Ketchum (1985).
[28] Huber, J.,Zwerina, K.: The Importance of Utility Balance in Efficient Choice Designs, *Journal of Marketing Research*, vol. XXXIII, pp. 307-317 (1996).

A Speech-to-Speech Translation based Interface for Tourism

M. Cettolo, A. Corazza, G. Lazzari, F. Pianesi, E. Pianta, L.M. Tovena
ITC-irst – Trento, Italy
(cettolo|corazza|lazzari|pianesi|pianta|tovena)@itc.it

Abstract

This paper presents a speech-to-speech translation system for tourism application developed in the context of the C-STAR consortium. Potential users can communicate by speech and by using their own language with a travel agent in order to organize their travel. The system uses an interchange format representation of the semantic contents of utterances, which is flexible and simplifies the system portability to new languages. A demonstrative prototype, developed at ITC-irst, is now working for the Italian modules and was integrated with the English counter part developed at the Interactive System Laboratory at CMU.

1 Introduction

In the field of tourist information, users from every part of the world may want to access an information system to get information for organizing their travels. However, potential users are not computer scientists nor are keen onto use artificial languages for interacting with the system. They would rather exploit their own language. This is why multi-lingual and translation-based interfaces are so important in tourist information retrieval applications.
Also, traditional computer based interfaces severely limit the number of potential users to those who are familiar with keyboards. Instead, the use of tourism information systems can be greatly enhanced by allowing a speech-based interaction, say by means of a telephone.
At present, general purpose speech-to-speech translation is too ambitious a target. The effort of the research community is directed towards making available domain-dependent speech-to-speech translation systems, which permit to limit the vocabulary size of the speech recognizer and the set of possible expressions to be considered in the analysis and generation steps.
With the goal of exploring the use of the speech-to-speech translation for tourism applications, the C-STAR consortium designed a possible scenario so that partners from different countries could cooperate by sharing data and experiences on a common task to build an actual system. At the moment six laboratories are participating to the system implementation: ATR (Japan), CLIPS++ (France), ETRI (Korea), ITC–irst (Italy), ISL at CMU (USA), ISL at UKA (Germany). Different partners from the consortium use a common formal language, called the interchange format (henceforth, IF), for encoding the information content of each utterance. This permits each partner to focus on the development of

modules mapping its language onto IF representations, and from the latter back to its language. The authors of this paper are involved in the development of analysis, and generation modules for Italian.[1]
The following section describes the application scenario considered. Sections 3 and 4 consider the two main characteristics of the system: the speech based interfaces, with its problems and advantages, and the interchange format approach. In Section 5, the system is described, in its general architecture and the particular methodologies applied for the single modules. Finally, general conclusions and future work are discussed in the final section.

2 The scenario

In the C-STAR application scenario, a customer is planning a trip to several countries around the world. He/she relies on a travel agency with agents in each of the considered countries that arranges for flights, trains, hotels, sight-seeing tours, tickets for cultural events, etc..
The scenario is designed in such a way that the conversation does not involve more than two people at a time. A typical conversation consists of a sequence of two-partners dialogues and takes place over the telephone, so that visual or gestual communication is excluded.
The contact point for the client is an agent, $A1$ (the *primary* agent), in the first city of the trip. The conversation, a phone call between $A1$ and the traveler, concerns the transportation settlements for the *whole* trip, and hotel booking and tourist arrangements for the country of $A1$. When $A1$ has finished his/her task, he/she transfers the line to another agent, $A2$ (*secondary* agent), in one of the other countries involved in the trip. $A2$ will only take care of room reservations and tourist information for his/her own country. Once the client has finished with $A2$, the latter transfers him/her back to $A1$ who might then dispatch the client to another secondary agent in another country, and so on. Three main subdomains characterize the scenario: the travel information, the hotel reservation and the tourist information. In addition, there are minor subdomains related to call transfers.

3 Speech based interfaces

The system interface is very important for the system usability. Speech based interfaces are very effective. Indeed, they leave the user hands free for performing other tasks (like handling documents or taking notes) and permit the whole exchange to be accomplished through a telephone line. Moreover, when the dialogue is among people, speech is the most natural way of communication.

[1] The idea of using an interchange format can be profitably extended to other application domains, e.g. to dialogue-based human-machine systems. In these cases, the interchange format can be translated into SQL queries for accessing a database [5].

The choice of a speech based interface, however, conditions the design of all the modules of the system. The idea of considering speech modules as parts which can be simply connected with a pre-existing (or an otherwise already specified) system has been definitely abandoned in the last years.
This is due to the fact that both the speech signal (input), and the spoken language (output) are extremely variable and difficult to model. Acoustically, *spontaneous speech* is characterized by highly variable speaking rates and by a series of extra-linguistic phenomena, like hesitations, pauses, coughs, and so on which have to be taken into account. Table 1 reports on the occurrences of such extra-linguistic phenomena in the corpus collected for the development and assessment of the system we are going to present.

phenomenon	eee	inhalation	exhalatiob	mouth	vowel lengthen	mmm	ehm	ah
# occurrences	1974	1497	1360	496	490	303	222	172
# affected sentences	1389	1117	1176	449	432	258	204	167
% affected sentences	25.3	20.4	21.4	8.2	7.9	4.7	3.7	3.0

Table 1. Most frequent human noises occurring in the corpus (# stands for "number of" while % for "rate".

To model these and other phenomena, and obtain acceptable recognition accuracy with spontaneous speech, accurate acoustic models are required. In this respect, only some of the relevant phenomena can be handled by current techniques. For example, modeling such frequent phenomena as breaths, filled and empty pauses, coughs, etc. is a feasible task, but modeling speaking rate variations is more difficult. Finally, handling out-of-vocabulary words, or word fragments are still research issues.
Another important point is that spoken language is often very different from written language (refer to [9] for a deeper discussion on this item). For example, it is commonplace to find utterances consisting of sentence fragments, sequences of fragments, or fragments combined with complete sentences. Building models capable of dealing with all possible variations is a difficult task.
Finally, recognition errors must be carefully controlled and minimised. They cause, in fact, the insertion of unuttered words in the recognized word sequence, the omission of uttered words or the substitution of uttered with unuttered words. This, in turn, causes problems to modules devoted to language processing, which are therefore expected to be very robust with respect to recognition errors. All these considerations are all the more important when dealing with spontaneous speech, as compared with read/dictated one.

4 The interchange format approach

The adoption of an interchange format based approach has several advantages and potentialities. The most obvious advantage is the reduction of the number of different systems which have to be implemented. Given n different languages, an analysis chain (starting from from the spoken input and delivering an interchange format representation) and a synthesis chain (taking the interchange format representation and prividing a linguistic form for it) for each language suffice to yield a system capable of dealing with speech-to-speech translation between all of the possible language pairs. That is, the resulting system would require n separate analysis and synthesis chains, instead of the otherwise required quadratic number of modules. Furthermore, given that each module involves only one language, the development can be done by native speakers of that language. Another important advantage concerns portability to a new language; given the described configuration, a lower effort is necessary to make an existing system capable of dealing with a new language. This strikingly contrasts with the case of a direct translation system, where the addition of a new language to a set of n pre-existing languages requires the construction of n new complete modules to link each old language to the new one.[2]

In addition to this, the techniques developed to build and process a formal representation of the information content of utterances can be exploited to meet the demands of many other applicative scenarios. For example, in a speech-based information retrival system, the interchange format can be used to build the formal query. Both in this case and in speech-to-speech scenario, the interchange format representations can provide the means to produce summaries of the transactions occured between the human and the machine, and among the different parties, respectively.

4.1 The interchange format design

For the interchange format based approach to work properly, the interchange format design is crucial. This is a difficult problem because many aspects need be taken into account. In the first place, the interchange format must be (as) language independent (as possible). That is, we want it to focus on the information contained in utterances rather than the way in which such information is expressed.

On the other hand, in order to control the complexity of the task, and often to make the taks feasible at all, the interchange format must be allowed to be both application- and domain-sensitive. Indeed, the applicative scenario provides strong indications as to the type of information which must be extracted, while the domain defines the actual data to be identified in the utterance. For example, the application might request the identification of the topic of the utterance, and the domain might restric the choice to a finite set [11].

[2] This short discussion is somehow reminiscent of the long debate between interlingua- and transfer-based approaches in traditional Machine Translation. This is not by chance. Actually, we believe that the IF-based philosphy described in the text can make the best of both approaches. Obviously, this requires that some constraints be relaxed; e.g., that the domain-independence pursued by interlinguas be abandoned. Yet, as we argue in the text, it is possible to maintain a high degree of language-independence.

To exemplify, suppose that the application is a system retriving data from a relational database. In this case the information which has to be extracted from the input utterance is that relevant to building the SQL query; that is, the topic, which usually corresponds to the table to be searched, the data to be retrived, which correspond to the column, and the constraints on the data. Therefore, in this case the database structure gives the structure of the interchange format. [5] describes a system working according to these principles which exploited a frame based language as interchange format. An interchange format example is reproduced below, and corresponds to the Italian sentence *vorrei i voli da verona a pittsburgh in partenza prima delle dieci* (i'd like to know about the flights from verona to pittsburgh which leave before ten o'clock).

(TABLE = flight)
(COLUMN = flight_id)
(ORIGIN = 'VERONA')
(DEST = 'PITTSBURGH')
(DEP_TIME IN 00:00 10:00)

Speech-to-speech translation scenarios feature dialogues with a richer structure than that of speech-based information retrival, which the relevant interchange format must be able to capture them. For instance, the number of parties active in the conversation is always greater than one and track must be kept of who is speaking at each time. To this end, the C-STAR IF provides a label to encode the speaker: *a:* for the agent and *c:* for the traveller. Furthermore, the users do not only ask for data or information. They also perform, and request the other party to perform, a number of different actions. Users greet the other speaker, seek and give information and clarifications, accept and reject proposals and suggestions, and so on. All these actions are represented in the *speech-act* level of the C-STAR IF. Moreover, each action may concern and involve a number of objects in the world and properties thereof. Such objects and properties are encoded by means of *concepts*, usually ordered by importance and (decreasing) generality. Examples of the relevant concepts are *availability, price, hotel, room, trip, ...* Finally, there is an *argument* level, consisting of *attribute-value* pairs such as *time=sunday, location=downtown* etc. Each concept admits one or more attribute-value pairs.
In summary, the C-STAR IF consists of four levels: 1) the speaker label, 2) the speech-act part, 3) a (sequence of) concept(s), and 4) the arguments. If the utterance considered in the example above had been uttered by the traveller in the C-STAR scenario, the IF representation would have been the following one:

c:request-information+features+flight
(origin=verona, destination=pittsburgh, time=(before=10:00))

Here, the four levels are: 1) *c:*, indicating that the speaker is the traveller and that he 2) asked for information *request-information*, concerning 3) flights *features+flight* 4) from Verona to Pittsburgh with departure time before ten am *(origin=verona, destination=pittsburgh, time=(before=10:00))*.

The architecture of the IF permits to clearly distinguish the domain dependent part (concepts and arguments) from the domain independent one (speaker and speech-act). This facilitates the porting from a domain to another. For example, moving from the hotel reservation domain to the travel information one will only require the addition of new concepts and new arguments.

5 The system

As said, the C-STAR consortium consists of several partners from many different countries. Each partner is required to develop system modules for its own language; the interface between each pair of partners/languages is provided by IF representations, which are sent and received through the geographical network. Partners can organize their modules the way they like, provided that the IF interface works properly.

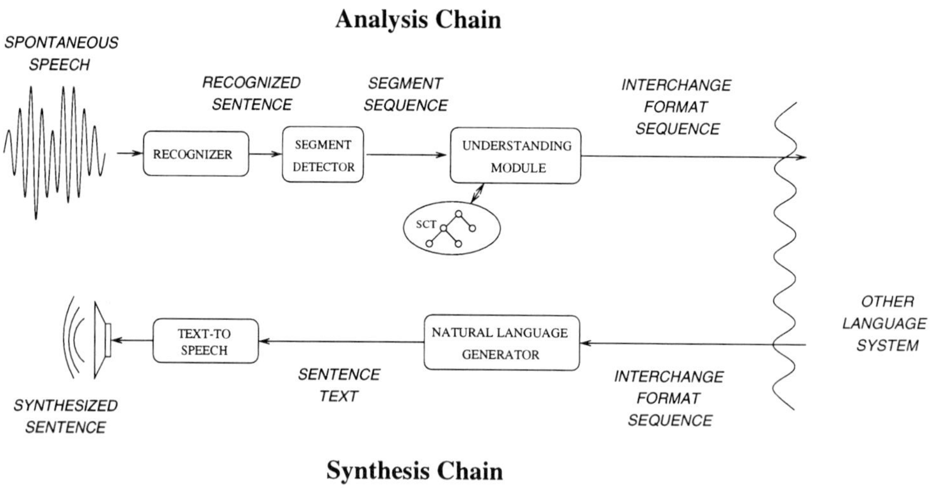

Fig. 1. System architecture.

At ITC–irst, two main processing chains have been implemented for Italian: the analysis chain and the synthesis chain (cf. Figure 1). The analysis chain converts the input speech signal into a (sequence of) IF representation(s) by going through: (1) the *recognizer*, which produces a sequence of word hypotheses for the input signal; (2) the *segment detector* which detects semantic boundaries inside the utterance on the basis of acoustic-prosodic features and simple statistics on words in correspondence of such boundaries [8]; (3) the *understanding module*, which exploits a *robust parser* and a statistical classifier to deliver IF representations [1].
The synthesis chain starts from an IF expression and produces a synthesized audio natural language message expressing that content. It consists of two mod-

ules. The *generator* first converts the IF representation into a more language oriented representation and then integrates it with domain knowledge to produce sentences in Italian [12]. Such sentences feed a speech synthesizer, namely the text-to-speech system Eloquens® developed by CSELT.

5.1 The Acoustic Recognizer

The goal of the speech recognizer is to find the word sequence that most likely caused the acoustic signal. For each sentence hypothesis, the likelihood can be computed on the basis of two probabilistic models: the *Acoustic Model* (AM), concerning the relation between each word and the acoustic signal, and the *Language Model* (LM), which considers how words are concatenated in a sentence. Speech sound is first converted into electrical signals by a microphone; the analog signal is then digitalized through sampling and quantizing; the digital signal is finally processed to estimate significative parameters [10].
The recognizer used in our system is based on the platform developed at ITC-irst [7] for Italian large vocabulary dictation tasks (20K words). It uses an AM based on hidden Markov models (HMMs) [13] of phonemes. Each vocabulary word is modeled by concatenating the sequence of phoneme HMMs corresponding to its pronunciation. HMMs were initialized on a phonetically rich database, APASCI, collected at ITC-irst [1], while a re-training phase was carried out on the training set of the spontaneous speech corpus considered here. Specific models were trained for most frequent extra linguistic phenomena. The adopted LM is represented by Shift-β trigram [7] including extra linguistic models as if they were real words. Such a model gives the probability of each sentence segment consisting of three words. These probabilities can then be combined together to find the LM probability of each possible sentence.
Intra-word acoustic constraints (phonetic transcriptions of words) and inter-word linguistic constraints (trigram language model) are compiled into a sharing-tail tree-based network that defines the search space, at phoneme level, for the decoding algorithm [3]. For each word, only a single canonical pronunciation is considered. Extra linguistic models are inserted into the search space by using their trigram distributions as given by the LM.

5.2 The Understanding Module

The input to the understanding module is represented by a sequence of words and speech phenomena like pauses and hesitations corresponding to a *semantic unit*, that is, a part of the utterance identified by two semantic boundaries. The role of the understanding module is to construct the corresponding IF representation.
The first level of the IF representation, i.e. the speaker, is known. The rest of the IF representation is built in two successive phases, each devoted to a single task. In the first phase the utterance is processed by a local parser which tries to extract information concerning argument-value pairs. In the second phase, a statistical classifier identifies the speech act and the concept sequence.

Therefore, our system conceives the first task (identifying argument-value pairs) as requiring consideration of the syntactic structure of portions of the utterance. The second task (building the speech-act and the concept sequence) is seen as a classification one in such a way that the word sequence output by the acoustic recognizer (and processed by the local preprocessor) is the object to be classified by means of IF labels.

Among all possible approaches to the classification task, the extreme variability or total absence of a global structure in the input utterance suggests the application of a statistical based approach. In fact, if a corpus of example utterances is available, it is necessary to find all and only the elements of the input utterance which have highest correlation with the IF label. Therefore, we use a preprocessor to extract the phrases which are relevant for the IF construction. The classification proper is left to a statistical classifier based on Semantic Classification Trees (SCTs) [6], which are derived from CARTs (Classification and Regression Trees) [2].

SCTs can be automatically built from a corpus of labelled examples (training set). In the current implementation [5], a variant of the procedure described in [6], the classification is based on the presence of particular *keywords.*

In a way, keywords are the simplest and most straightforward elements which can be identified in a sentence, while in principle statistical classifiers could be applied to any structure built on the input. On the other hand, in the system here considered, the application of SCTs is preceded by the application of the local parser which, in addition to extracting the arguments, preprocesses the input data by substituting important phrases with labels which can be used as keywords. In this way, the statistical relevance of the data improves because equivalent phenomena are clustered in the same event.

5.3 The generator

The goal of the generator is to produce the Italian translation for the source sentences encoded in IF representations. Since IF is in not a linguistically oriented semantic representation, first the generator uses a sentence planning module mapping IF into a functional representation similar to the f-structure of Lexical Functional Grammar. This step usually does not take place in current machine translation systems.

The sentence planning algorithm allows for three strategies, which can be mixed. *General heuristics* are used to map parts of the IF representation in linguistically relevant functions. These rules give medium quality results, but can be applied in a large number of cases. However, before resorting to these general rules, the system can consider more *specific* ones which produce a more accurate output but can be applied in a smaller number of cases. Should both strategies fail, a *backup strategy* applies, which merely translates the components of the IF representation, see [12].

The actual generation step makes wide use of flexible templates, which guarantee high efficiency and at the same time allow us an elegant treatment of linguistic phenomena such as phonological adjustment, morphological agreement and syntactic constituency.[3]

6 Conclusions and future work

At present, a demo version of the Italian modules is available. All the analysis chain modules were developed by using `C/C++`. Some simple filters are written in `perl`. The synthesis chain modules are implemented in `Prolog`. The user interface is written in `Tcl-tk`, but currently a new version in `Java` is under developement. All these choices guarantee a high degree of portability of the system across hardware platforms and operating systems (OSs).
The current demo is running both on PC and laptop equipped with `Linux` OS.

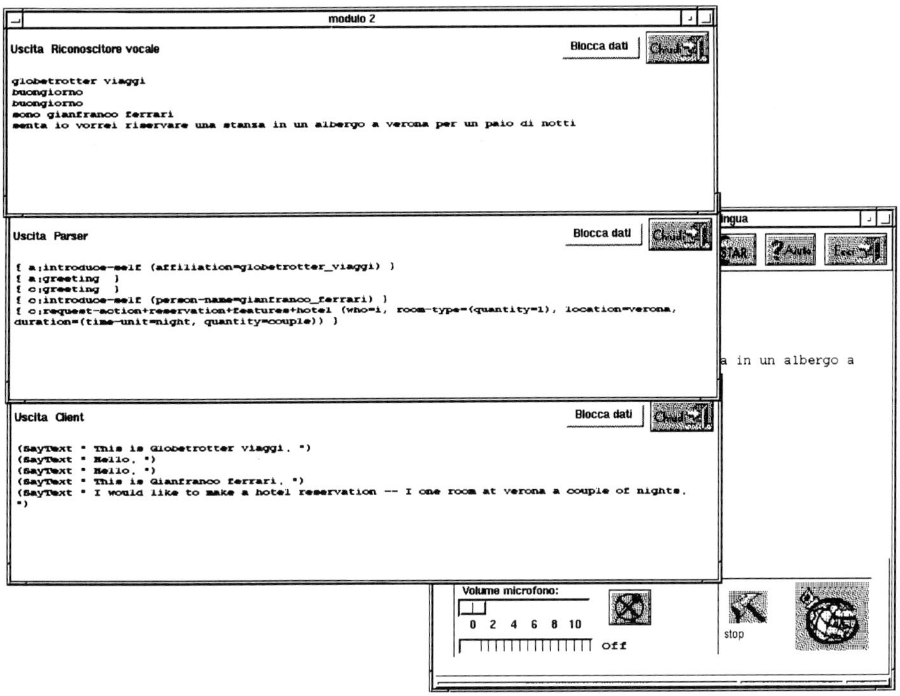

Fig. 2. Interface of the Italian-English demo.

[3] Our templates are expressed in Hyper Text Planning Language (HTPL) [4]. An HTPL expression can include different kinds of objects: linguistic items at different degrees of abstraction (from frozen strings to semantic representations), calls to template definitions, slot specifications to be filled at run time, conditional and disjunctive expressions, operators allowing to specify character formatting, speech syntesis annotations.

Other versions are available for `Unix`-based workstations (Sun and HP). Currently, the recompilation of all the modules under `Windows NT/95` OSs is being completed. In Figure 2 a screen dump of the Italian-English system is shown, which integrates to our modules those developed and implemented at the Interactive Systems Laboratory at CMU (Pittsburgh, USA).

References

1. B. Angelini, M. Cettolo, A. Corazza, D. Falavigna, and G. Lazzari. Multilingual Person to Person Communication at IRST. In *Proceedings of the IEEE International Conference on Acoustics, Speech and Signal Processing*, Munich, Germany, April 21-24 1997.
2. L. Breiman, J. Friedman, R. Olshen, and C. Stone. *Classification and Regression Trees.* Wadsworth Inc., 1984.
3. F. Brugnara and M. Cettolo. Improvements in Tree-based Language Model Representation. In *Proceedings of the 4th European Conference on Speech Communication and Technology*, pages 1797–1800, Madrid, Spain, 1995.
4. Nicola Cancedda, Gjertrud Kamstrup, Emanuele Pianta, and Ettore Pietrosanti. Sax: Generating hypertext from sadt models. In *Third Workshop on Applications of Natural Language to Information Systems*, Vancouver, 1997.
5. M. Cettolo, A. Corazza, and R. De Mori. Language Portability of a Speech Understanding System. *Computer Speech and Language*, 12:1–21, 1998.
6. R. De Mori and R. Kuhn. The Application of Semantic Classification Trees to Natural Language Understanding. *IEEE Transactions on Pattern Analysis and Machine Intelligence*, 17(5):449–460, May 1995.
7. M. Federico, M. Cettolo, F. Brugnara, and G. Antoniol. Language Modelling for Efficient Beam-Search. *Computer Speech and Language*, 9(4):353–379, 1995.
8. M.Cettolo and D.Falavigna. Automatic Detection of Semantic Boundaries based on Acoustic and Lexical Knowledge. In *Proceeding of the International Conference on Spoken Language Processing*, Sidney, Australia, 1998. To appear.
9. R. C. Moore. Integration of Speech with Natural Language Understanding. In D. B. Roe and J. G. Wilpon, editors, *Voice Communication between Human and Machines*, pages 254–271. National Academy Press, Washington D.C., USA, 1994.
10. R.De Mori, editor. *Spoken Dialogues with Computers.* Academic Press, San Diego, CA, 1998.
11. Fabio Pianesi and Lucia M. Tovena. Using the interchange format for encoding spoken dialogues. In *Proceedings of AMTA SIG-IL Second Workshop on Interlinguas and Interlingual Approaches*, pages –, 1998.
12. E. Pianta and L.M. Tovena. Generating with flexible templates from C-STAR Interchange Format. Technical Report 9808-04, Istituto per la Ricerca Scientifica e Tecnologica, ITC–irst, 1998.
13. L.R. Rabiner. A tutorial on hidden Markov models and selected applications in speech recognition. In A. Waibel and K.F. Lee, editors, *Readings in Speech Recognition*, pages 267–296. Morgan Kaufmann Publishers, San Mateo, CA, 1990.

Hotel Reservation Systems on the Internet – Custom Design vs. Standard Software

Sedat Güler; Stefan Klein
Institute for Information Systems, University of Muenster
{gueler|klein}@wi.uni-muenster.de

1 Introduction

The fast proliferation of electronic commerce applications on the Web has led to the emergence of a new field of research: Web Engineering or Web Information Systems Development (see e.g. the CACM special July 1998[3]). While Web Engineering initially was little more then the analysis of adequate tools for HTML or discussions about good HTML design, it has now become a full fledged area of software engineering with topics such as Web site modelling and maintenance, database integration, Java programming, choice of development tools etc. In many ways extreme contingencies for the development of Web software, such as time pressure, brief development and modification cycles, a trend towards throw-away software, highly volatile development environment in terms of tools, standards etc. may require specific methods and architectures. While their functional scope is expanding, Web application become more and more differentiated, in particular industry and application context specific.

Online booking and reservation systems in tourism are in most cases self developed, standard software is rarely used. We would therefore like to challenge this approach and discuss whether software packages, which are designed to sell consumer products via the internet, can be used to sell tourism products, e.g. a hotel room or even a complete journey. However, available standard software is focused to sell *physical* products, which can be described by certain attributes like size, weight, price per unit etc. Products have a certain article number, the availability can be checked by the stock level. So-called "shops" are often preconfigured and only little adaptation is necessary. Solutions for the tourism industry have to be different because the requirements are much more complex: the goods, e.g. hotel rooms, are dependent of the time period and are of perishable nature.

Following a software life cycle model we will focus on the identification of tourism industry and case specific requirements. Tourism Web applications are conceptually challenging because functional specification and technology selection are intertwined. Applications like TIScover, Expedia or Travelocity follow the rules of tourism as much as the rules of EC on the medium WWW. Building on the requirements analysis, we will assess development strategies based on existing tools and standard packages vs. individual programming.

We will present a prototype for a touristic information system in the Muensterland region which is conceptually based on TIS but has a different software architecture. Furthermore the user interface has been modified. Based on the experience with the prototype development we would like to discuss the raised issues of WebEngineering and suggest a few areas for future work.

2 Framework

In order to scrutinise the specific requirements for the development of tourism Web applications we have sketched a simple framework (Fig 1).

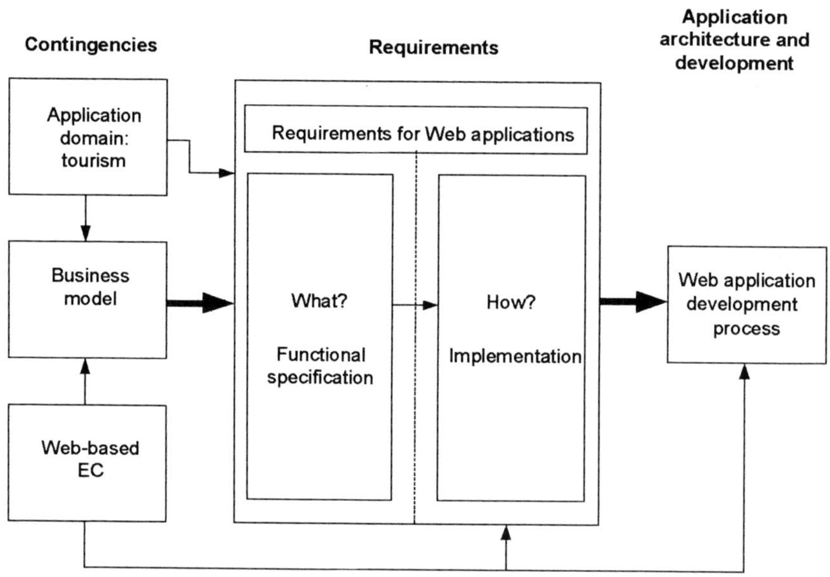

Fig 1: Determinants of Web application development in tourism

Three contingencies determine the requirements for Web applications: characteristics of the application domain, specific features and rules of Web-based EC and EC business models.

2.1 Application domain

Several authors have tried to capture the specific requirements tourism poses to IT support [14], [18], [19]. The major dimensions are:

- fragmented industry structure,
- a market of global suppliers and customers,
- almost anybody is a potential customer, leading to a high degree of diversity and heterogeneity,

- tourism products are typically perishable products with a high information content, their electronic representation has to take the temporal structure into account.

Shrinking airfares among other factors are increasing global competition of destinations. Changing patterns of customer behaviour, such as more frequent but shorter trips, more flexible products, last-second booking, are adding to the requirements for tourism IS:

2.2 Web-based EC

While the World Wide Web has been invented as a hypermedia communication infrastructure for academic purposes, it has been quickly appropriated by other user groups and turned into a differentiated and versatile communication environment or medium. In comparison to other communication media, the Web is characterized by the combination and integration of four functional properties.

- *Information and knowledge representation.* The Web enables the representation of complex hypermedia information, including three dimensional virtual reality representations (VRML). Powerful retrieval and search mechanisms assist the user to locate information in a global network of information providers.
- *Communication and interaction:* The Web has become a new communication channel among business and between business and consumers. It integrates various communication services such as email, file transfer, exchange of forms and video conferencing. Empirical evidence proves that the Web has considerably lowered the communication barrier: those people that have access to this medium communicate much more. Companies that are on the Web, typically receive much more customer communication and feedback than before. While the Web was initially seen as a medium of customer initiated advertising, recent developments like WebCasting have enabled companies to actively send information to selected customers.
- *Community building.* The analysis of successful commercial Web applications has shown that most of them initiate or support online-communities [15]. People are not only on the Web because they want to have access to the world's largest pool of information but they use it as a medium to communicate and establish virtual communities [2]. The concept is similar to that of relationship marketing.
- *Business transactions.* The commercial usage of the Web ultimately focuses on the execution and support of all phases of business transactions. The challenge and attraction of this medium lies in the combination and integration of the various ways of communication, interaction and transactions.

2.3 Business model

Successful Web sites have a clear value proposition that often is related to other communication media, e.g. convenience, accessibility, decoupling of time and space, customization, etc. The overall challenge of this new interactive medium of communication and commerce is to "mobilize customers to create their *own* value from the company's various offerings" [13]. The business model of TISCover, which has been the reference model for our prototype, reflects both, the characteristics of tourism and rules and requirements of Web-based EC.

TISCover is a destination-oriented information platform with a focus on regional small and medium sized tourism suppliers [19]. While it attempts to facilitate - as application domain - incoming tourism into Tirol, the major tourist destination in Austria, it does so on a Web platform. Thus the business model is inseparably linked to the underlying technology. Table 1 gives a stylized description of TISCover's features.

Dimensions of the Web	Features of TISCover
Information and knowledge representation	Comprehensive destination information with a focus on hotels.
Communication	E-Mail communication.
Community building	Extranet for regional tourism suppliers.
Business transactions	Hotel reservations and bookings.

Table 1: Dimensions of the Web and features of TISCover

TISCover features different modes of communication for different target groups: an Intranet for the Tirol Tourist Board, an Extranet for the participating suppliers and an open part for everybody, targeted at potential visitors and guests. TISCover functions as intermediary, or rather cybermediary, between suppliers and customers. Consequently, TISCover has to maintain huge amounts of data with more than 100.000 Web pages covering among others 1.500 local or regional tourist boards and over 15.000 suppliers.

Based on the brief sketch of contingencies and preliminary design decisions we have inferred IS development and implementation requirements.

2.4 Functional specification and conditions

The functional specification of TISCover has been based on previous versions of TIS, which already covered the core functions, and extensions which were enabled by the technology or driven by the market, in particular competition from other tourism Web sites. By comparison, TISCover's content has become much more comprehensive, the user interface has become more flexible and user-friendly, the interactivity has been expanded.

TISCover has to meet the standard of the leading tourism Web sites in terms of concurrency, topicality, availability etc. The user interface has to meet the needs of heterogeneous customers from various countries.

Functional requirements	Implementation requirements
Perishable products , Huge amount of data; frequently updated, from multiple sources, Complex network of content	Data base: server/client; replication mechanisms Service levels should be guaranteed Economically, technically and informationally sustainable application Scalable to increasing load Maintenance a) technical b) content Referential integrity (pointers) when changing layout/content
Overview of available products is necessary; Products have to be explained	Electronic product catalogue
Purchase of product should be possible	Booking functionality; secure transactions; (electronic) payment
Market/customer	
Experienced & inexperienced customers	Different modes of navigation; guided tour for newbies
Different customer preferences (business & leisure tourists)	User profiles; appropriate navigation; adequate representation of content; graphical user interface (GUI)
Customers from different countries	Multiple languages
Target groups: Tourists Suppliers Tirol Tourist Board	Access modes: (public) application Extranet for data management and management information Intranet for marketing analysis

Table 2: Basic requirements for TISCover

2.5 Implementation

The ongoing progress and differentiation in Web applications has led to a dynamic development of a rich set of software products, development and administration tools. While the developer has ample choice, the decision making process can be quite difficult and challenging. A brief analysis has confirmed that there is not a single integrated product that fulfils nearly all of the requirements. Consequently a layered and modular architecture has to be developed and it has to be secured that the individual modules that come to the market in a very high frequency, often barely tested, fit with each other.

2.6 Application architecture and development

As the Web is emerging quickly in almost any dimension, like users, suppliers, infrastructure, applications, software, standards, we will outline, based on anecdotal evidence, some general classes of software products and tools for the development of tourism Web sites. We will discuss and assess architecture options. While the findings are only preliminary, they shall nevertheless convey a better sense about on-going trends in Web Information Systems and their implications for tourism.

3 Description of prototype

We have used TISCover as a pattern or template for TIM (Tourismus Information Münsterland) and tried to reverse engineer the basic ideas of TISCover using standard software. Our aim was to examine if a system that offers the functionalities of TISCover can be realized by standard tools and whether any savings of time and effort can be achieved.

TIM, a functional prototype was implemented by 7 graduate students between December 1997 to February 1998 using Microsoft Merchant Server 1.0. The fo-

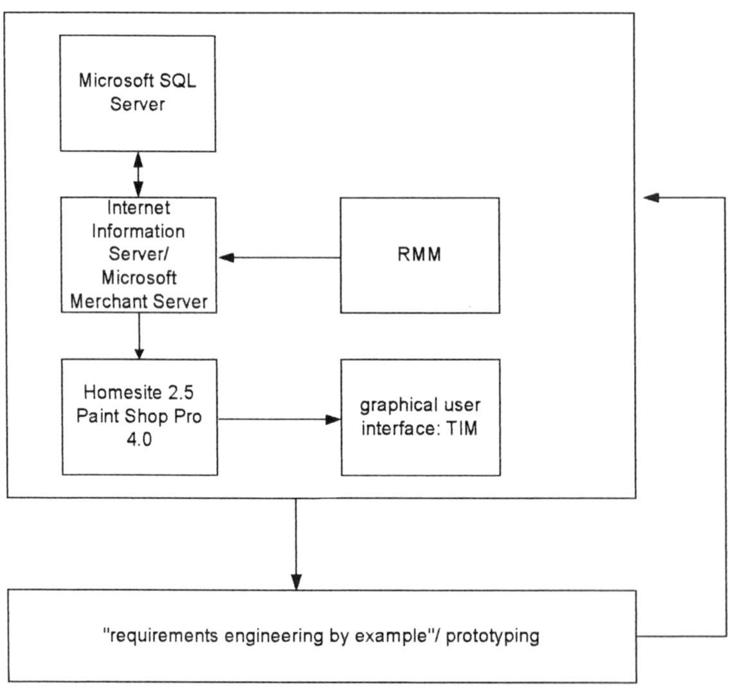

Fig 2: Web application development process for TIM

cus of TIM is on providing relevant information about hotels and regions and enabling the booking process.

3.1 Web application development process

For the application development process (Fig 1) the following tools and packages have been used:

- RMM was used as design and documentation tool.
- Microsoft Merchant Server 1.0 was the server platform.
- Home Site 2.5 was used as an additional tool for building HTML templates.
- Most of the user interface, such as navigation, guided tour, were individually developed.

Fig 2 gives a stylised overview of the development steps and modules.

3.2 Design with RMM

In a first step the relevant data were modelled. For this purpose the Relationship Management Methodology (RMM) was chosen because it allows to model the basic navigational structure of a Web site. Fig 3 shows the simplified navigation structure of the TIM-site from a customer's view.

Starting with *main.html* the customer can get information about regions, towns and villages and hotels. At a certain hotel he can request information about offers from this hotel. The remaining templates show how the booking process takes place. The slice-symbol indicates that there is a corresponding database-based content to the templates. For details see [8].

3.3 Microsoft Merchant Server and Microsoft SQL Server

We have chosen the Microsoft Merchant Server because it promises a higher degree of openness and support for the integration of self-developed components compared to other commerce servers. Microsoft has positioned its Merchant Server as a "platform" for programmers/ developers who can modify components for their purposes.

3.3.1 System architecture

A Merchant Server-Store consists of a number of Web pages which are generated dynamically by database queries. The appearance of the Web pages is defined by Merchant Server templates, which consist of standard HTML code and server-commands. The server commands (like *fetchrows, money, xlink*, see below) control which data are shown on a Web page and which SQL-queries are performed.

The database contains the relevant data about customers, about product description and price and statistical information.

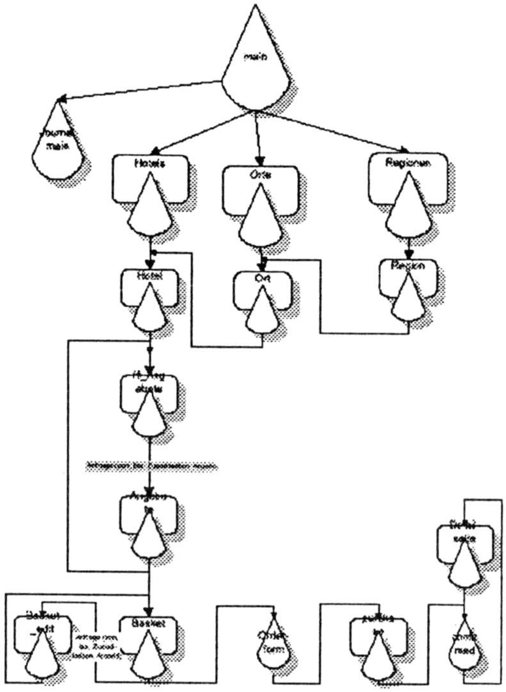

Fig 3: RMM model of TIM

The Merchant Server registry mainly contains data about country settings, server addresses, local indexes, components used for order-processing etc. Special entries in the registry define what directories of the shop are visible to the customers and to which directories the store-administrator has access. The so-called "order-pipeline", e.g. which components are used during order processing, is defined in the registry. Important are database-related entries in the registry: the names and locations of required tables and queries are also defined in the registry.

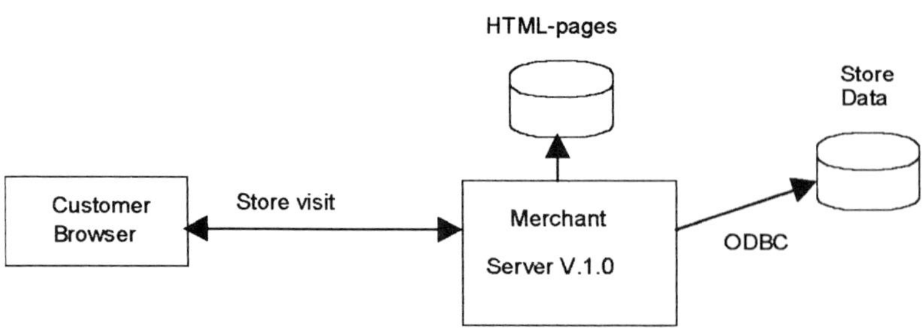

Fig 4: Architecture of the Microsoft Merchant Server

HTML templates consist of server-commands for page generation and standard HTML code.

Together with the Merchant Server four pre-configured shops (called "starter stores“) are delivered which Microsoft claims are sufficient for most purposes. We will briefly explain the functionality of one of these stores – the “clock peddler shop“- and then illustrate how we modified the “clock peddler shop“ for our purposes.

3.3.2 The Merchant Server concept

The basic structure of the database and its tables are outlined in the following figure and table.

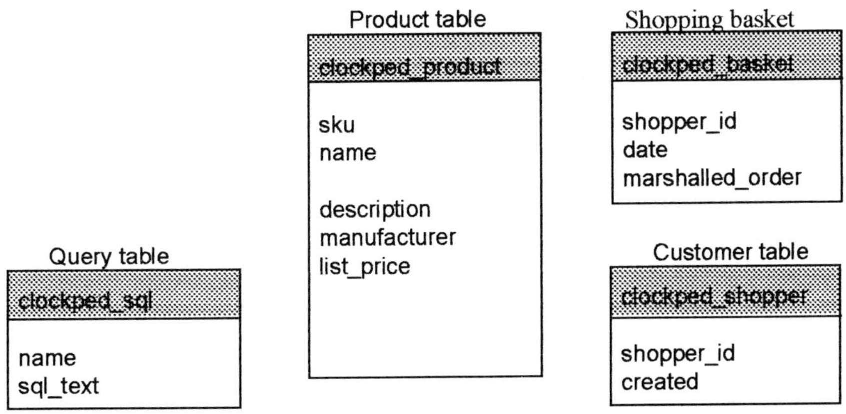

Fig 5: Database scheme of the clock-peddler (simplified)

Table name	Description
Clockped_sql:	Stores all SQL queries needed to generate the Web pages and or for order processing. Has to be inserted into the registry.
Clockped_product:	Stores information about the products.
Clockped_basket:	Stores orders of the customer. Has to be inserted into the registry.
Clockped_shopper:	A unique customer identification (shopper_id) is created by the system and is stored in the customer table.

Table 3: Clock peddler tables

Database-related entries in the registry are:

- "db_table_shopper"="clockped_shopper"
- "db_query_sql"="clockped_sql"
- "db_query_order_product"="product"

The query "product" is defined as ('select' * from clockped_product where SKU= :1').

Several HTML templates are used to generate Web pages during the order-process:

Function	Templates	Description
Presentation of the products	1) product.html	Generates product page
Purchase process	2) basket.html	Generates the shopping basket
	3) orderform.html	Reads address of customer
	4) purchase.html	Reads credit card data
	5) confirmed.html	Shows confirmation to customer when purchase is done

Table 4: Merchant Server HTML templates

Ad 1) The template product.html generates the Web page for every product. Product.html especially uses the already mentioned SQL-query product:

- *[fetchrows product "product" args.sku]* invokes the query "product" and hands over the argument "SKU" [SKU is an acronym for **stock keeping unit**]. The query returns a result from the table clockped_product.
- *[money product.list_price]* requests the attribute list_price of the "product" data.
- *[xlink order.additem SKU=product.sku]* produces a link with the process order.additem. The process order.additem puts the product with the argument SKU into the shopping basket. The order.additem generates a new page and uses the template basket.html for this purpose.

3.3.3 Specific requirements

The product table in "clock peddler" uses SKU as primary key with the list price as attribute. But SKU, designed for physical products, is inadequate in our case: staying in a hotel for two days instead of one is much more complex than buying an additional unit of a physical product. Furthermore different lengths of stay in the same hotel room make it a different product. We also introduced "additional beds" which makes the problem even more complex. An additional bed could be needed when parents want to stay in the same room with their little children. In order to reduce complexity, discounts for certain groups of customers and special seasonal offers were neglected. Besides the problem of finding an appropriate representation of the product, e.g. hotel room, we do not have a list_price to calculate the price of the product.

3.3.4 The design of TIM

The following figure and description illustrate how the booking process was realized, which modules of the Merchant Server were used and which parts of the solution were self-developed.

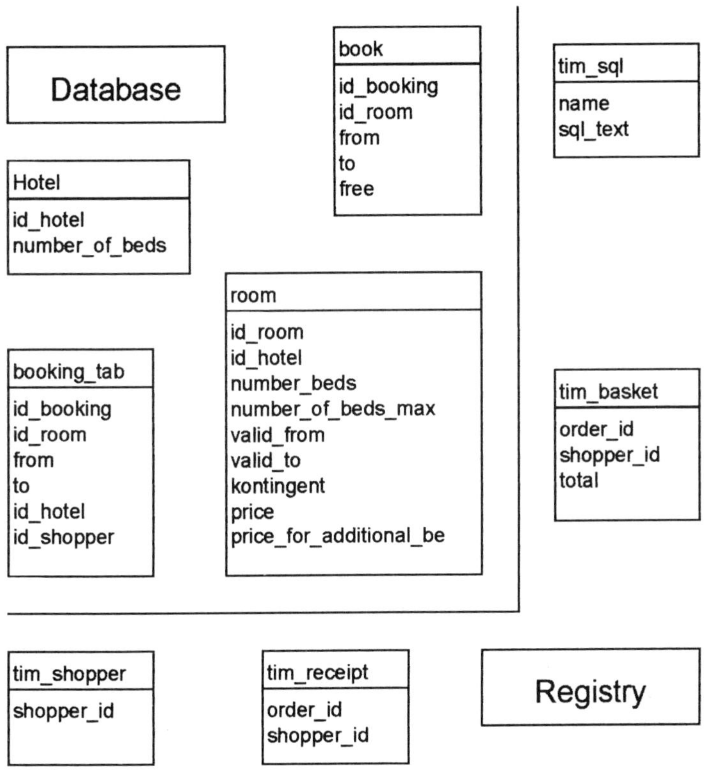

Fig 6: Structure of TIM-database (simplified)

The Merchant Server distinguishes between "normal" tables, SQL-queries and queries which are part of the "order pipeline", i.e. part of the order processing, and therefore need to be entered into the registry.

The SQL-queries are num_booked, booked, "db_query_order_product"="product", room_free. The stored procedure num_booked determines the number of stays already booked for a certain room and period. For this purpose it uses the tables book, booking_tab, room and number_booked.

Whereas the tables hotel and room correspond with the relative "static" part of the room representation the tables number_booked, book and booking_tab are needed to simulate the temporal structure and to check the availability. Tim_sql, tim_receipt, tim_basket, tim_shopper are Merchant Server specific tables needed for order processing. number_booked contains the information how often the requested room the is already booked.

The registry entries are

- "db_table_receipt"="tim_receipt"
- "db_table_sql"="tim_sql"
- "db_table_order"="tim_basket"
- "db_table_shopper"="tim_shopper"
- "db_query_order_product"="product"

The following HTML templates were used.

Function	Templates	Description
Presentation of the products	1a) h_offers.html	Rooms of a hotel for a certain period
	1b) offers.html	1a) with availability check
Purchase process	2) basket.html	
	3) orderform.html	
	4) purchase.html	
	5) confirmed.html	

Table 5: HTML templates of the TIM order process

First of all the representation of our "products" had to be changed: the template product.html was substituted by h_offers.html and offers.html. The remaining templates had to be adjusted to the product representation.

h_offers.html. generates an overview of the rooms a certain hotel offers. The relevant data to be displayed are the rooms of the hotel, the price per night and person for each room, it's number of additional beds and information (if available) about the location/region the hotel is located in.

Instead of invoking *[fetchrows product "product" args.sku]* in the "clock peddler" four different *[fetchrow ...]* commands had to be invoked.[1] By entering the number of requested rooms, the day of arrival and departure and the number of additional beds the customer can see the if the requested room is available by invoking

offers.html (id_room, number, from, to, additional_rooms, argsIDHotel)

offers.html displays the available room the customer has specified in 1a). If the customer wants to book the room it is put –if available- into the shopping basket.

The query room_free first checks if the entered period is valid. If it is valid the query delivers back all relevant data about the hotel and calculates the price per night and person. The queries booked and num_booked check if the room is available e.g. if the contingent is not exhausted. booked invokes the stored-procedure num_booked. The procedure num_booked writes into the table number_booked, how often the room in the requested is already booked. The query num_booked reads the result from the table number_booked.

---

[1] For this purpose the use of additional tables not named in figure 5 are necessary.

The next step is to create a unique id_booking for the table booking_tab. This is done by adding one to the highest entry of all entries in the shopping basket and appending this value to the order_id (table tim_basket). Then an unique SKU has to be generated by linking through concatenation room id and the number of additonal beds, i.e. *concat id_room "xa" number_of_additional_beds "xb"* with "xa" and "xb" as delimiters.

The command [order.additem] puts the room into the shopping basket. The price for the room can be calculated using the query product and the generated SKU:

```
SELECT    room.*, id_room as SKU, (room.number_of_beds * room.price
          + convert (smallint, substring(:1, PATINDEX ('%xa%', :1)+2,
          (PATINDEX('%xb%', :1) – PATINDEX ('%xa%', :1) -2))) *
          bed_extracharge) as list_price
FROM      Room
WHERE     id_room = convert (smallint, substring(:1, 1, PATIN-
          DEX('%xa%, :1)-1))
```

4 Analysis and outlook

It is a common cliché that Web applications can be developed quickly, easily and with limited investment. The development of the past years has led to a high degree of differentiation: At the high end there are huge Web sites with development and maintenance cost in the millions, at the low end there are still the small and simple sites. So what are the lessons learnt from a fairly simple Web application development example?

4.1 Assessment of the prototype

We have shown that a Web Application which enables the basic functionalities of TISCover can be implemented using standard software. By using the "clock peddler" shop as a template we had a running shop from the beginning which simplified "rapid prototyping" for our TIM-shop. Several built-in functions of the Merchant-Server, e.g. administration of customers, were useful. The platform idea of the Merchant Server and the openness of its order pipeline enabled us to use it for a purpose which has been not anticipated by its developers. However, this deviation from the foreseen path had its price. Major problems were:

- Functions, which were not supported by the Merchant Server, were implemented in SQL. With the exception of "concat" the Merchant Server does not provide functions to manipulate strings. The students had to built "workarounds" of complex SQL-queries doing string operations. The SQL-queries consumed most of the time during the implementation process and additionally made the source code difficult to understand.
- The Merchant Server requires that (some) changes have to be made in the registry of Windows NT. In some cases developers/shop administrators and (Windows NT-) system administrators may not be identical and therefor frequent communication between them will be necessary.

- Some missing/false documentation of the Microsoft products, especially the order-pipeline could have been explained in more detail [9], [10].
- Our approach of dynamically generating products had the effect of very long parameter lists.
- The Merchant Server 1.0 does not enable "Active Server Pages" (ASP). However, the successor of the Merchant Server, the site server [0], supports them.

Coming back to the mentioned cliché: TIM has been developed in fact relatively quickly (2 months of preliminary works supported by TISCover and about 3 months for implementation) but it required a basic knowledge of the application area and a sound knowledge of IT. Have the basic requirements (cf Table 2) of TISCover, especially of a economically, technically and informationally sustainable solution, been met by TIM?

- *Scalable to increased load*: We do not have evidence to give a clear indication. We tested TIM with a maximum of a hundred records for each table. The SQL-Server, which is commercially used, should be able to handle quite some load. By using ODBC a distribution of data to several databases is possible.
- *Maintenance (technical):* TIM depends on Microsoft's product strategy.
- *Maintenance (content):* TIM allows the shop manager to create, change, and delete destinations, hotel and rooms by using the browser. Tourism suppliers can, in principle, change the data of their rooms in the same way. The design with RMM proved to be quite useful with respect to maintenance.
- *Referential integrity:* This is a general problem with Web sites. However, during the implementation and test phase layout and content were changed several times without major problems.

4.2 Implications for Web application architectures and Web engineering

Our experience has not led to a clear answer in terms of make-or-buy and customize. We suspect that we will see more hybrid solutions in the future, combining prefabricated modules or components and self-made parts. But what are criteria to decide between customizing and developing?

- When standard products are sold, which are - for example - covered by the functionality of the Merchant Server's starter stores. I.e., if the functionality of the application is covered by the chosen EC package and expected maintenance is low or supported by the package, such a package should be chosen.
- The advantages of integrated EC packages are rapidly decreasing if the application in question is more complex or the Web application comprehends extra features in order to differentiate it from competitors' applications.

- As there is a constant flow of new software tools and the scope of EC packages is changing quickly, it is a challenging task to find which functions (cf Table 2) are provided by packages and which ones need to be developed.

Costs can be categorized into :

- building costs: requirements specification; software development (including license fees and customisation), organisational adaptations;
- maintenance costs: costs for store manager/ system administrator because of regular information updates; modifications caused by changing requirements;
- switching costs: any solution implies investments, switching to another solution, another supplier or even a new release incurs switching costs.[2]

Though it is difficult to estimate these costs it is likely that a completely self-developed solution will have much higher building and maintenance costs than a integrated standard solution. Prototyping helps to assess these costs. As suppliers of EC packages have a strong influence on the cost level, e.g. by providing flexible and simple interfaces or by ensure downward compatibility of new releases, their ability and readiness to provide functionally superior and cost efficient solutions will become a competitive advantage.

While there is a lot of technical literature about hypertext (for literature about HTML, dynamic HTML, XML, SGML and cascading style sheets see for example [6], [7]) and there are many tools to edit a single Web page there are only very few approaches about designing a large Web site: RMM [8], HDM [4] and W3DT [5].

To make things worse, the connection between these "abstract" and "technical" levels is not clear. A potential developer has to find and evaluate isolated information about WebSevers and Database applications for himself. Operational aides and decision criteria for this purpose "Use a tool like X when you want to do Y and your problem is like Z" would be very useful. In our case we have tried to do this. But more general frameworks for the "Web application development process" are required, but only few are available.

With the exception of the distinction between layout and content ("Navigational Design" and "Information Structuring") Fig 7 could be taken from a classical textbook for software engineering (SE), see for example [16]. However aspects like

- the distinction between layout and content, referential integrity is hard to ensure,
- the speed of changing of requirements,
- maintenance is more important than in classical SE,

---

[2] We are planning to migrate TIM to the Microsoft Site Server. It will be made available at http://ec.uni-muenster.de/tis/

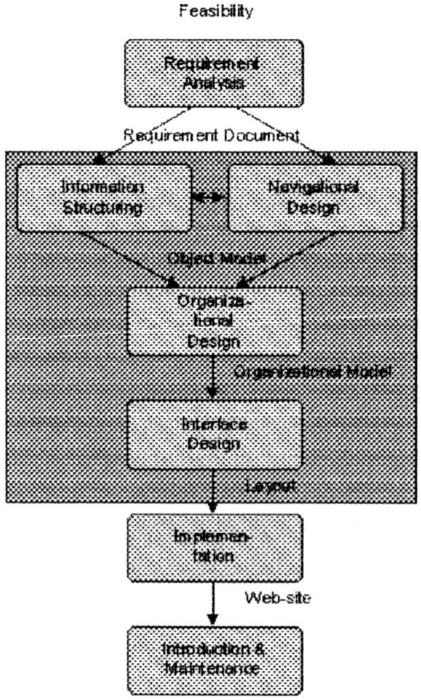

Fig 7: WWW development steps [5]

- different prototyping strategies

need to be explored.

More work is needed to elaborate the specific requirements of Web Engineering, in particular for tourism applications.

References

1. Amirfaiz, F. (1998): Official Microsoft Site Server 2.0 Enterprise Edition Toolkit. Microsoft Press, Redmond. 1998.
2. Armstrong, A.; Hagel, J. (1996): The Real Value of On-line Communities. *In: Harvard Business Review,* 134-141, May-June 1996.
3. *Communications of the ACM,* July 1998, 41(7), 78-118
4. Garzotto, F; Paolini, P.; Schwabe, D. (1993): HDM - A Model-Based Approach to Hypertext Application Design. ACM Transactions of Information Systems, Vol. 11, No. 1, 1-26
5. http://wwwi.wu-wien.ac.at/w3dt/gif/steps.gif [5.10.98]
6. http://www.w3.org [5.10.98]
7. http://www.w3j.com - World Wide Web Journal
8. Isakowitz, T.; Stohr, E., Balasubramanian, P. (1995). "RMM: A Methodology for the Design of Structured Hypermedia Applications". *Communications of the ACM,* 38 (8), 34-44
9. Microsoft: Microsoft Merchant Server 1.0 Documentation.

10. Microsoft: Microsoft SQL Server 6.5 Documentation.
11. Microsoft: http://www.microsoft.com/merchant [30.07.98]. The Website does no longer exist, it is automatically forwarded to [12].
12. Microsoft: http://www.microsoft.com/siteserver/commerce/default.asp [4.10.98].
13. Normann, R; Ramirez, R (1993): From Value Chain to Value Constellation: Designing Interactive Strategy. In: Harvard Business Review, 65-77, July-August 1993.
14. Schertler, W. (1990) Dienstleistungseigenschaften begründen Informationsgeschäfte - dargestellt an Tourismusdienstleistungen. In: Schertler, W. Tourismus als Informationsgeschäft. Überreuter, Wien. 1990, pp. 17 - 42.
15. Selz, D.; Schubert, P. (1998): Web Assessment - A Model for the Evaluation and the Assessment of Successful Electronic Commerce Applications. In: Proceedings of the 31. HICSS. IEEE, Los Alamitos, CA, Vol. 444, 222-231, 1998.
16. Sommerville, I. (1996): Software Engineering. 5th Edition. Addison Wesley 1996. 16-17.
17. Tourismus Information Münsterland (1998): Technical Documentation (in german).
18. Werthner, H. (1996) Design Principles of Tourist Information Systems. In: Klein, S., Schmid, B., Tjoa, A. & Werthner H. (1996) Information and Communication Technologies in Tourism. Proc. 3rd ENTER Conf., Innsbruck, 1996, Springer Verlag, Wien, New York, p. 70-77.
19. Werthner, H.; Klein, S. (1999) Information Technology and Tourism, Springer, Wien, 1999 (in preparation).

The cost and benefits of Information Technology and the Internet for small and medium-sized tourism enterprises

Dr Dimitrios Buhalis
Department of Tourism, University of Westminster
buhalid@wmin.ac.uk

Abstract

Small and medium-sized tourism enterprises (SMTEs) have always suffered from the distribution function of their marketing. Distribution and intermediation are increasingly recognised as critical factors for the competitiveness and success of the tourism industry in general, and SMTEs in particular. In Northern European countries SMTEs need to develop effective distribution channels to approach their independent clientele, while Southern European SMTEs need to provide direct booking mechanisms to reduce their dependency on Tour Operators. Hospitality organisations receive a growing percentage of their customers through the Internet. Hotel chains have demonstrated their commitment to exploit the Internet as a prime distribution tool and have already allocated a significant proportion of their gross annual revenue for technological development. It is reported that in a recent survey 51% of the hotel chains already receive reservations from the Internet, whilst another 33% are planning to do so in the next 12 months. Unless SMTEs improve their visibility on the electronic marketplace they will lose significant market share and perhaps will be unable to survive in the long term.

This paper builds on research undertaken in Greece, France, England and Wales. Most of the research was based on personal interviews and this qualitative analysis of the research results attempts to illuminate the cost and benefits of the SMTEs representation on the Internet and the usage of ITs. This paper demonstrates that gradually SMTEs start to take advantage of the Internet proliferation and gradually develop their presence in the electronic marketplace. This enables them to compete with their larger counterparts at affordable costs. Exploratory research illustrates the factors often considered by SMTEs in adopting ITs and the Internet, whilst a comprehensive cost and benefit analysis is demonstrated. The paper also argues that there is some evidence that investment on electronic presence and distribution through the Internet represents good value for money, as bookings start to materialise for innovative operators. Hence, innovative entrepreneurs who re-engineer their business processes and take advantage of the emerging opportunities will gain major benefits and enhance their profitability and viability in the global marketplace.

The significance of Small and Medium Tourism Enterprises for regional economies

Small and medium enterprises dominate the European economy as illustrated in Table 1. In particular, small and medium tourism enterprises (SMTEs) prevail the tourism and hospitality sectors throughout Europe and offer great benefits to regional development and local economies by diffusing tourist expenditure to local markets. Unlike larger chain-based organisations, they are normally privately owned, family-run, employ local people and purchase goods and services from suppliers within the local economy. SMTEs also provide tourists with direct contact to the character of the destination. It is estimated that 99.95% of the existing 1.41m European HORECA (HOtel REstaurant CAtering) enterprises employ less than 250 employees [20]. SMTEs are not only characterised by their small size, but also by their independence, flexibility, seasonality and often family ownership and management. SMTEs frequently feature informal organisational structures, with the role of family members forming a key component within the decision making process [7].

Table 1: Main indicators of private enterprises in the European Union in 1996

	Very Small	Small	Medium	Large	Total
No of Enterprises (000)	17,285 93%	1,105 5.9%	165 0.9%	35 0.2%	18,590 100%
Employment (1000)	37,000 33.2%	21,110 18.9%	15,070 13.5%	38,220 34.4%	111,410 100%
Average size (employees)	2	20	90	1035	6
Turnover per enterprise (ECU million)	0.2	3	16	175	0.8
Value added per occupied person (1000 ECU)	30	40	50	55	40
Share of labour cost in value added %	38	63	60	53	53

Source: [20] European Commission, 1997, The European Observatory for SMEs, Brussels

However, research into the marketing and management of SMTEs suggests that they are increasingly threatened by the growing concentration and globalisation of tourism supply, as well as by internal weaknesses, namely lack of professionalism and inadequacy of management and marketing skills. They also lack economies of scale available to larger, often chain-based, accommodation establishments in terms of access to necessary capital, human resources, marketing expertise and technology and are frequently over-dependant on few distribution partners. Insufficient formal education or training also means that proper business practices and skills are often absent, placing SMTEs at a competitive disadvantage. As a result, they are unable to market their products adequately and suffer a wide range of deficiencies, which have dramatic effects on their profitability and ability to survive in the emerging global competition era [7,11,17,22].

ITs revolution and Internet: New threats and opportunities for SMTEs

The development of Information Technologies (ITs) may threaten the existence of the traditional SMTEs. More people use ITs (including computer reservation systems (CRS), Global Distribution Systems (GDSs) and the Internet), to locate and purchase tourism and accommodation products. Thus, SMTEs may find themselves becoming isolated from the marketplace and face severe competitive disadvantages, should they fail to develop suitable interfaces [2,3,4,13]. However, it becomes evident that competent accommodation operators, regardless of their size or location, perceive the Internet as a major opportunity which will enable them to improve their interactivity with their consumers and other stakeholders. Consequently they invest heavily in technology in order to improve their efficiency and enhance their presence in the electronic marketplace. Tellini [28] demonstrates several models of hotel promotion featured on the Internet and demonstrates that the whole range of accommodation establishments is represented.

Research in 575 larger hotels globally, as illustrated in Table 2, demonstrates that most companies plan to increase their expenditure on ITs dramatically. They also regard investment on ITs as part of their strategic development. Most of the major hotel chains have already doubled their ITs investment budget for the next five years and they aim to develop systems which will empower their long term interactivity and profitability [23].

Table 2 Expected expenditure on IT investments by hotels in the next five years

Approximately how much will be spent on technology during the next five years?					
N=512	Less than $50,000	$50,000-$249,000	$250,000-$499,000	$500,000 or more	No answer
	14%	38%	22%	19%	6%

Approximately what percentage of gross revenues will be spent on technology during the next five years?						
N=63	Less than 1%	1% - 2%	2% -3%	3%-4%	More than 4%	No answer
	11%	21%	33%	21%	8%	6%

Source: adapted from [23] Hensdill,C.,1998, Hotels technology survey, Hotels, p.51.

The development of the electronic tourism marketplace through the Internet

The Internet and the ITs revolution have introduced a wide range of new marketing tools which are both accessible and affordable for smaller organisations and hence can also be regarded as a major opportunity [27,5,19]. The proliferation of the Internet revolutionises all best practices. The Internet is doubling every 100 days and electronic businesses should reach £178 billion by 2002 [1]. It is predicted that by the year 2000 over 700 million people will have access to the Internet and that by 2001 e-mail will outstrip conventional mail [29]. Weinstein commenting on the possibility of 500,000 to 750,000 on-line hotel bookings by 1998 comments that hotels that are not featured on the Internet "will be lost" [29]. Although GDSs currently dominate hotel bookings as they represent 54% of the hotel bookings made by travel agencies (whilst 24% came from central reservation facilities, 17% directly to the property and 5% non specific)[30], the Internet emerges as the prime media for receiving travel bookings from individuals. Hence, technology has pervasive applications and ITs penetration within the accommodation industry seems inevitable. "It is no longer a question of whether to computerise, but which system will give the most benefits and should be installed first" [25]. Understanding the pull and push factors for adapting ITs in SMTEs is therefore of great importance for assisting SMTEs to adapt to the new realities [14].

Perhaps more importantly for the commercial viability of SMTEs' Internet presence is whether hospitality organisations will be able to receive bookings through the Internet. Surprisingly, a great number of hotels recently surveyed already receive bookings through the Internet and the majority of the remaining properties develop their facilities in order to be able to generate Internet bookings in the near future. TravelWeb (www.travelweb.com) which already represents 18,000 hotels belonging to 90 chains illustrates the scale of on-line representation and opportunities emerging on the Internet. About 17,000 of these hotels are bookable on-line and the site attracts 6.5 million page accesses per month. At the end of 1996 TravelWeb generated $6.5 million as annual net reservation revenue, whilst the total predicted on-line travel sales by the year 2000 is expected to reach $4.7 billion [22]. Dennis [18] also illustrates that innovative and advanced hospitality organisations can benefit enormously from their Internet presence. Marriott (marriott.com) already enjoys "13,000 visits per day and is now conducting well over $1.5 million of business every month over the net". This performance not only increased the revenue and market share of the company, but it also reduced its distribution, promotion and marketing costs contributing directly to the bottom line.

However, as demonstrated in Figure 1, not only is it disappointing that only 39% of independent properties currently receive Internet bookings, in comparison to 51% and 46% for hotel chains and management companies respectively, but also 26% of independent properties are not even planning to develop their facilities in comparison to 15% and 13% from hotel chains and management companies [23]. The future of SMTEs which will be unavailable on the electronic marketplace and thus inaccessible to consumers and intermediaries is questionable. It seems therefore that independent properties will lose market share, increase their dependence on intermediaries and jeopardise their profitability, unless of course they develop their Internet presence and interactivity as part of their marketing strategy.

Figure 1: Using the Internet for reservations by accommodation establishments

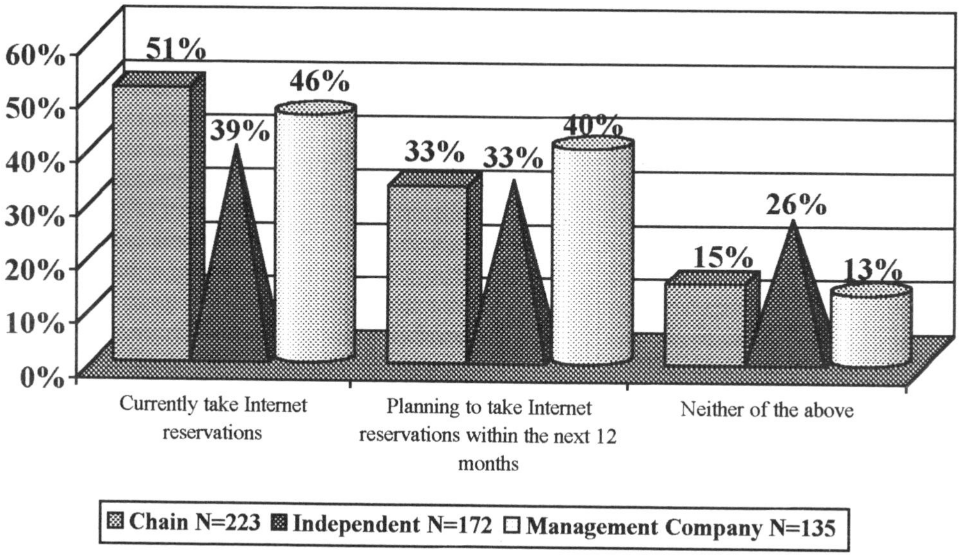

Source: Adapted from [23] Hensdill,C.,1998, Hotels technology survey, Hotels, February.

Cost and benefit analysis of SMTEs presence on the Internet.

The lack of professionalism, technical and managerial skills often observed in SMTEs effectively means that a thorough cost and benefit analysis is rarely undertaken in order to decide whether ITs will be utilised and whether an Internet presence will be developed. Often SMTEs, forced by persuasive salesmen, follow a piecemeal approach in purchasing hardware and software they do not necessarily understand and appreciate. This is often the reason for the lack of any evidence between the ITs expenditure and productivity in

SMTEs [26]. However, the attitude and enthusiasm of knowledgeable decision-makers, often determined by their young age and higher educational level, have consistently been identified to produce a positive correlation between the productivity of the enterprise and the level of ITs utilisation [8,26,15].

The willingness of SMTEs to spend on ITs and their expected returns on their investment need further investigation. Research in Greece, Wales, France and England [8, 13, 14, 15, 12] demonstrates that entrepreneurs compare their Internet presence with conventional advertising in catalogues and brochures. Designing and maintaining an Internet presence can cost as little as £300 pounds per year [27]. This compares favourably with a single advertisement in the travel section of a Sunday newspaper or a single advertisement in one guidebook. The short life expectancy of an advert in a newspaper or a magazine effectively means that there is a much greater possibility to break even by advertising on the Internet rather than in conventional media. The rule of thumb in the industry is therefore that SMTEs can break-even for a modest presence on the Internet by generating as little as 5-10 bookings per year. Enthusiastic Internet and IT users who appreciate the power of interactivity and electronic marketing generate a much greater number of bookings and gain greater benefits [8, 13, 14, 15,12].

Table 3 illustrates a comprehensive framework of all cost and benefit elements for developing an Internet presence for SMTEs. All items have been suggested as important during discussions with entrepreneurs and tourism marketing experts. It is illustrated that the majority of the costs and benefits are management and marketing based, rather than IT based. Hence it can be concluded that competent and innovative entrepreneurs will find the Internet more beneficial than their counterparts who lack marketing or management skills, abilities and knowledge. It is evident therefore that the costs can be reduced by intensive management, marketing and IT training for SMTEs which will enable them to develop a more comprehensive marketing strategy and to utilise ITs as a strategic tool for their long term development.

Not only several SMTEs appear to have developed their own Internet site but also a number of new dedicated sites promote exclusively SMTEs and B&Bs [12]. The size and prices charged by SMTEs are not barriers to establishing their Internet presence. This is supported by recent research which demonstrates that with technology costs falling and hotel revenues rising, expenditure on technology is no longer the main concern for hoteliers [23]. It is evident therefore that once the hype about the Internet has elapsed, some SMTEs realised that great opportunities emerge for promotion and distribution of their products.

Hewson [24] illustrates how a six bedroom guest house in the West Country in the UK introduced a web page using a PC running Windows 95 Office software. The proprietor

Table 3 Cost and benefit analysis for developing Internet presence for SMTEs

COSTS

- Cost of purchasing hardware, software and communication package
- Training cost of users
- Design and construction of internet presence
- Cost of hosting the site on a reliable server
- On-going maintenance and regular updating
- Marketing the Internet service and registration of domain
- Development of procedures for dealing with Internet presence
- Commissions for purchases on line by intermediaries
- Advertising fees for representation in search engines and other sites
- Interconnectivity with travel intermediaries such as TravelWeb, ITN, Expedia

BENEFITS

- Direct bookings, often intermediaries and commission free
- Global distribution of multimedia information and promotional material
- Low cost of providing and distributing timely updates of information
- Global presence on the Internet, 24 hours a day, 365 days a year
- Durability of promotion (in comparison to limited life of printed advertising in press)
- Reduction of promotional cost and reduction of brochure waste
- Great degree of attention by visitors to web site
- Reduction of time required for transactions and ability to offer last minute promotions
- Low marginal cost of providing information to additional users
- Support of marketing intelligence and product design functions
- Development of targeted mailing lists through people who actively request information
- Great interactivity with prospective customers
- Niche marketing to prospective consumers who request to receive information
- Interactivity with local partners and provision of added value products at destinations
- Ability to generate a community feel for current users and prospective customers

designed and maintained the web pages by downloading Netscape for free from the Internet. It is reported that for an average monthly outlay of approximately £41 the establishment achieved monthly bookings amounting to £750. This compared favourably with his advertisement on the Yellow Pages as well as on all other promotions in tourism guides, which the owner was not surprisingly considering relinquishing. Choosing the right search engines and using the right keywords are of paramount importance for attracting hits and bookings. The proprietor of this guesthouse uses words such as B&B, Lodging, Cornwall and United Kingdom. These keywords enhanced the visibility of the property and generated a greater number of bookings. To the degree that Internet users are more affluent, professionals and better educated people, they can match the profile of independent travellers. Hence the Internet can enable SMTEs to develop their target markets and reduce their dependence on intermediaries [8, 13, 14, 15,12].

A word of conclusion

Increasingly SMTEs realise the opportunities emerging through the development of the Internet and utilise the new media in order to support the design, promotion and distribution of their products. As Internet users are more likely to be active, independent, educated, affluent and frequent travellers, SMTEs can gain major benefits. A reduction of SMTEs dependence on current distribution channels, i.e. tour operators, travel agencies, travel information centres, tourist guides, will enable them to dissintermediate their distribution channel and perhaps improve their profitability. In addition, enhancing interactivity with consumers will support SMTEs ability to appreciate their needs and requests better and to improve their flexibility and adaptability. Not only can SMTEs reduce their seasonality by producing customised and themed tourism products, but they can also develop individualised bundles of products in order to satisfy niche markets. The Internet empowers the amalgamation of specialised produces as well as promotes and distributes them at a fraction of the time and cost required by conventional media. The fact that SMTEs are family run and managed can create several opportunities as it can enable the creation of authentic local experiences and traditional hospitality. It also enhances the commitment of employees to the enterprise and reduces personnel turnover. However, family members will need to be trained adequately in order to be able to outperform hospitality professionals operating in larger tourism organisations. More importantly SMTEs need to realise that technology and their Internet presence should not be stand-alone initiatives, but they should advocate a revolution of best operational and strategic practices. Hence, a re-engineering of all their strategic and operational practices is required, as well as the development of entrepreneurs' managerial skills and professionalism. Training on marketing and management as well as on the use of ITs will enable SMTEs to appreciate the new developments and take full advantage of the emerging tools. Marketing and management should drive technological development, rather than the opposite. ITs should be regarded as part of the core competence of SMTEs and should attract long term commitment, investment and appreciation.

Finally the development of Destination Integrated Computer Information Reservation Management Systems will enable destinations to develop networks of SMTEs and promote them under their brand name[6,7,9]. This will encourage SMTEs to stop competing fiercely at the destination level, and to develop networks of wealth creation and mutual benefits in order to deliver seamless tourism products and to compete against remote destinations and SMTEs [11]. Cano and Prentice [16] argue that the Internet can provide opportunities for endearment between tourists/consumers and destinations or principals. The ability of destination organisations to develop and maintain such systems will be critical for their ability to optimise the impacts of tourism locally and to enhance the competitiveness of local enterprises and their prosperity in the new millennium.

Bibliography

1. Anon., 1998, Every 100 days 'use of Internet doubles' report by the United States Commerce Department, The Times 17/4/98.
2. Archdale, G., 1996, The Internet in context, Tourism Insights, BTA, July 1996, Vol.8, pp.1-8.
3. Beaver, A., 1992, Hotel CRS an overview, Tourism Management, Vol. 13(1), London, pp.15-21
4. Beaver, A., 1995, Lack of CRS accessibility may be strangling small hoteliers, the lifeblood of European tourism, Tourism Economics, Vol.1(4), pp.341-355.
5. Briggs, S., 1997, Marketing on the Internet-Tangled web or powerful network?, Insights-Tourism Intelligence Papers, British Tourism Authority, March, pp.41-48.
6. Buhalis, D., 1993, Regional integrated computer information reservation management systems as a strategic tool for the small and medium tourism enterprises, Tourism Management, Vol.14(5), pp.366-378.
7. Buhalis, D., 1994, Information and telecommunications technologies as a strategic tool for small and medium tourism enterprises in the contemporary business environment, in Seaton, A., et al (eds), Tourism-The state of the art: the Strathclyde symposium, J. Wiley and Sons, England, pp.254-275.
8. Buhalis, D., 1995, The impact of information telecommunication technologies on tourism channels: implications for the small and medium sized tourism enterprises, PhD Thesis, University of Surrey, Guildford, UK.
9. Buhalis, D., 1997, Information and Telecommunication Technology as a strategic tool for economic, social and environmental benefits enhancement of tourism at destination regions, Progress in Tourism and Hospitality Research, Vol.3(1), pp.71-93.
10. Buhalis, D., 1998, Strategic use of information technologies in the tourism industry, Tourism Management, Vol.19(5) (forthcoming).
11. Buhalis, D., and Cooper, C., 1998, Competition vs co-operation: Small and Medium sized Tourism Enterprises at the destination, in E., Laws et al (ed.), Embracing and managing change in tourism, Routledge, London, pp.324-347.
12. Buhalis, D., and Keeling, S., 1999, Distributing B&B accommodation in York, UK: Advantages and developments emerging through the Internet, in Buhalis, D., and Scherlter, W., (eds) Information and Communications technologies in Tourism, ENTER 1999 Proceedings, Springer-Verlag, Wien.
13. Buhalis, D., and Main, H., 1997, Catalysts in introducing information technologies in small and medium sized hospitality businesses, in Tjoa, A.M., (ed), Information and Communication Technology in Tourism, ENTER'97, Springer-Verlag, Wien-New York, pp.275-285.
14. Buhalis, D., and Main, H., 1998, Information Technology in small and medium hospitality enterprises: Strategic analysis and critical factors, International Journal of Contemporary Hospitality Management, Special Theme Issue: Small hotels: The peripheral tourist sector (forthcoming).
15. Buhalis, D., Keeling, S., Lacorte, A., Reynolds, N., 1997, Technology in hospitality organisations: The case study of La Plagne in France, in Tjoa, A.M., (ed) ENTER 1997 Conference Proceedings, Edinburgh, Springer-Verlag, Wien.

16. Cano, V., Prentice, R., 1998, Opportunities for endearment to place through electronic "visiting": WWW homepages and the tourism promotion of Scotland, Tourism Management, Vol.19(1), pp.67-73.
17. Cooper, C., and Buhalis, D., 1992, Strategic management and marketing of small and medium sized tourism enterprises in the Greek Aegean islands, in Teare, R., et al, (eds), Managing projects in hospitality organisations, Cassell, London, pp.101-125.
18. Dennis, P., 1998, Marriott International on the Internet: A success story, Presentation at the ENTER'98, Istanbul.
19. Ensman, R., 1996, Hospitality in Cyberspace: Designing your World Wide Web site, HSMAI marketing Review, Vol.13(3),Winter 1996/97, pp.35-37.
20. European Commission, 1997, The European Observatory for SMEs, Fifth Annual Report, DGXXIII, Brussels.
21. Go, F., 1992, The role of computerised reservation systems in the hospitality industry, Tourism Management, Vol. 13(1), London. pp 22-26
22. Hart, P., 1998, Travel Servers on the Internet, Presentation at the ENTER'98 Conference, Istanbul.
23. Hensdill, C., 1998, Hotels technology survey, Hotels, February, pp.51-76.
24. Hewson, D., 1996, To the seaside via hyperspace, The Sunday Times, 26th May, p.10.
25. O' Connor, P., 1996, Using computers in hospitality, Cassell, London.
26. Peacock, M., 1994, Dear Doctor Ludd: some questions on the hospitality industry and advanced technological change, International Journal of Hospitality Management, Vol.13(1), pp.19-24.
27. Revolution, 1998, The Internet for small businesses, Revolution, June, Haymarket Business Publications.
28. Tellini, A., 1995, Models of hotel promotion on the WWW-Sourced from the Internet [http://gwis.circ.gwu.edu/~iits/journal/modelwww.htm].
29. Weinstein, J., 1995, More Hotels Plug Into Internet, Hotels, June 1995
30. Worcester, B., 1998, GDS's rule reservations: HEDNA survey shows Internet not replacing traditional means of booking accommodation, H&MM, June 1, pp.48-51.

Distributing B&B accommodation in York, UK: Advantages and developments emerging through the Internet

Dr Dimitrios Buhalis and Steve Keeling
Department of Tourism, University of Westminster
buhalid@wmin.ac.uk,
steveandjo@btinternet.com

Abstract

Small and medium tourism enterprises (SMTEs) provide the majority of establishments within the European accommodation sector. SMTEs tend to offer a unique, locally owned and independent accommodation product, and hence have a unique character. This paper offers a comprehensive case study on the bed and breakfast (B&B) establishments in York, UK and demonstrates how they gradually take advantage of the Internet. Increasingly B&Bs incorporate the Internet in their marketing and distribution policies and aim to attract consumers from overseas and to compete with larger counterparts. A brief overview of the tourism industry in York demonstrates the importance of SMTEs whilst an analysis of the main distribution channels for local B&Bs is provided. Although guide books and the local Tourist Information Centres (TICs) have been the main primary and secondary sources of information about local B&Bs, there is evidence of a growing presence of the destination and B&Bs on the Internet. As the profile of independent travellers attracted at the area often matches the profile of Internet users, it is anticipated that the Internet will overtake printed guides for this market segment and will enable innovative B&Bs to attract a greater percentage of clientele.

This paper is based on primary research undertaken with 54 B&Bs in York, England. The methodology followed is compatible with research in Greece, France and Wales and thus results are comparable with previous research results. The paper demonstrates that surprisingly most B&Bs in York are aware and have access to the Internet (79.6%), whilst a great percentage (61%) already receive part of their reservations through the Internet. This demonstrates a turning point as SMTEs start realising the emerging benefits of the Internet and develop their presence in the electronic marketplace. The primary research illustrates that whilst SMTEs can benefit from the Internet without possessing high levels of ITs knowledge, establishments with their own web page attract a higher number of visitors and have greater satisfaction levels. Amongst proprietors awareness of new threats and opportunities is high. A clear majority of respondents cite new budget/motel accommodation as a threat to the B&B, whilst acknowledging the growing importance of the Internet as a tool to compete with hotel chains and large counterparts.

Marketing and distribution of SMTEs in the United Kigdom

The contribution of small and medium tourism enterprises (SMTEs) to tourism destinations and regional development has been analysed in other papers in this volume and elsewhere [1,2,3,4,5]. The importance of the Bed and Breakfast (B&B) and guest house sector necessitates research into its effectiveness within the context of the changing tourism industry globally. The rationale of this paper is to provide an in-depth analysis of the marketing and distribution functions of SMTEs and in particular B&Bs through a case study in the City of York, UK. The paper also aims to assess the opportunities and threats emerging through technological change for these enterprises as well as their ability to compete in the new millennium.

Most SMTEs and B&Bs use a combination of marketing sources to reach their target markets. Their clientele is primarily originated in the independent budget sector. Most B&Bs have advertising boards outside their premises and often advertise through national and/or local media. In many prime destinations a room booking service is available via a local Tourism Information Centre (TIC), which also provides information on local tourism products, facilities, attractions and accommodation. TICs are often provided, operated or organised by the local council and are run in partnership with the private sector. The details of the accommodation booking service vary in different destinations, but SMTEs are usually asked to register and pay a fee (either an annual charge or/and a commission on bookings). In return they receive inclusion in the tourist information brochure supplied by the TIC to prospective visitors and where an accommodation booking service exists, inclusion in the register within the TIC. Additionally, the regional and national tourist boards such as the Yorkshire Tourist Board (YTB), the English Tourism Board (ETB) and the British Tourism Authority (BTA) and most local authorities produce tourist guides, which include details of B&B accommodation within their area.

In addition, a number of specialist annual publications, such as The B&B Guide, The AA B&B Guide, The RAC B&B Guide, and the ETB B&B Guide, list B&Bs and SMTEs. Many guide books to Europe, the UK or England (such as Lonely Planet, Rough Guide or Lets Go) also feature B&Bs in their accommodation sections. Most of these guides require the establishment to pay an annual fee for inclusion, whilst some of the guide books (e.g. Lets Go England) only include B&Bs which have been recommended by readers. Increasingly, however, destination information as well as accommodation and tourism guides appear on the Internet and are freely accessible by prospective consumers world-wide.

York as a tourism destination and the significance of SMTEs

The city of York is a major international tourism destination, featuring an impressive portfolio of significant tourist attractions. These include the York Minister and the Jorvik Centre which attract 2 million and 700,000 visitors per annum respectively [6]. The city is established on what Davidson and Maitland have described as a cultural 'milk run' which includes other cities such as: Canterbury, Stratford Upon Avon and Chester, characterised by a high proportion of historical and cultural attractions and attracting overseas visitors completing a circuit of these towns [7]. Tourism is one of Yorks' major employers, being directly and indirectly, responsible for approximately 10,000 jobs.

As far **tourist demand** is concerned, the City actively targets high spending overseas tourists from North America and Northern Europe. The latest visitor survey demonstrates that over 4 million people visit York annually. About 51% stay overnight within the city. Most overnight visitors are short break independent travellers (88%) with an average stay of 3 nights. Visitors also tend to be from higher than normal socio-economic groups, with approximately 64% of visitors coming from socio economic groups A, B and C. However, this factor is more prevalent amongst overseas visitors, with some 57% of the UK visitors coming from socio-economic groups C2 and DE. About 34% of visitors live outside the UK, with a high percentage of visitors from North America (16%), Australasia (5%) and Europe (10%). European visitors are more likely to be from Northern European countries. The visitor survey shows only 1% of overnight visitors originating from the Far East. Of the total number of overnight visitors some 37% were from overseas, 57.6% of which were from the USA/Canada. Half of all North American visitors stayed in B&Bs with a further 20% staying in 1 or 2 star hotels [8,10].

As far as **tourism supply** is concerned, York is a major centre for tourism accommodation at all levels. The total accommodation capacity in York is estimated at 7000 beds [9]. No definitive figure for the number of B&Bs (including unregistered ones) exists, although it is estimated that approximately 200 B&Bs and other accommodation SMTEs are located within a 2 mile radius of the city centre itself. Hence, B&B accommodation establishments provide an important part of the supply, as research demonstrates that some 27% of overnight visitors stayed in B&Bs with a further 47% staying in independent 1 or 2 star hotels [8].

Two competing organisations operate York's TICs, which undertake the majority of **marketing and distribution** activities for the destination and SMTEs. Guide Friday is a private sector organisation that operates two TICs on franchise from the city council. The York Tourism Bureau operates a further TIC on behalf of their members. Membership is widespread amongst the key tourism players in the city including the city council, First Stop York, local attractions and accommodation establishments who all pay an annual subscription. There is a clear element of duplication, as both organisations produce official visitor guides to the city. York also hosts the headquarters of the Yorkshire Tourism Board who have responsibility for tourism across the county of Yorkshire.

Research Methodology

The primary research section of this study focuses on the marketing channels currently used by SMTEs within York and attempts to identify the effect of the Internet as a marketing tool for B&Bs. The main source of primary data was obtained by conducting interviews with owners of B&Bs and also by leaving questionnaires for completion within the primary location of York. The opportunity to collect large amounts of information in a relatively short period of time made this kind of survey the only practical method in order to produce reliable results. The sampling criteria were broad to include not just establishments that defined themselves as B&Bs but also guest houses and small independent hotels. The basic criteria for inclusion were a budget and independent properties offering bed and breakfast accommodation for less than £30 per night per person. A sample frame of 145 B&Bs was identified from personal observation as well as a wide variety of sources including the following:

- Guide Friday City Guide
- York Tourism Bureau Guide
- British Tourism Authority web site
- Yorkshire Tourism Board web site
- Smooth Hound/UK Hotel and Guest House Directory web site
- B and B My Guest UK web site
- Stillwells web site
- UK B&B guide book,
- AA and RAC B&B guide books,
- Lonely Planet guide to England
- and Lets Go England

The questionnaire featured both quantitative and qualitative variables in a format whereby a quantitative answer could be followed by a qualitative answer/explanation to illicit richer data. This method allowed respondents to give impressions and opinions, which can then be coded under general categories. As a result, qualitative data can be used in order to enlighten several areas of exploratory research. Mail-back questionnaires were hand delivered. This method enabled a larger sample frame of establishments within the city to be established and approached. Also in approximately 20% of cases as the questionnaires were being delivered, face to face contact was made between the proprietor or key decision maker and the researchers. This gave the opportunity to explain the purposes of the study, to encourage participation and to collect some qualitative data through informal discussions. Response rate was high (37%) with 54 completed questionnaires being returned out of a total of 145 delivered. In addition, several visits and informal interviews took place to SMTEs to collect qualitative data and to verify some interesting results emerging through the quantitative research.

Current distribution channels for York tourism and SMTEs

Analysis of the data demonstrates several critical factors. Within the city of York a number of **distribution channels for SMTEs and B&B** exist. There are 2 separate officially recognised tourist information companies running 3 TICs. They all offer a telephone room booking service and produce 2 separate official brochures. They are also the contact point for the national Bed Ahead scheme. A further accommodation bureau located at the railway station is run by Thomas Cook, which offers 33 separate bed and breakfast establishments. The accommodation sector is also served by a number of external sources. As York is a major tourist destination it is represented on most UK tourism related Internet sites and SMTEs are featured. Additionally national B&B guides and guide books popular with international independent travellers, including Lets Go and Rough Guide, feature SMTEs within the city. There is a great deal of overlapping between the various distribution channels enabling SMTEs to spread travellers awareness and to reduce dependency risks. Respondents use a wide variety of marketing outlets and have high satisfaction levels with the outlets used.

The city of York has a variety of non-tourism related **Internet pages**. The city council runs WWW/Gateway York, which has general tourist information. First Stop York runs a web page devoted to promote York for economic development. The University of York also maintains a web site. The BTA run an official web-site (www.visitbritain.com) which includes information on all B&Bs and guest-houses which are registered with the Yorkshire Tourist Board. However the BTA web-site only displays 20 establishments at a time. The listing provides details on price, location and facilities for each establishment, but on-line booking is not available. The YTB also run a web site that features links to accommodation establishments with their own web sites. These web sites provide the opportunity to book on-line via e-mail. Out of 19 properties featured on the YTB accommodation page for York, 11 are B&Bs or guest houses with the smallest only possessing 5 rooms. Surprisingly, of the major hotels in York only Novotel is listed on the YTB web page. There is no overall accommodation guide purely for the city of York, or indeed no York based tourism guide that features large numbers of accommodation establishments. The YTB web page perhaps offers the best potential for providing links to B&Bs, but currently it is limited to establishments with a web page and hence fails to achieve significant coverage.

Although some York B&Bs maintain their own web pages these establishments are atypical. The majority are included in listings developed by marketing organisations. Information regarding B&B accommodation in York is to be found on national B&B web sites including: "Smooth Hound UK" Hotel and Guest House Directory (www.SmoothHound.uk); and "B&B My Guest UK" (www.BandBMyGuest.uk). Smooth

Hounds' site features 82 B&Bs or guest-houses. On these sites where an establishment has an e-mail address or its own web page a link is provided. However most SMTEs appear as a listing with a phone number and fax number for bookings. Few establishments appear on only one site, whilst the majority appear on several of the sites.
Table 1 demonstrates that altogether some 12 distribution channels were used by at least by 2 of the respondents. Guide books were used by 92.6% of respondents, and the TICs were used by 85.2% of respondents clearly indicating them as the most significant sources of bookings. Over 80% of SMTEs reported that they use at least 3 channels, illustrating that they aim to reduce dependency and to cover as many outlets as possible. Interestingly, 61.1% of respondents stated that they received bookings via the Internet, overtaking advertising, recommendation and the travel trade as a reservations generator. A remarkable feature is the absence of tour operators as a primary source and the small percentage of respondents reporting tour operators as a second or third source of bookings. This underlines the independent patter of tourism in York and the nature of its visitors.

Table 1: Distribution mix and relative importance for SMTEs and B&Bs in York

Distribution Channel Used	Response SMTEs N	%	Primary source of bookings	Contri-bution %	Secondary source of bookings	Contri-bution %
Guide Books	50	92.6%	21	39.6%	14	27.5%
TIC York Railway Station	46	85.2%	6	11.3%	7	13.7%
TIC De-Gray Rooms	46	85.2%	2	3.8%	7	13.7%
TIC George Husdon St	34	63.0%	1	1.9%	3	5.9%
Internet	33	61.1%			4	7.8
Advertising in Newspapers and magazines	21	38.9%	3	5.7%	1	2.0%
Tour Operators	21	38.9%			3	5.9%
Passing-by trade	17	31.5%	7	13.2%	4	7.8%
Thomas Cook	14	25.9%	1	1.9%	2	3.9%
Recommendation	11	20.4%	6	11.3%	4	7.8%
Word of Mouth	3	5.6%	1	1.9%	1	2.0%
York Visitor Guide	2	3.7%	5	9.4%	1	2.0%
Total	54		53		51	

Note: Multiple response- Percentages do not add to 100%

Guide books are by far the largest primary source of bookings accounting for almost 40% of respondents, with the remaining 60% being split between TICs, recommendations and passing-by trade. Surprisingly, given the large numbers of B&Bs receiving bookings from them, the 3 TICs accounted for only 17% of the establishments as primary sources. No respondents stated that the Internet was a primary source. Apart from guide books, the largest secondary sources were the 3 TICs with the York Railway Station and De-Grey Rooms TICs. However, the Internet was featured as an important secondary source for 8% of the respondents, whilst another 7% identified the Internet as the third most important generator of bookings.

Discovering Information Technology and the Internet by SMTEs in York

Altogether 49 respondents completed the section on IT penetration. As demonstrated in Figure 1, 49% of SMTEs had a PC, 67% had a fax machine, and 57% had a word processor. The number of establishments reporting an Internet presence at 79.6% was higher than the 61% figure quoted for establishments who receive reservations from the Internet (even allowing for non-respondents to this section the figure was 72%). If respondents were accurate in their answer, that effectively means that some B&Bs have developed their Internet presence without having a PC, as well as that some SMTEs do not receive or are not aware of any bookings generated through their Internet presence. Almost 29% of establishments stated that they have developed and maintained their own web page.

Figure 1 Level of IT penetration in York SMTEs

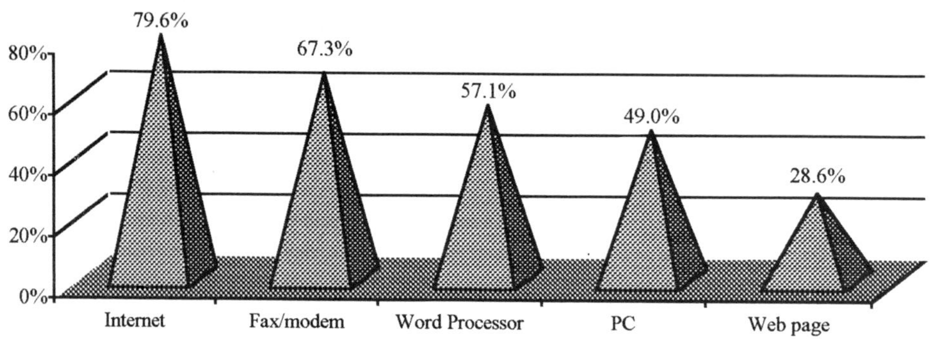

Reservations through the Internet for SMTEs and B&Bs

Some 67% of the respondents reported a percentage figure for reservations received via the Internet as demonstrated in Figure 2. The average percentage of bookings received via the Internet was 6.54%. However, a standard deviation rate of over 6.14% demonstrates a wide range of individual percentages. In some cases B&Bs report that up to one fourth of their reservations come from the Internet, whilst in other occasions they cite figures of below 1%. Not surprisingly establishments with a web page registered higher percentages of reservations received with a mean total of 10.1% and a standard deviation of 5.8%. Interestingly, the highest single percentage of bookings received via the Internet was by an establishment without a web page.

This was achieved by The Hobbit Hotel which received 25% of their reservations via the Internet and clearly demonstrates the effect of visibility on the Internet. Although the Hobbit's percentage figure is impressive at 25% it is interesting to speculate how many reservations they would receive via the Internet if they maintained their own web page and had direct connectivity via email. The hotel is represented on various web sites including the BTA site, Smooth Hound and B and B My Guest UK. Customers booking via the Internet are almost entirely North Americans. The owner states the key advantages of Internet booking as being "the absence of people phoning up to book in the middle of the night from North America." Instead she states: "I come down in the morning and there are a pile of bookings waiting for me on the fax machine."

Figure 2: Percentage of bookings received via the Internet by SMTEs in York

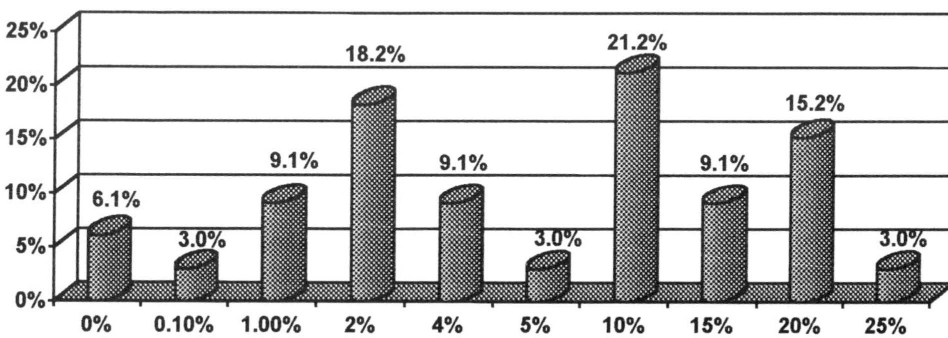

The owner believed that the name of the establishment was a key element in achieving visibility on the Internet. The Hobbit is the name of a fantasy novel by the author R.R. Tolkien. Tolkiens' works are particularly popular in North America. The owner acknowledged "I don't think we would get as many customers if we were called the City Hotel. I think people look down the list (on the Internet) and it (The Hobbit) leaps out at them." The owner states that she has no intention of getting a web page and considers herself "a bit of a Luddite!"(i.e. anti- technology). This reinforces the point made by Hewson [11] regarding the choice of keywords on the Internet and illustrates that an overall marketing strategy is required for developing SMTEs' visibility on the Internet.

Also the ability of the Internet to generate bookings from American and Northern European visitors should also be noted if SMTEs would like to develop these markets. Additionally, it demonstrates how the Internet can bring benefits to organisations via centralised databases such as the BTA or Smooth Hound B&B guides at no additional cost and with little investment in knowledge or technology.
The level of satisfaction recorded with the Internet is slightly lower to this experienced by the third largest source of bookings, with some 42% of respondents fairly or "very satisfied", 25% fairly or "very dissatisfied" and 33.3% "neutral". It is worth noting that as the Internet is the second or third source of customers in only 13% of cases, this score is impressive. Again, not surprisingly establishments with a web page have a higher level of satisfaction with 25% of establishments registering that they were "very satisfied" and a further 40% saying that they were "satisfied". Only one establishment with a web page was dissatisfied with the Internet as a marketing tool. The higher level of satisfaction experienced by SMTEs which maintain their own web page is predictable, when one considers that this offers one of the main advantages cited by establishments, that of on-line bookings. Additionally, as noted above, the ownership of a web site allows greater control over marketing and gives B&Bs the opportunity to maximise their visibility to prospective users. It is natural therefore that ITs active SMTEs which maintain a web page receive a higher percentage of reservations via the Internet and record higher satisfaction ratings.

Conclusions and recommendations

This study demonstrates some important new developments in the field of information technology and accommodation marketing. The primary research confirmed the growing significance of the Internet as a marketing tool for tourism and accommodation establishments. Most previous studies of SMTEs had demonstrated a low take up of ITs. However, the evidence presented here shows that in an area where the majority of customers are educated, middle class and independent, establishments start taking advantage of the Internet, despite the fact that many of them do not actually possess a PC. After years of speculation and encouragement SMTEs start realising the benefits of technology and the ones which adopt an active and innovative approach can already identify significant benefits.
Although the nature of SMTEs may differ in several destinations, there are still great similarities and strategic weaknesses, which characterise them. It is expected therefore that as the Internet grows the clear advantages ITs offer will lead to a significant increase in their use and desirability by B&B establishments in York and elsewhere.
It is evident that increasingly ITs and the Internet offer greater marketing advantages unmatched by other distribution channels. The Internet enables a global coverage of the market, allows interactivity 24 hours per day and costs relatively less to develop and maintain than any other form of communication, promotion and advertising. Although the

ability to receive bookings is mainly observed in SMTEs that have their own web page, there is evidence that even B&Bs without a computer and their own web site can benefit enormously from recent developments. Closer collaboration at the local level and the development of appropriate Destination Management Systems will also enable the destination to develop its marketing and to maximise the tourism impacts for both the public and the private sectors [12,13]. Training on on-line marketing and practical advice on using the Internet as well as promoting innovative tourism products should be undertaken by key decision-makers in SMTEs. This training should be facilitated through local partnerships between the private and public sectors as well as the European Community development funds. This process will enable SMTEs to enhance their presence and their profitability in the new millennium and to contribute to regional development.

Bibliography

1. Buhalis, D., 1999, The cost and benefits of Information technology and the Internet for small and medium tourism, in Buhalis, D., and Schertler, W., (eds) Information and Communications technologies in Tourism, ENTER 1999 Proceedings, Springer-Verlag, Wien.
2. Buhalis, D., 1998, Strategic use of information technologies in the tourism industry, Tourism Management, Vol.19(5), (forthcoming).
3. Buhalis, D., and Main, H., 1998, Information Technology in small and medium hospitality enterprises: Strategic analysis and critical factors, International Journal of Contemporary Hospitality Management, Special Theme Issue: Small hotels: The peripheral tourist sector (forthcoming).
4. Buhalis, D., and Main, H., 1996, Information technology in small/independent Welsh and Aegean hotels, Hospitality Information Technology Association. Third World Wide Annual Conference, Napier University, Edinburgh.
5. Cooper, C., and Buhalis, D., 1992, Strategic management and the marketing of small and medium sized tourism enterprises in the Greek Aegean islands, in Teare, R., et al (eds), Managing projects in hospitality organisations, Cassell, London, pp.101-125.
6. City of York Council, 1997, York Data File.
7. Davidson, R., and Maitland, R., 1997, Tourism Destinations, Hodder & Stoughton, Bath.
8. First Stop York, 1996, York Visitor Survey, City Of York Council, York.
9. Anon, 1997, Total number of hotel beds in York now 7000,Yorkshire Evening Press, 27 July, York
10. First Stop York, 1997, Annual Report, City of York Council, York
11. Hewson, D., 1996, To the seaside via hyperspace, The Sunday Times, 26th May, p.10.
12. Buhalis, D., and Cooper, C., 1998, Competition or co-operation: Small and Medium sized Tourism Enterprises at the destination, in E., Laws, B. Faulkner, G. Moscardo, (ed.), Embracing and managing change in Tourism, Routledge, London, pp.324-346
13. Buhalis, D., 1997, Information and Telecommunication Technology as a strategic tool for economic, social and environmental benefits enhancement of tourism at destination regions, Progress in Tourism and Hospitality Research, Vol.3(1), pp.71-93.

Comparing Operating Ratios for Small and Medium Hotel and Restaurant Businesses. A Decision Support System Using Internet Technology

Karl W. Wöber
Institute for Tourism and Leisure Studies
Vienna University of Economics and Business Administration, Austria
karl.woeber@wu-wien.ac.at

Abstract

In this paper the author discusses a generally acceptable method for analysing the financial performance of hotels, restaurants, and similar units and suggests an approach to the formulation of accounting and control strategy in the context of hotel operations. The system developed here is accessible on the World Wide Web (http://tourmis.wu-wien.ac.at/bv/index.htm) and based on data obtained from Austrian small and medium sized hotel and restaurant enterprises. It uses a 'multi-attributed weighting model' to identify similar hotel and restaurant businesses and to guarantee representative samples to avoid misinterpretations. The author gives a comprehensive description of the conceptual approach, the technical realisation and experiences with the prototype version of the system.

Keywords: SMEs (small and medium enterprises); Management and strategic information systems; Internet/Intranet/Extranet/World Wide Web.

Introduction

When planning a new hotel or restaurant or subsequently measuring its performance, certain essential relationships between various quantities are to be expected (Kotas 1982, Kotas and Kreul 1987). Thus we expect a certain relationship between the investment in assets and net profit, between net sales and net profit, between rooms available and rooms occupied, and so on (Andersson 1995, Applebee 1995, Sutton 1983). All such relationships may be expressed by ratios. Downie (1997) investigated the use of accounting information in hotel marketing decisions. The results of her study showed that managers in hotels have identified gaps in the current provision of information. The essence of accounting is the provision of information for decision making. An accounting system is usually the major quantitative information system within a company and has proved to be extremely helpful in assessing the performance of business enterprises (Altman 1968, Sharma and Mahajan 1980, Geller 1985a, 1985b, 1985c). Any deficit in this information is caused not only by a lack in business administration knowledge, but also by poor technical support in gathering and processing the various data sources in a cost-effective way.

The Austrian Professional Hotel and Restaurant Associations, situated within the Federal Chamber of Commerce, have realised that Austrian small and medium sized enterprises cannot cope with this information deficit on their own. Therefore they decided to fund a research project which allows the industry to exchange data on business operations on a global basis in order to benchmark individual performances. The system developed here is accessible on the World Wide Web and based on data obtained from approximately 1,300 Austrian small and medium sized hotel and restaurant enterprises.

The program was the natural extension of some work carried out on the standard system of hotel accounting and the justification for this system is similar to the uniform system of accounts of the American Hotel & Motel Association (AH&MA 1996). It was prepared for the 40,000 hotel and restaurant owners who are not accountants but wish to obtain information for the control of their business. Basically, the system does two things:

- It suggests methods of management accounting for both small and large hotels to provide hotel management with the information required to plan and control hotel operations.
- It provides a standard classification of accounts so that information can be presented in a form which is common throughout the hotel and restaurant industry. By adopting a standardised accounting method, the development of a inter-hotel benchmarking system enables Austrian entrepreneurs as well as consulting companies specialising in tourism to compare the performance of hotel and restaurant enterprises with others of a similar nature.

The system is operated by the Austrian Society for Applied Research in Tourism (ASART) at the Vienna University of Economics.

Variables and concepts

Financial information is collected annually on a confidential basis from approximately 1,300 hotels and restaurants. The data comprises information from the balance sheet, the profit and loss statement and information obtained from an additional questionnaire (e.g. type of business, capacities, number of employees, opening days, number of overnights, location, ownership, etc.). The data is processed by ASART and expressed through aggregated values (means and medians) for various forms of companies. In order to guarantee meaningful comparisons hotels and restaurants are classified according to their size, their location (country or city), number of closing days, and seasonal operation. The system, which was first launched in 1967, provides 'standards' or 'yardsticks' by which hoteliers can assess their performance. Originally, these standards, measured as ratios, percentages or indices, were published in paper format and distributed to all participating entrepreneurs.

Examples of the sort of accounting and operating ratios generated and reported in the project are:

- return on investment,
- debt to equity ratio,
- profit margin,
- departmental gross profit ratio,
- current ratio,
- acid test or quick ratio measures,
- rate of inventory turnover,
- hotel occupancy,
- average rate per overnight,
- sales mix,
- gross operating profit,
- cash flow,
- working capital,
- after wage profit, and
- various cost-based ratios (e.g. average labour cost),

Since 1994 the statistics are available in an annually published report which is accessible to anyone, including those who did not contribute to the regular survey (Wöber 1997). Currently 32 key ratios are calculated and grouped for 37 different types of hotel and restaurant businesses. The sample size in the survey represents approximately 2% of the hotel and restaurant industry in Austria.

The processing of the data

One of the major problems in the study is the trade-off between the comparability of businesses as a result of the classification system and the representativity and therefore accuracy presented in those groups. For instance, requests concerning the database are usually very specific, like: 'What is the average occupancy rate for a 80 bed hotel-garni in Tyrol?'. Those questions usually cannot be processed as the database will not contain enough hotels which fulfil all requested criteria and therefore guarantee representativity. However, in some cases the system could provide the user with slightly different hotels which also may satisfy his needs. In fact, user requests to the ASART hotel and restaurant database are usually very fuzzy in nature and sometimes hard to define.

Traditional forms of publications do not allow the flexibility and interactivity which is necessary to build a system which adopts to individually varying information needs. Presented below is a system which allows this functionality using a 'multi-attributed weighting model' to identify similar hotel and restaurant businesses and to guarantee representative samples to avoid misinterpretations.

The Multi-Attributed Weighting Model

The stratification of the survey aims to form as homogeneous groups as possible clustered in such a way that the maximum coherence and reliability of the information is guaranteed when added together. The ASART hotel and restaurant panel survey looks at six stratification criteria. The stratification is done on the basis of the type of services offered by the establishments CV_1 (Table 1), the number of opening days CV_2, the geographical area the enterprise is located CV_3 (Table 2), the ownership CV_4 (Table 3), the size CV_5 (measured by turnover and number of employees) and the category CV_6 (Table 4).

Table 1 Type of services offered by the establishments in the panel study

		1	2	3	4	5	6	7
1	Hotel garni	100						
2	Hotel incl. F&B	80	100					
3	Spa hotel	60	80	100				
4	Restaurant	0	50	40	100			
5	Inn, Pub, Tavern	0	40	30	80	100		
6	Cafe house/shop	0	10	0	50	80	100	
7	Espresso/Bar	0	0	0	20	50	80	100

Table 2 Geographical Area where the enterprise is located

		1	2	3	4
1	Vienna	100			
2	> 50,000 inhabitants	80	100		
3	15,000-50,000 inhabitants	60	80	100	
4	< 15,000 inhabitants	40	60	80	100

Table 3 The ownership

		1	2
1	Complete ownership	100	
2	Rented or leased	70	100

Table 4 The category

		1	2	3	4	5
1	*****	100				
2	****	80	100			
3	***	50	80	100		
4	**	30	50	80	100	
5	*	10	30	50	80	100

Selection of the comparability values is a crucial decision as it has a significant influence on the performance of the decision support system. There is no real theory in hospitality research concerning the criteria which determine competitive pressures among hotel and restaurant enterprises. As a result the values had to be assigned by expert judgements in co-operation with the Austrian Professional Hotel and Restaurant Associations and various consultants specialised in hotel and restaurant operations.

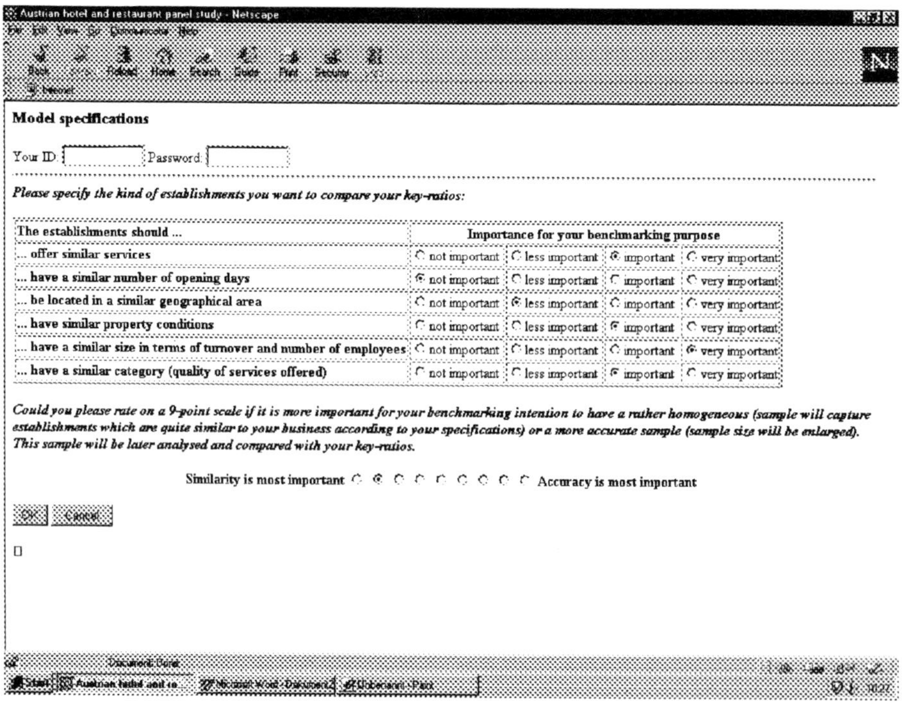

Fig. 1. The user has to decide whether representativity or accuracy is more important to his decision problem

A general comparability equation is suggested in the form of an additive function which also includes an additional weighting procedure to adapt to the situational needs of the user accessing the system. The total weighted comparability value C for each individual enterprise i is:

$$C_i = \sum_{j=1}^{6} CV_{ij} * \omega_j \qquad (1)$$

The weights for ω_1, ..., ω_6 are assigned by the user according to his requirements by a simple scale from 0 to 3 (0 = not important, 1 = less important, 2 = important, 3 = very important).

After rating each establishment represented in the panel database, the enterprises can be easily sorted by their comparability with the user's case. Representativity and accuracy are determined by the number of establishments in the sample which will be drawn after this sorting procedure. According to the users interest in the accuracy of the counselling task he will specify a high or low number of establishments which will go into the sample file. This trade-off is made explicit by a bi-polar rating scale where the user has to decide which objectives have more importance in his decision problem (Fig. 1).

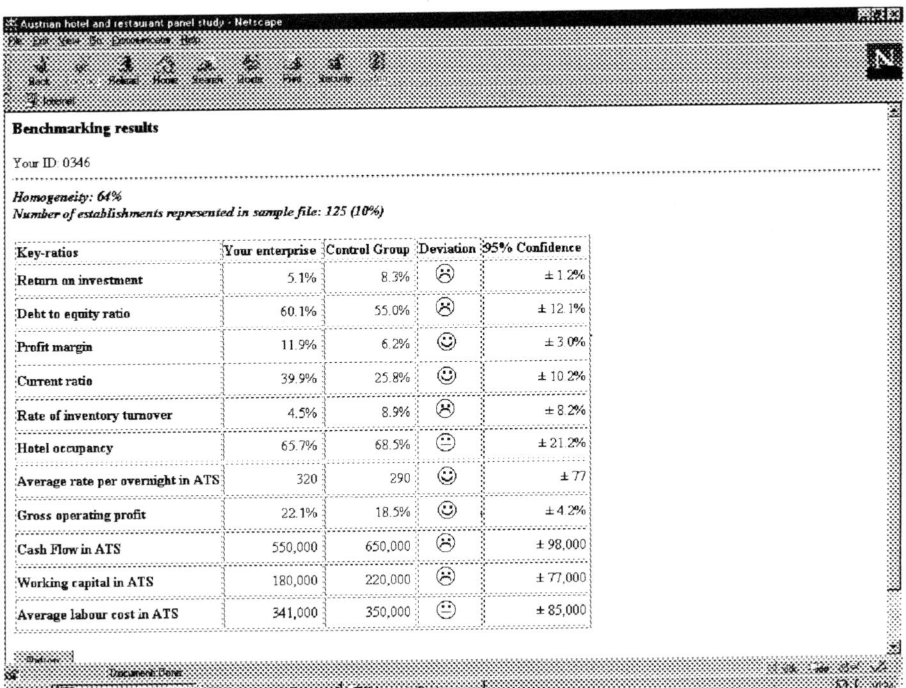
Austrian hotel and restaurant panel study - Netscape

Benchmarking results

Your ID: 0346

Homogeneity: 64%
Number of establishments represented in sample file: 125 (10%)

Key-ratios	Your enterprise	Control Group	Deviation	95% Confidence
Return on investment	5.1%	8.3%	☹	± 1.2%
Debt to equity ratio	60.1%	55.0%	☹	± 12.1%
Profit margin	11.9%	6.2%	☺	± 3.0%
Current ratio	39.9%	25.8%	☺	± 10.2%
Rate of inventory turnover	4.5%	8.9%	☹	± 8.2%
Hotel occupancy	65.7%	68.5%	😐	± 21.2%
Average rate per overnight in ATS	320	290	☺	± 77
Gross operating profit	22.1%	18.5%	☺	± 4.2%
Cash Flow in ATS	550,000	650,000	☹	± 98,000
Working capital in ATS	180,000	220,000	☹	± 77,000
Average labour cost in ATS	341,000	350,000	😐	± 85,000

Document: Done

Fig. 2. Sample output page of the hospitality benchmarking programme

In order to keep programming effort simple the prototype system uses an integer 9-point-rating ($r = 9$) to decide on the relation between accuracy and similarity. The necessary transformation also considers a minimum sample size (e) of 30 establishments to guarantee a certain level of precision:

$$n = \frac{e}{r} * (N - t) \tag{2}$$

n = sample size
N = number of establishments in panel database
t = minimum sample size
e = importance of accuracy for the user

The respondents to the ASART panel study form a sample which is not randomly selected but self-selected. There is little that can be done about this except to make every effort to achieve a high response rate. In Austria some information is available on the structure of the hotel and restaurant industry which is used to weight the sample to correct certain sources of bias. For example, in the case of the ASART survey businesses with more employees tend to participate more frequently in the survey. To correct this misdistribution information about the real size of hotels and restaurants, available through a regular survey of the Austrian Central Statistical Office, is used.

In a random sample the size of the standard error depends on the size of the sample and is unrelated to the size of the population. For a manager interested in benchmarking it will be important to know a confidence interval of his statistic.

$$\bar{x} \pm 1.95 * \sqrt{\frac{\sigma^2}{n}} \tag{3}$$

$\bar{x}$ = mean ± confidence level + 1
σ^2 = variance
n = sample size

The homogeneity of the resulting sample can be best expressed by an indicator which derives from formula (1) and is expressed in (4).

$$C = \frac{\sum_{i=1}^{n} \sum_{j=1}^{6} CV_{ij} * \omega_j}{6n * \sum_{j=1}^{6} \omega_j} \tag{4}$$

The indicator, which is standardised between 0 and 100 (100 = complete similarity with the case example entered by the user; 0 = no comparable establishment found in the total panel data set), is displayed together with the key ratios calculated by the program and supports the manager in interpreting the representativity of the results (Fig. 2).

The program was developed in PERL and is accessible within the tourism marketing information system TourMIS (Wöber 1998). The CGI interface uses an Xbase – Perl module (version 5.001) written by Pratap Pereira (pereira@ee.eng.ohio-state.edu).

Conclusions

The desired level of precision may be selected by giving the amount of error that we are willing to tolerate in the sample estimates. This amount is determined, as best we can, in the light of the uses to which the sample results are to be put. Sometimes it is difficult to decide how much error should be tolerated, particularly when the results have several different uses. In the present application, for instance, an entrepreneur who is interested in opening a new hotel will certainly have completely different information needs in comparison to a manager of a an operating establishment. Part of the difficulty is that not enough is known about the consequences of errors of different sample sizes as their effect on the decisions are difficult to observe.

The advantage of the proposed system is that the user can go back and forth and learn from the output. He can change the sample size and therefore the accuracy of the results, as well as the criteria which decides on the competitive situation he is facing. He is not bound to a strict classification as is usual in ordinary printed publications of panel studies. Hence he will realise soon that results may vary significantly, sometimes even through minor changes in his preliminary assumptions. Therefore he can gain more insights and a better understanding how to interpret benchmarking results and how to use them for managerial purposes.

There are three research problems which have been experienced during the development phase of the hospitality benchmarking program and which have to be discussed in the future. First, it is still unclear which criteria determine competition in the hotel and restaurant sector. Much research effort has been put into the evaluation and analysis of strategic marketing planing processes (Adams 1997) but almost no theory based investigation of this phenomenon is known by the author. Maybe one of the reasons marketing methods, for instance portfolio- or SWOT-analysis, are rarely used by hospitality managers, is that they simply lack practical advise in how to determine their own competitive environment.

A second research problem arises during the weighting process of the various competitive criteria. It is clear that the ideal set of weights depends on the decision problem the user is faced with. However, someone could argue that the user could have difficulty to objectively estimate how relevant this is to his decision problem. In fact, first empirical tests of the prototype program show that users tend to indicate that all criteria are very important for their benchmarking task. Future improvements of the system could incorporate an evaluation of the various decision problems and perform a self-determination of the weighting values. These values could be adapted by a small feed-forward neural network which uses managerial judgements to calibrate the system's output.

Finally, the third research problem tackles the question of whether there is an optimal relation between the representativity and the size of sample derived from the panel database. Decisions on the significance levels of confidence intervals and the necessary preciseness in the benchmarking results have a major impact on this optimisation problem. Obviously, the optimal adjustments will also depend on the underlying application which has to be investigated more thoroughly.

References

- Adams, D. (1997), Management Accounting for the Hospitality Industry, London: Cassell.
- Altman, E.I. (1968), Financial Ratios, Discriminant Analysis and the Prediction of Corporate Bankruptcy, *Journal of Finance*, 23(4), pp. 589-609.
- American Hotel & Motel Association (1996), Uniform System of Accounts for the Lodging Industry, 9th revised edition, New York: Educational Institute.
- Andersson, T.D. (1995), Traditional Key Ratio Analysis Versus Data Envelopment Analysis: A Comparison of Various Measurements of Productivity and Efficiency in Restaurants, in: N. Johns (Ed.) Productivity Management in Hospitality and Tourism, London: Cassell.
- Applebee, A.C. (1995), Accounting and Finance for the International Hospitality Industry, P. Harris (Ed.), Oxford: Butterworth-Heinemann.
- Downie, N. (1997), The Use of Accounting Information in Hotel Marketing Decisions, *International Journal of Hospitality Management*, 16(3), pp. 305-312.
- Geller, A.N. (1985a), Tracking the Critical Success Factors for Hotel Companies, *Cornell Quarterly*, 25(2), pp. 76-81.
- Geller, A.N. (1985b), The Current State of Hotel Information Systems, *Cornell Quarterly*, 25(5), pp. 14-17.
- Geller, A.N. (1985c), How to Improve Your Information System, *Cornell Quarterly*, 25(8), pp. 19-27.
- Kotas, R. (1982), The European Hotel: Methodology for Analysis of Financial Operations and Identification of Appropriate Business Strategy, *International Journal of Hospitality Management*, 1(2), pp. 79-84.
- Kotas, R. and Kreul, L.M. (1987), Management Accounting for Hotels & Restaurants, 9th edition. New Jersey: Hayden.
- Sharma, S. and Mahajan, V. (1980), Early Warning Indicators of Business Failure, *Journal of Marketing*, 44(4), pp. 80-89.
- Sutton, D.F. (1983), Financial Management in Hotel and Catering Operations, 2th edition, London: Heinemann.
- Wöber, K. (1997), Betriebskennzahlen des Österreichischen Gastgewerbes. Bilanzjahr 1995. Wien: Österreichischer Wirtschaftsverlag.
- Wöber, K. (1998), Improving the Efficiency of Marketing Information Access and Use by Tourism Organisations, *Information Technology and Tourism*, 1(1), in print.

A comparative study of ICT and Tourism and Hospitality SMEs in Europe

Professor Graeme Evans and Dr Martin Peacock,
Centre for Leisure and TourismStudies,
University of North London, England
g.evans@unl.ac.uk

Introduction

The paper is based on the first phase of a two year European Union LEONARDO Da VINCI Survey and Analysis project which investigates the application, training needs and potential for ICT in small and medium-sized (SME) tourism and hospitality firms in three European areas. The study is being carried out in London, UK; the Aragon region of North East Spain and the Netherlands, providing a contrast between destination areas and types, from a *World City* to peripheral rural tourism and national tourism systems.

The focus on SMEs is intended to assess the extent of awareness and development of ICT applications in comparison to both the global tourism system and national, regional and local tourism information and promotion. This will include the relationship between SME tourism suppliers and travel agent and tour operator online reservation systems (CRS) and between tourism information and booking systems operated by local TICs and regional and national tourist boards. The study encompasses a wide range of tourism organisations including hotel and accommodation providers, visitor attractions, cultural, heritage and entertainment venues, to small tour operators, guides and tourist information centres. Here the links between the local and regional tourism area will be evaluated in terms of the use of intranet, joint promotion and marketing through web sites and reservation systems and other shared ICT and promotional efforts. A questionnaire-based survey of a cross-section of 500 SMEs is designed to measure the usage, range and awareness of various IT applications and their development potential and training need, including barriers to ICT development.

The paper reports on the results and analysis of this survey, initially in the UK (London), highlighting the key issues arising and barriers to ICT application and development by SMEs. These include capital investment, lack of specialist training and design and maintenance of ICT systems and structural weaknesses within the tourism and hospitality system and EU policy itself. The study also presents on the one hand an antidote to the technological determinism ('optimism') and domination of ICT and online reservation systems by major travel and tour operators and integrated chains (e.g. hotels, car hire, tour operators, travel agents and transport carriers) and the problems of accessing such systems by SMEs. The results of the first year of this study also form the basis of a the second year's investigation which will develop in depth case studies of individual SMEs, their training needs and ICT skills and awareness, from which opportunities for ICT product development and design, training programmes and dissemination/technology transfer are likely emerge.

ICT in Tourism Development

The opportunity and impact of greater use of ICT by small and medium-sized tourism enterprises (SMTEs) can be viewed on the one hand in the light of global competition from the transnational tourism and hospitality industry and their domination of global reservation and integrated IT systems, and on the other, from the changing nature of the tourism product and market in Europe. The development of speciality and niche markets is evident for instance in the growth of the independent travel market which grew from 10 million holidays in 1990 to 13.4 million in 1998 (MINTEL, 1998), in part driven by low cost airline and budget hotels, whilst *"in the meantime, teletext information and internet booking services have enabled travellers to create their own itineraries"* (op.cit.). In the UK outbound market, France is the leading independent destination (5m), followed by Spain (2.25m) and the USA. The growth of long-haul independent travel has also boosted average spend as consumers travel for longer periods (spending £3.8m in this sector in 1998). In the USA, the most advanced in online travel and ICT access, the percentage of travellers who use online services to make travel plans or reservations jumped from 11% in 1996 to 28% in 1997 (e.g. 13.8m Americans used the internet to plan trips and 6.3m to make reservations). In 1997 there was a 19% increase in those who prefer the Internet for travel reservations than travel agents, although over half still prefer the agency system. The TIA in 1997 estimated that online travel bookings would increase by 200% in that year.

The official UK web-site 'visitbritain' is, not surprisingly, most popular with tourists from the US (both the highest visitor and online user), but British domestic tourists are the next highest user of their "own" online marketing and booking system, followed by other English-speaking countries, Canada and Australia, and then Germany and the Netherlands (BTA, 1998). Whilst ICT penetration by the mainstream travel and tourism sectors can effectively reduce the market share and market entry of SMEs, ICT as a local area resource, particularly Destination Marketing Systems (DMS) and web-based marketing, bypassing retail and tour operator intermediaries in key generator countries (e.g. USA), offers a response for SMTEs at the destination. As Archdale observed, *"a destination particularly attractive to the independent traveller is often one (which includes) a substantial number of small and independent businesses... theoretically well-placed to benefit from a fully functional (DMS)"* (1994: 249).

SMEs/SMTEs in Europe

Implementing effective and viable ICT strategies and solutions is however hampered by structural weaknesses in SMEs generally, and particularly in tourism and hospitality, bearing in mind the fragmented nature of this 'sector' (CEC, 1996b:2) which is made up of autonomous services and suppliers, from accommodation, transport, visitor attractions, cultural venues and sites, and information, tour and promotion bodies, public and private. The exponential growth in online usage and travel reservations, above, also exaggerates the potential for SMTEs since this activity is largely represented by airline sales (90% of all online travel sales in the USA), with hotel and car rental chains dominating the remainder. US-based activity also dwarfs other online users (28.7m US households on-line, estimated to reach 60m in 2000), however by the year 2000 Europe is predicted to have 36.6m and Asia/Pacific Rim 16.6m households on-line. After the USA, Canada and Japan, the UK has the next highest online household penetration and the Netherlands is 7th in this league table.

Whilst the SME is føted by European governments and the European Union (EU) as representing the key to sustained employment and economic growth, and tourism and related services are similarly targeted as growth sectors (6% of the EU's GDP and employment), the skewing of SMEs in relation to medium and larger firms underlines the fundamental barriers to growth and efficiency gains through ICT. Their small size therefore means fewer staff and specialisms; limited technology; under-capitalisation and diseconomies of scale in any investment such as in technology, training and in product development generally (Wanhill 1997). The next table profiles the employment structure in Europe which clearly shows the inverse relationship between the high proportion of micro-enterprises (93%) to lower proportions of Employment (30%) and Turnover.

Table 1. SMEs Contribution to the European Union Economy

Type of firm	**Employees**	**Firms in the EU**	**% of Firms**	**No. of jobs**	**% of the EU Employment**	**% Total turnover**
Micro	0-9	14.5 m	93.05	26m	30	22
Small	10-99	1 m	6.42	22m	25	48
Medium	100-499	70,000	0.45	14m	16	
SMEs	0-499	15,570,000	99.9	62m	70	70
Large	500+	12,000	0.08	26m	29	30
Total		15,582,000	100	88m	100	10700

Source: EIM and EC (1993) in Buhalis and Cooper, 1998: 325

The high number of micro-enterprises as a proportion of all firms in Europe has also been fuelled by a growth in self-employment, as the flexible labour market and 'contract culture' has become established within the post-industrial services economies (tourism represents one third of the EU trade in services). This is evident in greater contracting-out and franchising within larger hospitality firms and the privatisation of public transport operations (rail and bus). In Europe as a whole self-employment has grown, particularly in southern Europe, but also in the UK which has since the 1980s moved towards a greater flexible labour market and deregulation (e.g. Sunday Trading, privatisation of rail, bus and airport operations).

Table 2. Self-employment (non-agricultural) as a proportion of Total Employment: 1979 vs 1993

Country	1979	1993	Change
Spain	16%	18%	+2%
United Kingdom	6%	12%	+6%
Netherlands	7.5%	7.5%	-
EU (15)	12.5%	14%	1.5%

Source: DTI Small Firms in Britain Report, 1996

In the UK, the focus for the SMTE Survey of ICT application, below, the distribution of firms within the hotel and restaurant sectors provides a further analysis in terms of the number of firms, employees and turnover in Table 3. Here smaller firms measured by the number of employees was even more concentrated than in the EU, with 99% of firms employing under 50 staff (vs 99% under-100 in the EU as a whole, Table 1.)

Table 3. Distribution of UK Hotel and Restaurant Businesses by Size

Hotels and Restaurants	1996	Size (number of employees)			
		1	2-49	50-249	250+
No. of Businesses	148,866	28%	71%	1%	0.2%
Employment '000s	1,469	3.9%	48.9%	9.5%	37.7%
Turnover £million	£45,788	3%	41%	10%	46%

Source: DTI Labour Market Trends, October 1997

ICT and SMTEs

The attention given to SMEs and the development of IT generally and ICT in particular, has also been disproportionate to the global ICT and tourism activity which, not surprisingly, focuses on the national and international market and online systems. In a study of UK hotels, mostly SMEs (48% under 50 and 73% under 100 employees), Technology was rated well down in the factors for perceived competitive advantage (14 out of 16) and less than 5% felt that 'superior technology' contributed to out-performance by their hotel competitors (Harrington and Akehurst 1996: 143-4), although this is somewhat contradicted in the findings of the wider *Hospitality 2000 Research Study* (wherein 90% of respondents evaluated technology as an 'important tool' and 88% said that it would enable firms to improve the delivery of services - in Rimmington and Kozak, 1997: 61). Textbooks on IT and tourism also give scant coverage of SMTEs – for instance Inkpen's standard text (1998), even in the second edition makes three or four passing references in 375 pages. He does acknowledge however the issue of booking and reservation of independent hotels/B&Bs which do not generally have any kind of automation *"simply because they do not need it"* (p.254) and he posits: *"How can a tourism Web site visitor book accommodation with SMEs in the destination?"*. One solution offered is an IT inventory control system connected to the Web site server. But this is discounted in the case of the micro-firms with perhaps less than 10 rooms and no credit card facility. The other solution is the third party booking system that guarantees visitors accommodation with the advantage that:

a) It leaves the tourism firm free to focus on its core role, which is the promotion of tourism in domestic and overseas markets;
b) it would enable the booking service company to enjoy a new revenue stream, which would not be bundled up with the tourism organisation's finances, and
c) it would provide visitors with an on-line booking tool.

An example of a SMTE network arrangement which provides a joint Web-site and on-line booking system is discussed in Evans (1998) and on the Aegean region see Buhalis (1994) and Buhalis and Cooper (1998). Increasingly, local area tourist or visitor information bureaux provide this intermediary booking service for accommodation suppliers (but seldom for other suppliers such as transport, visitor and cultural attractions). In Huesca, Aragon NE Spain, the *Tourism Verde* service provides a centralised booking and reservation system for a network of rural accommodation suppliers, however this is not strictly on-line and requires telephone or personal visit to the office in order to make a booking. Following the establishment of the 'visitbritain' web site by the BTA in 1997, accommodation online bookings have been highest in B & B category, more than hotels, with touring by car the most common. This bodes well for the independent and SMTE supplier, since the online user is also more discerning - most likely to be a couple travelling without children, higher educated and aged between 25 and 54 years (BTA, 1998). In London however, aside from the London Tourist and Visitor Convention Bureau Offices, only one local TIC provides an on-line booking facility (Evans 1998) and this link and opportunity for local tourism suppliers is therefore still undeveloped.

Much of the focus on ICT benefits to local and regional SMTEs has therefore been Destination Management Systems (DMS), often publicly funded and administered by local or regional tourist information offices, local authorities or enterprise development agencies. Archdale estimated in 1994 that there were in excess of two hundred local area DMS databases: *"However the vast majority are limited in their scope and ambition either by their ownership or by their technology"* (1994: 247). Their success to date has however been mixed (Sussman and Baker 1996; Archdale, 1992, 1994), with evidence of inadequate risk assessment, project management and market analysis having been undertaken in several cases. Baker et al (1996) suggest the following factors for success and failure for a DMS:

- IT Project Risk (as with any other IT investment or development);
- Regional Advantage Factor (vs national competitive advantage);
- Political Dimension (Performance evaluation and indicators, Policy rationales).

Particular contractual issues also arise in terms of allocation of fees and commissions; relationships (or not) with TICs and travel agency networks, and the preference for tourists to book accommodation, as well as transport and other services such as visitor and cultural attractions and tours, direct. For a DMS to be making a significant contribution to a region or local areas's competitive advantage, it has to be handling a significant amount of traffic (Baker et al 1996), and to pass the 'additionality' test. If commission payments are its prime source of income the scale of bookings will need to be high enough to maintain the system itself. The benefits for individual SMTEs are therefore difficult to assess, until a critical mass of improved (quality and quantity) trade is evident, a Catch-22 for SMTE and DMS feasibility at the outset. As Wanhill concludes writing on peripheral area tourism and SMTEs in Europe (1997): *"what is now required is a fully networked computerised reservation system for SMEs... In order to move from a cost-oriented stance to one that is proactive, there is a need to create an interactive database which can be accessed from PC networks to research and analyse market trends"* (p.66). Buhalis (1997) also presents an ambitious version of the DMS with wider coverage of suppliers and facilities than the more limited destination sites and TIC systems.

ICT in SMTE Survey

As the first stage in the EU LEONARDO project, a questionnaire was designed which would be used in each of the three countries. This was initially drafted in English, then a final a version translated into the other host languages for piloting. Standard questions were coded for analysis by SPSS. Issues around the level of IT application within what were quite different geographic and economic regions, simplified the range of IT and degree of 'jargon' used, whilst measurement of accommodation sectors by bed spaces or bed rooms reflected the different classification and types which existed in the London, the Netherlands and in Aragon, Spain. At the time of writing, survey data for the Netherlands and Aragon was being collected, and the following analysis is therefore based on the survey of tourism and hospitality SMEs in London. In the next stage of the study, this data will be consolidated enabling both combined and comparable survey analysis across the three destination areas.

A database of 500 SMTEs was created based on firms located in the Greater London region. Thus was drawn from existing local area lists of tourism, hospitality, cultural and TIC facilities which had formed part of SME, training needs and other surveys undertaken in the previous two years. These were supplemented with directory searches, tourist board, TEC and guide lists from which larger, chain and ineligible companies were excluded. In order to achieve a spread of firms across the full range of service and supply types, additional firms were included during the first survey period. A response rate of 30% has so far been achieved which is higher than average. Respondents were asked whether they would be willing to participate in a follow-up interview, as envisaged in the next stage of the study (45% responded positively).

SMTE status

Firstly, the status of respondents was sought, in terms of their legal/corporate nature: whether they were private or public, charitable ('not for profit') or self-employed individuals ('sole trader').

Table 4. Status of organisation

Status Type	**n=146**	**%**
Public (local) Authority/TIC	52	36%
Private Company	42	29%
Charity/Not-for-profit	33	23%
Public Limited Company (plc)	19	13%
Other	6	4%
Sole trader	4	3%

Public local authorities were the most common, representing local tourist information centres and offices which were physically independent from Council Offices and Town Halls, and in a few cases, authority museums and visitor attractions. The next highest category was private companies, the standard small trading company format, followed by charitable trusts or companies, most used by museums and other cultural attractions. A significant minority were public companies but the smallest category of respondent was the sole trader, such as tour guides.

Range of SMTE Activity

The purpose of the study is to consider ICT within tourism and hospitality and these sectors embrace a wide range of visitor, information and accommodation services, particularly in the case of the diverse London urban tourism market (Evans, 1995). Higher response was observed from the cultural organisations, perhaps reflecting a greater receptiveness and awareness of ICT opportunities – museums, heritage and cultural venues represent over half of the sample. Hotel and other accommodation providers represent 13% of respondents (15% including catering), as did visitor attractions.

Table 5. Main SMTE Activity

Service/Sector	**n=144**	**%**
Museum, gallery or heritage site	46	32%
Arts or entertainment venue	33	23%
Hotel/ accommodation/camping	19	13%
Visitor attraction	18	13%
Tourist information/TIC	9	6%
Other	7	5%
Café or restaurant	3	2%
Travel/bookings agency	5	3%
Tour guide	2	1%
Activity/tour organiser	2	1%

Size of Firm

As discussed, the size of SMTE is significant both for policy, e.g. national, EU, and structural reasons, with SME micro-enterprises prevalent generally. This sector was no different in this respect with over half of firms employing 10 or less and a further 29% employing up to 50 staff. Only 5% employed over 100 people and 3% over 200. This regional SMTE sector is therefore largely made up of small and micro-firms.

Table 6. Size of organisation

Number of employees	n=145	%
0-10	80	55%
11-25	27	19%
26-50	15	10%
51-100	12	8%
101-200	7	5%
Over 200	4	3%

Although most SMEs are located at a single site, this sector had more instances of multi-site operation, despite their small employee base – 28% operated from more than one location and 70% of these had 2 to 4 sites, suggesting that IT network systems would be appropriate (and borne out by the 10% operating an intranet system – Table 7). Another common measure of accommodation providers is bedrooms or beds, with establishments with less than 50 beds categorised as 'small' (Buhalis 1994: 256). Respondent SMTEs in this sector were divided between 40% with under 50 bedrooms, but over half medium-sized, including 4 with over 200.

ICT usage and plans

In order to assess the extent of ICT usage, details of current and planned usage of a basic set of IT applications was requested. This revealed nearly 60% usage of Email; 50% of the Net and 43% CD Rom (now standard on new PCs). Over 10% used intranet and online reservation systems. Usage of systems does not of course mean ownership of dedicated IT facilities, but could also represent shared access or networked systems such as travel agency teledata and other CRS provided by tour operators and airlines. If those that planned to use IT actually did so, online systems would be applied in 80% of these SMTEs, but with less than 20% using online reservation systems, suggesting a gap in reservation/booking opportunity and barriers to entry (ref. DMS above). A significant minority of firms would also have established intranet, notably TIC and information providers, but also cultural institutions who had started to look to IT-based archiving and interpretation.

Table 7. ICT currently used or planned

Application/system	Currently use	Plan to use
Teletext	7.4%	0.7%
E-mail	59.7%	23.5%
World Wide Web (www)	50.3%	28.2%
Intranet	10.7%	8.9%
CD Rom	43.0%	12.7%
Online reservations – CRS	10.7%	7.4%
Virtual reality (VR)	-	1.0%

Booking Systems

Booking systems are obviously key to any tourism supplier, particularly ones relying on individual rather than block or contract booking arrangements. Telephone and fax was the common method, but over 30% also used Email and 18% the Net for reservations.

Table 8. Methods to take bookings/reservations and payment

Application/system	Reservation/ booking	Payment for services
Teletext	1.3%	1.3%
Telephone	75.8%	29.5%
Fax	65.1%	20.8%
E-mail	31.5%	8.7%
Internet/Web	18.8%	4.0%

Where payment is concerned however, the 63% accepting credit cards did so mostly after booking, although some still did this via phone/fax. Online methods were seldom used for payment. A significant proportion did not accept credit, and this group would therefore be unable to exploit online booking and payment arrangements without an intermediary (e.g. DMS or TIC)

Training in IT

A prime goal and outcome of the LEONARDO project and funding criteria, is the identification of training to meet SME enterprise needs (LEONARDO is the EU's vocational education and training programme). Given the barriers to SMEs training take-up, whether in-house or externally provided (Evans, 1998), the level of expertise and training provided in the various IT applications was elicited. Email was the application where SMTEs felt most experienced and also where training was provided, followed by the Web and CD Rom (self-learning programs are now widely incorporated into such software). There was a shortfall however in those using ICT (Table 7) and the expertise and training available.

Table 9. Expertise held or Training provided in the following

Application/system	Expertise	Training
Teletext	2.7%	2.7%
e-mail	43.0%	21.5%
World Wide Web (www)	35.6%	16.8%
Intranet	10.7%	5.4%
CD Rom	23.5%	12.8%
Online reservations (CRS)	6.0%	4.7%
Virtual reality (VR)	0.7%	0.0%

The second stage of the survey, which will be carried out at the same time in each of the three destination areas, will be to undertake in depth case studies through interview with selected SMTEs (over 45% expressed willingness to participate in the next stage of the study). This will include an audit of IT facilities and training, and a training needs assessment. The type of training provided will also be assessed and the extent to which this is felt to be effective by the organisation and individuals involved. The final phase of the 2 year project will be the response in terms of ICT training support and delivery, including IT-based learning materials.

Policy Summary

The level of ICT application within this SMTE survey group is higher than expected and in terms of EMail and Net usage, two to three times that found amongst SMEs in 1996 and 1997 (in Evans, 1998). This perhaps reflects the aggressive marketing and speed of expansion of ICT applications (e.g., Microsoft's Net Explorer on new PCs); as well as advocacy by national and regional tourism bodies (BTA and LTB in this case), but less so the EU itself. In a review of the Community Action Plan to Assist Tourism in 1993-1995 (CEC, 1996a) IT development by tourism suppliers does not feature in this largely bureaucratic and inward looking assessment of the EU Tourism Unit's programmes. Of the various marketing, training and campaign measures supported, over 50% received a 'Poor, Very Poor' or at best 'Average' Technical Assessment in 1993 and 1994 (op.cit.:13). The only measure aimed at Information and Booking systems, which looked at standardisation of TIC services was judged to be *"largely obsolete because of the development of the Internet"* (p.16). A project to improve yield management in SMTEs was judged to be high cost, because of unclear relevance to SMEs!

In the case of technology-based projects assisted by the EU in this period, the most innovative aspects have been their transnational character and the attempt to apply new technology to new areas such as information handling, previously addressed through guide books and maps. In all cases projects failed to address post-project sustainability (*cf.* DMS, above). The report also raises the relevance to SMEs since, as the authors of this report note: *"Technology offers both a barrier and an opportunity to SMEs, and this has not satisfactorily been addressed... some projects omit any link to suppliers at all, concentrating on tour operators and travel agents"* (p.21).

The opportunity to improve on EU policy and intervention measures is provided in the subsequent Programme for the period 1997 to 2000 (CEC, 1996b). The "Philoxenia" (*Hospitality,* Greek trans.) programme outlined the EU's plan and measures for assistance. Objectives such as 'Improving Knowledge' included the development of information systems, but these were solely statistical data gathering and standardisation, not supply-based IT effectiveness measures. This programme is disappointing and despite the poor performance of previous Actions, presents 'more of the same', and fails to address the supply and growth needs of the tourism sector, notably its largest component, SMTEs, preferring to target Community Funds on further marketing and standardisation efforts. Support and development of SMEs does of course take place within other departments of the EU (DGs), however the Tourism Unit is located in DGXXIII which does encompasses trade, enterprise and co-operatives, and this lack of integration in policy programmes would appear to perpetuate this plan's view of Tourism as *"a diverse and highly fragmented industry, most of which are SMEs, often resulting in less coherent policy formulation and ineffective co-ordination at many levels"* (p.2). Wanhill independently concludes that *"there should be an action programme targeted at SMEs to improve their competitiveness"* (1997: 68) and that improved communication and intelligence particularly through ICT, should underpin any programme in this area.

The initial results and interest shown in ICT development by respondent SMTEs, are however, encouraging and when comparable findings are made with the two other surveys in Spain and Netherlands, the degree of convergence or otherwise will be of interest, particularly if transnational collaboration and exchange between SMTEs is beneficial (CEC, 1996a) and ICT and training opportunities further developed. This is likely to engage and link SMTEs cross-sectorally within tourism and hospitality, and within local area/destination regions (Buhalis 1997), rather than through a top-down EU or even national approach.

References

- Archdale, G. (1992) *A new direction for effective destination marketing and quality customer service*, In Yee J. (ed) Proceedings of the 1992 PATA Destination Database Conference, Singapore, December 9-10: 13-18
- Archdale, G. (1994) Destination databases: issues and priorities, in A.V.Seaton et al, *Tourism: The State of the Art*, West Sussex: Wiley: 246-253
- Baker, M.G., Hayzelden, C. and Sussman, S. (1996) Can destination mangement systems give you competitive advantage? *Progress in Tourism Hospitality Research* 1(3): 89-94
- BTA (1998) *Marketing Britain on the Internet*, London: British Tourist Authority
- Buhalis, D. (1994) *ICT as a Strategic Tool for Small and Medium Tourism Enterprises'*, in A.V.Seaton et al, *Tourism: The State of the Art*, West Sussex: Wiley: 254-274
- Buhalis, D. (1997) Information Technology as a Strategic Tool for Economic, Social, Cultural and Environmental Benefits Enhancement of Tourism Destination Regions, *Progress in Tourism and Hospitality Research* 3: 71-93

- Buhalis, D. and Cooper, C. (1998) *Competition or Co-operation? Small and medium-sized tourism enterprises at the destination*, in *Embracing and Managing Change in Tourism'* (Laws, E. et al, eds.), London: Routledge
- CEC (1996a) *Report on the Evaluation of the Community Action Plan to Assist Tourism 1993-95*, 92/421EC, Brussels: European Commission
- CEC (1996b) *First Multiannual programme to Assist European Tourism "PHILOXENIA" (1997-2000)*, Brussels: European Commission
- Datamonitor (1997) *New Technologies in Travel and Tourism,* London
- DTI (1996) *Survey of IT Usage in the UK*, Department of Trade & Industry
- Evans, G.L. (1995) *Planning for Tourism in London: World City-Whose City*, Urban Environment: Tourism Conference, South Bank University: 55-62
- Evans, G.L. (1998) *Networking for Growth and Digital Business*L Local Urban Tourism SMTEs and ICT, ENTER '99 Conference, Innsbruck, January 1999
- Evans, G.L. and Taylor, M. (1997) *Destination Marketing Strategy for East London*, LDDC
- Harrington, D. and Akehurst, G. (1996) An Exploratory Investigation into Managerial Perceptions of Service Quality in UK Hotels, *Progress in Tourism and Hospitality Research*, 2: 135-150
- Inkpen, G. (1998) *Information Technology for Travel and Tourism* (2nd ed), Harlow: Longman Main, H. (1995) IT and the Independent Hotel – Failing to make the Connection, *International Journal of Contemporary Hospitality Management* 7(6): 30-32
- MINTEL (1998*) Independent Travel*, London
- Molina, P. (1998) *Rural Tourism in the Province of Teruel: Contribution to the stabilisation of its population and sustainable development*, MA dissertation, University of North London
- Rimmington, M. and Kozak, M. (1997) Developments in IT: Implications for the Tourism Industry and Tourism marketing, *Anatolia* 8(3): 59-80
- Sussman, S. and Baker, M. (1996) Responding to the electronic marketplace: Lessons from Destination Management Systems, *Int. J. Hospitality Management* 15(2): 99-112
- TIA (1997) *Travel and Interactive Technology: A Five Year Outlook*, Travel Industry Association of America, Washington D.C.
- Wanhill, S. (1997) Peripheral Area Tourism: A European Perspective, *Progress in Tourism and Hospitality Research* 3: 47-70

Distribution of Danish holiday cottages via the Internet/WWW

Carl H. Marcussen, PhD,
Research Centre of Bornholm, Denmark
marcussen@rcb.dk, http://www.rcb.dk/staff/chm/carl.htm

Introduction

Holiday cottages accounted for 16.3 million out of 44.1 million registered tourist nights in Denmark in 1997, i.e. 37% of the volume, but 'only' about 25% measured in value. Of these 16.3 million tourist nights spent in holiday cottages, Germans accounted for 83%, and Danes for 10%. So holiday cottages are a major type of accommodation for tourists coming to Denmark, and Germany is the main market for this product, with the home market being significantly smaller.

During the first half year of 1998 there was a rush amongst the holiday cottage letting agencies in Denmark to establish solutions to the distribution of Danish holiday cottages via the Internet, partly tailored for each of the two the main markets, Germany and Denmark, with the former clearly a priority.

This paper reviews the solutions implemented by five - more or less directly competing - Danish letting agencies, ranging in size from one of the smallest to the second largest, i.e. from one with only about 30 to one with more than 5,000 cottages. The distribution strategy varies between the agencies, e.g. in the main market (Germany). Some almost only sell directly to the end consumers, whereas one (in fact the largest) only sells through travel agents on the German market. This is also reflected in the WWW-solutions which each of the letting agencies have implemented.

In each of the five cases the extent to which each of the elements in the distribution process for the cottages is carried out via the Net will be shown. The areas covered are: Description, price information, availability (real-time or with less than instant updating), booking function, issuing of renting contracts and payment.

The meaning of the term 'real-time booking' over the Internet - especially with regard to the updating frequency of the underlying availability data - is discussed.

Acknowledgement: This paper is mainly based on one of the chapters of a report in Danish prepared for Destination Bornholm, www.bornholminfo.dk/turist, by the author on behalf of Research Centre of Bornholm, www.rcb.dk.

The solutions implemented by five Danish holiday cottage letting agencies

dansommer (about 5,000 Danish holiday cottages) [1]

dansommer (always spelled with a lower case 'd') is one of the four largest Danish holiday cottage letting agencies. It was founded in 1979 and has about 70 employees. In 1996 dansommer thought the time was not at all ripe to "put the catalogue on the Internet" but has now done so both in German, Danish, and Norwegian - including prices, availability data and reservation function.

dansommer's solution for the German market

In the beginning of March 1998 dansommer launched the possibility of real-time *reservation* of holiday cottages via the Net.[2] Availability data for given cottages are completely real-time, since they are extracted directly from dansommer's central, internal electronic database (booking system). There is one photo of each of the cottages, and there are prices. dansommer's solution for the German market means that the final booking must be undertaken at a travel agency. dansommer still thinks that it will take *a whole generation* before the German holiday makers start deviating from their traditional purchasing pattern, buying through travel agencies. The results for the first five and a half months until 12th August 1998 of the German version of the Website was 137 bookings. This corresponds to less than one percent of all dansommer bookings made by Germans during the period 1st March to 12th August.

dansommer's solution for the Danish market

On 20th April 1998 dansommer opened a Danish version of their Website.[3] This functions largely just like the German solution but the Danish (and Scandinavian) tourists can choose between booking their holiday cottage stay directly with dansommer or with an agency near their home. The results for the first four months until 12th August 1998 of the Danish version of the Website was 270 bookings. This corresponds to about three percent of all dansommer bookings made by Danes during the period 20th April to 12th August. - The Norwegian version was opened as late as 10th June, and by 12th August only two bookings had been made by Norwegians.

So, by 12th August dansommer received a total of 409 bookings for 503 weeks, which generated a revenue of DKK 2.24 million. All in all, dansommer reports that 0.6 percent of their bookings (during 1998 until the middle of August) came via the Net. After opening for bookings for 1999 bookings in August 1998, bookings started coming in at the rate of one per day already during the first month without any promotion. - In the course of four years, i.e. by the year 2002, dansommer expects that 30% of all their bookings will come from the Net.

Discussion and perspectives in relation to dansommer

A couple of statements about dansommer from 1995 still seems to be valid:

- the director is very interested in IT, and can see some business advantages in being at the forefront of developments.
- dansommer is leading the use of IT among the Danish holiday cottage letting agencies.[4]

It is certainly a fact that dansommer is among the leaders within IT as far as the application of the Internet is concerned - among the Danish holiday cottage letting agencies as the sites appear in the spring and summer of 1998.

It should perhaps be mentioned that dansommer was not the first holiday cottage letting agency in Europe which started on-line real-time booking over the Internet. One Finnish agency opened a site as early as in 1996, and is now receiving 8% of all their bookings over the Net.

In an international - specifically a German - context the term holiday apartments is used (Ferienwohnungen, FEWO). Holiday cottages are part of this category. Among the ten largest "FEWO" operators on the German market as many as *seven* now have an Internet booking solution: specifically TUI, Inter Chalet, dansommer, DER, Sol & Strand, ITS and Ameropa.[5] TUI, which is one of the very largest tour operators in Europe and also the largest operator/supplier within the "FEWO" category, has had its solution for a couple of years. However, all the holidays at TUI's Website are - as is the case with ITS - solely charter package tours to southern European and distant destinations. The "FEWO" suppliers on the above mentioned top ten list, who do not yet have an Internet booking solution are Novasol, DanCenter and Wolters (now owned by TUI).

Among the major suppliers within the "FEWO" category, only the Internet booking solution of Sol & Strand is based on sales directly to the consumers as far as the German market is concerned (i.e. not through travel agencies).

Sol & Strand (about 3,700 cottages)

Sol & Strand is the fourth largest of the Danish holiday cottage letting agencies. In 1997 Sol & Strand stated that they would go for Internet technology - instead of CD-ROM. In April 1998 Sol & Strand actually opened a real-time booking function for their holiday cottages - without making any big event out of it. They have put the whole of their paper catalogue on the Web, and availability data updated every five minutes. Bookings can be made. The solution has been established in a Danish and a German version.

The basic graphical work transforming the catalogue into Internet format has been undertaken by the same bureau which produces Sol & Strand's printed catalogue.

Catalog International A/S (formerly called The Vision Factory) has - with the help of their product called Cat@log - undertaken the more technical, i.e. the linking of Sol & Strand's internal booking system and their Website. The internal booking system is based on an Oracle database and is executed on a Unix computer, while a PC functions as a Web-server. All information, to which the Internet user has access, is copied to the Web-server, including photos, text, prices and availability data.

It is Sol & Strand's strategy to distribute directly to the consumers - among others on the Danish and German markets. Therefore it is also quite natural that they have chosen to utilise Internet/WWW as an extra direct sales link to consumers. (There are also other examples of on-line sales of other holiday and travel products directly to consumers on the German market, e.g. last-minute holidays.[6]) Already during the first couple of weeks about ten bookings were received via the new Website, in spite of the fact that the booking facility as indicated was hardly being promoted at all. It was interesting that the bookings came from markets in which Sol & Strand does no active selling (through agents). This indicates that the WWW can be a sales channel to *new markets*.

In the middle of 1998 the expectation of Sol & Strand is that a couple hundred bookings will come via the Net in the course of the 1998 season. Many catalogue orders are also received via the Net. In five to ten years Sol & Strand expects that a third of all sales will take place through the Net.[7]

Ulfborg-Vemb Holiday Cottage Letting Agency (about 560 holiday cottages)

Ulfborg-Vemb Holiday Cottage Letting Agency was established in 1972, and has since 1979 shared buildings and personnel with Ulfborg-Vemb Tourist Bureau, which was founded in 1950. There are a total of ten employees apart from a number of occasional/seasonal workers for cleaning etc. of the holiday cottages. It is not the strategy of the Ulfborg-Vemb Holiday Cottage Letting Agency to distribute via travel agencies in the German or other markets. Ulfborg-Vemb has about 560 cottages included in their main catalogue. The houses are located by Nissum Fjord and on the west cost of Jutland.

Ulfborg-Vemb is part of Urlaubsring Dänemark (Holiday Partner Denmark) together with a dozen other middle sized bureaux - with an average of 500 cottages each, i.e. about 4,500 cottages in total.[8] Holiday Partner Denmark has a common sales office in Hamburg, which was previously used solely by Ulfborg-Vemb.

85% of Ulfborg-Vemb's bookings come from Germans. Each house is let for about 20 weeks per year. Ulfborg-Vemb has had a Website since September 1997, which is common for the tourist bureau and the letting agency, and in the course of ten months until the end of April 1998 there were almost 40,000 hits distributed on about 1,600 visits (~24 hits per visit). It is the holiday cottages especially, which are of interest to the Web-surfers. The Website also contains a link to weather forecasts. New ideas for further development of the Website continue to surface, and the site will continually be further developed.

The availability data on Ulfborg-Vemb's Website are based on an automatic up-dating of the Web-server from the internal electronic booking system once a day. The availability data on the Web-server are thus not quite real-time, but the updating frequency can be increased if needed. The Web-server is physically placed at a Web-hotel, and data communication takes place via an ISDN line.

The possibility of searching for available holiday cottages and booking these through the Net was established in the beginning of April 1998.[9] The procedure is as follows: the Web user must first fill in some search criteria, i.e. arrival date, number of weeks, number of persons, and the required number of bedrooms. Furthermore, by checking boxes the user can select cottages where pets can be brought along and it can be specified whether the cottage should be equipped with sauna, telephone, dish washer, washing machine and satellite TV. The result of the search is a list of available cottages during the desired week(s) which fulfils the user's requirements. *Reservation* can be undertaken via a screen on WWW. The rental contract is posted by ordinary mail and likewise payment must take place by traditional means, i.e. as far as the German market is concerned typically via bank transfer. In future, by clicking on one of the numbers of the cottages it will be possible to see photos and text in addition to prices for given cottages, just like in the printed catalogue, and in due course it will be possible to pay via the Net.

Römö Holidays (about 125 holiday cottages)

Römö Holidays is a holiday cottage letting agency which was established in 1996, and which exclusively lets holiday cottages on the island of Römö, in a tidal area on the Danish west cost, just north of the Danish-German border. There are four employees at the bureau including the owners, and additionally 25 occasional workers for cleaning the cottages. The bureau had 70 cottages in its 1997 catalogue, which was its first, while there are 110 cottages in the 1998 catalogue. A further 16 cottages were added after the catalogue was printed, i.e. as many as 15% more.[10] These are described on eight pages, which are inserted as loose leaves in the 1998 catalogue. The printed catalogue, which is published in German and in Danish, has been put on the Web largely unchanged. Furthermore, the agency intends to put an English version on the Web, but there will be no printed catalogue in English.

As many as *97%* of the weeks let with Römö Holidays are booked by *Germans*, 2% by Danes and 1% by others. Römö Holidays has chosen not to promote itself much on the Danish market since it feels that holidays on Römö are perceived as a high price product by the domestic market. As many as 95% of the bookings from Germans come directly to the bureau on Römö (from the consumers). Before the start

Römö Holidays expected that 25% of its German bookings would come from German bureaux, and "only" 75% "directly", but it turned out that a significantly larger share comes "directly".

Römö Holidays is still on T-Online (previously Btx) in Germany, but it will reconsider its continued participation because of a fall in the number of messages received from that channel. From the middle of 1997 the bureau has had a Website in German, which was updated in the beginning of June 1998, and it is now available in German and Danish. From April 1998 and onwards the Internet (which here means e-mail) has become the channel through which Römö Holidays receives the greatest number of enquiries. This has been achieved after advertising in a German magazine for car owners with mention of its WWW and e-mail address.

From its foundation in April 1996 Römö Holidays has had an electronic, internal, booking system. It runs on an IBM AS400 platform supplied by Østergaard Data in Esbjerg, Denmark. PCs are used as work stations, and these are linked in a local area network, and of course connected to the central booking system. Østergaard Data has now developed an Internet module for their existing holiday cottage booking system, *Book/400.*[11] An early version of the new module was introduced to Østergaard Data's customers at the end of 1997.[12] Römö was expected to become the first of at least three bureaux to install the system, which was originally was planned to take place in May 1998. At the same time the catalogue was to be put on the Net in both German and Danish. This actually took place in the middle of July 1998.

In its introductory text in German about the revised Website the bureau writes that it has "the world's newest on-line booking system for the Internet", and in the corresponding text in Danish it even claim to have "the world's most advanced booking system on the Internet". The first statement was no doubt true at the time it has written, and probably also at the end of September 1998. For how long the statement will continue to be valid is another question. The system is no doubt *one of* the most advanced booking systems on the Internet, and if limited to systems *especially for small and medium sized holiday cottage letting agencies* it may be true that it is *the most advanced* one. The reason for the 'SME' part of the proposed limitation is that dansommer's solution as previously described seems equally advanced - in terms of the degree to which the availability data is real-time. With respect to number of photos, Römö Holidays shows four per cottage, including a ground diagram of the building, whereas there is only one photo per cottage at dansommer's Website, so here "Römö" beats dansommer, but "more photos" does not necessarily mean "more advanced". Similarly, Römö's principle of updating the availability data is *different* from dansommer's, but this in itself does not make in more advanced, cf. below.

The internal (central) booking system is linked with an Internet server, which will enable real-time booking of holiday cottages via the Net. The Web-server is physically placed at a Web-hotel in Copenhagen, but could be placed anywhere.

The communication between Römö Holidays and the Web-hotel in Copenhagen takes place via a "sleeping" ISDN line, which is automatically opened as and when needed. It is thus opened each time a booking is undertaken, either via one of the terminals in the local area network or via the Internet. ISDN lines are generally opened very promptly when the dialling up is undertaken by a computer. Although there is no constant communication between the Web-server and the central booking system, the two computers keep each other *constantly updated* anyway, since an updating takes place each time a booking is made.

This updating principle seems right for small and medium sized letting agencies and similar organisations, since:

1) telecommunication costs are limited, and at the same time
2) bookings via the Net are based on availability data which are completely real-time - in the practical sense of the term.

Figure 1. The elements in real-time booking via the Net - for Römö Holidays

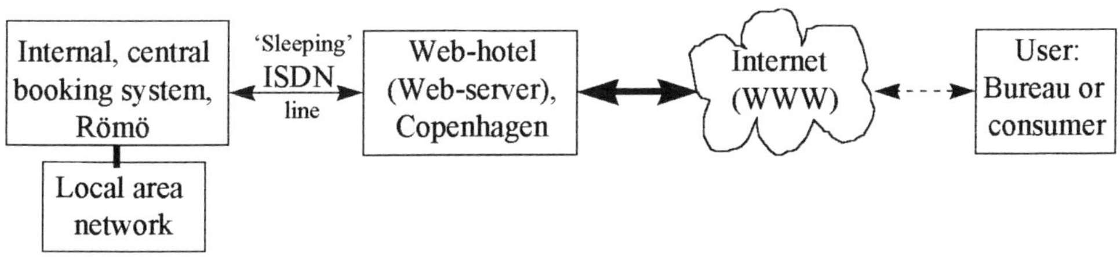

It may be agents and/or the consumers (holiday makers) themselves who will book via the Internet on the system. It must be assumed that it will primarily be end-consumers who will book via the Internet at Römö Holidays' new Website. But Römö Holidays also expects that the real-time booking function on the Net will be used a good deal by small bureaux ("kitchen table agents"), the type of agents with whom "Römö" co-operates in the German market. - "Römö" agrees that large German travel agencies, as previously, will prefer to undertake all bookings of all types of holiday and travel products via their CRS-terminal (typically Start), with which about 90% of all German travel bureaux are equipped. But an Internet connection is considerably cheaper than a connection to Start. Therefore Internet access (as user) is an interesting alternative for the smallest bureaux/agents.

Bureaux, which have a different booking system from Book/400, can of course not use specifically this Internet module just like that, since in such instances modifications are required which will require special programming. It is impossible to give a general answer as to what such special adaptation will cost.

Farsö Tourist Bureau (about 30 cottages).

By the end of 1997 *only one single* - very small - holiday cottage letting agency in Denmark supplied availability data at their Website. It was Farsö Tourist Bureau with only 30 cottages.[13] The solution is based on a weekly manual up-dating of the home-page, which first of all is a time-consuming exercise, and secondly provides far less than desirable timeliness than desirable. There are also small letting agencies (with fewer than 100 cottages) which stated in 1997 that they had considered the matter carefully, but decided not to provide availability data for "their" holiday cottages on the Net, partly not to disclose information which some owner may like to keep confidential (for example because they wish to receive requests, even if the cottage is not available during the period preferred by the customer).

DanCenter and Novasol

DanCenter and Novasol - along with dansommer and Sol & Strand - constitute the largest holiday cottage letting agencies in Denmark. DanCenter is developing its current modest Website so that in future it will comprise the entire catalogue *plus availability data*, and so is Novasol. With respect to *payment* DanCenter would welcome the possibility of payment by bankcard (in Denmark known as the dankort) as far as the Danish market is concerned. With respect to the *German* market DanCenter will not reveal its plans, since the solution for that market has not been fully developed. One would, however, assume that inspiration would be taken from the dansommer solution, since DanCenter like dansommer and many tour operators in the German market relies, to a large extent, on sales through travel bureaux.

Novasol was the last of the four national holiday cottage letting agencies to open a Website with basic information, which took place at the beginning of 1998.[14] Novasol's brief information is provided in Danish, Swedish, Norwegian, German and Dutch - but remarkably enough not in English, which must be explained by the fact that it does not publish any catalogue in English. Catalogues can be ordered at the site, but at the moment there are no availability data, and no photos, etc. of the individual cottages. Like DanCenter and dansommer Novasol is bookable through Start in Germany and the corresponding CRS called Smart in Scandinavia. This reflects its strategy of primarily or exclusively distributing through travel bureaux in the German market and partly also in Scandinavia. This is probably also why the Novasol Website was opened rather late and, like that of DanCenter, it only contains very basic information and functions.

Summary - and discussion of "real-time bookings over the Net"

In the course of the first half year of 1998 a most remarkable development has taken place in the field of letting Danish holiday cottages via WWW. Both large bureaux with several thousand cottages and medium sized bureaux with from 100 to 600 cottages have established themselves on the Net with more or less real-time availability data, prices, photos and booking functions. In this paper all the different types of systems used by Danish holiday cottage letting agencies (five of them), which so far (i.e. by the autumn of 1998) provide availability data on their Website have been mentioned. A summary is shown in table 1.

Table 1. Letting of Danish holiday cottages - with availability data - via the Net.

Bureau	No. of cottages in Denmark	Web-address:	Up-dating of availability	Photos?
Dansommer	5,000	www.dansommer.dk	Constantly	Yes (1)
Sol & Strand	3,700	www.sologstrand.dk	Every five minutes	Yes (2+)
Ulfborg-Vemb	560	www.ulfborg-turist.dk	Once a day	Not yet
Römö Holidays	125	www.romo-holidays.dk	After each booking	Yes (3+)
Farsö Turistbureau	30	www.farsoe.dk/turist/	Once a week	Yes (1)

Source: Own research.
Note: '+' means that a ground diagram of each cottage is also shown in addition to photos.

The five agencies in table 1 represent a total of 9,415 cottages, corresponding to 27% of the total number of cottages for letting in Denmark. (In the middle of 1998 two more agencies with a total of 270 cottages have implemented the same solution as Römö Holidays - after which the calculated percentage remains at 27%). If or when the final two of the four major letting agencies actually implement the Internet solutions, as they claim they will, the percentage will increase to 65%. The remaining 35% of cottages for letting are represented by small and medium-sized letting agencies (with less than 600 cottages each). Some of these agencies can also be expected to implement solutions for on-line booking via the Net along the lines of the examples described in this paper. This would bring the penetration of Websites with availability data and on-line booking functions beyond 70% of the total number of cottages for letting in Denmark by the spring of the year 2000.

- Table 1 indicates that there are solutions for the letting of holiday cottages for any size of bureau - and for any budget.
- Availability data for any given cottage is provided by all five solutions, but with the degree of currency of the availability data generally varying with the number of cottages.
- Prices (which vary by time of year) of all the cottages are provided by all five agencies, and for four out of five *photos* of all the cottages are shown. Showing photos will be one of the next steps for the fifth of the bureaux.
- The reservation function is undertaken via the Net in all instances.

- Renting contracts are typically posted by ordinary mail.
- Payment is not carried out via the Net in any of the cases examined. In one instance payment is undertaken at the travel agency (dansommer). In other instances payment is undertaken by traditional means, for example by bank transfer.

Booking via the Internet may be based on availability data, the updating frequency of which may vary. The expressions on-line bookings and real-time bookings over the Internet can be found on many tourism Websites.

The meaning of *on-line* is very unclear, since it may just mean that Internet is used in some way, e.g. in as vague a sense as "we have no availability data on our Website at all, but send us an ordinary e-mail with your booking enquiry, then you may get an answer in a day or two if we remember to empty our e-mail box".

Real-time, on the other hand, implies that the underlying availability data are absolutely current, combined with instant and automatic feed-back to booking requests. But in exact time-units, does real-time mean that the underlying availability data have been updated within ... the last 24 hours ... or the last hour ... or the last five minutes ... or the last seven seconds ... or the last second or two ... or does it mean that the availability data have been extracted directly from a central computer in the split-second after the Internet user has submitted the enquiry to the Web?

The developer of one of the Website mentioned in this paper which updates every five minutes (Sol & Strand) wishes to call this frequency of up-dating real-time - whereas the writer in his initial description had termed it *almost* real-time.
Obviously there is no exact definition of what deserves the description real-time availability data on the Net. In general, the more booking objects and the more bookings per object, the more frequent the updating should be.
To determine an appropriate updating frequency of availability data provided to Web-users requires the balancing of the updating costs against the costs involved in the Web-user being presented with incorrect data.
For medium-sized letting bureaux and similar organisations a good solution is to update the availability data on the Web-server each time a booking is undertaken as illustrated by one of the examples in this paper (Römö Holidays).

End-notes

1 Additionally, dansommer lets 500 Norwegian cottages.
2 Advertisement in the national paper *Jyllands-Posten* on Sunday 8 March 1998. The Web-address of the German version is: www.dansommer.de.
3 This was loudly announced by a full page ad in one of the national newspapers - the price of which was be almost DKK 200,000.

4 Petersen, Anders og Zinck, Niels C. B., 1995, *dansommer*, student paper from the Aarhus Business School, 11 pp., put on the Web in February 1997, http://www.hha.dk/management/msccourses/cm96to98/sis/dansommer1.html

5 The Internet addresses are: www.tui.de; www.interchalet.com; www.its.de; www.der.de; www.ameropa.de.

6 www.ltur.de. "L'TUR - Europas Nummer 1 für Last-Minute-Urlaub. ... Neu: Mit Kreditkarte 24 Stunden online buchen. Jetzt können Sie in AOL und T-Online 24 Stunden täglich online buchen." Not all German Internet users can book on-line with L'TUR, only those who subscribe to America On-Line (AOL) or T-Online.

7 Sales direktor Peter Fogh Nissen, Sol & Strand, *Jyllands-Posten*, Digitalt, 24 June 1998.

8 http://www.feriepartner.dk/feriepartner/engelsk/framegb.htm

9 Internet version of *Jyllands-Posten*, 10 April, 1998. The new facility is located at this Web address: http://www.ulfborg-turist.dk/Feriehuse/indexdk.htm

10 This high number of 15% underlines the fact that "Römö" is in an expansion phase, since the corresponding figure nationally is 5% or 6%.

11 http://iws.as400.ibm.com/denmark/denmark.htm. Römö Holidays: www.romo-holidays.dk.

12 Press release dated 23 October 1997, www.oestergaard-data.dk/pressemed.htm.

13 www.farsoe.dk/turist/ - here under: www.farsoe.dk/turist/optaget.htm

14 www.novasol.dk / www.novasol.com

Electronic Invoicing for a Hotel Management Computer Network System

Guevara, A., Caro, J.L., Aguayo, A., Gálvez, S.
Dpto. Lenguajes y Ciencias de la Computación
Escuela Universitaria de Turismo
University of Málaga. Spain
<guevara,caro,aguayo,galvez>@lcc.uma.es

González, L.
Dpto. Economía Aplicada (Estructura Económica)
Escuela Universitaria de Turismo
University of Málaga. Spain

1 Introduction

The current work is part of a larger research and development project undertaken by the Department of Computer Languages and Science at the University School of Tourism in Malaga University, in collaboration with certain software development companies plus the support of more than fifteen hotels in Malaga and Almeria, Spain.

The aim of the main project is to develop an integrated system of hotel management able to maintain a fully up-to-date and interactive Database ensuring that any transaction with the system occurs in real-time. These transactions could be generated within the system or made by clients via the Net securely and confidentially.

The project has been divided into several modules among which we could mention: interactive TV from the hotel room which will allow the client to check his records, pay the bills or order services; information points; real-time connection to the hotel database via the Internet or from central booking offices; an electronic invoicing system fulfilling the requirements of Spanish legislation; and other traditional hotel management modules (front-office and back-office).

Here we introduce the electronic invoicing module which constitutes a global system of electronic invoicing capable of handling the exchange of invoices as required by Spanish tax legislation.

2 Traditional invoicing and Electronic invoicing

Before introducing the features of our electronic invoicing system, we need to briefly look at the requirements imposed by Spanish tax law regarding any legal electronic invoicing system. We will also look at the different invoicing systems available in the market.

2.1 Legal Requirements

Any invoice must have three parts: header, body, and footer. The address of the buyer and seller should be indicated in the header as well as their tax identification number, invoice date, and invoice number, which has to follow sequential numbering. The body shows services or items sold, together with the cost and VAT. Finally, the footer must include total net cost, total VAT and the Grand Total.
Other data can appear in the invoice, but only those indicated are legally required. It is important to note that it is compulsory to keep a sequential numbering in the invoices within each tax year, in other words, no numbers can be missed on the invoices issued by the hotel.

2.2 Types of invoicing system

We are going to classify the systems according to the current Spanish legislation for the hotel sector:

INVOICING SYSTEMS			
NON-ELECTRONIC		ELECTRONIC	
Traditional (hardcopy in paper required)	Automatic (hardcopy in paper required)	Automatic + E.D.I. (hardcopy in paper required)	Automatic + E.D.I.+ transaction control (hardcopy in paper NOT required)

Let us now explain the differences between electronic and non-electronic invoices and their subtypes.

Non-electronic invoicing:
Traditional: This system is quickly becoming obsolete. For example, a hotel provides a client or business company with a set of services and the transaction is recorded in an invoice written by hand on paper.

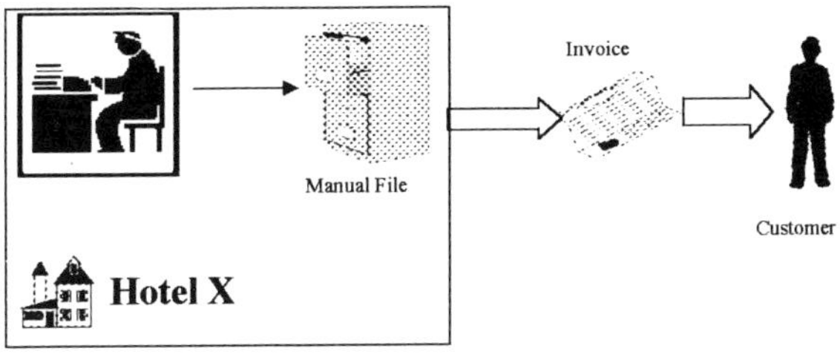

Fig. 1. Traditional

Automatic: Currently, this is the system most widely used. In this case, the hotel uses a software application to issue the invoice. The services and data are introduced into a database which is automatically updated, and a proof of the transaction is printed in the form of an invoice.

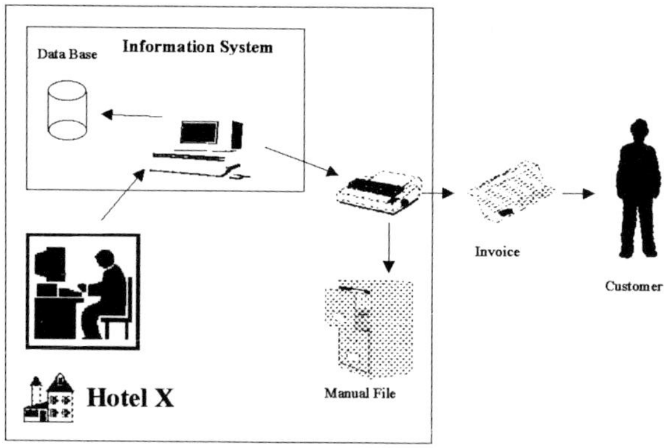

Fig. 2. Automatic

In both instances, Spanish legislation demands the filing of these invoices on paper which have to be produced in case of tax inspection.

Electronic Invoicing:
Automatic + E.D.I.(Electronic Data Interchange) [3]: This system is also widely used. In this case, the hotel issues an invoice to the client using a software application and sends it to the client via internet or a network. This electronic invoice has no legal validity within Spanish legislation and so the hotel will have to issue a printed copy and file it for possible inspection as above.

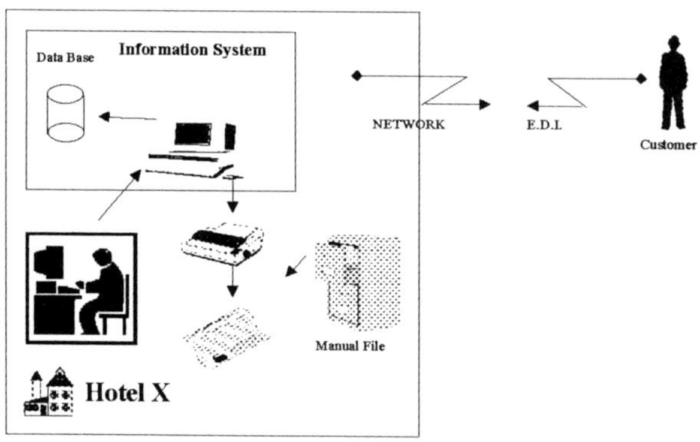

Fig. 3. Automatic + E.D.I.(Electronic Data Interchange)

Automatic E.D.I. + Transaction control: This system is not used very much as yet, due to the fact that there are very few software packages which comply with Spanish legal requirements. In this instance, the hotel issues an invoice using a software application and sends the document, which is certified by an authorised centre, via internet or another network. This invoice can be stored in digital form and has tax validity in case of inspection. Our project focuses on this system.

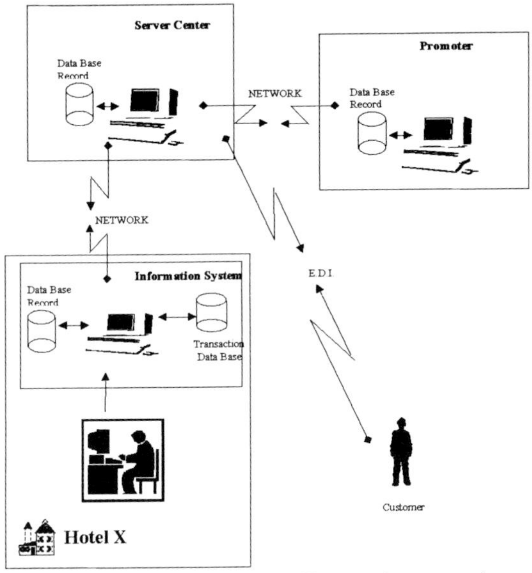

Fig. 4. Automatic E.D.I. + Transaction control

3 Electronic Interchange Invoicing System

Spanish legislation regarding the interchange of electronic invoices was ratified on the 29th of March 1996. However, very few tourism companies have included this system in their information systems due mainly to the fact that there is no efficient and reliable software in the market to carry out these transactions within the requirements of Spanish law [5, 6].

In order to understand the features of the software we are developing it is necessary to become familiar with Electronic Invoicing Interchange Systems as defined by Spanish law (known as SIFT).

An electronic invoicing interchange system is understood as a system which includes a promoter, one or more servers, users, and when required, computer service providers able to create a system according to Spanish regulations.

The hotels operating with several servers must adopt a single standard regarding electronic data interchange, so that the physical format of the document exchanged between issuer and recipient is fully maintained. Equally, the interchange mechanisms used between servers must be specified to ensure that the tax authorities have easy access to the information.

Let us now define the agents involved in a SIFT:

- *Promoter*: business persons, professionals or their associated organisations holding a SIFT licence compliant with the law.

- *Users*: business persons, professionals or their associated organisations that are authorised to work with any of the fully approved systems.
- *Server centre*: provider of an electronic data service that can ensure transparency and integrity of data interchange between users.
- *Computer service provider*: businesspeople, professionals or their associated organisations that develop software or systems able to work with SIFT.

In Spain, the setting up of a SIFT is not an easy matter, mainly due to the quantity of conditions required by the tax authorities in order to give their authorisation. Some of these requirements, which our project is compliant with, are:

- Reasons motivating the implementation of a SIFT.
- Rules and regulations that will govern the relationship established between the different agents.
- Economic study demonstrating the benefits deriving from the implementation of a SIFT.
- General description of the SIFT and proposals of standards.
- Physical and logic configuration of the system including:
  - Communication protocol.
  - File format and structure during the transmission of the document as well as storage.
  - Analysis and design of software related to electronic invoicing.
  - Source and executing programs provided by the promoter or server to the users.
  - Full encoding messages tables, including communication errors.
- Description of security measures incorporated by the server centres as well as the formula and mechanisms which ensure integrity and accuracy of the data transmitted.
- Technical characteristics and general specifications of the user environment, and accepted by the promoter, regarding platforms as well as software, user and technical manuals, etc.
- A model of the subscription contract to a SIFT as well as proving that the system is compliant with the legislation.
- Identification of the server centres the user is going to employ.

Given the amount of requirements demanded, very few hotels have adopted such a system. Our project opens a way for this to happen so that many hotels can adopt the system and improve their overall efficiency, speed and accuracy.

4 Our project and SIFT software

So, the aim of our project is to create software able to solve this situation. We are developing a model of SIFT able to handle the processes involved in a hotel-client interaction, from the request of services on the part of the client to the hotel, to the issuing and sending of an electronic invoice reflecting the transactions and in full accordance with Spanish regulations.

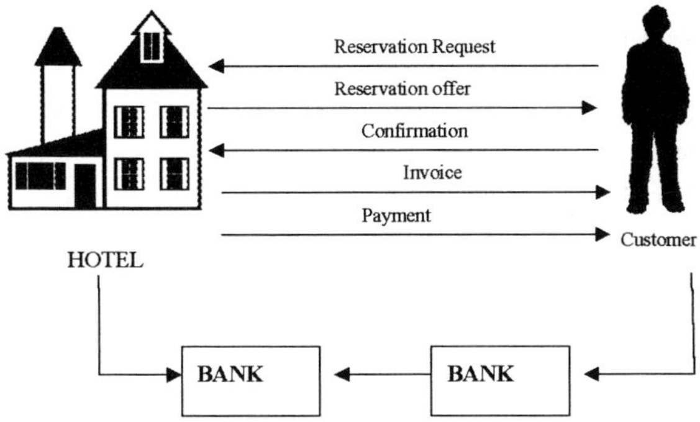

Fig. 5. Our SIFT software

Now, we will analyse the obligations of each party involved in a SIFT and how our system deals with them.

a) *Promoter's obligations*: The promoter is responsible of maintaining a control system to make sure that the conditions and the requirements established by the law are fully met. In order to fulfil this obligation, we have adopted the rules of the AECOC (Asociación española de codificación comercial) [1]. In this way, it will be possible to obtain any kind of data, required by the administration, obtain copies and carry out tests to verify whether the system complies with the regulations.
Records of all users will be kept, indicating the date of contracting the service and when they stopped using it, as well as their address, tax identification number and an internal code identifying the user.
The servers will have a control system to guarantee the original content of the information, in chronological order, which they have to give to the administration during the prescribed period.
A log will be kept during the same period using a double entry method for the operations of each server centre. Received invoices will appear recorded and balanced on receipt and issued invoices will show their source. Each entry will have its unique, sequential internal number. The content of the log will be stored in optic or magnetic media:

The entries will include:

- Internal sequential number of the operation, taking the first one of the year as number 1 without breaks in the sequence.
- Identification of the type of operation carried out, i.e., ordinary sending or receiving documents or invoices.
- Code of the server.
- Code of the user (sender or receiver).

- Number of transaction, sequential for each user taking as number 1 the first transmission of the year without breaks in the sequence. This number will be given by the server's control system.
- Date and time of the beginning of the transaction.
- Transmission time.
- Bytes transmitted.
- Number of invoices transmitted.
- Code for transmission confirmation.

Additional Information:

- Reference containing the internal number of the entry source.
- Code of the server used for the transmission.
- Code of the user (receiver or sender).
- The number of invoices dealt with.

In the case of using more than one server centre, the code of the source and destination centre will have to be included.
On the other hand, it will be necessary to keep a log of messages regarding eventualities identifying the users affected, the item, the date, and the kind of problem. To begin with we have pared down the codes for transmission confirmation to just three:

- *COR*: syntactic and semantically correct
- *ERR*: syntactically incorrect: incorrect EDI
- *ERC*: content error: EDI correct but incorrect for SIFT

b) *User's obligation*: The user will send or receive invoices according to the rules dictated by EDIFACT [7](EDI For Administration, Commerce and Transport). These are the standards proposed by the International Standards Organization and the United Nations Economic Commission for Europe.
Full copies of invoices sent and received in the same order of having been sent or received will be stored in magnetic or optical media. These files will be kept separately from any other kind of document sent and received electronically.
The software will include security measures such as a backup copy; storage media and devices will be in accordance with the legislation i.e., MS-DOS floppy disks or magnetic tape. In our case, the media employed will be magnetic tape since floppy disks are too small for storing this sort of information, and any other storage system would need special permission. The characteristic of the magnetic tape will be as follows:

> 9 tracks, Density 1600 0 6250 BPI
> Code EBCDIC or ASCII in capitals with non-packed numerical fields, no control characters or tabulation.
> The beginning of the tape will have no labels or marks but the end of each file will be marked as well as the end of the tape.

The users will also have to keep a list in magnetic or optical media as well as on paper of each transmission received or sent. Alternatively this can be done as a daily summary list of all transmissions made during the day, keeping the order of transmission sequential and maintaining the following structure:

Header:

SIFT version and option.
Transmission date.

Body:

Each invoice must be in a line.
Number of the communication.
Time of starting data transmission
Invoice number.
Invoice data.
Code of server involved.
Invoice Sender (issuer) and recipient.
Number of lines in the invoice.
Gross amount of the invoice.
Deductions to Gross amount.
Special discounts.
Tax base.
Net amount to be paid.
Grand total of the invoice.

Footer:

Total of the numeric fields.
Obviously, the software will allow printing the invoice should this be requested as a hardcopy in paper.

c) *Other agents' obligations*: Server centres as well as service providers must cooperate with the tax authorities and provide them with any information they request.

5 Conclusions

We have introduced the features of a project we are developing at the Dept. of Computer Science of the University School of Tourism at Malaga University, which will lead to the implementation of a SIFT in more than 15 hotels on the Costa del Sol, Spain.
At the beginning of this project we studied the EDI software already on the market and we also looked into the projects of some international associations working with hotel management systems such as HITA (Hospitality Information Technology Association) and HITIS (Hospitality Industry Technology Integration Standards) [4], both pioneers in the field. However, we found that given the legal requirements of the Spanish tax system it was not possible to apply any of these systems to our situation.
Therefore, this project is novel within the field of hotel-oriented-computing. It is only one of the modules within a future and more global project that will include the incorporation of interactive television, automatic payment systems, etc., applying co-operative work and workflow [2] control techniques.

6 References

[1] AEOC. Prepárese para la factura electrónica. http://www.aeoc.es/notes/aeoc5/24e2.html. (1996).

[2] Aguayo, A, Caro, J.L., Guevara, A. et al.: Workflow Technology: An Application for Tourism Management. ENTER'97 Information and Communication Technologies in Tourism 1997 A Min Tjoa ISBN: 3-211-82963-6 SpringerComputerScience. (1997).

[3] E.D.I.: The UK confederation for E.D.I. standards. http://www.eca.org.uk/ukcedis. (1987).

[4] HITIS. Hospitality Industry Technology Integration Standards. White Paper. http://www.hitis.org/background. (1998).

[5] OECD: Electronic Comerce and Tourism Policy. OECD Policy Brief. N° 1 November 1997 on Electronic Comerce. http://www.oecd.org. (1997).

[6] Serrano, C. et al: Planificación de Sistema de Información en la empresa. El intercambio electrónico de datos. http://ciberconta.unizar.es/Biblioteca/0003/SerLabFab96.html. (1996).

[7] Yellow Henry's, H., UN/EDIFACT Book: Introduction to UN/EDIFACT Messages. http://www.harbringer.com/secure/edifacts. (1997).

From intra-regional competition towards intra-regional cooperation in tourism : The concept of Telecooperation and Virtual Enterprises in the regional tourism business

Michael C. Laubenheimer
Madeira Tecnopolo (P), Director of Projects, TourISt Project Manager
mclaubenheimer@madinfo.pt
Thomas Carlsson, CINS (S); Franco Cordero, Consultant (I); Ari Makinen, Kemi-Tornio Polytecnic (FIN);

Abstract

Tourism is a complex service business combining many players at the *Point of Offer* – the tourist destination. Small and medium sized tourism enterprises (SMTEs) have to find their way between competition and co-operation within this rapidly changing market.
New organisational, technical and work concepts are being discussed within the scientific world as suitable for improving the ability of organisations to respond to fast changing market conditions : (Tele)Co-operation, networks, virtual enterprises. Although the key issues are clear and evident, there are no guidelines for implementing these concepts.
The paper gives an introduction to these concepts and presents the situation of SMTEs as analysed through seven tourist destinations in Europe. The paper then gives some examples of what these regions have done in the last twelve months in trying to implement the concepts.

1 Introduction

1.1 Tourism today

Tourism is widely regarded as being the world's largest industry, making significant contributions to the economies and employment of most countries. It is worth recalling some of the characteristics of the tourism business in general :

- Tourism is a *complex product*, involving the integration of services from diverse organisations: private and public, large and small, local and remote.
- Effective *collaboration* between these organisations is essential for the delivery of a quality product.
- The availability *of up-to-date, accurate, attractive and accessible information* is regarded as crucial for the success of a tourist product.
- Tourism is *information* rather than a physical product that needs to be *distributed* and made available to both intermediaries and end consumers; it is almost entirely dependent upon representations and descriptions to help consumers make a purchase decision.

1.2 Current and emerging business models

What generic business models are suitable for coping with market situations arising in the tourism sector ? For the following discussion we wish to keep in mind the marketing approach which says that any enterprise should be managed as from the market and towards the market [1/p 3-10].

According to Heinen [2/p 215] *co-operation* is collaboration based on contractual agreements between legal and economically independent organisations with the aim of following and achieving a common goal. Co-operations can be seen from different angles [3/p 281]

- as vertical co-operations between organisations from different successive levels of the value-added chain
- as horizontal co-operations between organisations from one sector and the same level of the value-added chain
- as diagonal co-operations between organisations from different sectors
- purpose, e.g. joint marketing
- scope : regional, national or international
- duration
- level of information and communication technology (ICT) support.

The objective of co-operation (bilateral or multilateral in the form of networks) is to achieve a strategic advantage vis-à-vis enterprises which act alone : mainly minimisation of investments, time advantages, acquistion of skills, reduction of business risks, market entries, etc. [3/p 279]. A key element is that the partners involved continue to act autonomously and with equal rights. Despite the contractual relation aiming to reduce the costs of control, a major success factor of co-operation is the level of trust among the partners. Without trust the strategic advantage will be reversed.

Progesses in ICT, telecommunications and multimedia and their applications [4/p31-152 ; 5/p 29-68 ; 6] bring a new dimension into co-operations: *Tele*-cooperation means computer supported collaborative work between organisations or parts of organisations which are spread throughout several sites [7/p 24-30]. Organisations become independent of time and location despite the fact that they are working jointly with others in order to carry out specific common tasks. In theory, resources can be used wherever they are cheap and available. We see here the fading out of traditional working locations.

While technlogical progress is behind this development, the phenomenon is at the same time responding to current market trends (providing the services there where they are required : near the customer) and traffic, regional development and structural policies of governments and international organisations [3/p 368-372].

The additional advantage of tele-cooperation vis-à-vis traditional co-operation is limited by the availability of powerful telecom infrastructures, by the capacity of networks to handle multimedia applications/information and by security and legal risks [3/p 303-306]. As a consequence additional control mechanisms have to be implemented to guarantee reliable co-operations. Beside these technical and organisational barriers studies have also focussed on the human aspect : tele-cooperation applications and scenarios have only been accepted by people who are familiar with the use of PCs and who are willing to change their traditional working methods for co-operative and collaborative environments [5/p 59 ; 3/p 458f][1]. Thus awareness and training become a crucial element when implementing ICT based working methods.

From the conceptual point of view there is no difference between *co-operation* and *tele-cooperation*. Both collaborative forms concern the internal relations between organisations and people involved.

The concept of *virtual enterprises* goes beyond this point of view completementing it through its market approach.

Any business activity aims to create income and profit resulting from a contractual relation between a supplier and a customer, i.e. between a seller and a buyer. This buyer-seller relationship is actually not a co-operative relation as defined above. Nevertheless, the purpose of co-operation is to sell a product or service to generate income. As a consequence, the companies jointly involved in a co-operation can be considered as the supplier or seller. It is obvious that a customer or buyer prefers to deal with only one single organisation able to provide a complete product or service instead of with many. Thus, the new issue entered by the concept of virtual enterprise is the relationship of a (tele)co-operation partnership or network with the market, the seller.

Virtualisation can be illustrated through an analogy in computer technologies where the distinction between physical and logical components aims to overcome capacity and flexibility limits. The *client* (i.e. the seller) only sees the logical system, the procedures of co-ordination and the tasks completion are hidden. Each system component enters its core skills and capabilities. Through a clever combination of these components and skills one can create the impression of being as fast as the fastest, big as the biggest and cheap as the cheapest. [3/p 396ff].

An example of a virtual organisation might be a translation service. It is unlikely that a single translation office can provide translation services in every language and in every field. Through the combination of specialised translation services (language and field) which might be spread throughout the world nearly every client can be served

---

1 Picot lists a series of requirements concerning people engaged in tele-cooperations : openness, high productivity, good specialised knowledge, self-motivation, self-control, planning capacities, adequate ICT skills.

individually. Information and communication technologies enable rapid exchange and service delivery.

Virtual enterprises are built through networking of distributed organisations which contribute to a co-ordinated process of product/service creation.

Picot presents the following characteristics and realisation principles of virtual enterprises [3/p 403].

Characteristics	Realisation Principles
Modularity relatively small and clear system with decentralised responsibility for decision making and results	*Open-Closed-Principle* closed market appearance based on open and dynamic structures
Heterogeneity different performance profiles (strengths and skills)	*Principle of complementarity* skills possed by the elements are complementary
Distribution Physical and time related, possibility of dynamic reconfiguration	*Principle of transparency* client only specifies his requirements, he is not concerned by internal processes : "black box"-effect

Organisations with the characteristics and following the principles mentioned are able to react to fast changing market conditions and requirements and to provide a set of complex individualised products or services (mass customisation).

1.3 Situation of tourism regions

While important industry sectors already benefit from networking and co-operation and are forerunners in the implementation of virtual organisation concepts, the service sector in general is hesitating to implement new organisational and infrastructural concepts. This is also the case for tourism even if airlines are ICT specialists, big tour operators (TOs) are starting to offer individualised holiday packages and more and more tourist information can be found on the Internet.

Many tourism regions and many tourism organisations, in particular small and medium sized tourism enterprises (SMTEs) hesitate to use advanced technologies and to implement new business concepts. A series of barriers impede co-operation within the tourism sector or between tourism and other business sectors.

The TourISt project[2], whose aim is the introduction of the so-called Information Society into regional tourism, analysed

[2] Seven European tourism regions - Aosta Valley (I), Burgenland (A), Guadeloupe (F), Hampshire (UK), Lapland (Fin), and Västerbotten (S) under the leadership of Madeira (P)

i. the situation of SMTEs from economic, organisational and technological aspects,
ii. the market situation of the regions concerned,
iii. the form of co-operation at regional, national and international level among public and private organisations and
iv. the use of information and communication technologies.

Despite the fact that the tourism offer differs considerably between the regions involved, despite the fact that TOs have market shares in these regions between 95 % (nearly total market control) and 5 % (nearly no TO activity at all), despite the fact that the regions have full year tourism or only very few activity peaks, there is a series of findings [8/p 15-18] common to the regions; and we are sure that these findings are identical for other destinations. The findings can be divided into organisation and region-related issues.

The tourism organisation is confronted with specific market situations :

- often it is a family managed organisation and is rather small ;
- clients – the tourists – are far away, direct contacts are difficult to establish ;
- short-term profit targets do not make it possible to invest in skills/qualifications, technologies and marketing ;
- low-level skills in the use of information and communication technologies ;
- large international TOs are dictating the prices and controlling the market (development) ;
- there are many competitors at the regional level

At the regional level, additional problems can be identified which do not facilitate the life of SMTEs :

- there is little structured co-operation between public and private tourism organisations ;
- tourism is not recognised as an industry with a value added chain, industrial working concepts (co-operation, networking) are not considered as useful or applicable ;
- public organisations and TOs do not make major awareness-raising effort to promote the use and implementation of advanced ICT in tourism ;
- no regional ICT strategy in tourism ;

– formed a partnership with the common aim of finding practical solutions to meet the new challenges of the tourism market : increasing the performance of regional tourism professionals and improving the information flow to the end consumer through the use of advanced information and communication technologies. TourISt (**Tour**ism towards the **I**nformation **S**ocie**t**y) is funded by the European Commission under Article 10 of the European Regional Development Fund as a pilot application project relating to the joint "Regional Information Society Initiative" (RISI2) of DG XVI and DG XIII.

- little information is available about the tourists' expectations, behaviour and reactions and about overall market trends, because of limited market observation and dissemination information ;
- holiday makers have only limited information about a given holiday destination with its large variety of activities and places of interest.

Thus the situation for implementing promising work and organisational concepts in regional tourism was not very encouraging while starting the exercise of implementing ICT in regional tourism. SMTEs are used to co-operating with other organisations. But we have seen that this happens in a generally *ad hoc,* unstructured way without any planning or co-ordination.

However, regarding the main market characteristics of tourism – high complexity of product and high market instability and uncertainty – virtual organisation concepts are considered as particularly suitable for overcoming these obstacles [4/p 251]. And Schertler explicitly pointed out that "the tourism business has a high potential for the successful application of what we call the *virtualisation*" [9/p 279]. The question was and is how can we implement new work and organisational concepts based on advanced ICT in the service business and in particular in regional tourism with its aforementioned characteristics. The literature analyses and discusses the advantages and disadvantages, the potential and the limits, the requirements and results of tele-cooperation and virtual enterprises in detail. But few answers are given as to how to progress from the situation today towards sustainable co-operations and virtual tourism enterprises.

2 Steps towards sustainable cooperation in regional tourism

Some authors mention issues which concern this transition process : *trust* and a system of common values [10 ; 11/ chap 9]. Mathews proposes 10 rules of trust creation which concern the maintenance of trust between organisations rather than the creation of trust [12/p 16-19]. Knetsch asks for intensive training as a prerequisite of for all those persons concerned with tele-cooperation [5/p 59].

Training, trust, common sense, community - these are the items on which the TourISt regions have focused their first steps towards the introduction of the Information Society into the tourism business. These tasks have not yet been fully completed but we can already present at least one result - that without building a community the provision of technology will fail[3]. Those who progressed too fast and focused on technical issues rather than human and social issues did not achieve their objectives and are likely to have major problems in further deployment of their ICT based solutions and services.

---

3 Interesting information about virtual communities and their creation and development can be found by Hagel [13/ part II]

Thus the lessons we have learned so far are :
Lesson One : Go slow, take your time
Lesson Two : Clarify the relations between the potential partners, speak together
Lesson Three : Create a (regional) community with win-win situations

In the following we present examples of actions undertaken and processes introduced in some of the regions. All activities can be assigned to the three elements which constitute a virtual enterprise : *People/Organisations – Purpose – Connections.*

2.1 People / Organisations

Mutual understanding

The six-month starting period of the project where each region was obliged to analyse its situation enabled multiple bilateral and multilateral meetings and discussions to be held. All meetings were controlled by regional project managers who play rather a neutral role than being directly involved in the tourism business. While the bilateral meetings provided a deep insight into the relationships among regional tourism organisations, the multilateral meetings made for a better mutual understanding. Thus, it was possible to fully integrate competitors who were rather reluctant to co-operate at the beginning of the exercise. The creation of mutual understanding concerns not only the tourism organisations of a given region, but also the relation between the regions involved (which are to a certain extent also competitors on the global market). The SMTEs and the public tourism organisations of a given region learned that their problems are not unique but general. As a consequence, the enabling of these exchanges and learning processes was in the interest of all, and this process is still going on.

Training

As the common decision was to go ahead with the introduction of Information Society Technologies[4] it was natural to deploy a comprehensive training programme in ICT based applications bearing in mind the low skills of regional SMTEs and public organisations in charge of tourism.

While the starting phase concerned the management level of tourism organisations, the training focused on the operational level. However, many managers, too, were very interested in attending the training sessions. For many of the tourism professionals it was the first time they had followed a training programme.

---

4 The TourISt partner regions agreed on the implementation of two major applications : (i) developing and implementing an intranet system to enhance the intra-regional co-operation and communication – the Back Office ; (ii) providing access to the regional tourism information system through 24-hour access public terminals and the Internet – the Front Office

Three steps have been selected to ensure that the maximum is obtained out of the training :

A. *Information Technology: a new way to communicate*
   This step is targeted to make either regional professionals or SMTEs understand "how to communicate" in the emerging Information Society : Marketing, Customer profiles in the 90s, Players and rules in tourism, Technologies for tourism, Designing and handling a database, Direct marketing, Internet – the new challenge.
   The objective of the modules is twofold : capturing the attention of the audience through the targeting on professional issues attractively presented and raising the awareness of the potential of ICT for the tourism.
B. *Office automation: basic training*
   In this phase the focus is laid on the importance of using up-to-date office tools in day-to-day work (e.g. introduction to Word, Excel, Access, Powerpoint, DTP) The objective of these modules is to make the professional familiar with the use of a computer. Each of the modules is built around a typical business scenario, and thus know-how is acquired through a kind of "learning on the job" and "learning by doing"

C. *System and application training*
   The modules lead professionals and SMTEs to the "core" of the Information Society applied in tourism, showing them technically how to handle tourist information using the new telematic tools (e.g. BBS, e-mail, Internet browsing, design of html pages).
   These modules are directly related to the back and front office applications mentioned above.

As the regional tourism organisations jointly followed the courses, the training sessions also supported the creation of communities either on a intra-regional level (part B and C) or on an inter-regional level (part A). Some of these training modules were realised in dense workshops combining tourism professionals, multimedia specialists, schoolteachers, secondary school pupils, researchers and politicians.

2.2 Purpose

All actions followed the overall objective of the TourISt project to better market a given tourism region through the use of information and communication technologies. All regional organisations had agreed on this, no decision and strategy met with any outside opposition. It is obvious that the decision processes took time (they were however guided by the regional project managers) but otherwise the SMTEs and public organisations would not have committed themselves for an active participation.

For marketing a product through the use of ICT it is first of all necessary to have information available in a digitised format and secondly, several information needs to be packed into an attractive product.

Thus, as soon as the basic hardware and software was installed (see 2.3 connections) the professionals could start to digitise existing material and/or to create new material. Here they could already apply the know-how gathered in the training courses of part B – continued "learning by doing". As a consequence, one of the regions has a comprehensive databank of regional tourist information which can be viewed from all local tourist offices : tourists can be provided for the first time with complete, prompt and up-to-date information concerning the entire regional offer and not only from the local offer.

Regions where the tourism sector is more privately driven focused their efforts more on the development and creation of saleable products. This process is more time consuming because besides the pure combination of information the regional partners also have to discuss and to agree on a marketing strategy. But, based on the discussions engaged so far and the marketing plans forwarded to the other regions, all regions have decided to develop and market jointly one product which can be offered in each of the regions except one. The product concerns a specific niche market which does not overlap with the offers provided by international TOs.

2.3 Connections

Connections are all physical, technical, organisational, personal and social channels, interactions and relations which help create a team or a community on which virtual enterprises are built.

The installation of computers, office and communication tools constitutes the prerequisite for supporting the co-operative work. This happened at the same time when the local and regional tourism organisations started to digitise their information base and to enter new data.

But the regions had already invested in the establishment of human and organisational relations. Regular (face-to-face) meetings and participation in training courses created new relations where non-existent or extended and strengthened existing relations.

In one case, there was a private initiative of cottage owners since the 80s aiming to better organise the renting of holiday cottages. Based on previous good experience and probaly due to the fact that the core group of independent organisations had over the years established some kinds of rules and common sense and had learned to trust one another, the extension of service offer (i.e. the extension of partnerships) seemed opportune and realistic : hotels, shopkeepers, safari entrepreneurs and other specialised tourism service providers have been integrated into this co-operation initiative. This is what we said earlier by mentioning lesson three "create a (regional) community".

Today they have a central office and run joint marketing (resource sharing and service improvement). The customer (tourist) has the impression of dealing with one single organisation (black box effect), and of obtaining an exclusive service.

Thanks to the TourISt project, the regional SMTEs were able to benefit from ICT and to enlarge their partnership. For the cutomer, this kind of ICT supported co-operation claims to have a virtual significance despite real smallness [3/ p 407]. In addition they are able to reduce their internal communication costs through the use of an Intranet and e-mail and of a comprehensive local information service.

Trust, once again, is the key to the success of co-operative relations. Otherwise sales people will not sell beds for other organisations or will find service providers more concerned with meeting tourists' requirements than pursuing a policy of income optimisation for their own organisation.

3 Conclusion

We have not yet reached the end of the project and neither have we fully implemented the technical infrastructures necessary to meet the challenges of the emerging Information Society. But based on the experiences gathered so far we think that we are on the right track and that the concepts of virtual enterprises have proven their relevance. Scientific discussion is not always very helpful, but at least it indicates some fields where and how regional tourism organisations may intervene in order to create and exploit sustainable intra-regional co-operations rather than stimulating intra-regional competition.

Keys to successful intra-regional co-operations (which will be extended later to other regions (inter-regional co-operations) and to other tourism related sectors (inter-sectorial co-operations)) are

i. *time* for the deployment of the transition from competition to co-operation,
ii. *trust* in people/organisations, purpose and connections,
iii. *training* and awareness in order to exploit the potential of information and communication technologies and applications.

ICT is available and affordable as well as specific applications facilitating the use of electronic information (Internet, Intranet, Extranet ; trip planners, geographical information systems, booking and payment services). Virtualisation is more of a social issue than a technical one.

Through the application of new business and working concepts, through the creation of confidence and the establishment of partnerships and through the use of existing ICT tools, we have now the condition that our tourism destinations and SMTEs will enter into new markets and increase the tourist satisfaction and build the basis for long-term prosperity.

The overall idea which the TourISt regions are going to realise is illustrated in this final scheme.

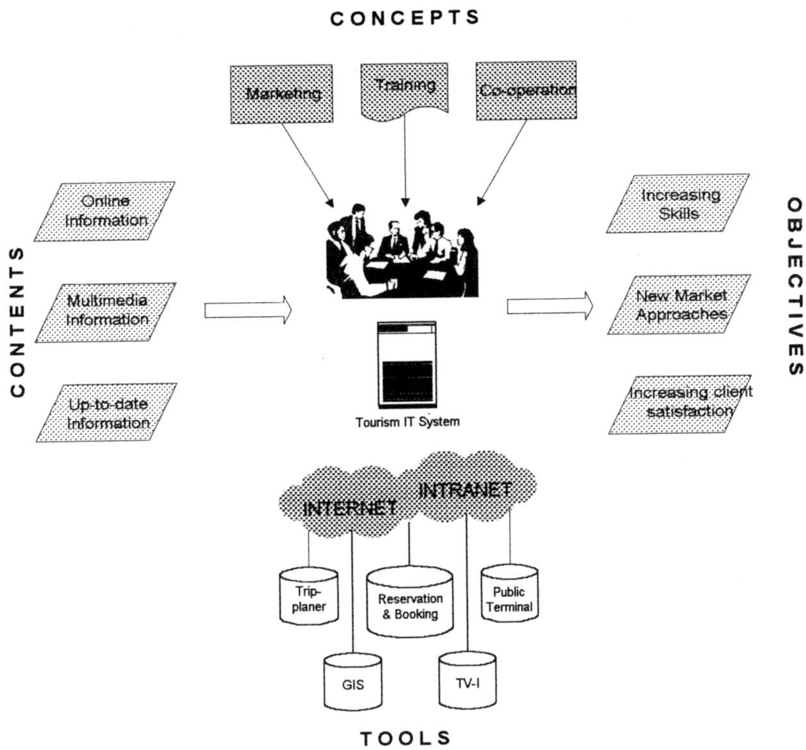

4. References

[1] Raffée, H. (1979), Marketing und Umwelt, Stuttgart 1979
[2] Heinen, E. (1983), Industriebetriebslehre, 7. Aufl., Wiesbaden, 1983
[3] Picot, A. (1997), Die grenzenlose Unternehmung, 3.Aufl., Wiesbaden 1998,
[4] Pribilla, P. (1996), Telekommunikation im Management, Stuttgart 1996
[5] Knetsch, W. (1996), Die treibenden Kräfte : Der Weg zum vernetzten Unternemen, in: Arthur D. Little, Management im vernetzten Unternehmen, Wiesbaden 1996
[6] France Telecom Expertel (1996), Business Solutions Analysis and Demonstrations, Deliverable 1 of "INFORMS : Dissemination of Euro-ISDN Benefits for SMEs", 1996
[7] Reichwald (1994), Telekooperation und Telearbeit, in : Office Management (1994) 10
[8] TourISt (1997), Feasibility Study, Funchal 1997, for internal use
[9] Schertler, W. (1998), Virtual Enterprises in Tourism : Folkore and Facts – Conceptual Challenges for Academic Research, in : Information and Communication Technologies in Tourism 1998, Wien 1998
[10] Handy (1995), Trust and the Virtual Organization, in : Harward Business Review, Nr. 3, p 40-50
[11] Lipnack, J. / Stamps J. (1998), Virtuelle Teams, Wien 1998
[12] Mathews, J. (1994), The Governance of Inter-Organisational Networks, in: Corporate Governance, Nr. 1, 1994, p 14-19
[13] Hagel /Armstrong (1997), Net Gain – Profit im Netz : Märkte erobern mit virutellen Communities, Wiesbaden 1997

Factors Affecting the Contribution of Information Technology in the Hospitality Industry

Michael Baker and Silvia Sussmann
School of Management Studies for the Service Sector
University of Surrey
mss1ss@surrey.ac.uk

Introduction

Although at a practical level there is beginning to be a reasonable body of literature on the application of information technology to the hospitality industry, there are indubitably questions, which are of interest to both researchers and practitioners, which need further investigation. Of particular interest is the question of success and failure of information technology projects. This paper describes research which employs comparative analysis of case studies to investigate the factors which make one information technology implementation successful and another, apparently similar, seem to fail. The research is at present under way, and the paper discusses the pilot case, and considers how this pilot has validated the research approach. Of course there are already some case studies published which bear on this question (see for example, Baker and Sweeney, 1998; and Baker, Wild and Sussmann, 1998) but these have been one-off opportunities to research material of particular interest.

Success and Failure in IT Projects

IT projects have a poor reputation. According to a study by OASIG, a special interest group concerned with the organisational aspects of IT, up to 90% fail to meet their performance goals. Around 40% fail completely or are abandoned. Less than 25% properly integrate business and technology objectives (OR Newsletter, 1996; Caulkin, 1997). Others have come to similar conclusions (for example Dertouzos, 1990, Bailey, 1996), Strassmann (1985, 1990). In hospitality, there is no reason to believe the record is any better. Indeed, the attitudes and education of many managers in the hospitality industry make them ill equipped to embrace innovation (Gamble, 1991).

A number of authors have made suggestions about the factors most influential in the success or failure of IT projects. The summary of the OASIG study results referred to above identified a number of reasons why IT projects fail (OR Newsletter, 1996). Collins and Bicknell (1997) state that in virtually all the IT disasters the same ten themes occur. Dutton *et al* (1995) draw attention to a number of factors management and others should attend to in order to avoid major IT disasters. To the extent to which a successful project is an avoided failure, and on the basis of the OASIG study,

Collins and Bicknell's analysis, and the advice of Dutton *et al* referred to above, successful projects would be expected to have the following features:

- Business- rather than technology-led; buy-in by line management from the start;
- Weight given to other values and goals along with a focus on economic efficiency;
- A management agenda which concentrates on business effectiveness;
- Close attention to human and organisational factors;
- Consideration of organisation of work and job design;
- Significant users' influence on systems development;
- Incremental development through small steps;
- A healthy scepticism about claims of suppliers and consultants;
- Carry out effective regular project reviews.
- Create an open culture which encourages self-reporting, making it clear that admissions of mistakes will not be punished; and encourage a willingness to accept that mistakes are opportunities to learn, not chances to score points;
- Insist on systematic risk assessment, detailed disaster management and contingency plans for each project;
- Make practical efforts to gain the commitment of all direct stakeholders at all stages of the project life cycle.
- Ensure pressures for greater efficiency do not cause demotivation amongst key professionals;
- Institute a "quality culture";
- Avoid top-down or external deadline setting that takes insufficient account of local needs; and
- Preferring cheap, proven, off-the-shelf packages rather than costly, unproven, custom-built software; or, worse, the tailoring of a standard proven package.

This list provides a number of hypotheses about implementing IT in the hospitality and tourism industries which research is required to test.

The Research

The research programme planned is of a number of case studies of information technology in hospitality and in tourism, using a common template, to obtain comparative material for measuring strategic and operational benefits. The methodology is adapted from that used by Fearon and Philip (1998). This procedure involves a comparison of pre-implementation benefit expectations with post-implementation perceptions of realised benefits. Three "benefits states" are used to denote the degree of the gap between expectations and perceptions of realised benefits. If a shortfall is experienced throughout the company as a whole, then this benefit state is described as a “deficiency”. If there is no gap, the state is termed “neutrality”. If the perceived realised benefit, on the other hand, exceeds the original benefit expectations, then this is regarded as “efficiency”. The assessment is through the use of a benefit rating instrument and personal interviews. It is thus possible to draw conclusions about the relationship between the benefit states and factors such as implementation approach, and put forward some analysis of the reasons for relative success and failure. The methodology takes into account that pre-implementation expectations overall may be high or low, and that the change may be radical or incremental.

For the purpose of the pilot, the eight categories of strategic benefit and ten categories of operational benefit used by Fearon and Philip were employed (Tables 1 and 2 show which they are). However, whilst Fearon and Philip measured, for each category, benefit for both pre-implementation expectations and post implementation outcomes as either high, medium and low, in the pilot this was simplified to identifying under which categories benefits were expected and experienced and which were of particular importance to the company.

Available documentation was collected and used but the research relies mainly on semi-structured interviews, with subsequent confirmation of the data as presented written up as a case study, including the tables as shown below. The case study below summarises the pilot.

The Golf and Country Club[1]

The Golf and Country Club comprises two international competition golf courses, a 24-bedroom international standard hotel, 32 lodges, and extensive sporting and leisure facilities. The luxurious lodges provide accommodation for four, six or eight guests. There are four bars and two restaurants. The leisure facilities include swimming pools, squash courts, fitness suite, and a spa centre. The banqueting and conference facilities are capable of handling a wide range of events. There are resident professionals offering golf tuition; the retail function sells equipment and clothing.

The Golf and Country Club offers a range of memberships, depending on which of the facilities the guests want to take advantage of, over what period, with what frequency, and whether as a group, family or individually. Overall there are some 2000 sport and leisure members and around 1000 golfing members. The company turns over around £6m ($10m) annually. It employs about 180 full and part time staff in the summer, falling to around 100 in the low season. The company is unusual (and fortunate) in the hospitality industry in having very low labour turnover amongst the

---

[1] The names are not the real ones and the company has been disguised in the text. The author is very grateful to the managers in the company who have given their time and advice. All errors, omissions and inaccuracies are entirely the author's responsibility.

permanent staff, with some members of staff having joined when it first opened. About four years ago the owners determined that major changes were needed to improve performance, control and the service offered by the club to its clients, in order to respond to competitive challenges. A new management team set about introducing a new organisational structure, redefining job roles and accountabilities.

There were then few IT systems in the company, and they were stand-alone and relatively primitive. There was little in the way of management information. The decision to introduce first a Property Management System (PMS) linked to a Food and Beverage (F&B) system (from Company A, a leading supplier of this type of package), followed by a system to cover the golf, leisure, membership and retail functions (from Supplier B, also a well known supplier, to the sports and leisure industry) heralded a major change for the company and the people working for it. These systems have now been installed. This case study focuses on the introduction of these two systems, and the assessment by the management of their success.

Property Management and Food and Beverage Systems

The PMS and F&B systems were introduced about four years ago. The supplier, Company A, is a leading supplier of these products with a significant worldwide client base. The PMS is a standard package covering front office, guest accounts, conference and banqueting, and back office functions. The F&B Package is also a standard product, and covers the restaurants and bars. It provides inventory and portion control and supports touch screens. Objectives for the investment included better control, improved co-ordination, easier operation, and a belief that a major venue should be able to benefit from modern technology. The management recognised that the introduction of the integrated PMS and F&B system represented a radical change for the company, and the staff, who were already dealing with the difficulties of changes in roles, accountability and organisation which the new management was introducing, faced the introduction of these systems with trepidation.

Managing the Change

Introducing the new IT systems inevitably meant additional work in planning, preparing and implementing the new system, training staff and ensuring new tasks were carried out effectively, and this fell on already busy people. However, managers recollect that on the whole the implementation went reasonably smoothly. Hardware had to be introduced and tested, with the installation of the cabling possibly giving the most headaches. For each of the PMS and the F&B systems, a team of key personnel was responsible for preparation of the files which hold the tables of static information such as rooms details, menus and prices, and for taking the project forward and co-ordinating implementation. In the case of the PMS, an additional member of staff, familiar with hospitality IT systems, was recruited on a short-term contract, and worked in a team with the Head Receptionist and front and back office staff members. For the F&B system the team consisted of the Conference and Banqueting Manager, the F&B Services Manger, the F&B Controller and two others. Staff training was run on site in one of the lodges. Generally there were few problems with the software.

The few technical problems were resolved, and managers comment that the suppliers "stayed with it". Overall they were satisfied with the performance of the system once installed and with the support provided by the suppliers during and after installation.

Implementation took, from start to finish, about a year to 18 months, and although the new systems were a bit of a shock for some of the staff, particularly those with long service, they have all adapted. Once the new systems were in, the staff could see there were benefits, and management believes that no one would now want to go back to the old way of doing things. It was, however, a radical change and a culture shock for the company.

Table 1: Expectations and Outcomes: PMS and F&B System

	Expectations	Outcomes	Importance
Strategic			
Increased Profit	✓	✓	
Reduced Long term Risk			
Market Share			
Competitive Advantage			
Customer Service	✓	✓(eventually)	
Improved Image	✓	✓	
Faster Trading			
Operational			
Cash Flow			
Paperwork Cut	✓	✓- (not in accounts)	
Admin Costs Reduced			
Errors Reduced	✓	✓	High
Payment Processing Improved	✓	✓+	
Reduced Staff Levels	✓	N	
Lower Inventory Costs	✓	N	
Fewer Stock-outs	✓	N	
Improved Customer Information	✓	✓+	
Better Management Information	✓	✓+	High
Better Control	✓	✓+	High
Lower Costs	✓	✓+	High

Key

Column 3	✓	expectations met
	✓-	some improvement but not to expectation
	✓+	expectations exceeded
	N	no improvement
Column 4	High	Indicates this aspect was of particular importance to the company

Expectations and Outcomes

Now the system has been running for some time, managers are aware that it could provide them with much more information than is currently used. The company has inevitably found out that there are ongoing costs to an IT investment. Support and hardware and software upgrades have to be paid for. However, the company is satisfied with the support provided by the supplier. Overall the managers are more satisfied with the PMS and F&B system than they expected.

Table 1 shows for strategic and operational aspects what the company expected of the PMS and F&B system and, in the third column, the extent to which these expectations were met. So, in column 2, a tick indicates that improvements were expected in this area. Column 3 shows how well these were met (see the key below the table). The fourth column shows how important this aspect was for the company.

The Golf, Leisure and Membership System

The company then set about providing systems to deal with membership, golf and leisure bookings and the retail function, including stock control. There were already some systems in this area. Although the membership files were held manually, the golf bookings used a basic computer programme, and a till. The leisure bookings were manual, again using a till. The retail function had a computer system, and the stock control was run on a PC using Lotus 1-2-3.

The Process of Change

The implementation, over some six months, did not go well. When introduced, the system was found not to be able to deal with some aspects of the operation; for example, the retail module was unable to distinguish, as the old system could, between different sizes, colours and styles of garment. The system seemed unable to cope with the very wide range of membership options the company offered. There was no conversion of existing computer files to the new system, which meant that all existing bookings had to be rekeyed. The process of transfer took about six weeks, and the management of the bookings on the old and new systems together represented a significant problem during implementation. The software had errors, which took time to correct. Training was inadequate and staff suffered considerable levels of stress. However, whilst the company is inclined to identify the supplier as responsible for a poor implementation, there are aspects which the company recognises as its responsibility. The requirements specifications appears to have been inadequate (with the system unable to deal with aspects of the company's business, as indicated above). Furthermore, the supplier had recommended 40 hours of training that the company had cut to 12 hours to save expense.

Expectations and Outcomes

Table 2 shows how the company assesses its expectations for this system, and the outcomes. As the table shows, the company had expectations of benefits in many areas. Although in most of these there have been improvements, few have fully reached expectations. Furthermore, the system continues to give problems, and the company is not as satisfied as for the hospitality systems with the ongoing support given by the supplier. One cause of continued difficulty is the underdeveloped link with the PMS. Transactions created in the Golf, Leisure and Membership System eventually update the accounting system in the PMS. However, if the PMS goes off-line, transaction updates created in the Golf, Leisure and Membership System do not get stored for later updating, but have to be manually rekeyed into the PMS. Overall, although it represents improvement, the system has not met expectations. The managers judge that it was also a major change for the company, and for the employees affected.

Table 2: Expectations and Outcomes: Golf, Leisure and Membership System

	Expectations	Outcomes	Importance
Strategic			
Increased Profit	✓	?	
Reduced Long term Risk	✓		
Market Share	✓		
Competitive Advantage	✓	✓	
Customer Service			
Improved Image	✓	✓	
Faster Trading			
Operational			
Cash Flow	✓	✓-	
Paperwork Cut	✓	✓-	
Admin Costs Reduced	✓	✓-	
Errors Reduced	✓	✓-	
Payment Processing Improved	✓	✓	
Reduced Staff Levels		?	
Lower Inventory Costs			
Fewer Stock-outs	✓	✓-	
Improved Customer Information	✓	✓-	
Better Management Information	✓	✓-	High
Better Control	✓	✓-	High
Lower Costs	✓	✓-	High

Key

Column 3	✓	expectations met
	✓+	expectations exceeded
	✓-	some improvement but not to expectation
	N	no improvement
	?	not known
Column 4	High	this aspect was of particular importance to the company

Factors Affecting Success: some conclusions and speculations.

Why did one IT system exceed expectations and the other one not meet them? First, there are technical aspects. The products of Company A appear to be robust, whilst the Golf, Leisure and Membership System is technically less satisfactory. Managers at the company identified a significant difference between the two. The PMS and the F&B system are both true *packages.* The package incorporates a data model and process structures, which (it is hoped) cover all eventualities and therefore there should be no requirement for reprogramming to fit the needs of a new customer. The company enters the static data into tables, thus particularising the general data model. If there is a suitable package available, it is likely to offer a cheaper solution than a bespoke system offering the same functionality. If it is necessary to modify the programming of a package, this implies that the data model is insufficiently comprehensive to cover the particulars of the company in question. For this reason doing this (modifying the programming of a package) is generally held to be getting the worst of both worlds; a better option in such a case is a bespoke system. It is not clear whether the suppliers of the Golf, Leisure and Membership System were modifying the programming of an existing package, or constructing a new system, using some existing program modules. However, whichever it was, it is not surprising that the package proved the more satisfactory.

Second, the requirements specification seems to have been more comprehensive in the case of the hospitality systems. The extent to which the suppliers or the company management helped in this cannot be differentiated after all this time. Third, there was a clear determination to allocate and manage the use of resources in the implementation of the PMS and the F&B systems. A systematic approach seems to have paid off. Finally, training seems to have been adequate in the case of the hospitality systems, whereas the company's cutting the amount of training recommended by the supplier of the Golf, Leisure and Membership System may have been a false economy.

Overall, however, whilst more resources and more training over the period of the implementation might have ameliorated the trauma of the experience for those concerned, it seems unlikely that these would have affected in the long term the dissatisfaction with the Golf, Leisure and Membership System. On the other hand, good organisation and adequate training in the implementation of the hospitality systems probably ensured a favourable response by the users, which may well have affected perceptions of how satisfactory it is.

Benefit Success Matrix

Fearon and Philip (1998) suggest that a matrix can be used to conceptualise empirical evidence for the relationships between benefit success, implementation success and implementation approach. The matrix is divided into left and right sides: the higher the position of the company on the left side ('B' quadrant) or the right side ('C' quadrant), the better the company has been at achieving its expected benefits. The right side of the matrix represents radical change aimed at achieving high benefits, including strategic advantage. The left side of the matrix represents incremental change, with overall low expectations of benefits, and mainly operational ones. The diagonal "line of neutrality" is the "ideal" benefit state, where expectations are exactly met. Clearly moving from left to right involves more careful planning and higher risk, with greater chance of unsatisfied expectations.

Figure 1 shows this matrix, with the position of the two system implementations shown. Clearly the PMS/F&B system exceeded expectations, whereas the Golf System did not. Both are reckoned a radical change for the company, although the focus on operational benefits suggests a position not too far into the right hand quadrants. The PMS/F&B system thus is in the High Realised Benefits/High Benefit Expectations and above the diagonal line of neutrality. Positioning the Golf System is more problematic. Clearly it falls below the line of neutrality, as the benefits fall short of the expectations. It is still the case that significant benefits were achieved, which suggests a position on or just below the border between low and high implementation success.

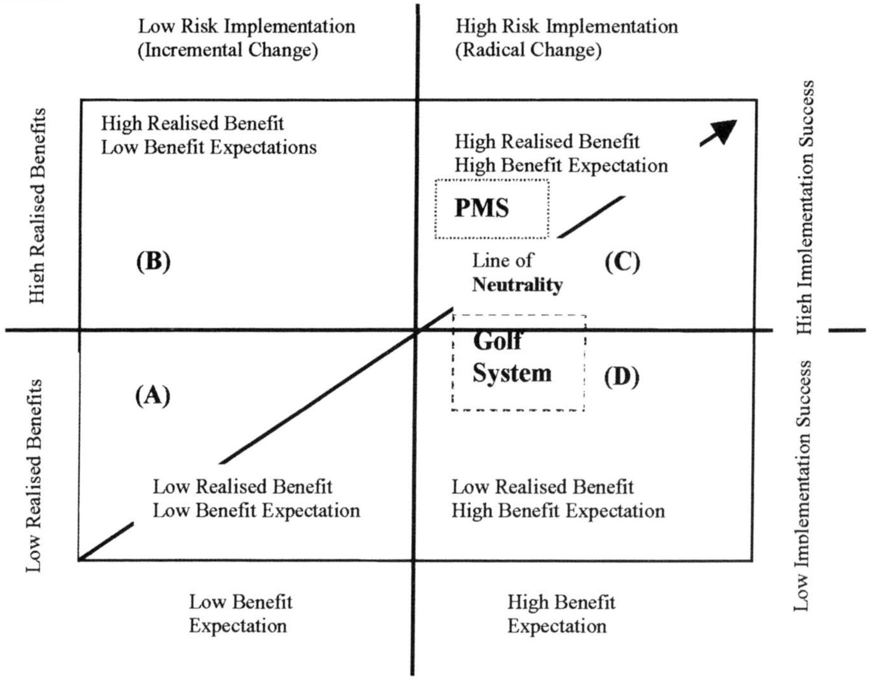

Figure 1. The Benefits Success Matrix

Assessment of the Pilot

At this stage the pilot is still being assessed to see whether further case studies require a modified approach. One change that will probably be put in place for future case studies will be reverting to Fearon and Philip's method of assessing expectations and benefit outcomes for each category as high, medium and low, rather than the simplification employed in the pilot. However, in principle, the methodology is practical, and it is the intention to continue to use it. The Benefit Success matrix promises to be a useful analytical tool, even though the implications of assuming a close correspondence between high risk implementation, seeking strategic as well as operational benefits and radical change (and conversely between low risk implementation, seeking only operational benefits and incremental change), implicit in the model, need to be considered. As the programme continues, it is hoped that the speculations about factors affecting success and failure in individual cases will be generalised to more concrete conclusions, thus shedding useful light on how to get the most out of IT in the hospitality and tourism industries.

References

- Bailey, M. (1996) "What has happened to productivity growth?", *Science* (234), 443 - 451.
- Baker, M.G. and Sweeney, G. (1998) More lessons on business process re-engineering on the tourism and hospitality industries: the case of ALPHA Flight Services, in Buhalis, D., Tjoa, A.M. and Jafari, J. (eds.), *Information and Communication Technology in Tourism 1998*, Proceedings of the International Conference, Istanbul, SpringerWein, New York, 21-23 January.
- Baker, M.G., Wild, M. and Sussmann, S. (1998) Introducing EPOS in Bass Taverns: a report of the case and an exploration of the issues, *International Journal of Contemporary Hospitality Management*, pp 16-23, 10(1).
- Caulkin, S. (1997) "You've got IT - but are you attractive", *The Observer*, 25 May.
- Collins, A. and Bicknell, D. (1997), *Crash: Ten Easy Ways to Avoid a Computer Disaster*, Simon & Schuster, London
- Dertouzos, M.L. (1990), *Computers and Productivity*, MIT Laboratory for Computer Science, Cambridge, Mass.
- Dutton, W.H., MacKenzie, D., Shapiro, S. and Peltu, M. (1995), *Computer Power and Human Limits: Learning from IT and Telecommunications Disasters*, PICT Policy Research Paper No. 33, PICT Programme Office, Uxbridge, UK
- Fearon, C. and Philip, G. (1998) Self-assessment as a means of measuring strategic and operational benefits from EDI: the development of a conceptual framework, *European Journal of Information Systems*, Vol. 7, no. 1.
- Gamble, P.R. (1991) "Innovation and innkeeping", *International Journal of Hospitality Management*, Volume 10 No 1., 3-23.
- OR Newsletter (1996) "Why do IT projects so often fail" September, pp. 12-13.
- Strassmann, P.A. (1985), *Information Payoff: The Transformation of Work in the Electronic Age*, The Information Economics Press, New Canaan, CT.
- Strassmann, P.A. (1985), *Information Payoff: The Transformation of Work in the Electronic Age*, The Information Economics Press, New Canaan, CT.
- Strassmann, P.A. (1990), *The Business Value of Computers: An Executive's Guide* The Information Economics Press, New Canaan, CT.

The Productivity Paradox and the Hospitality Industry

Michael Baker, Silvia Sussmann, Marisa Meisters
School of Management Studies for the Service Sector,
University of Surrey
Michael.Baker@surrey.ac.uk

Introduction

During the '60s and '70s computers were first used to automate clerical procedures such as record keeping, accounting, billing and report generation; and in manufacturing they were used to automate the manufacturing process itself. In this phase of IT's introduction, there is some evidence of their contribution to overall productivity, but by the end of the '80s there was increasing concern about the real contribution computers had made, particularly to productivity. This was dubbed the "productivity paradox". This paper considers relevant published research on this subject in the hospitality industry and elsewhere, and describes the results of a recent survey which sheds further light on the issue. It goes on to identify a research agenda on this subject which is being followed at the University of Surrey.

The Productivity Paradox

Stephen Roach (Senior Economist, Morgan Stanley, New York) showed that, during the '80s in the US, whilst 80% of the investment in IT hardware had gone into the broad service sector (services, communications, wholesale and retail trade, finance and insurance), its productivity had grown at 0.7% per year, less than one fifth of the productivity growth in of the goods sector (manufacturing, mining and construction). Roach also showed that between 1960 and 1987, productivity of information workers general in the US economy did not rise (Roach, 1991). Others have come to similar conclusions. Strassmann (1985, 1990) in a review of studies by others and in his own research, was unable to discover convincing evidence of computers having made a productive contribution in the US economy. On the other hand, Brynjolfsson and Hitt (1993), in an econometric study, identified positive effects of computer investment on productivity. This study indicated that the firms that gain the most from IT are those with the greatest experience of the application of IT.

Causes of disappointment

There may be a number of reasons for the apparent failure of IT to improve industrial productivity. Frequently IT projects suffer significant cost overruns or fail to meet their deadlines, and when the users come to assess them, are found to be seriously flawed, not achieving the desired business benefits. Because software development products tend to run over budget and fail to achieve their planned benefits so dramatically, the consequent failure to achieve their planned rate of return on investment can significantly drag down the firm's average rate of return. This is compounded by a rapid rate of obsolescence and difficulties in achieving inter-operability. Furthermore, computers also probably encourage wasteful activity by tempting users to pursue analysis beyond the point of diminishing returns. Being able to calculate with ease three scenarios provides useful information about the range of possible outcomes, well beyond that arising from calculating point estimates. But the tenth, twentieth, thirtieth scenarios? Similarly, documents go through multiple drafts because changes are so easy. The computer's ability to produce management reports usually exceeds management's ability to read them, thus wasting managerial time (to the extent that managers actually try to master the paper mountain) as well as computing resources.

Landauer (1995) suggests the main problem causing the lack of productivity improvement from the use of IT over the last twenty-five or thirty years lies with the design of software. He suggests that software fails both in its usability (i.e. how easy it is to do the things it is mostly called on to do) and usefulness (i.e. the extent to which the things it can do are of any real value to those who use it). He attributes failures in these areas to poor design method, and prescribes user-centred design, development and deployment.

The Hospitality Context

Although the hotel industry has moved very slowly to adopt computerisation (Chervenak, 1993), and has often been unkindly regarded as a technological dinosaur by those unfamiliar with the intricacies of an industry which is primarily people- and service- oriented, this situation is now beginning to change. However, it would be a surprise if the record of IT in hospitality was in any way better than elsewhere. Certainly, the existing literature on IT in hotels provides very little convincing "hard" evidence specifically demonstrating that the use of IT leads to improvements in business performance.

Were there evidence of superior managerial skills in the application of IT in the hospitality industry, there might be reason to hope that the industry would avoid the productivity paradox; but there is not. Gamble has written extensively about IT in the hospitality industry, alternately exhorting it to take advantage of what the technology can provide, and expressing concern about the industry's management's' ability to do so (see, for example, Gamble, 1988, 1990, 1991). Hospitality already has its shares of IT disasters. Oz (1994) describes the collapse of the CONFIRM project. Pringle (1994) describes how HI-LINE swallowed public funds before expiring. Archdale (1992) shows how by the time BRAVO eventually collapsed it was at the expense of both public and private funds. Presumably, for each disaster publicised, there will be many more quietly written off in corporate discretion. And for each computer failure, like other industries, many more are delivered well over budget, work badly, are unstable and unreliable, or fail fully to meet their objectives.

Recent Studies

There have been two recent studies on the productivity paradox as it manifests itself in the hospitality industry. One is by David *et al* (1996), who surveyed a number of US hotel groups (owning or managing between them a significant number of hotels). The second is by Baker and Li (1996), who compared perceptions of potential and performance of IT investment with financial performance indicators in a number of Taiwanese hotels. These are discussed below before the results of a recent general study are compared.

The US Study

David *et al* (1996) surveyed nine respondents from hotel groups to gain their perceptions of the contribution IT made to a number of aspects of the performance of the hotels in their groups. They asked several open-ended questions about what management information technology had been installed and the impact of the equipment on productivity. The survey asked about the respondents' beliefs about their information systems' contribution to productivity, service quality, guest services and competitive advantage. The respondents rated their expectations for increases in productivity (front office, back office and guest interfaces such as in-room vending) with their view of what the outcomes actually were.

The respondents believed that information technology helped improve the quality of business operations. Several thought IT helped to expand their guest services and contributed to improved customer services. Although it was found that managers in the survey often implemented new computer systems without specifically expecting measurable productivity improvement, respondents generally reported productivity improvements in excess of expectations in both front office and back office applications, although this was not the case for guest-operated technology. However, it might be argued that guest-operated technology may well be installed with other objectives than productivity improvements.

The authors concluded that the connection between technology and productivity in hotels is still not well understood; they suggest that the explanations for any lack of correlation between IT investment and productivity improvement in the industry may lie with managers' objectives' being other than productivity improvement; in particular these managers may be focussing on improving service quality.

This study provided some useful insights on the problem in the hospitality industry. The main weakness of this study is that it is based on managers' perceptions of the expectations and the outcomes of IT investment, rather than hard data. This was something that the study discussed below attempted to address.

The Taiwan Hotel Study

Baker and Li (1996) were able to obtain financial and other business performance data for 1993 on 42 hotels in nine regions of Taiwan. They compared this with data from a postal survey of the hotels themselves. Of the 42 hotels surveyed, 29 usable replies were returned (69% response rate).

The questionnaire sought, *inter alia*, to determine, for each of occupancy rate, business performance and manpower productivity, whether: IT had significant potential to change it positively; computer systems had been mainly installed to change it positively; the respondent was satisfied with the IT the hotel used for this; and the hotel was planning over the next 2-3 years new or updated IT systems for this purpose. Only for occupancy rate did the authors find significant correlation between responses to questions one ("IT has significant potential to...") and questions two and four (".... .....you have mainly introduced computer systems which aim to...." and "....are planning new or updated IT systems which..."). In no case was these significant correlation between actual performance (e.g. occupancy rate or manpower productivity as derived from the hotels' published financial/business performance data) and question three ("....you have mainly introduced computer systems which aim to....").

In the final section of the questionnaire, the respondents were asked for their subjective rating of all their competitor hotels' effectiveness (and their own) in the use of IT. The responses to this question were aggregated to provide a mean peer evaluation of each hotel in the sample. Correlations between this evaluation and Overall Return on Sales (ROS) and Return on Investment (ROI) were calculated. There was a significant correlation between ROS and peer assessment of IT competence. However, the authors did not consider this link between IT competence (as assessed by peers), and corporate performance, convincing.

The authors concluded that these data demonstrated that the managers in these hotels made their investment decisions in IT rationally, in the sense that *views* about IT's past contribution to their businesses tended to guide future IT investment. They were unable to discover a significant correlation between past investment in IT and corporate performance. The authors acknowledged the difficulty in isolating the contribution of IT from other factors affecting business performance, and the problems of developing satisfactory measurements of aspects of business performance; they also acknowledged that for practical reasons the study had shortcomings, including the small sample size (this last is supported by the study by Rai *et al* (1997) described below).

A Recent General Study

Rai *et al* (1997) obtained data from two sources: *Information Week*, a weekly magazine for business and information technology managers, and Computstat, a database of financial and market information on public companies. Using a survey by Information Week of Computstat's top 500 firms for data on IT budgets, replacement costs of computers, client/server expenditure, and a breakdown of IT budget in terms of hardware, software, telecommunications and IS staff expenditure were isolated. Corresponding financial data for these firms were obtained from the Computstat database. The usable sample was 497 firms, although for some categories the data was available for only half of this. The authors used six performance variables: business output as measured by value added and by sales; two accounting measures, ROA and ROE; and administrative productivity and labour productivity. Administrative productivity is value added divided by total administrative costs; productivity was measured by added value per employee. The table below shows where the study did and did not find positive, significant, associations (a + shows a positive, significant association; a – shows a significant negative one).

Table 1: Results at a Glance

	Firm Output		Business Performance		Intermediate Performance	
Variables	*Value*	*Sales*	*ROA*	*ROE*	*Labour Productivity*	*Administrative Productivity*
IT Capital	+	+	+		+	
IT Budget	+	+			+	
Client/Server Expenditure	+	+	+		+	
IS Staff Expenditure	+	+			+	-
Hardware Expenditure	+	+			+	-
Software Expenditure	+	+				-
Telecom Expenditure	+	+				-

The authors note that there is a lack of clear association between aggregate IT investment and business performance. They suggest, however, that the correlation between IT capital and ROA might indicate that cumulative investments in IT have begun to reach a critical mass that can affect the overall performance of firms. However, the disaggregation of the components of IT expenditure and the use of intermediate performance measures, with a substantial sample, has shed some useful light on the contribution of IT expenditure to manpower productivity. Expenditure on IS staff, telecom and hardware are positively associated with productivity. The contribution of client/server expenditure is also clearly identified. The authors comment that the insignificant and negative results for the effects on administrative productivity indicate that IT does not necessarily reduce the costs or increase the productivity of management. They note, with Strassmann (1988), that computers will not make badly managed businesses better, because they automate dysfunctional management processes, increase sunk costs and reduce management flexibility to respond to change. The authors in their conclusions noted that IT investment has differential effects on various aspects of business performance, and this needs to be taken into account in attempting to isolate its contribution.

The Internet Survey

From these studies there is strong evidence that, in the hospitality industry, as elsewhere, the contribution of IT investment to improved performance in any department depends strongly on the competence in management generally and competence in implementation and management of IT systems in particular. This dependence may be stronger in hospitality than it would be in a typical manufacturing industry, where shop-floor investment in IT may well bear productivity benefits despite shortfalls in management performance elsewhere in the organisation. It was in the light of this speculation that the analysis of a recent hotel survey, conducted at the School of Management Studies at the University of Surrey, is of interest.

This study was of UK hotels with Internet sites. If it is managerial action which is the determinant of success in applications of IT in hospitality, then it was expected that those who were more optimistic about the Internet's contribution would be those which were getting the most out of it and that they would be doing more to gain the most from it. Eighty-six hotels responded to the survey, from which there were 75 useful responses. Fifty-three of these hotels are independent, 11 are members of chains, nine are consortium members, and two are unknown. Ten of the hotels have a five star rating, eleven are four star hotels, thirty are three star hotels, seventeen are two star hotels, and one is a one star hotel.

Three groups were distinguished, on the basis of their opinions of the statement "the Internet today is an important channel for hotel reservations". One group is sceptical of the usefulness of the Internet ("disagree" or "disagree strongly"), a second group is somewhat unsure of the benefits of the Internet ("neither agree or disagree"), and a third group believes that the Internet is important now ("agree" or " agree strongly"). It was hypothesised that the enthusiasts would be getting more out of their Internet presence, and that there would be evidence that their getting more out of it would be because they were putting more in. It would also not be surprising if they were more optimistic about the Internet's contribution in the future.

Findings

In terms of results, the enthusiasts were doing better, on average, than the sceptics and the unsure. On average they achieved many more website hits, and got about twice as many reservations per month over the Internet. However, the number of reservations and web site visits per month vary greatly in this group of hotels with some reporting very few web site visits and bookings per month while others report a very large number of hits and reservations. Internet reservations make up as much as 25% of total reservations for some of the hotels in this group, with one hotel reporting that up to 70% of its reservations come from the Internet. Over 80% said that actual reservations had increased because of their Internet presence, compared with about 55% for the unsure and about 30% for the sceptics. As far as optimism about the future of the Internet, in responding to the statement "the Internet will grow in importance as a distribution channel for hotel reservations in the future", the mean score for the enthusiasts placed them between "agree" and "agree strongly", whilst the scores for the other two groups placed them only on the "agree" side of "neither agree or disagree".

Chart 1: Enthusiasts & Sceptics

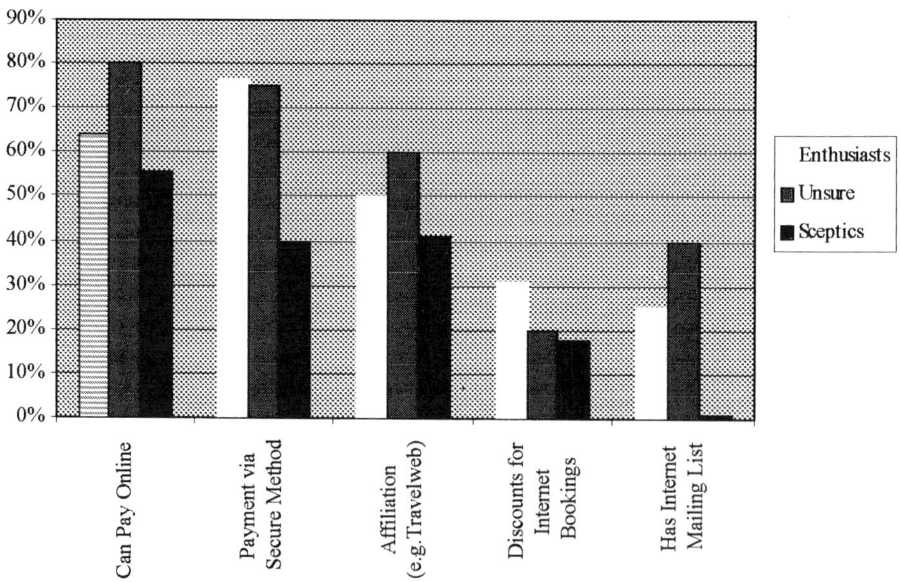

Respondents' comments can provide further insights into how they view the Internet. One sceptic said that the Internet "is not working yet because it is not organised." Another asked, "How many people do you know who have a PC at home? Therein lies the problem." A third said that the Internet is "vastly overrated at present, too slow, and there is too much rubbish on the 'net." Only two of the unsure hoteliers made comments. One said, "the response to date is disappointing. Hopefully use will increase." Another said that their hotel is very small, "but we do believe our presence on the web is an asset." A number of the Internet enthusiasts commented. One hotelier credits the success of the Internet to the fact that the hotel supports six different languages on the web site and that it contains a lot of useful information about the hotel itself. Another mentions the growing use of e-mail: "An increasing number of people who may have had Internet access for some time are now beginning to use e-mail as a normal method of communication." Some hotels credit their Internet success to the fact that they are listed on multiple booking web sites. Even small hotels are seeing benefits from using the Internet, with one commenting: "We are a tiny hotel but we have seen benefits from Internet exposure that we couldn't have afforded to attempt with any other high profile medium."

The differences between sceptics and enthusiasts

All three groups are compared in the bar chart. The enthusiasts overall have taken more steps to ensure that their hotels' web sites are well promoted. More are affiliated to other web sites which offer reservations (such as Travelweb), more have created their own mailing lists that people can subscribe to in order to be notified of special deals, and some also offer special Internet discounts that are not advertised anywhere else. Enthusiasts are more likely than sceptics to offer online payment, and those that do are more likely to offer secure payment methods. By using more forms of self-promotion to get their web sites recognised, the Internet enthusiasts have been successful in receiving larger numbers of bookings and inquiries. More of the Internet sceptics and neutral hoteliers, on the other hand, have not joined travel reservation web sites, do not run mailing lists and never offer special Internet deals.

Some Speculation about the Hospitality Industry

The study by Rai *et al* (1997) sheds some useful light on the studies in hospitality. First, there may, at the total company level, only just be a sufficiently critical mass of IT investment in many companies to be showing through now in corporate performance. Second, as well as looking for measures of intermediate performance such as productivity, these should be considered in the light of disaggregated IT investment, if the effect of the latter on the former is to be identified.

Third, the strong correlation between measures of disaggregated IT investment and manpower productivity, and the negative correlation with administrative productivity, has significance when considering a service industry such as hospitality. As Rai *et al* (1997) comment, where IT is applied to administrative productivity, the contribution of competent management is critically important. In a service industry, business processes tend more to be administrative, or management, processes. In the light of this, the results of the Baker and Li (1996) study can be reinterpreted. The strong correlation in the Baker and Li (1996) study between Return on Sales and peer assessment of the competence of the organisation in applying IT supports this thesis. Similarly, the results of the recent Internet survey also support this conclusion.

A Research Agenda

This does leave some new questions to be answered. First, there is the concept of "critical mass" arising from the Rai *et al* (1997) study. What exactly does this comprise? Investment in hardware and software is implied, but it might be suggested that investment in training would also be important. But attitudes are also important, particularly at management level, and so the notion might embrace the proportion of the employees, particularly managers, who had appropriate attitudes to IT. There is also the question of experience, both of implementation and operation, a point made by Brynjolfsson and Hitt (1993). Second, intermediate performance measures such as productivity need to be considered in the light of disaggregated IT investment, and this itself gives rise to practical research problems. It is unlikely that disaggregated IT investment could be identified by a postal survey. Third, there is the question of the technical excellence or otherwise of the systems, the point made by Landauer (1995). To what extent is poorly specified and badly written software still a source of major disappointment? Finally, there is the question of judgements about "managerial competence", as well as those of attitude identified earlier.

Given the complexity of the issues that need to be untangled, the research questions seem to call for a case study approach. However, it seems unlikely that just one or two case examples will give sufficient cross bearings on the issues, so a significant programme is called for. It is for this reason that the School of Management Studies for the Service Sector is now embarking in a research programme based on case studies, looking at the factors affecting success and failure in IT projects in hospitality.

References

- Archdale, G (1992) "A new direction for effective destination marketing and quality customer service", in Yee, J., (Editor), Proceedings *of the 1992 PATA Destination Database Conference, Singapore, December 9 - 10*, PATA Intelligence Centre, San Francisco, 13-18
- Baker, M.G. and Li, B. (1996), "A little of what you fancy does you good? Does IT make a positive contribution to the hospitality industry?" Paper to the HITA Conference, Edinburgh, 17-20 May.
- Brynjolfsson, E., and Hitt, L. (1993), *New Evidence on the Returns to Information*

Systems, MIT Press, Mass.

- Chervenak, L. (1993), "Hotel technology at the start of the new millennium", *The Council on Hotel, Restaurant and Institutional Education,* **17**(1), 114-120
- David, J.S., Grabski, S. and Kasavana, M. (1996), "The Productivity Paradox of Hotel Industry Technology", *Cornell Hotel and Restaurant Administration Quarterly*, April, 64 – 70.
- Gamble, P.R. (1988) "Attitudes to computers by managers in the hotel industry", *Behaviour and Information Technology*, 7(3) 305-321.
- Gamble, P.R. (1990), "Building a yield management system -the flip side", *Hospitality Research Journal*, 14(2), 11-22.
- Gamble, P.R. (1991), " An information technology strategy for the hospitality industry of the 1990s", *Int. J. Hosp. Manage.* 3(1) 10-15
- Landauer, T.K. (1995), *The Trouble with Computers*, The MIT Press, Cambridge, Mass.
- Oz, E. (1994) "When professional standards are lax: the CONFIRM failure and its lessons", Communications-ACM, Vol. 37, No 10: 29
- Pringle, S.M. (1994) "Destined to fail? An investigation of the Hi-Line destination marketing system", in Seaton, A.V., ed., *Tourism State of the Art*, Wiley, Chichester.
- Rai, A., Patnayakuni, R. and Patnayakuni, N. (1997), "Technology Investment and Business Performance", Communications of the ACM, Vol. 40, No 7, 89-97.
- Roach, S. (1991), "Services under Siege – the Restructuring Imperative," *Harvard Business Review*, Vol. 69, No 5, 82-92.
- Strassmann, P.A. (1985), *Information Payoff: The Transformation of Work in the Electronic Age,* The Information Economics Press, New Canaan, CT.
- Strassmann, P.A. (1990), *The Business Value of Computers: An Executive's Guide,* The Information Economics Press, New Canaan, CT.

The Future is Feminine
Gender issues and information systems in hospitality and tourism

Dr. Martin Peacock
Business School, University of North London, England
m.peacock@unl.ac.uk

Introduction

Throughout the literature on gender and technological innovation within tourism and hospitality, there is an assumption of a link between computerisation and masculinity. As far back as 1987, McCool found that the manager who is introducing a computerised management information system is likely to be male. And, as recently as 1995, Main noted that "male managers [are] more likely to use computers than their female counterparts" (p.31).

Research on the hospitality and tourism industry within London conducted over the last two years, suggests that this association between gender and information technology is the result of deep-seated inequalities within the structures of the two industries. Within hospitality, for example, women managers figure disproportionately in the small, independent hotel sector. Among the large, independent restaurants (a highly remunerative and computerised sector of the industry) women managers represent a tiny minority.

The large establishments are most likely to use information technology. However it is within these companies that women have the smallest share of power. This is not necessarily a causal relationship. This paper suggests that the association of computerisation and disproportionately male management reflects the prevailing structures of power within the industry. Most managers within the tourism and hospitality industries perceive technological innovation as an external, autonomous process. While in reality "technology interacts with the subjectivity of those who develop or use it" (Scarbrough and Corbett, 1992, p.21). "The way that technology is related to work organisation is seen to be the product of negotiation and political action" (Child and Loveridge, 1990).

Gendered Innovation

Berg (1995) takes up the above point and notes the absence of women in the technological innovation process. She speaks of a gendered innovation process and a gendered technology. Not only are women largely excluded from the creation of the process, but they are also made the targets of this process.

Most work groups experiencing computerisation within the industries are predominately female. Within the hotels both front and back office receive the highest levels of information technology (counted as average numbers of computers to employees). Male dominated departments, such as food production and engineering still have relatively low rates of computerisation. When Werneke (1990) writes "as women have entered the labour market certain activities in the service sector and occupations have become increasingly 'feminised'" this applies particularly to departments within tourism and hospitality which interface directly with consumers.

From reservations to reception, to checkout, the consumer will generally be speaking to female operatives operating with a sophisticated information system. This is the traditional picture of technological innovation within hospitality and tourism. Innovation is 'imposed' by a male management on departments consisting predominately of female operatives. As Wood (1994, p.178) writes "power is gendered. Hospitality organizations are no exception".

The Female Operative

This image of male management imposing technical innovation on a female workforce is in trouble. At its simplest, it is not delivering the expectations of the male management: staffing levels are not being reduced, revenue is not increasing, operating costs are not being reduced. The industries are seeing the high-cost information system, which fails to deliver. At another level however, technological innovation is undermining the male-dominated 'managerial tabernacle', which imposes the technological 'solution' in the first place.

The development of new skills, which the predominately female operative has acquired through the computer, has led to a shift in power. Traditionally the male manager tends to "associate personal computers with clerical work" (Craver, 1990, p.16) and avoids involvement. However Buchanan noted that to the great dismay of management, users of computers develop expertise and "a feel for their functioning that supervisors who merely observe do not have".

What constitutes a skill and how it is valued is very much socially constructed, and gender plays a key role in this construction. To an extent tourism and hospitality lead to work which can be construed as domestic (e.g. housekeeping) and this can lead to it being perceived as low status. Thompson (1989) includes a detailed discussion of these issues. It would be interesting to question to what extent the use of computers has changed the *perception* of the skill as opposed to its real level. However, the computerised operative is generally recognised as having increased in status.

The data from our survey confirms the work of Daniel (1987), that operatives within the industry generally welcome and enjoy technological innovation. The data also suggests that (in the view of surveyed managers) operatives are seeing an increase in responsibility and skill, while at the same time undergoing decreasing levels of supervision. These are broadly in line with the 'informated' employee model outlined by Zuboff (1988).

When McLoughlin and Harris (1997, p.47) point out that organisations can often "know less than their members", this can be seen in the teams of computerised female operatives (universally entitled "the girls") who often have a more precise picture of booking levels and consumer price sensitivity than their line managers. In one example a female reservations team was disregarding one potential performance bonus based on the percentage of customers who were charged full price so that the team could achieve the percentage occupancy target. The team was maximising its bonuses, while hotel revenue was declining. The solution (suggested to senior management by the team) was a bonus scheme tied to total booking revenue. This option was declined, as senior management were unwilling to reveal this (actually quite accessible) information.

Women Managers and Computer Confidence

It is not just at the operative level that the link between a male management imposing 'solutions' on a female workforce is being undermined. Women managers themselves are significantly more computer confident than men. At the UNL Business School, a survey consisting of interviews with over five hundred hospitality managers was completed last year. In a question designed to assess computer confidence, it found that a quarter (25%) of the male sample felt that it took over a year to learn to use a computer. However the proportion of women managers who agreed was only a third (8.8%) of the male sample (Chi-square significance 0.02221).

In part this link between gender and computer confidence is related to educational levels, which were found to impact on computer confidence. Women managers within the tourism and hospitality industries tend to be more qualified (though less senior) than their male counterparts. In the hospitality industry, for example, almost half the proportion of female as opposed to male managers were qualified just at GCSE level (that is, leaving school at 16). However, even if this education effect is taken out of the statistical analysis, there is still a relationship between women managers and computer confidence.

Another reason for the more computer-literate female manager could be in gender-based career patterns. As seen above, computerisation tends to target female dominated departments: departments involved in large-scale data manipulation or in selling, from customer reservations to the reception of guests. One result of this has been a new career pattern where the female operative is poached by the software company to provide an industry focus to their sales and customer support. This salesperson or technical advisor is subsequently poached by a computerising company to lead the introduction of a new system.

Anecdotal evidence would tend to support this linking of computerisation and feminisation. Claridges (previously rigidly sexually demarcated) recently employed its first female receptionist at the point at which it upgraded its front-of-house system. The "sorting out" (interviewed male system manager) of the Dorchester systems was completed by a woman manager. This was a significant and prestigious achievement.

The Systems Managers Association (recently demised) saw a steady increase in the number and influence of its women members. The female managers tended to have a background from within operations as opposed to the generally more technical background of the male members.

Gender and Managerial Culture

Another reason for the undermining of the link between 'maleness' and technological innovation could be a difference in managerial culture based on gender. In a survey of both male and female managers, Doherty (1997, p.62) found that women are perceived as more employable. The managers felt "that women had better communication skills, that they handled interpersonal relationships better and that they were better at dealing with complaints". There are significant differences in the manner in which male and female managers manage.

In our survey of managers, women were less than half as likely to label their management style as autocratic (10.5% of female managers as opposed to 24.4% of males). This link between gender and management style plays a significant role in the relationship between gender and information technology. Managers who define success in terms of the perception of their superiors were overwhelmingly male, but these were also managers who worked in places with both highly autocratic styles and information systems, which reduced the discretion and autonomy of the individual manager. In these more 'masculine' workplaces the strategy behind the development of information systems was the control of subordinates. Computer systems are a means of achieving predictability from subordinates.

The 'Male' Hotel

As a way of illustrating the two contrasting approaches to information technology, two case studies are submitted. The first one is an installation at a large four-star hotel, the second is a small two-star hotel, both in central London. In the first hotel the head office decided to purchase the Fidelio package at a cost of over £100,000 excluding installation and training. The primary motivation for this purchase was the integration of this (recently purchased) hotel's systems with the other hotels in the chain.

There was no consultation, in fact the decision was kept a secret for six months. Then, each operative received a week's training which covered all departments, not just their own. At the end of this week, the majority of the receptionists came out of training feeling nervous about the system, and dreading the set-up date.

When the system eventually arrived, a month after the booked date, installation meant that neither the old nor the new system could be used and for six hours, five hundred guests had to be checked in manually. Following this "chaos" (hotel receptionist) 15% of front office staff resigned within a month as a direct consequence of the installation.

Guests are unhappy too, with a 37% increase in complaints since the installation. These are mainly complaints about long waits at reception or bills being mistotalled. Ironically, some of the most frequent complainers were members of the hotel's 'regular guest programme' singled out for special treatment. It was these guests in particular who objected to Fidelio's 'scripting' of receptionists, when the machine tells the operator what to say. At the end of the first month, most receptionists were not using the prompt at all. Fidelio has been observed being successfully installed at different establishments, so management's suggestions that some of the problems were the product of the software package do not carry much weight.

The financial consequences of this installation were not negligible. The cheapest rooms, previously sold at £145 rack rate, were being offered at £45, or (for users of Teletext) £25 per night inclusive of breakfast. Although head office, when questioned, could suggest that installation costs would have been covered "in a matter of weeks", data suggested that loss of customer goodwill and the loss of experienced staff was having serious implications for the finances of the hotel months after the installation.

There is an irony in a culture which can carefully calculate the percentage increase in complaints while fostering the same complaints. This culture is perceived within the hotel as predominately 'male'. The majority of the computer operatives were female, but managers were overwhelmingly male. Values tended to emphasise targets rather than process, authoritarian values and an emphasis on sensitivity to the higher level of authority tended to override issues connected with guest satisfaction.

Ironically and contrary to its legitimising coda, there appeared to be no link between this 'male' authoritarian culture and increased profitability. Although the new property management system represented a considerable advance in technological sophistication over the old system, it has not generated additional revenue or reduced operating costs.

Far from increasing profitability, there is no evidence that it made any contribution to its cost of over £100,000.

The 'Female' Hotel

In contrast to this 'male' hotel, the 'female' hotel is a small hotel situated less than three hundred metres away from the large. It is owned and managed largely by Dutch people, and it is interesting that Hofstede (1984) makes the point that the Dutch and British are particularly different on the masculinity scores. Britain tends to favour what are perceived as the masculine values of assertiveness and competition over the feminine values of personal relations and quality of life.

The hotel itself is owned by a husband/wife team who live in the Netherlands and the majority of the managers are female. Our 'feminine' hotel (as characterised by its operatives and managers) is technologically sophisticated, with, for example, membership of an internet marketing consortia, which our 'male' hotel still lacks. All managers receive two months training working as receptionists on the front desk. This means that they all know the system well, in contrast to the previous hotel where managers see direct knowledge of the system as operative status. There is no distinction in dress between managers and operatives.

The emphasis on teamwork means an emphasis on multi-skilling, with one receptionist denoted a 'springer' (from the Dutch 'springen': to jump) who covers whatever needs doing. This job is rotated among the receptionists. In contrast to the previous establishment, management did not believe that the increasing sophistication of information systems would reduce the number of operatives.

There is a highly co-operative style visible in the hotel. There are monthly meetings of receptionists and managers where revenue figures are reviewed. In contrast to the secrecy of the 'male' hotel, all financial data is available for this meeting. This is important for the bonus scheme: "It was the obvious thing to do" (owner): "the receptionists' level of efficiency and commitment certainly has an impact on the overall revenue".

Operatives are directly involved in solving business problems and maximising revenue, and this means that management is not always present. It is left to the judgement of the receptionist what rooms to sell and at what rate. The computer system is used to test the impact of a variety of approaches and results are shared in informal conversations and at the monthly meetings. Staff enjoy their level of responsibility and find their jobs more interesting. Doing and thinking are not separated in the manner of the hotel described above.

Although the picture of the 'feminine' hotel detailed above is very untypical for the British tourism and hospitality industries, it is not a product of the difference in sizes between the two hotels. There was some evidence from the data that the establishments which tended to favour the more autocratic 'male' style of management were the smaller ones. Certainly, in Britain, the most strongly autocratic establishments are either owner-managed or public houses.

The 'feminine' hotel is more successful on a number of levels. Firstly it recruits and retains staff much more successfully than our 'male' establishment. It has higher profitability when related to number of staff, and its customer base is more loyal and increasing. Finally it uses information technology more successfully. The application of IT is directly related to the solution of day to day operational problems ("what rate do I charge today?"). This approach to information technology uses what Zuboff (1988, p.201) characterises as a "collegial" style of decision making, based on group hypothesis formulation and testing.

Summary

The title of this paper is taken from the Joint Hospitality Congress report: *Hospitality into the 21st Century* (1996, p.20). This report suggested that, increasingly, women are of key importance to the hospitality industry both as customers and as employees. This paper is suggesting that gender differences in approaching information technology are making a significant impact on its effective use. As the point of purchase becomes more of a complex negotiated process based on information systems (both for vendor and purchaser), then the social and IT skills of vendor's representative will play a more key role. The purchase price itself becomes little more than a daily shifting set of parameters, used by the seller to test future selling strategies. In this scenario feminine social skills (used by either gender) become more valuable.

Companies within Tourism and Hospitality are looking for the competitive advantage long promised by information technology in the creative combination of organisational changes and new approaches to selling. After all, "in a world where value is created by understanding, obedience no longer fulfils the demands of production" (Zuboff, 1988, p.290). The future is feminine.

References

- Joint Hospitality Industry Congress, *Hospitality into the 21st Century, a Vision for the Future*, Henley Centre, London, June, (1996).
- Buchanan, D. and McCalman, J. 'Confidence, Visibility and Pressure: The effects of shared information in computer aided hotel management', *New Technology, Work and Employment*, pp. 38-46, (1988).
- Craver, David, 'Training the Hybrids in their Own Image', *Computer Weekly*, p.16, (1990).
- Daniel, W., *Workplace Industrial Relations and Technical Change*, Frances Pinter, Shaftesbury, (1987).
- Doherty, Liz, 'The Future is Female', Paper for the *Hospitality Business Development Conference*, Sheffield, (1997).
- Hofstede, G., *Culture's Consequences: International Differences in Work-Related Values*, Sage, London, (1984).
- Main, Hilary, 'Information Technology and the Independent Hotel - failing to make the connection?' *International Journal of Contemporary Hospitality Management*, Vol. 7, No. 6, pp. 30-32, (1995).
- McCool, A.C., 'Some Considerations in developing expert systems for the hospitality industry', *International Journal of Hospitality Management*, Vol. 6, No 4, pp. 191-198, (1987).
- McLoughlin, Ian, and Harris, Martin, *Organizational Change and Technology*, Thomson Business Press, London, (1997).
- Scarbrough, Harry, and Corbett, J. Martin, *Technology and Organisation - Power, Meaning and Design*, Routledge, London, (1992).
- Thompson, P., *The Nature of Work: An Introduction to Debates on the Labour Process*, Macmillan, London, (1989).
- Werneke, D., in Forester, Tom, (editor) *The Information Technology Revolution*, Blackwell, London, (1990).
- Wood, Roy, *Organizational Behaviour for Hospitality Management*, Heinemann, Oxford, 1994.
- Zuboff, Shoshana, *In the Age of the Smart Machine: the Future of Work and Power*, Heinemann, Oxford, (1988).

Combinatorial Optimisation Based Decision Support System for Trip Planning

Jean-Marc Godart

University of Mons-Hainaut
Warocqué Faculty of Business Sciences
Department of Applied Mathematics
godartjm@mercure.umh.ac.be

Abstract

This paper investigates how Combinatorial Optimisation - a very active branch of Operations Research - can be used to set up a Decision Support System for trip planning. Consecutive alterations of the well-known Travelling Salesman Problem (T.S.P.) led to define a model which is more appropriate for that purpose and which was thus called "Trip Planning Problem" (T.P.P.). This brand-new approach for designing trip planning Decision Support Systems algorithms takes advantage of the specificities of computers, rather than expecting them to simulate human brain activity.

1. Introduction

The Internet and other recent information and communication technologies clearly have a major impact on tourism. As stated in the first announcement for Enter '99, these new technologies "have become the backbone of the industry - for the planning, development, marketing and delivery of tourism products." [12] Hence, innovative tools are necessary to help move the tourism business into the electronic marketplace and to make the best possible use of emerging technologies to serve tourists in the future.

Moreover, "over the last ten years, the world has seen a substantial shift in the preferences and behaviour of tourism consumers - away from standardised packages designed by tour operators with bulk economics in mind, to individualised products specified by the customer, increasingly targeted at unique and authentic experiences, special interests and activities. Information technology will play a powerful role in enabling customers to select and purchase tourism products to meet their specific requirements". [12]

The topic of this paper is at the centre of these recent developments that revolutionise tourism. As a matter of fact, it proposes an innovative approach, based on Combi-natorial Optimisation, to design Decision Support Systems (D.S.S.) aimed at helping users to select and combine the most appropriate tourism products, considering a tourist's personal values, wishes and constraints (this is what is referred to as "trip planning" in this paper).

Although tourists can already book many travel components (e.g. transportation and accommodation) online, only little has been done so far with regard to the trip planning process as a whole. Yet, given the very large number of available products and the interdependence of their choice, assisting users in choosing and arranging these components turns out to be essential, both to take advantage of the marketing opportunities offered by the new information technologies and to make tailor-made trips possible.

Briefly, the purpose of this paper is to summarise the way in which Combinatorial Optimisation can be used to build up a D.S.S. for trip planning. First, the focus will be on Combinatorial Optimisation and on the main mathematical tools which are to be used. Then, the trip planning process will be sketched in a few words. Finally, the paper will look at the design of a D.S.S. and investigate how the tools presented before can be of help. The conclusion will highlight a few specific characteristics of the approach.

2. Combinatorial Optimisation

Combinatorial Optimisation is an extremely active branch of Operations Research that deals with the problems of finding the best (or one of the best) element(s), according to a given objective function, in a finite non-empty set (of which the elements are usually called "solutions"). In the mathematical form, a Combinatorial Optimisation problem consists thus in finding a solution $s^* \in S$ such that :

$$f(s^*) = \underset{s \in S}{\text{opt.}}\ f(s)$$

where : $0 < \#S < +\infty$
"opt." can be either "min." or "max."

The solutions of such a problem generally consist in combinatorial assemblages (e.g. combinations or permutations, with possible specific constraints to be satisfied) of given items. Therefore, when the number of these items increases, the cardinality of S, though finite, usually gets tremendous, and the problem of finding an optimal solution thus quickly turns out to be intractable.

A famous example of a Combinatorial Optimisation problem is the Travelling Salesman Problem (T.S.P.), which can be defined as follows :

(n + 1) different places $p_0, p_1, ..., p_n$ (n integer ≥ 1) are considered and it is assumed that a salesman being in p_0 must go through each of the remaining n places - $p_1, p_2, ..., p_n$ - exactly once, before coming back to his starting point at p_0. The set T of possible tours for this salesman can thus be stated as follows :

$$T = \{ (p_0, p_{i(1)}, p_{i(2)}, ..., p_{i(n)}, p_0) \mid \{i(1), i(2), ..., i(n)\} = \{1, 2, ..., n\} \}$$

Given a value (e.g. distance, cost, duration...) v_{ij} for the move from p_i straight to p_j (where i, j $\in \{0, 1, ..., n\}$), the total value (e.g. distance, cost, duration...) of a tour $t = (p_0, p_{i(1)}, p_{i(2)}, ..., p_{i(n)}, p_0)$, such that $\{i(1), i(2), ..., i(n)\} = \{1, 2, ..., n\}$, will be v(t), where :

$$v(t) = v_{0i(1)} + v_{i(1)i(2)} + ... + v_{i(n)0}$$

Then, the T.S.P. consists in finding the best (e.g. shortest, cheapest, fastest...) tour for the salesman, that is a tour $t^* \in T$, such that :

$$v(t^*) = \min_{t \in T} v(t)$$

Figure 1 represents what could be an optimal solution for a T.S.P. with n equal to ten. The black square and the white circles symbolise the point of origin/destination and the ten places that have to be visited on the tour.

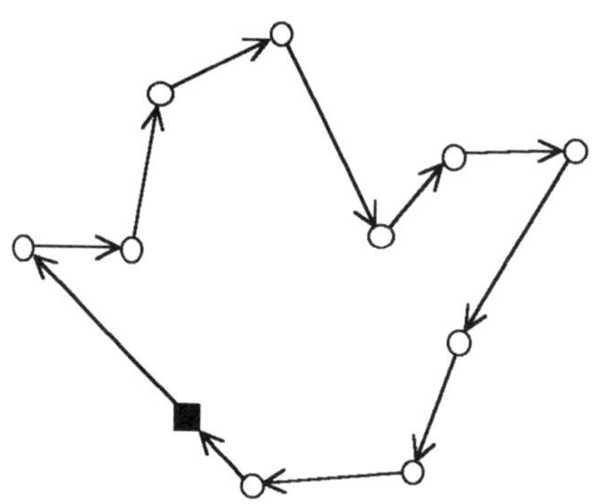

Fig. 1. A T.S.P. solution

The above mentioned terms of the T.S.P. make it clear that the number of possible tours is equal to n!. Table 1 illustrates the strong intractability of the T.S.P. when many places are taken into account. Since no exact algorithm was ever found with computation times always shorter than a given polynomial of n, the T.S.P. is said to be "NP-hard". To tackle large-size instances of the T.S.P. and other NP-hard Combinatorial Optimisation problems in a reasonable time, one often resorts to heuristic methods, which sacrifice solution quality to shorter computation times.

Table 1. #T for a few values of n

n	#T
6	720
8	40,320
10	3,628,800
12	479,001,600
14	87,178,291,200

3. Trip Planning

As defined in the introduction, trip planning is selecting and combining, in a trip, the most appropriate tourism products considering a tourist's personal values, wishes and constraints.

Since any trip starts when the tourist leaves his/her home and finishes when he/she gets back to it, trip planning can be viewed as a tour construction problem. For the purpose of this research, three categories of components to the tour will be considered : transportation (car, airplane...), lodging (hotel, camping...) and activity (museum, amusement park...).

Trip planning is normally performed by the tourist himself/herself or by a travel industry intermediary (travel agent, tour operator...), or even split between several of these actors.

As mentioned before, a shift has been noticed in the last years, towards a higher involvement of the consumer in this planning process. As a result, a great many tourism companies have offered new possibilities to assist and sometimes encourage the tourist in this activity : "hotel only" brochures and bookings, toll-free access to reservation desks, etc. The Internet and other networks have grown up in this context and made a handsome contribution to it by enabling the general public to access Global Distribution Systems (e.g. Sabre...) and Computer Reservation Systems (e.g. Best Western, Hilton...), and thus directly make their own reservations online.

Though search tools exist to help users select the most appropriate travel products (e.g. flights, hotels...), little has been done so far to assist these users in combining components into a complete trip.

4. Decision Support System

A lot of attempts have been made in the last years to build up tools aimed at aiding tourists or intermediaries in their travel-related decisions : destination choice (e.g. [8], [11]), inclusive tour selection (e.g. [5], [6], [7]), and others (see for example [2], [3], [9] for more details).
Only a few papers deal with, or tackle, the question of designing a trip planning D.S.S. Among these :

- Halatsis *et al.* (1994) wrote about MaTourA, which would provide an interactive way to construct personalised tours in Greece [4] ;

- Loban (1997) mentioned the idea of developing computer-assisted travel counselling towards itinerary building, with tourism components which would not have been prepackaged [7, p. 830].

To date, most D.S.S. designed for tourism, including the above mentioned MaTourA, are expert systems that rely on artificial intelligence concepts to attempt to "model the human reasoning process" [3, p. 3]. Here a different approach is applied that is based on mathematical optimisation, which Loban [7] also suggested to use, notably for tour packages selection, as an alternative to the expert system approach.

More precisely, this approach consists in using and adapting Combinatorial Optimisation tools, which have been used with success in many different fields (routing, scheduling...), and which seem to be appropriate for the modelisation of trip planning situations too.

The Travelling Salesman Problem (T.S.P.) appears as a suitable starting point to modelise trip planning. As its name indicates, this problem was initially designed for travel, even though it was essentially used and developed in other applications after that.

The T.S.P. can be helpful in solving very basic trip planning decision problems. For example, if the white circles of Figure 1 symbolise tourist attractions, a solution of the T.S.P. could be one of the cheapest tours through all those activities. The point of origin/destination (the black square in Figure 1) can be the tourist's place of residence but also any other place where a tour starts and finishes (e.g. a hotel or an airport).

Of course, the benefit of the T.S.P. is rather limited for trip planning, and the enlargement of this model to more intricate, but also more realistic, tourism situations has hardly been investigated. Therefore, starting from the T.S.P., the problem formulation was progressively amended to take specific trip planning features into consideration. This series of improvements and the extensions of the T.S.P. to which they led are summarised in Figure 2.

From a trip planning point of view, a first major drawback of the T.S.P. is its inability to select activities to be included in the tour. A second inadequacy comes from the fact that the T.S.P. does not deal with lodging at all and can thus only be appropriate for travel in a "happy-go-lucky" fashion (where the traveller makes no provision for lodging in his/her plans). Figure 3 represents the background the T.S.P. disregards (black circles symbolise lodging possibilities).
Accordingly an initial alteration of the T.S.P. will consist in enabling selection of activities (T.S.P.-A.S.), lodging (T.S.P.-L.S.) or both (T.S.P.-A.L.S.).

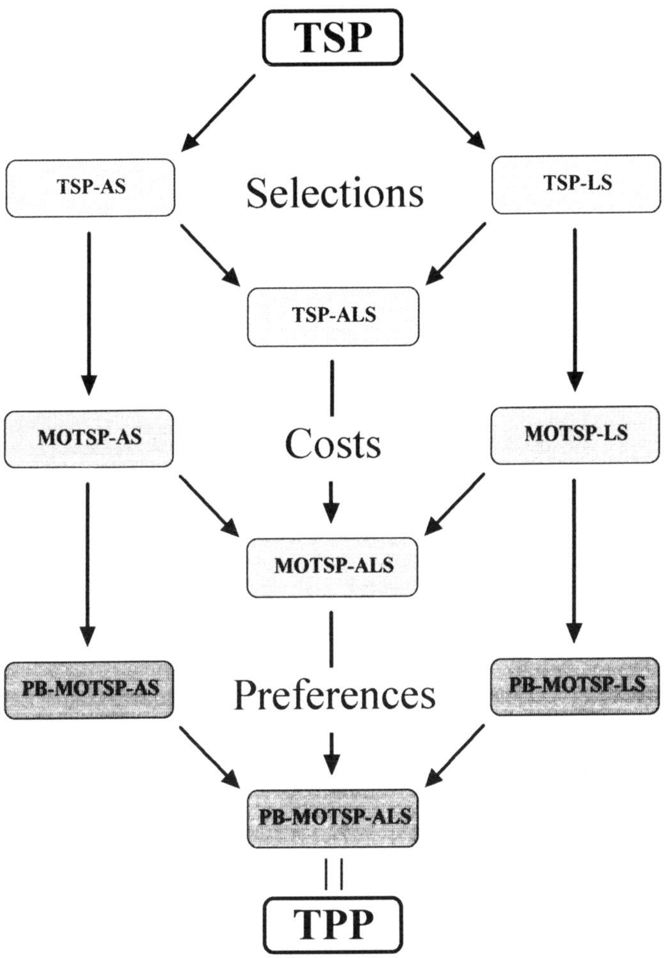

Fig. 2. From the T.S.P. to the T.P.P.

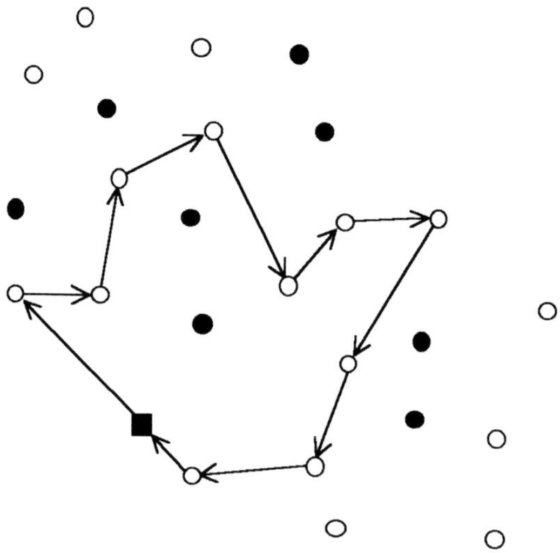

Fig. 3. A T.S.P. solution, from a trip planning point of view

A solution of the T.S.P.-A.L.S., as schematised in Figure 4, is a sequence made up of activities and lodging possibilities, and of the point of origin/destination, that will be considered here as initial/final imposed lodging. As for the T.S.P., the objective is finding a sequence (tour), with a minimum transportation cost.

The number of lodging possibilities to be selected from a "lodging database" set - with repetitions allowed, since several nights can be spent in a same hotel - is defined by the user.

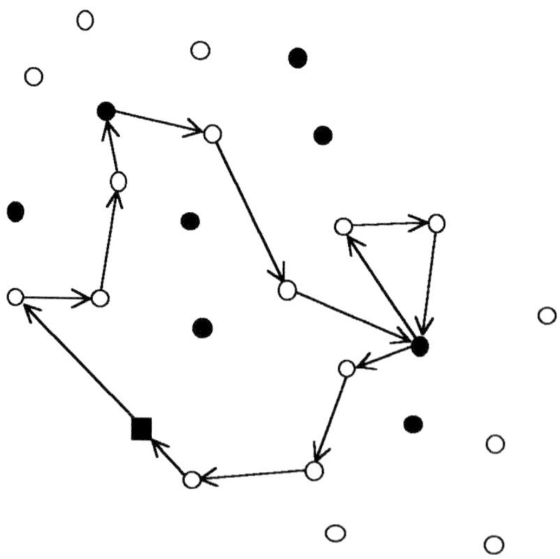

Fig. 4. A T.S.P.-A.L.S. solution

Given the time needed for every activity and for the movement from one place (activity or accommodation) to another, the number of activities to be selected from an "activity database" set - this time without repetitions allowed - is governed by a length of day rule : the duration of the journey between two consecutive lodging places in the sequence always has to fall in a given time interval.

Appropriate tools to solve this extension of the T.S.P. are the meta-heuristics, which are a class of flexible heuristic methods that can be implemented to tackle a whole range of Combinatorial Optimisation problems. Meta-heuristics are known to perform well for the T.S.P. and their high flexibility makes them easier to adapt to derived problems than specific heuristics (see for example [1], [10] for more details).

Even though the solution structure of the T.S.P.-A.L.S. is now appropriate to represent trips, shortcomings remain regarding the objective of the problem. Indeed, in most trip planning situations, selection based on transportation cost only is not conceivable. Activity and accommodation costs should also be considered.

Since total costs of transportation, activity and lodging usually do not have the same importance in the tourist's eyes, minimising those costs does not simply amount to minimising their sum. Therefore, three separate objectives have to be taken into account at the same time : minimising total transportation cost, minimising total lodging cost and minimising total activity cost. This new alteration gives rise to the Multiple Objective T.S.P.-A.L.S. (M.O.T.S.P.-A.L.S.).

A lot of attention has been devoted to Multiple Objective Combinatorial Optimisation (M.O.C.O.) problems in the few last years and knowledge of those problems, and of the best ways to solve them, progresses quickly. In particular, multi-objective versions of meta-heuristics give promising results to determine quasi-efficient solutions of large-size M.O.C.O. problems.

Finally, a last major improvement which is necessary to modelise trip planning consists in taking into consideration not only the components' costs but also the tourist's preferences. Besides minimising the three costs, maximising lodging and activity attractiveness leads to define a problem with five objectives : the Preference-Based M.O.T.S.P.-A.L.S. (P.B.-M.O.T.S.P.-A.L.S.).

The extra objectives brought in by the P.B. versions of the models pose new specific problems which are related to the need to quantify and aggregate the tourist's preferences, and to which Multiple Criteria Decision Aid (M.C.D.A.) is dedicated. Depending on the measuring scales of preferences, several solutions can be considered.

The last problem defined can play a central part in trip planning, just like other extensions of the T.S.P. do in various fields (e.g. the V.R.P. to plan delivery rounds). Consequently, it was nicknamed "Trip Planning Problem" (T.P.P.).
The T.P.P. as such is especially appropriate as a basis for modelising sightseeing tours, where a whole area is visited, from and back to the specified point of origin/destination, with accommodation in hotels and transportation by car or bus. However, it could most probably also be used as a starting point for trip planning at large, and this will be a topic for further research.

A first consistent implementation of multi-objective versions of two meta-heuristics, called Tabu Search and Simulated Annealing, gave promising results for fictitious instances of the T.P.P. (with make-believe data for preferences, costs...), based on the case of sightseeing tours in Florida. This brought to light many future prospects to design D.S.S. aimed at planning sightseeing tours and possibly other kinds of trips.

5. Conclusion

Only a few years ago, the idea of building a D.S.S. for trip planning would have been considered science fiction. Until then, information and communication technologies were not advanced and widespread enough to make this possible. Moreover, as shown above, the T.P.P. proves to be difficult to manage in several respects and requires techniques that have only recently been approached in Operations Research and about which many studies are still in progress. From a tourism research point of view as well, the T.P.P. is at the focus of various research directions : hotel and activity selection criteria, trip patterns, etc.

In the very near future, even more tools and knowledge will be available to build helpful trip planning Decision Support Systems, based on Combinatorial Optimisation. Such systems could assist all tourism consumers, intermediaries and providers in selecting travel components (transportation, accommodation and activities) and combining them into coherent products, aimed at maximising tourists' satisfaction.

A trip planning D.S.S. could be useful in lots of different situations with varied purposes : independent traveller's assistance on the Internet, tour packaging, and hotel marketing to name a few. Of course, the trip arrangements obtained from such a system, which is based on mathematical algorithms, should not be expected to be the best possible ones or to be definitive. However, they can be very good starting points for further "manual" improvements.

Finally, it is worth noticing that the Combinatorial Optimisation models and methods presented in this paper do not pretend to come under Artificial Intelligence. The algorithm does not devise trips, but goes through a tremendous number of trip possibilities to select the most appropriate one(s). Thus, unlike expert systems, it does not attempt to simulate human brain activity, but just uses computers to do what they really can do much better and faster than people, that is, repeated data processing.

References

1. Aarts, E.H.L., Lenstra, J.K., "Introduction", *in* Aarts E., Lenstra J.K. (eds.), "Local Search in Combinatorial Optimization", John Wiley & Sons, United Kingdom (1997), pp. 1-17.
2. Bennett, M., Radburn, M., "Information Technology in Tourism : The Impact on the Industry and Supply of Holidays", *in* Sinclair, M.T., Stabler, M.J. (eds.), "The Tourism Industry, An International Analysis", C.A.B. International, United Kingdom (1991), pp. 45-65.
3. Crouch, G.I., "Expert Computer Systems In Tourism : Emerging Possibilities", Journal of Travel Research, vol. 29, no. 3 (winter 1991), pp. 3-10.
4. Halatsis, C., Stamatopoulos, P., Karali, I., Mourlas, C., Gouscos, D., Margaritis, D., Fouskakis, C., Kolokouris, A., Xinos, P., Reeve, M., Véron, A., Schuerman, K., Li, L.L., "MaTourA : Multi-Agent Tourist Advisor", *in* "International Conference on Information and Communication Technologies in Tourism, Innsbrück, 1994" proceedings, Springer-Verlag, Austria (1994), pp. 140-147.
5. Hruschka, H., Mazanec, J., "Computer-Assisted Travel Counseling", Annals of Tourism Research, vol. 17, no. 2 (1990), pp. 208-227.
6. Lenz, M., "IMTAS : Intelligent Multimedia Travel Agent System", *in* "International Conference on Information and Communication Technologies in Tourism, Innsbrück, 1996" proceedings, Springer-Verlag, Austria (1996), pp. 11-17.
7. Loban, S.R., "A Framework for Computer-Assisted Travel Counseling", Annals of Tourism Research, vol. 24, no. 4 (1997), pp. 813-834.
8. Mulye, R., Rickard, J., "A Decision Support System for Tourism Destination Choice", *in* "International Conference on Information and Communication Technologies in Tourism, Innsbrück, 1995" proceedings, Springer-Verlag, Austria (1995), pp. 299-307.
9. Ng, F.Y.Y., Sussmann, S., "A Personal Travel Assistant for Holiday Selection - A Learning Interface Agent Approach", *in* "International Conference on Information and Communication Technologies in Tourism, Innsbrück, 1996" proceedings, Springer-Verlag, Austria (1996), pp. 3-10.
10. Osman, I.H., Kelly, J.P., "Meta-Heuristics : An Overview", *in* Osman, I.H., Kelly, J.P. (eds), "Meta-Heuristics : Theory & Applications", Kluwer Academic Publishers, U.S.A. (1996), pp. 1-21.
11. Vanhoof, K., Molderez, I., "An Advice System for Travel Agents", *in* "International Conference on Information and Communication Technologies in Tourism, Innsbrück, 1994" proceedings, Springer-Verlag, Austria (1994), pp. 120-132.
12. First announcement of the Enter '99 conference, Innsbrück, Austria, January 20-22, 1999.

User Interfaces in Information and Reservation Systems: Classification and Development Issues

Dr Andrew J Frew
Napier University, Edinburgh
a.frew@napier.ac.uk

Elaine Crichton
Napier University, Edinburgh
e.crichton@napier.ac.uk

Abstract

This work derives from a broader investigation of usability in information and reservations systems and although these systems are now commonplace, research on system usability in the sector is scant. It is envisaged that this usability field will expand significantly and thus an attempt is made here to lay some foundations for this future work Difficulties in seeking to define and classify systems, users and user interfaces as a first approach to investigating usability, are described and pending subsequent refinement, a working definition is ascribed to information and reservations systems and users. However the central focus is the user interface itself since this is the key to usability. The paper concludes with an approach to classifying user interface configurations which may facilitate future research by applying a common approach to usability assessment for both system users and software developers.

1 Introduction

Almost every area of the tourism industry has benefited significantly from the recent progress in computer and communications technology, especially those systems designed to enhance and simplify information and reservations processes. These systems, in a profusion of guises, are now ubiquitous in the sector, from the supersystems such as the global distribution systems (GDS) and the large international hotel central reservations systems (CRS) through to Destination management systems (DMS) accessible through high street kiosks. They may be encountered in travel agencies or on hotel front desks, railway terminals or tour operators, ski resorts or car hire outlets. There are thousands of developers, hundreds of thousands of systems, millions of operators and hundreds of millions of users. The scale of activity of these systems is expanding as access to such systems is progressively enabled in homes, offices and in the high street through enhanced telecommunications and in particular through the penetration of the Web. We are all becoming consumers in a growing electronic marketplace.

The authors' research interest in the field of information and reservations systems encompasses an investigation of usability aspects of such systems with the aim of examining both the development process and user-centred issues. The central goal of the research work upon which this paper draws, is the establishment of a rational and consistent basis for the examination of system usability issues within the tourism industry and in particular the impact of usability issues within information and reservations environments. Within the industry, information and reservations systems are widely regarded as mission critical systems and the way in which enterprises and their customers access information and make bookings is of paramount importance. These systems tend to be relatively expensive to purchase and to install and will often attract significant support and maintenance costs. Initial and ongoing training costs are high (emphasised by high staff turnover areas of the industry) and there are often substantial system interfacing and integration issues, and costs, which arise when seeking to combine or communicate amongst differing systems even within a single enterprise. These examples are only indicative but make it apparent therefore that usability will significantly impact upon all aspects of this process. There is a good case then for investigating usability and some have started to address usability specifics in the tourism sector [1,2]. It should be said that the research work described here does not attempt to investigate the theoretical and philosophical aspects of the relationship between humans and computer based systems, the thrust of the study is in exploring interface attributes from a practical perspective.

2 Background

It is our contention that most information and reservations systems have poor usability and that usability is given insufficient priority by system designers. -yet this need not be the case. *"Many fine words have been spoken about the notion of "usability", but it can be an elusive concept to pin down... embracing usability imposes additional performance criteria that can be specified in quantitative terms. Moreover a range of usability evaluation methods that yield data of various sorts and quantities has been developed."* [3]. That is the view of those working in mainstream HCI, however, in order to progress this work in tourism, an agreed practical means of measuring usability is required which in turn requires consideration of the systems , users and interfaces. A significant barrier was, however, encountered at an early stage when initial investigation of the literature revealed neither a rationale nor an agreed means of classifying the systems themselves, system users or indeed user interfaces.

The first of these aspects, systems classification, on initial examination appears less problematic than the others in that there is a considerable body of literature now devoted to global distribution systems, to central reservations systems, to destination management systems, to property management systems and so forth. Closer investigation of this literature revealed a confusing and contradictory use of many terms - as recently illustrated [4]. For practical research purposes in the current investigation, this was not seen as an obstacle since it was relatively easy to identify whether or not a given system was intended to address information and reservations tasks. Our interest lay in information systems only where linked directly or indirectly to a booking process, in other words the view taken was that it would be a straightforward task to identify whether or not any given system qualified for consideration.

Definitions of the system user and of the user interface were significantly more problematic and, other than generic work on user interfaces, there was in fact very little literature applicable to the tourism sector. The primary aim therefore of this paper is to attempt to provide a tentative classification of both users and user interfaces within the context of information and reservations systems.. Usability will influence not only business costs related to this core area but will in itself strongly affect the way in which business is conducted in this environment. The importance of user interfaces is highlighted by Myers [5] *"User interfaces are likely to be one of the main value-added competitive advantages of the future as both hardware and basic software become commodities"* Let us therefore turn to the user interface first before consideration of users and then finally re-visit the issue of systems classification.

3 The User Interface

The term user interface is taken from the broader area of human computer interaction (HCI) which can itself be regarded as a sub-set of the man machine interface (MMI). While MMI has of course been around since the industrial revolution, HCI is a comparatively new multi-disciplinary field which has been described as *"... the design of computer systems that are safe, efficient, easy and enjoyable to use as well as functional"* [6]. So, man may well have interacted with machines for centuries but it is only in the last 30 to 40 years that computing power has become part of many types of machine and indeed that humans have interacted with computers.

The study thus looked at conventional generic definitions of user interfaces and in attempting to uncover relevant research, the literature was approached from both tourism and computer science areas. It was hoped to place user interface aspects within tourism as a field in the broader area of HCI and to lay the groundwork for specific investigative approaches from this work. Comprehensive literature searches were conducted in an iterative manner, both manual and on-line, including electronic and Web sources and employing a range of tentative and progressively refined key words. The starting point for this process lay with the definition of user interface and such definitions like the area itself have evolved enormously in recent years.

For example, in the 1980s user interfaces were defined as *"those aspects of the system that the user comes in contact with"* [7] a rather vague interpretation improved upon to.. *"an input language for the user, an output language for the machine, and a protocol of interaction"* [8]. However, by the 1990s it was already becoming clear that the user interface comprises much more than merely what is palpable through the various peripheral devices. For example *"a user of a computer system is required to understand the meaning of commands and replies, to anticipate the effects of commands on what the computer programme will do, and to relate their own task goals and plans into system specific commands that will allow these goals to be achieved"* [9]. Ultimately the authors settled on an inclusive definition.. *"those aspects of the system with which the user comes into contact both physically and cognitively"* [10]

In our quest to establish a means of classifying or categorising user interfaces for use by systems researchers in tourism, there was little specific help from the literature. It is not that little research has been undertaken into the user interface, quite the reverse, but rather that the research discloses a bewildering selection of instruments with which to disassemble and uniquely identify a user interface. These tools and techniques benefit (HCI) computer scientists working on tightly defined aspects of systems, unfortunately for the researcher seeking some summarising descriptors, groups or classes of interface which may be used across a range of systems they are of little assistance.

A simple starting point is to look at the hardware and software available to the user and this does yield some helpful pointers. In the broadest sense, the hardware is seen as enabling the interface configuration options through which software interacts to provide the full user interface. It should in principle be simple to identify hardware aspects of any system. Software itself is often simply described through the terms environment software, application software and system software. Environment software describes how the user interacts locally with the software performing the users functional tasks - the application software, while system software is the underlying operating system. These terms have also been further sub-divided e.g. application software has been described as horizontal, vertical or bespoke software - and while this helps us understand who the software was designed for it tells us little about the interface. For many approaches this may indeed be considered a straightforward means of labelling systems e.g. a windows-based booking system running under Unix and so on, however, there are problems. There is not a clear demarcation of these software boundaries; operating system software is now routinely bound directly to the environment software, the level and type of system software underlying an application may vary depending upon the telecommunications environment in which the application is being employed and so forth. Where does the operating system stop? In terms of developer influence for example, a parallel may be drawn between the recent Windows 95/Internet Explorer issues and the GDS/Travel Agency systems issues.

In other words adopting a hardware/software approach as outlined above is possible but may not be especially informative for applied systems research. What is needed is a useful and portable means of classifying any particular user interface by its key attributes and which can be readily employed when investigating users and perhaps more tellingly, the approaches adopted by software houses and system suppliers to the industry. No obvious single approach emerged from the literature search, as has been said, nonetheless a classification approach arising from recent research and into which most of those examined seemed to fit was considered [11] and adapted. This preliminary user interface classification approach has four main aspects:

- *Interaction devices* - here the researcher can inventory the range of input, processing and output devices/systems available to the user - very largely the hardware dimension mentioned earlier. These devices comprise keyboards, handwriting recognition, speech recognition, positioning devices, screens, code readers, scanners and so forth.

- *Interaction styles* - early interactions with computers entailed simple text entry and response dialogue, form-filling dialogue was a more user-friendly development of this and gradually as more non-specialists used computers varied and hybrid systems were designed to address a wide range of user preferences. Evaluating interaction styles will thus involve looking at mixtures of style with each application. There are a number of common interface styles including command-line interface, menus, natural language, question/answer and query dialogue, form-filling, WIMP, point and click and 3D interfaces

- *Display Design* - the screen is the normal means of both presenting information and facilitating interaction with the system. How information is presented depends very much upon the kind of information to be presented and the purpose for which it is to be used. The aesthetics if screen design may conflict with practical utility and representations on screen may be passive or require interaction.

- *Modelling the users tasks* - the functionality of any piece of software will reflect the tasks that the user wishes to perform, however, there are often many ways of conceiving of and implementing these e.g. early hotel booking systems merely mimicked the approach of the manual systems which they replaced. This area is fundamental to interface design and is a key element in tackling research into the development process.

Each of these aspects is of course capable of much finer subdivision but present a practical starting point. In this approach, the user interface is defined by the application - it is application specific so in classifying any interface, the first task is therefore to specify and define the application itself - part of system classification. It will thus be seen that the user interface is independent of the functionality addressed through the application software, the same functionality may be offered through very different user interfaces - neither is it defined by the operating system. When approaching any information and reservations system, the way forward for the researcher would therefore seem to be to clearly identify the application in use and proceed to inventory the system characteristics in use through the above four aspects and across the full range of system functionality. It should be noted that the user interface is not a static description and will vary to some extent according the nature and frequency of functions accessed by the user, which leads us to the third dimension of the user interface that of the system user.

4 The System User

In providing a framework for examining usability it is important not only to standardise an approach to user interfaces but also to attempt a classification of the various users. Without even a preliminary means of grouping users, it is difficult to design research into usability aspects of systems. "*If adequate functionality has been chosen, reliability ensured, standardisation addressed and schedule plus budgetary planning is complete, then developers can focus their attention on the design and testing process. The multiple design alternatives must be evaluated for specific user communities...*" [12]. Who then are these communities of information and reservations systems users? The introduction gave an indication of the scale of system use and users may be drawn from those involved in private sector tourism supply; accommodation, transport, visitor attractions and so forth or perhaps those involved in indirectly selling or promoting this supply such as travel agents or tour operators. There is public sector involvement through the national and regional tourism organisations and other government agencies and then of course there are the consumers themselves. A comprehensive list of users would be beyond the scope of this paper. A common approach to the classification issue is to consider users as either suppliers of a product or service, intermediaries in the distribution chain or consumers of the product or service. This classification based on the role of the user in the distribution chain, has been used extensively in tourism and for example recently adopted by Inkpen [13] when describing the structure of IT in travel and tourism and is capable of some further refinement to take account of e.g. user roles, functions and skill levels. In addition to these primary system users, there are also those who use the systems during development, those who sell, install and perhaps support and maintain systems, system trainers and so forth. These may be regarded as secondary users.

Thus, it is also possible to sub-divide these user categories; for example, the needs of a hotel receptionist accessing a reservations system, is very different from the function of a hotel manager accessing a reservations system. The receptionist is likely to be heavily input-oriented e.g. making or changing bookings; whilst the manager is likely to have more of an output-orientation requesting management information, reports, forecasts and so on. The same may be said for intermediaries and consumers themselves may be typified by either leisure or business-oriented needs. Furthermore it is useful to categorise users by their level of skill or system expertise, the standard approach to this being to class them either as novice users, knowledgeable intermittent users or as expert frequent users. In summary we therefore have four user types each of which may be explored through for example role, function and skill level.

5 Systems

In the introduction to this paper it is stated that, despite confusing nomenclature, it is relatively easy to identify systems which address information and reservations tasks. If you are investigating system users accessing the SABRE system, you are dealing with a GDS, the Gulliver system in turn is a DMS (Destination Management System) while those accessing Fidelio are using a PMS (Property Management System) and in many ways systems are defined by their sphere of orientation - airlines, hotels, destination, travel agency, tour operator, visitor attraction and so on. In the main, usability investigations are likely to be user-centred, in which case the information and reservations system(s) in use will be 'defined' by their users or the research will be system developer-centred and again, developers will define their user markets. That said, we are beginning to witness significant vertical and horizontal systems integration from systems developers and the telecommunications revolution spearheaded by the Web is transforming these conventional definitions. Work elsewhere [14] is starting to examine this phenomenon in the shape of hotel electronic distribution channel characteristics and it is anticipated that this will in due course inform the user interface work by identifying systems through their attribute clusters rather than conventional terminology. In the interim, however, the conventional terms will be used.

Commons systems include the GDS, CRS and DMS mentioned earlier and also encompass Alternative Distribution Systems (ADS), Travel Agency Systems (TAS), Tour Operator Systems (TOS) and Property Management Systems (PMS) and provide the obvious starting point for usability research. System attributes may be usefully extended to include contextual dimensions such as location, ownership, scale and so forth.

6 Conclusions and future work

The approach arrived at produces a classification process which, while not perhaps entirely purist to the HCI community, should be both readily understood and easily applied by the those engaged in tourism systems research. Modelling the process of

Figure 1. Usability Evaluation

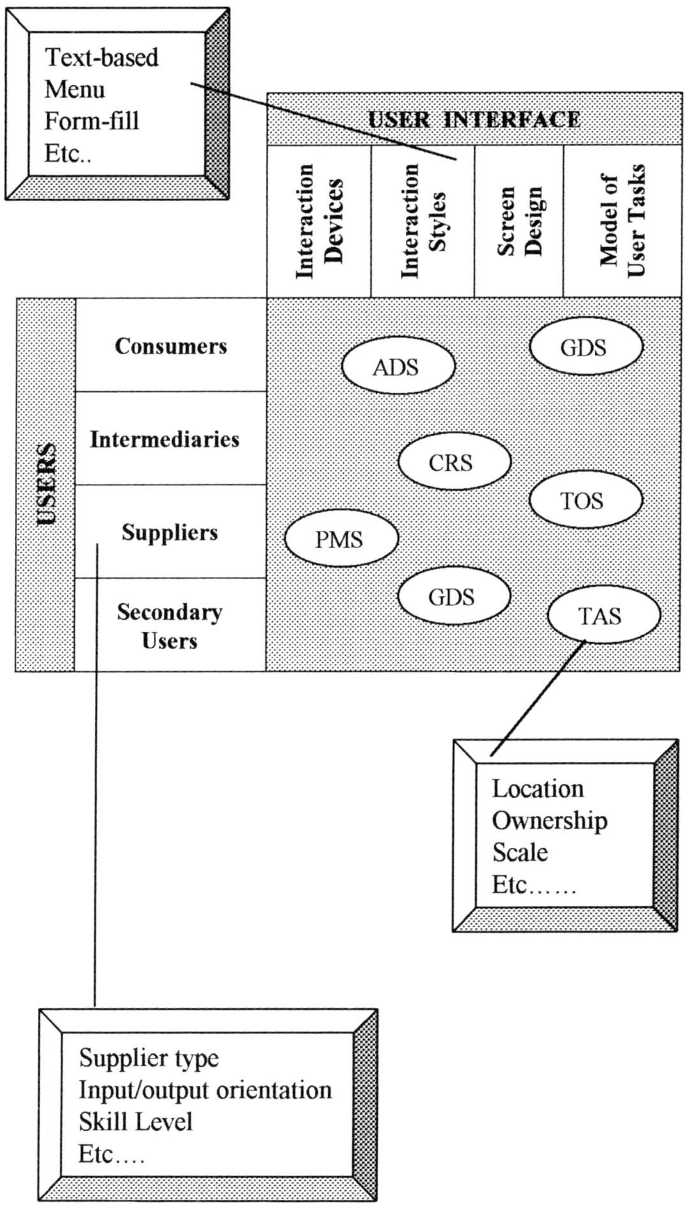

bringing user interface dimensions to bear on users and systems may be represented as in Figure 1. What is described is an approach which will identify user interface characteristics through four key aspects. Each of these should be considered for every class of user although their individual importance and emphasis will vary by user. Users are seen as belonging to any of four classes while systems are simply allocated their conventional label (with the limitations earlier noted). Each of these dimensions is capable to progressive hierarchical decomposition, the scale of which be set by the researcher as appropriate. In studying the development process, for example, the researcher may examine the model of the users tasks in a very detailed way. On the other hand it may be more appropriate to expand the interaction style aspect when exploring leisure consumers accessing DMS.

It is intended at the next stage of the work is to seek to evaluate DMS usability from the perspective of each of the user communities described above, however, in due course it is hoped that this approach may be widely applied to user and system classes and that comparisons and perhaps some generalisations may be produced across the field.

References

1 Loban, S. R., "Designing Effective Documents for Destination Information Systems", in *Information and Communication Technologies in Tourism*, Springer, New York, 1998.
2 Werthner, H., "Design Principles of Tourist Information Systems", in *Information and Communication Technologies in Tourism*, Springer, New York, 1996.
3 Crerar, A. and Benyon, D. "Integrating Usability into Systems Development" in *The Politics of Usability*, Tranner L, and Bawa J (eds), Springer,1998
4 Frew, A.J. and O'Connor, P, "A Comparative Examination of the Implementation of Destination Marketing System Strategies: Scotland and Ireland" in *Information and Communication Technologies in Tourism*, Springer, New York, 1998
5 Myers, B., "A Brief History of Human Computer Interaction Technology", Interactions, March & April, 1998
6 Preece J. et al, "Human-computer Interaction", Wokingham, Addison Wesley, 1994
7 Moran, T,P "The command language grammar: a representation for the user interface of interactive systems" International Journal of Man Machine Studies, 15 (1), 3-50 1981
8 Chi H U, "Formal specification of user interfaces: a comparison and evaluation of four axiomatic approaches IEEE Transactions on Software Engineering, vol. 11 (8) pp671-685 1985
9 Johnson, P., "Human-computer Interaction: Psychology, Task Analysis and Software Engineering", McGraw-Hill, 1992
10 Preece, J. (Ed), "A Guide to Usability: Human Factors in Computing", Addison Wesley, 1993
11 Crerar, A., Napier University, Department of Computer Studies, personal communication.
12 Shneiderman, B., "Designing the User Interface", (3rd ed), Addison Wesley Longman, Reading
13 Inkpen, G., "Information Technology for Travel and Tourism", (2nd ed.), Longman, 1998, p3
14 O'Connor, P., and Frew, A.J., "Hotel Electronic Distribution Systems", EuroCHRIE, Oslo, 1998..

The Airtours Cruise Intranet: Streamlining the distribution of information, knowledge and money

G. Jewell, B. Williamson, K. Kärcher

Abstract

Airtours PLC is one of the largest vertically integrated tour operator groups in the world, and is partly-owned by Carnival Corporation, the world's largest cruise ship operator. The Airtours Cruise Division currently operates four wholly-owned cruise ships, servicing passengers from many different states in Europe and North America. The Airtours Cruise Division has implemented an advanced Intranet, i.e. a virtual private corporate network based on Internet-technologies. This Intranet links, via land lines and satellites, the Airtours cruise ships and all offices of the Airtours Cruise Division worldwide. Using this communication infrastructure, both voice and data are distributed between different locations as required. This paper outlines, in case study form, the technical and organisational infrastructure and operations of this 'state-of-the-art' Intranet, which cost-effectively streamlines the distribution of information, knowledge and money.

1 Introduction

The Airtours Cruise & Hotels Division (CHD), based in Helmshore/Lancashire near Manchester, is a wholly-owned division of Airtours PLC (Airtours Group), Manchester, England. Airtours Group is one of the largest travel and tourism companies in the world, with substantial international interests in charter airline, cruise, hotel, tour, and leisure travel agency operations (Table 1).

In April 1996, Airtours PLC was partly acquired by Carnival Corporation, Miami/Florida, USA. Carnival is, with a fleet of approximately 40 cruise ships, the world's largest cruise ship operator. Airtours CHD, which trades as 'Sun Cruises', 'Sunwing Hotels' and 'Vacation Ownership' (i.e. the timeshare operation), was set-up in early 1994. By mid 1998, Airtours CHD operated four wholly-owned cruise ships (Table 2), carrying approximately 1.6 million passengers per year in total.

In late 1996 and early 1997, Airtours CHD formulated and approved a new IT strategy (see for example Airtours CHD, 1997). In essence, a decision was made to develop and implement a technical and organisational infrastructure to cost-effectively streamline the distribution of information, knowledge and money within all Airtours CHD business units. The two main commercial aims of this strategy were (i) to increase passenger revenue streams, and (ii) to control costs. As a result

Operations	Geographic Focus	Main Subsidiaries
Charter Airlines	Scandinavian Leisure Group (SLG)	Premiair (13 aircraft)
	UK Leisure Group (UKLG)	Airtours International (22 aircraft)
	West European Leisure Group (WELG)	Air Belgium
Cruise Ship Operations	Caribbean, Mediterranean	Airtours CHD (4 cruise ships) Costa Cruises (7 cruise ships)
Hotel Operations	Mediterranean	Airtours CHD (> 30 properties; 2 timeshare complexes)
Tour Operators	North American Leisure Group (NALG)	Alba Tours, Silver Wing, Sunquest Holidays, Sunquest Vacations, SunTrips
	Scandinavian Leisure Group (SLG)	Always, Saga Solreiser, Simon Spies, Tjaereborg Rejser, Ving Group
	UK Leisure Group (UKLG)	Airtours Holidays, Aspro Holidays, Bridge Travel Group, Cresta Holidays, Direct Holidays, EuroSites, Tradewinds
	West European Leisure Group (WELG)	Frosch Touristik / FTI, Sun International
Leisure Travel Agents	Scandinavian Leisure Group (SLG)	Ving Shops
	UK Leisure Group (UKLG)	Going Places (> 700 outlets)
	West European Leisure Group (WELG)	Flugbörse D+S Reisen (> 90 outlets), Sun International

Table 1. Main Airtours Group Interests in mid 1998

Cruise Ship	Acquisition	Cabins	Berths	Crew	Tonnes
MS Carousel	October 1994	528	1,160	400	23,200
MS Seawing	April 1994	339	916	300	16,607
MS Sunbird	May 1998	707	1,575	500	37,584
MS Sundream	August 1996	540	1,190	400	22,945
Total		2,114	4,841	1,600	100,336

Table 2. The Airtours Cruise Ships

of this IT strategy, the 'state-of-the-art' Airtours Cruise Intranet, which is discussed in this paper, was implemented between January 1997 and summer 1998.

Only the Cruise Intranet is described here; thus the paper does not include information related to the Airtours Hotels Intranet of Airtours CHD (Anonymous, 1998a) nor to any other Airtours Group Intranet, unless where directly relevant. No cost and financial information is published for reasons of confidentiality.

2 Technical Information and Communication Infrastructure

Airtours CHD decided to implement a common platform with common reporting processes across the division. It was also decided to adopt standard telecommunications and IT products whenever available, and only to implement be-spoke systems where necessary. With regards to reporting, systems had to support 'push-reports', rather than 'old-style' 'pull-reports'. This meant that financial and management information were distributed automatically by the systems rather than having to be retrieved on demand.

The main IT systems concentrated on initially during the project were (i) general ledger system and MIS (management information system), (ii) property database, and (iii) guest management system. Over time, more systems were added, and currently the main systems used by Airtours CHD are (in alphabetical order):

- **'Airtours Res'**: The be-spoke tour operator system of Airtours Holidays Limited, storing package holidays branded as 'Airtours' and 'Aspro' (Kärcher, 1997, pp. 139 - 140). The system operates on Data General (DG) MV60 machines in Helmshore. The system is accessed either via an internal front-end, or via a viewdata (videotex) emulator accessing the external Airtours Holidays viewdata front-end system.
- **'AMOS'**: The standard ship stock control and purchasing system of Airtours CHD, developed and maintained by Spectec, Norway. The system, which is based on fully distributed databases, operates on PC servers on the cruise ships, at the Fleet Management Office in Southampton, and at the Fleet Purchasing Office in Monaco. The system was implemented during June and July 1998.
- **'ASI'**: The standard cruise ship hotel management and catering system of Airtours CHD, developed and maintained by Automated Sciences Inc. (ASI), Sarasota, USA. The system operates on PC servers on the ships. It was implemented on MS Carousel in January 1997, on MS Seawing in March 1997, and on MS Sundream in April 1997.
- **'Fidelio'**: The standard (land-based) hotel management and catering system of Airtours CHD, developed and maintained by Micros Fidelio, Germany (and USA). The system was implemented in the first Airtours Sunwing Hotels in January 1997, but was not used on the cruise ships.
- **'Frango'**: The be-spoke corporate accountancy database system of Airtours Group, used in particular for generation of monthly and annual financial reports. The system operates in Helmshore.
- **'MS Explorer'**: The standard Microsoft Internet browser software, allowing access to the internal Windows NT web server in Helmshore and to public Internet web sites.
- **'MS Outlook'**: The standard Microsoft e-mail software, which was implemented by Airtours Group worldwide between January and August 1998.
- **'Scala'**: The standard financial system of Airtours CHD, developed and maintained by Scala, Sweden. Relevant information is extracted automatically

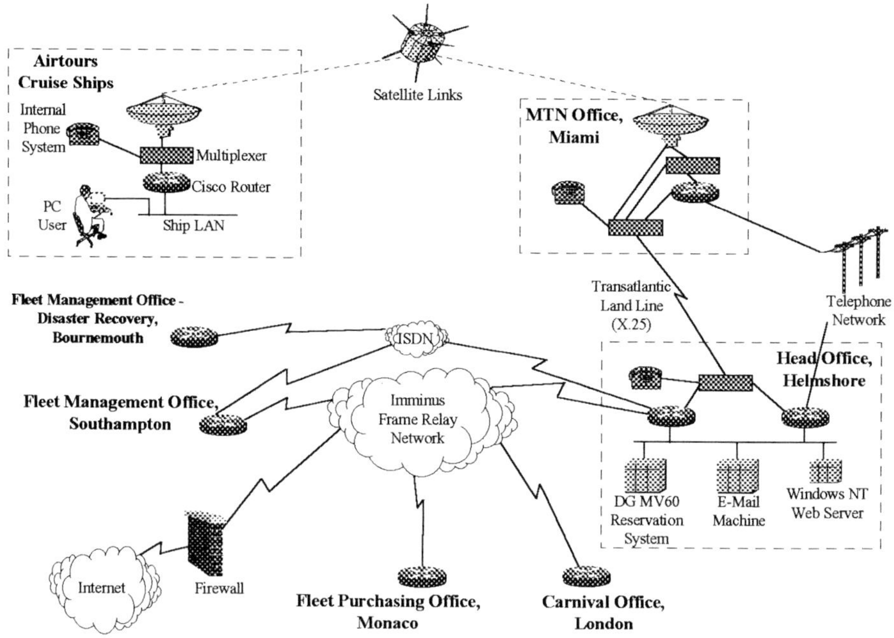

Fig. 1. Airtours Cruise Intranet Technical Infrastructure

from 'ASI' and 'Fidelio'. On a monthly basis, financial information is passed automatically to 'Frango'. The system operates in Helmshore and was implemented in February 1998.

Throughout the division, Windows NT has been implemented as the operating system, Ethernet as the LAN (local area network) standard, and TCP/IP as the LAN and WAN (wide area network) protocol. For cost reasons, ISDN is used for back-up and disaster recovery processes.

All IT systems are linked by a modern telecommunication infrastructure using Internet technologies (i.e. TCP/IP) to allow communication over various platforms, without the need to implement complex gateways. Fig. 1 gives an overview of the Airtours Cruise Intranet IT infrastructure.

Fig. 1 does not show additional links to the Airtours Group Head-Office in Manchester, and to other Airtours Group offices and subsidiaries worldwide, as these links are not part of the Airtours Cruise Intranet. While on-line access is available to 'Airtours Res', no other land-based systems can be accessed on-line by cruise staff for security reasons.

Most of the international Cisco router management and maintenance, and the land-traffic (limited only by bandwidth). Each cruise ship has eight voice chunks for passengers, one voice line for staff, and one fax (/voice) line. Each ship operates a telephone exchange (PABX) capable of supporting over 1,000 extensions per ship. In addition, voice internal traffic via routers is provided to the ships, as well as the Miami office and the Head-Office, allowing for up to four concurrent calls.

Connectivity to the Inmarsat, which is charged on a time-dependant basis, is maintained for emergencies. For example, the 'MariNet' store-and-forward system can be used via the Inmarsat as a back-up messaging system. Television and radio programmes are received via further satellite links. Moreover, the GMDSS (Global Maritime Distress and Safety System) was implemented during November 1997 to May 1998. This modern safety system made the role of Ship Radio Officer as well as the function of the Ship's Radio Room redundant.

While some links existed prior to the implementation of the Airtours Cruise Intranet (for example, Helmshore was linked during 1996), the main Intranet developments and implementations were conducted during January 1997 to summer 1998. The first cruise ship, MS Sundream, was refitted during February and March 1997 (Jordan, 1997). The routers on MS Carousel and MS Seawing were installed in September 1997 (Anonymous, 1997 and 1998b), the fleet purchasing office was linked in October 1997, the fleet management office in February 1998, and the disaster recovery site in early summer 1998. Finally, Internet access was provided in September 1998.

Prior to the implementation of the Cruise Intranet, all ship-to-shore and shore-to-ship communication was by voice and fax only. The Intranet allowed for the introduction of electronic mail and FTP (file transfer programme). With the introduction of 'MS Outlook', FTP has been replaced by more efficient file attachments to e-mail messages.

Each cruise ship had one to two IT staff, consisting of an Electronic Technical Officer (ETO) and, in some cases, a Communications Assistant. Overall, the entire IT department for both cruise and hotel operations consisted of approximately 20 staff. Additional IT support is provided by Airtours Holidays / EDS, and by the IT and telecommunication partner organisations.
based telecommunications infrastructure and support, is provided by Imminus / General Telecom Limited, Peterborough, England. The satellite links are provided by Maritime Telecommunications Network (MTN), Miami, USA. The software company ASI has dial-up access to the network in Miami via the public telephone network for on-line 'ASI' software support. Imminus / General Telecom has access to the Cisco routers for management via further separate public telephone dial-up links both in Miami and in Helmshore. The Fleet Purchasing Office is operated by Martinoli in Monte Carlo, Monaco, and the Disaster Recovery Centre of the Fleet

Management Office is operated by RGH Associates (Richard, Graham, Humphrey) in Bournemouth, England.

The MTN satellite links are used as the main communication links to the ships. This connectivity is paid for on a fixed charge for volume independent voice and data

3 Organisational Information and Communication Processes

Prior to the implementation of the Intranet, all data and other information was held on PCs on the ships and the various cruise offices locally. Information could only be transferred either by phone or fax, and it then needed to be re-keyed into the PCs. This process was very labour intensive and slow, and occasionally lead to errors through re-keying. Some land-based offices also used the e-mail software 'MS Mail', while the very restrictive 'Uniplex' was in use on some cruise ships. However, electronic communication between these systems was 'piecemeal' and perceived as unsatisfactory. With the introduction of the Intranet, many processes were completely re-engineered, as outlined in the following.

3.1 Corporate Information and Knowledge Management

- **General information and knowledge management:** 'MS Outlook' was introduced between June and 1 August 1998, replacing 'MS Mail' in land-based offices and 'Uniplex' on the cruise ships. This allowed for the integration of the internal electronic communication infrastructure, thereby leading to increased communication speeds and considerable cost savings, such as in reduced telephone and fax costs and in lower administration effort. Using 'MS Explorer', Intranet web-sites based in Helmshore displaying corporate information can also be accessed. In addition, through a guarded outbreak to the public Internet, staff can also exchange e-mail messages with company external contacts including their families and friends. Moreover, staff can access Internet web-sites. For example, the cruise ship doctors can access up-to-date medical information on-line via the Internet. However, it is worth noting that due to ship procedure, all cruise ship outgoing and incoming communication is seen by the Captain. Moreover, all safety-related communication is printed on paper and retained for records according to ISM (Institute of Safety Management for Shipping) procedures.
- **Financial information management:** 'Scala' (and 'Frango') replaced the Airtours Holidays accountancy system 'Miracle', as well as various 'MS Excel' spreadsheets. This implementation reduced system response times and, through interfaces to other systems, fully automated many manual procedures, thus gaining substantial savings in administration. In addition, flexibility and commercial control was increased as more financial information on the

operations of the hotels and cruise ships could be extracted from 'Scala', in particular due to interfaces to 'Fidelio' and (since summer 1998) to 'ASI'.

- **Human resource (HR) information management:** Staffing information is mailed electronically between the ships, head-office and the fleet management office. No HR system is currently used, but the 'ASI' HR module is planned for the end of 1998.
- **Ship layout information management:** In the past, all ship layout drawings were stored on paper both on the ships and in the land-based offices. These drawings are used for engineering, maintenance and passenger information purposes. In July 1998, a CAD (computer-aided design) software was implemented, developed and maintained by DHE, Southampton, England. CAD files are now sent as e-mail attachments and are stored on PCs on the ships and in the land-based offices, thus substantially reducing the workload of transferring, storing and handling the layouts. An automated interface between the CAD software and the 'AMOS' inventory system is also planned.

3.2 Supply Management

Prior to the implementation of 'AMOS', stock management was mainly manual, with the occasional use of standard PC word processing and spreadsheet software. The processes were little integrated and therefore slow and labour intensive.

- **Stock control management:** Since the implementation of the database stock inventory module 'AMOS-D' on 1 June 1998, all stock of water, fuel and spare parts (ranging from screws to major engineering components) held on the cruise ships is stored electronically. Updates of this stock information are e-mailed to Head-Office and the Fleet Management Office. In addition, food stocks are held in 'ASI', and medical stocks in 'MS Access' databases (which will be integrated into 'ASI' in the future).
- **Purchasing management:** When stock levels in 'AMOS-D' get below a certain amount, the 'AMOS-P' purchase order generator module, which was implemented in July 1998, automatically generates an electronic purchase order, which is e-mailed to the Fleet Management Office. The Fleet Management Office either orders the items directly, or passes an electronic order to the Purchasing Office in Monaco. Electronic messages confirming the delivery dates are returned to the ships. In parallel, food and medical supply orders are sent to and handled by the Head-Office in Helmshore.
- **Maintenance management:** 'AMOS' contains electronic preventative and planned / scheduled maintenance plans. These plans automatically update, via 'AMOS-D', the stock information, and generate, via 'AMOS-P', any necessary purchase orders. 'AMOS' also contains a hotel fault reporting module, which supplements 'ASI'. For example, when a passenger informs a crew member that a cabin toilet does not work, various pieces of paper (so-called 'AVOs' / 'avoid

verbal order') which had to be filled in manually were passed between that crew member, the engine control room, and the resident ship plumber. With the implementation of the hotel fault reporting system in 'AMOS', all fault reports are keyed into the system, which then automatically generates all reports, updates the database regarding spare part stock use, orders new parts, records times of each system entry and therefore the length of repairs, and finally automatically generates a letter of apology for the passenger.

3.3 Customer Service Management

- **Hotel operations:** The on-board passenger accommodation is operated as a hotel, and all hotel management and catering information is held in 'ASI'. 'ASI' is supplemented by the hotel fault reporting module of 'AMOS'. Passenger information is automatically transferred via FTP from 'Airtours Res' onto a PC word processor based charting system in Helmshore. The passenger lists are then e-mailed to the cruise ships and loaded into 'ASI'. While customer complaints were previously handled manually, they are now entered into the passenger complaint reporting module in 'AMOS'. This modules records what, when and by whom complaints have been reported, and passes this information to the individuals concerned. Dates and times of all activities are recorded, and these time stamps cannot be changed. The three new systems 'ASI', 'AMOS' and 'Scala' also allowed for, among others, monitoring of guest spending, identification of changes in customer demand, control of quality of service, and information on repeat bookings.
- **Payment handling:** Using the 'ASI' credit card module, any on-board credit card payments are captured in this passenger manifest system. Shortly before the end of each voyage, this information is electronically transferred to Helmshore and onto the NatWest bank host system for authorisation and settlement. Electronic messages confirming or declining the payments are returned. This semi on-line clearing process takes a few hours, but has substantially improved the previous manual process which took five to six days. Full on-line credit card authorisations, as well as ATMs (automated teller machines) for cash withdrawals in the ship casinos, are being considered for the future.
- **Travel agent operations:** Passengers can purchase on-board next year's Airtours holidays, with crew being able to access 'Airtours Res' on-line. An 'ASI' module for tour excursions from the ships is planned in addition. The operation of travel agent outlet on the ships allowing the bookings of a wide range of travel and tourism components and packages from different suppliers via the Imminus Travel and Tourism Intranet (Edwards et al., 1998) is also being considered.
- **General information handling:** Passengers have free access to daily electronic headline information including home news and sports, which is supplied by the Daily Mail newspaper and downloaded via the Inmarsat. Moreover, it is planned to give passengers access to Intranet web sites, displaying information on the

cruise ships and excursions, as well as to the public Internet to 'surf the Web' and send e-mails to family and friends. Stand-alone touch-screen systems, for example for information on ship and tour excursions, are also being considered. Digital images of every cabin on the ships have been produced, with the aim to display this information on an Intranet and an Internet site both to passengers as well as future customers.

4 Conclusions

Pickup (1998, p. 4) lists a number of direct and indirect business benefits arising from the implementation of intranets:

- Direct business benefits: Savings in paper; savings in print production and distribution of newsletters, policy documents and telephone directories; increased efficiency of staff; increased turn-around for sales quotations; savings in replacing legacy systems.
- Indirect business benefits: Knowledge management; improved motivation; shared common visions; communication and change; keeping in step with new technology; competing with external media; aiding communication in disparate organisations; modern working practices; synergy of the work force; free market research; innovation from everyone; relief from information overload; breaking down the 'silo' mentality.

In the case of the Airtours Cruise Intranet, all these benefits were achieved (to different degrees). Moreover, the Airtours Cruise Intranet has lead to a number of further benefits, ranging from increased quality of service to increased customer satisfaction. In particular, major improvements have been made to achieve the two main aims (i) to increase passenger revenue streams, and (ii) to control costs. Although it is too early to assess the full impact of the implementation of the Intranet on the business and financial performance of Airtours CHD, the Cruise Intranet is likely to have substantially improved the operations of and has added crucial short and long-term competitive advantage to the Airtours Cruise Division.

5 References

Airtours CHD (1997). *Project Gemini Strategy Paper* (4 February). Unpublished internal paper, Airtours Cruise & Hotels Division, Helmshore, Lancashire, England.

Anonymous (1997). 'Airtours Installs New Technology on Vessels.' Travel Weekly, 17 September.

Anonymous (1998a). 'Airtours Books Virtual Network Package.' Computer Weekly, 14 May.

Anonymous (1998b). 'Airtours Links up with Imminus.' Travel Bulletin, 3 July, p. 16.

Edwards, G., Dawes, C. and Kärcher, K. (1998). 'The Imminus Travel and Tourism Intranet.' pp. 190 - 200. In: Buhalis, D., Tjoa, A.M. and Jafari, J. (Editors). *Information and Communication Technologies in Tourism 1998*. Springer, Wien, Austria, and New York, USA.

Jordan, D. (1997). 'Airtours: Despite his passion for the great outdoors, Graham Jewell has enjoyed developing a career in IT; now Technical Manager at UK travel operator Airtours, Graham has switched sides from IT supplier to user.' Network News, 14 May, p. 36.

Kärcher, K. (1997). *Reinventing the Package Holiday Business: New information and communication technologies*. DUV, Wiesbaden, Germany.

Pickup, P. (1998). 'Money Matters: Constructing a strong business case for your intranet.' Intranet Communicator, 2(7), June, pp. 4 - 8.

About the Authors

- Graham Jewell is IT Director of the Airtours Cruise & Hotels Division, Helmshore, Lancashire, England.
- Brian Williamson is IT Manager at Airtours Cruise Division, Helmshore, Lancashire, England.
- Dr. Karsten Kärcher is Account Director at Imminus / General Telecom Limited - Travel Division, Peterborough, Cambridgeshire, England.

Contact e-mail: Karsten_Karcher@compuserve.com.

Emerging technologies and their role in developing a marketing information system(MKIS) for tourism and hospitality products

Hilary C. Main
Swansea Business School, Swansea, Wales, UK

Abstract

Destination management systems are in operation in several global locations, though recently their effectiveness in marketing tourism and hospitality for SMEs has been questioned in terms of cost/ benefit analysis. Also their connectivity and inclusion of SMEs within their systems have been neglected in many cases. As individual enterprises, there is evidence that SMEs fail to focus on strategic issues, such as marketing planning and intelligence gathering, as they are preoccupied with the tactical and operational running their businesses and consequently have neither the time nor the resources to focus on developing a role within a Marketing Information system, either at destination level or individual enterprise level.

There are many definitions of what constitutes an MKIS, Thierauf[22] describes an effective management information system as one that allows the decisionmaker(i.e. the manager) to combine his or her subjective expertise with computerised objective output to produce meaningful information for decision making.The ability to use management information systems effectively is essential to the successful operations of most organisations .Information is now considered to be a sixth major resource for most businesses and in this information age could be described as the most important resource for some industries and certainly for the tourism and hospitality sector it is a crucial resource, that is frequently poorly managed.

This paper seeks to identify the flow of information within a destination with particular reference to SMEs. Qualitative data was gathered by conducting semi-structured interviews within the destination with key stakeholders at micro and macro level regarding the current flow of information and determining the usefulness/ appropriateness of technology applications as an enabler to supply information in /out of the marketing information system and as a storage device. This paper will particularly focus on emerging "smartcard" technology as a source and channel for information flow and storage. This particular technology has gained wide acceptance in other business sectors as a tool for micro marketing and mass customisation as the cost is decreasing and does not require real- time connectivity ,which makes it particularly appropriate for SMEs. A model will be developed to identify key flows of information, highlighting technology as an enabler to these flows and demonstrating cost/ benefit analysis to SMEs and the destination.

Introduction

The hospitality / tourism sector has traditionally been at the forefront of efforts to monitor and track guest preferences. Many hotel groups maintained comprehensive and detailed banks of information about their guests' needs and spending habits as part of their guest history systems. While these were originally stored on paper index cards and updated manually, developments in computer technology now allow this data to be stored electronically and updated automatically in real time as guest transactions occur.[17]

Two technological developments in particular have had a great effect on how customer history data can be used. Firstly, the reduction in the cost of data storage which has occurred over the last three decades (from £1 per byte in 1960 to two pence per megabyte in 1997, according to Price Waterhouse, [6] this has made it both feasible and economical to store more data about each subject in the database. Instead of data being limited to the guest's name, contact details and summary information on the total number of times they have stayed and their total spend to date, there is an increasing trend towards what is know as "full folio" storage, where complete details of all transactions are stored for later analysis. Secondly, the growth in the amount of processing power which is economically available on the desktop allows more comprehensive analysis to be performed than could be achieved using manual methods

Certain attributes and factors are necessary for the successful operation of an MKIS. These include technical knowledge (to design the system), marketing knowledge (to implement a strategy based on marketing intelligence data) and a technology based network (to record the transactions and transfer them to the loyalty database). Within the tourism sector, only large companies such as the airlines and the major international hotel companies are likely to have access to such expertise and facilities.

Unfortunately, the vast majority of tourism enterprises around the world do not fit this profile [20]. Instead they are small or medium in size, are not part of a chain or consortium, and in general are owner operated and managed [2]. Tourism operations of this type tend not be users of technology, and their lack of marketing knowledge has consistently been identified as a key weakness [7] Apart from this, most SMEs have a rather limited range of services, and thus their attractiveness to the guest for repeat purchase is questionable and relevant marketing data difficult to accumulate and profile-build. Therefore, MKISs administered in the conventional way, are unlikely to be successful with individual SMEs.

However, SMEs have the potential to gain the most from the information provided by such schemes. Their small size gives them flexibility which they can use to rapidly respond to changes in their customer needs - assuming, that is, that they can identify these changes in the first place.

The Marketing of Tourism and Hospitality products

In the hospitality industry, marketing is a term frequently used when referring to selling and advertising [15]. A broader approach to marketing is required. Effective marketing requires planning from the initial conception of a product (aided by relevant by market intelligence information) right through to its delivery to the customer and thereafter to the retention of the customer. In a constantly changing market place, external and internal information is required to support strategic, tactical and operational marketing decisions and provide a competitive advantage. The investment generally in the UK hospitality sector in marketing activities and indeed in Europe is considerably less than in America, Canada or Australia and Pacific rim countries [23].

Also, there are some important differences in the way that large and small tourism and hospitality operators hotels seek to match their markets and product offerings. Large, usually chain, hotel operators are increasingly assessing their markets and setting out to sell their hotel products to identified market segments e.g. the business traveller. Smaller operators tend to approach their markets less formally and more intuitively from their detailed, close contact with their guests, and their requirements. Importantly, complementary tourism and hospitality products are packaged together forcing changes where channels of distribution and interconnectivity become important elements in the marketing mix and marketing strategies. There is evidence [3,10] that SMEs fail to focus on strategic issues, such as marketing planning and intelligence gathering, as they are preoccupied with the tactical and operational running their business.

Management Information Systems (M.I.S.)

At the macro level there are destination MISs functioning in several global locations though management and flow of information and its effective use in the marketing of tourism and hospiality products is questionable in terms of cost benefit analysis [18]. Thierauf [22] describes an effective management information system as one that allows the decisionmaker(i.e. the manager) to combine his or her subjective expertise with computerised objective output to produce meaningful information for decision making. Information is now considered to be a sixth major resource for most businesses , and in this information age could be described as the most important resource for some information intensive industries. Existing MISs tend to have subsystems which relate to traditional functional areas of the business i.e. corporate planning, manufacturing, accounting and finance, personnel and marketing subsystems.These systems and subsystems would not be appropriate for all industry sectors and the model may be too complex to be of use to the SME manager or destination manager. A simpler system which concentrates on continuous and dynamic data, information and intelligence flow to support marketing decisions may be more relevant [9]. For most organisations their marketing efforts can be enriched through the introduction of a system that ensures personnel are motivated and stimulated to communicate their impressions, opinions, factual observation providing bits of intelligence which gives insights into the market. There is evidence that the larger, usually affiliated, organisations have implemented MIS ,e.g. Marriott's "Marsha" but there is little evidence to suggest SMEs are utilising MISs..

Marketing Information Systems(MKIS)

Dibb [5] defined an MKIS as distinct from an MIS as,

"A formalised set of procedures for generating, analysing storing and distributing information from internal and external, to marketing decision makers on an ongoing basis"

Recent research [11,12,13] indicates that an effective MKIS enhances a products range and customer services and provide a comparative advantage and also[19] reinforces that information is a strategic marketing offensive weapon.

MKISs need not be restricted to large organisations and O'Brien [16] makes the point that smaller organisations, in other business sectors, have more advanced information systems than those that even the largest companies had ten years ago. The use of technology, nets and CD-ROM and easy to use databases has put more information at the marketing managers fingertips. However, early evidence [7] suggests that SMEs in the hospitality and tourism sector do not have MKISs, technology based or manual, collect or use information gained internally on market segments and rarely access external sources of information. Not only do they not know their customers but they do not know their market environment. External information is crucial for effective information systems. The demand for accommodation may change for reasons of government action, weather, business booms and busts, tourism fashions, special events, festivals, building projects or simply increased disposable income. Economic, political and environmental changes can quickly affect this volatile industry. A small operator, particularly, has to fit as a whole entity into the physical and social ambience of a city or local community. It has to have the relevant information to make wise marketing decisions in terms of positioning, market mix variables, segmentation and targeting.

MKIS MODELS

Buttery& Butter [4] suggest there are three main models for MKISs in general use and these are prescriptive, positivist and phenomenological. Other simpler models exist e.g models based on inputs i.e. from competitors, government statistics, market research findings, industry data and accounting and sales reports into the system , processes that manipulate these inputs and predetermined outputs in the form of reports etc . Li et al's model is based on a framework of the 4Ps (product, price, place and promotion) but linked into other subsystem's within the business.

In other industry sectors there have been extremely successful cases of effective MKISs e.g. banking and charities and possibly lessons could be learnt from their experiences. Other studies [9] would suggest there has been a tendency to keep MKISs separate from other information systems (IS) as DSS evolved in the eighties to support functional business activities and marketers jumped on the bandwagon of keeping MKISs separate from integrated ISs. Li et al maintain that an MKIS is a conceptual model and was never intended to operate in a stand alone manner as marketing must integrate its data from other subsystems and vice versa. Mitchell [12,13] suggests that MKIS should be a 'natural' element and utilised for a more 'sensory information' approach to collecting information and promote a wider degree of information sharing.

There are obviously several models, with appropriate inputs, processes and outputs, that have to be considered in the development of a MKIS and perhaps the best model appropriate to the SMHEs would incorporate the best features and practices of these different epistemologies. Though there is some published academic research on MKIS and large hospitality organisations there is little published data on the use or utility of MKISs to destinations and SMEs. Much of the current published information concentrates on large operators in the hospitality and tourism market and/ or focuses on the US market sector [8].

Emerging Technologies- Smartcards/ Internet/ Extranet/ Intranet

One of the main problems in operating an MKIS is collecting the data and sharing it with speed, accuracy and efficiency. Unless each customers transactions are correctly related back to their record in the database, the quality and usefulness of the data warehouse as a whole is compromised. A solution has been to issue participants with a magnetic strip based card, which aids identification and data entry. However, these are limited in the amount of data which they can store, and the sheer number of different cards which people must carry with them today (sometimes known as "card clutter") discourages them from sharing their marketing information.

Smart cards, however, can store more data and are also multi-purpose [14]. As a result, they can store extensive data about customer profiles and purchasing behaviour, and the same card could be used for a variety of different functions. In the travel sector, there are already some examples of multipurpose smartcard use. For example, passengers on Carnival Cruise Lines use smartcards as their electronic door key, for making purchases in the bars or beauty salons, to pay for telephone calls and even to operate video games.

As smart cards can also receive data from and share data with their reading device, they remove the need for an on-line connection between the EPOS and the loyalty database. Profile changes, such as for example, a change of address, can be made by the member on a kiosk, and the updated information stored automatically on the chip Dingley [6]. This transfers the responsibility for data integrity and maintenance onto the customer themselves.

Smartcards could prove to be the key to not only storing data but also providing the conduit to transfer the information stored on the card during transactions, into the marketing database. As costs decrease for this technology while storage capacity increases, this may prove an incentive to utilise the technology, particularly in the light of the success stories for the smartcard, particularly in the retail sector, which are providing invaluable marketing data which is immediately actionable.

Inter-extra-intranet technology for some industries have already proved their worth in enhancing marketing communications strategies. Not only do they provide global marketing opportunities but facilitate "keeping close to your customer". *Netting* provides easy movement up the value chain with *intranets* providing effective internal sharing of data in graphic form and *extranets* supporting customers and suppliers with effective interfaces which further enhances marketing communications.

Methodology and Research

Figure 1 was consequently extracted and developed as a MKIS model for destinations and SMEs in order to summarise and review the utilisation of current marketing data .

Firstly, a broad review of the secondary literature was conducted to form a foundation to the study. The literature abstracted and cited in the report is only that which relates directly to this paper. It must be emphasised that this research is at a *preliminary stage* and is part of an ongoing research project. At a *micro level* of individual operator, a telephone questionnaire administered to a selection (14) of small to medium sized tourism and hospitality enterprises in England and Wales to discover their level of utilisation of information for marketing purposes. These were

Figure 1- Marketing Information System for SMEs within a destination

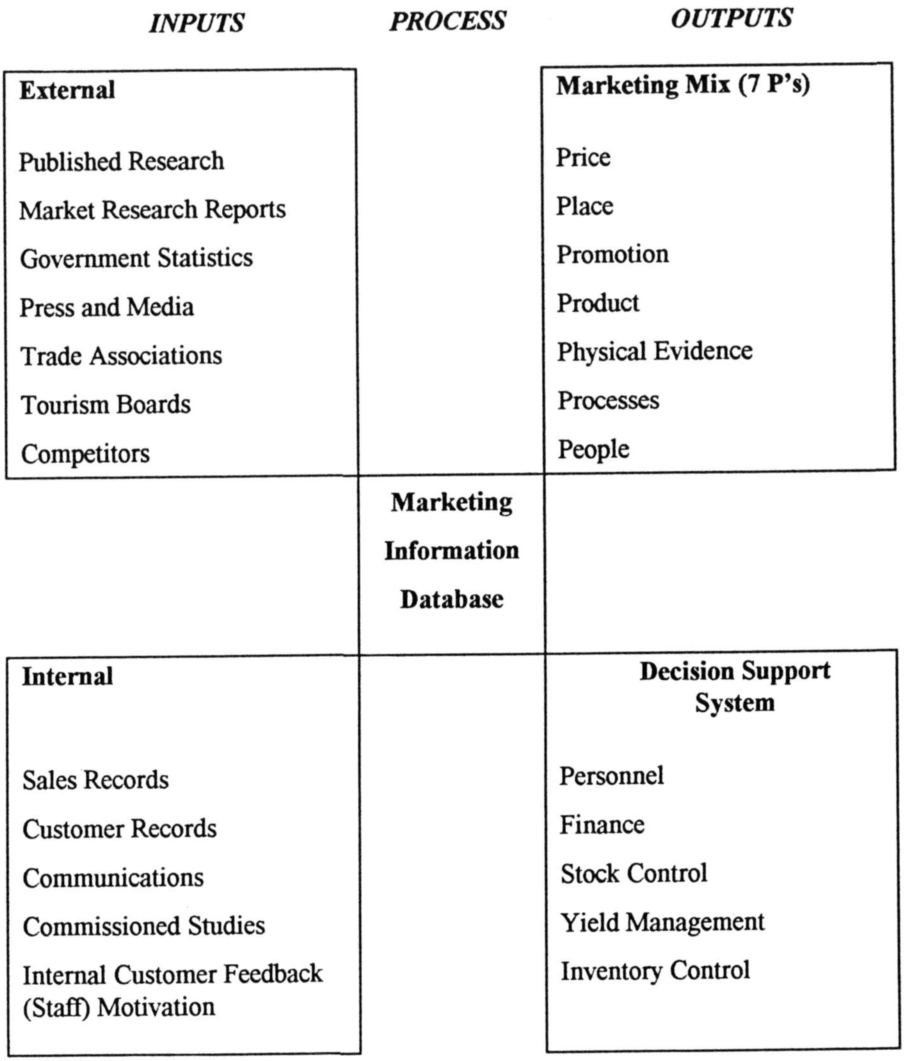

chosen from the English and Welsh Tourist Board publications using a randomisation process. The questionnaire was designed to discover what internal and external information was collected by the participant operators, how it was processed and how it was used.

At the *macro level*, the particular methodology for this research was a semi-structured questionnaire administered to key stakeholders (20) in the UK in the tourism and hospitality sector. This questionnaire focused on the key issues, flows of information, sources of information and areas where technology was used as an enabler to these processes. There was particular focus on what these results revealed in terms of perception of emerging technologies and their relevance to the marketing of the destination.

Preliminary Findings

Using Figure 1 as a framework for evaluation it was evident at a *micro level* from the survey of SMEs, and to the extent that our small sample reflects the SME sector, there are indications that operators are either information rich (very few) or information poor (the majority), with little in-between. The data collected from internal sources mainly consisted of guest records and accounting information, including data kept for taxation and other legal purposes. None of the SMEs produced any in-depth statistical analysis, rather the data tends to be lists and counts e.g. number of meals served., people passing through the turnstiles .Customer information was retained when collected, usually,at time of check-in, also some useful information is collected informally but seldom utilised. Many identified what data would be useful to collect and perceived a gap in their marketing data. Hotels, particularly, used little or no external information though some were members of professional bodies and associations but found them inadequate as sources of market intelligence.Technology was rarely used in the collection, processing or output of marketing data. Cost, time and lack of expertise were the main barriers to the use of technology.

At the *macro level* it was clear that technology was a main driver of the marketing function, as perceived by the marketing managers who completed the questionnaire. They of course do not have the same budget restraints as SMEs with most of the respondents having a budget between £100,000 and £3 million. In terms of information sources, externally they used a wide range of sources including published reports, industry syndicated report, press, media, exhibitions, though they rarely employed specialist technology or marketing consultants. However in terms of accessing the data , only one used technology , internet, to access the data. Internal sources of data were mainly customer focused, being feedback forms and customer data collected at point of booking. This data was *not* collected using technology, except in one case, and the storage and transmission of the data sources in and out of the MKIS was done manually, though one organisation had piloted a smartcard scheme in one of its regions. However implications of the management of the scheme (which needed to be contracted out due to technology expertise required) had halted the scheme thus far.

Conclusions

From both the micro(SME operator) and macro (destination)level the respondents indicated that they could see the potential benefits, particularly of net technology in terms of it being easier, quicker, cheaper, not only for the customers of their services and products, but also for the opportunities to *grab* information about their markets and customers. They perceived smartcards as an application applicable in a closed environment, e.g. an hotel, but the management of the card as problematic. The flows of information within and outwith the destination is not currently facilitated by technology. The collection of valuable internal data , at individual operator and destination level is frequently missed and if captured , never processed in an MKIS.

The drive to use technology as an enabler needs to come from destination level down to individual operators. Valuable historic data is currently *lost* and cosequently the opportunity to yield market intelligence for destination and individual operator. Evidence from other industry sectors are that effective marketing strategies can be enhanced by using technology. These emerging technologies would allow the effective capture , processing and dissemination of marketing intelligence , allowing both destination and operators to make best use of their valuable resources, respond to market demand and build close customer relationships. If destinations do not take control of their information resources they risk being marginalised and losing out to competitors who are better positioned to market their products and services to consumers.

References

1. Brassington, F and Pettitt , S (1997) Principles of Marketing, London, Pitman
2. Buhalis, D & Main, H (1996) Information technology in small/independent Welsh and Aegean hotels, HITA conference proceedings, Edinburgh, UK
3. Buhalis, D (1995) The Impact of Information Technologies on Tourism Distribution Channels: Implications for the Small and Medium Sized Enterprises Strategic Management and Marketing, PhD Thesis, University of Surrey, Guildford
4. Buttery, E A and Buttery E M (1991) Design of a Marketing Information System, European Journal of marketing,Vol 25 No 191,pp26-40
5. Dibb, S et al (1991) Marketing Concepts and Strategies, London: Houghton Miffin
6. Dingley, D (1997) Hilton Hotels Corporation Joins With American Express And IBM In Smart Card Pilot Tests, Infortec-Travel listserv.
7. Ingold, A & Main H (1997) The use of marketing information systems in the hospitality industry, (UK), HITA conference proceedings, Las Vegas, USA.
8. Kotler, P, Bares, J & Mahens, J (1996) Marketing for hospitality and tourism, London, Prentice Hall
9. Li E Y et al (1993) Marketing Information systems in the Fortune 500 Companies: past Present and Future, Journal of Management Information Systems, Summer 93 (10/1),pp165-193

10. Main , H (1994) The Application of Information Technology in the Independent Hotel, MPhil thesis, University of Wales
11. Martell, D (1988) Marketing and Information Technology, European Journal of Marketing,Vol 22 No 9, pp16-25
12. Mitchell J W and Sparks l (1988) Marketing Information Systems in the Major UK Banks, International Journal of Bank Marketing, Vol 6 No 5, pp 14-29
13. Mitchell, V W (1992) The Human Face of MKIS, Marketing Intelligence and Planning, Vol 9 No 191, pp19-27
14. Morrall, K (1995) Golden Handcuffs: Loyalty programs that retain customers, Bank Marketing, Vol27 No 8, pp52-58
15. Morrison, A. (1995) Hospitality Marketing, Oxford:Hospitality Press
16. O'Brien, T (1990)Decision Support Systems, Marketing Research, Dec., pp51-55
17. O'Connor, P (1996) Using Computers In Hospitality, Cassell, UK.
18. O'Connor, P & Frew A (1998) A Comparative Examination of the Implementation of Destination Marketing Strategies: Scotland and Ireland, ENTER conference proceedings, Istanbul
19. Pottruck D S (1988) Turning Information into a Strategic Marketing Weapon, International Journal of Bank Marketing, vol 6 No5, 9949-57
20. Sheldon, P (1993) Destination Information Systems, Annals of Tourism Research,Vol 20 No4 pp633-649
21. Teare R et al (1994) Marketing Management: A Resource Based Approach for the Hospitality and Tourism Industry, London: Cassell
22. Thierauf, R (1987)Effective Management Information Systems, Ohio: Merrill Publishing
23. Worlwide Hotel Industry (1991, 1992, 1993)Worldwide Industry Reports, London

The New Extranet for the Norwegian Tourism Industry

Tjostheim, Ingvar; Bergan, Marius; Lous, Joachim.
Norwegian Computing Center (NR)
ingvar.tjostheim@nr.no, marius.bergan@nr.no, joachim.lous@nr.no

Abstract

The extranet for the Norwegian tourism industry is part of a network project supported by the industry and national research council. After describing the features of the extranet, the first response of a test group is reported. The task of the test-group is to evaluate the extranet and to take part in the discussion of the usefulness of such an industry-net.

1 Introduction

In recent years the Research Council of Norway (RCN) has co-funded several projects within the Norwegian tourism industry. The 'Norwegian Tourist Guide'[1] on the web was developed as part of such a project [1, 2]. The RCN supports network projects in a number of industries through the NIN-program (National Information Networks), and the extranet presented in this paper is part of this research program.

To continue the network built around the Norwegian Tourist Guide, an initiative to develop an extranet was launched autumn 1997. At this time Marcussen [3] conducted a study of extranets for the tourism industry which included the planned extranet in Norway. During the next months several new partners were recruited, and in April 1998 the project officially started. Then, what we call an *industry-net* was developed for the purpose of testing the need for an extranet within the Norwegian tourism industry, and to discuss what kind of content it should have. The extra-net, the prototype has been developed at NR.

In this paper the aim is not to discuss extranets per se. For definitions and theory about extranets, we refer to Baker [4] and Marcussen [3]. The paper is organised in the following way; 1) a description of the extranet and some of the technical features, 2) how the extranet is anchored in the tourism industry - a presentation of the partners and the test-group, 3) the results from the first part of the test period.

2 Description of the extranet

Marcussen [3] suggests the defining characteristics for an extranet are that access to the net is controlled, and that the net is used by business partners (or collaborators) who selectively share information, knowledge, money or social values. The prototype version of the extranet clearly falls into this category. We will now give a brief

---

1 www.tourist.no

description of the main design objectives for the prototype and indicate how these were realised in terms of content and functionality on the web site.

Relevant content for tourism professionals in Norway. We chose the following main content sections for the prototype site after extensive discussions with selected professionals.

- *The Press page* contains quotes from the daily newspapers and tourism related journals relevant to the participants in the project. Links to the full articles on the web are included where these are available.
- *The Market page* contains digested information about the latest relevant market analyses. Again, links to the sources on the web are included where possible.
- *The Finance page* contains information about various grants and project finance arrangements available through the SND, The Norwegian Industrial and Regional Development Fund.
- *The statistics page* contains information primarily from Statistics Norway, the national bureau of statistics.
- *The Norwegian Links page* contains links to a number of tourism related web sites in Norway.
- *The Foreign Links page* contains links to major international sites for tourism professionals or tourists.
- *The Conference page* contains information about upcoming events in the tourism industry, with links where these are available.
- *The Discussion page* contains a threaded discussion group facility (see below).
- *The Address page* contains names, affiliations and email addresses for all participants in the extranet.

The prototype also contains a full electronic version of the September issue of the hotel & restaurant business journal *RBL News*. This issue is included on the extranet site whilst future versions may be linked in from the journal's site. Another means of improving relevance to the users is to limit access to the site to those users with a well defined interest in it. Currently, users are authenticated using the password mechanism provided by our Apache web server.

User contribution to site content. In the test period this will be achieved partly through the evaluation programme which is based on email questionnaires, and partly through the inclusion of a *discussion forum* on the web site. This is intended as a medium where participants can discuss and express preferences regarding the contents of the site, as well as a medium for conducting discussions on relevant topics from tourism. An effort was made to make the discussion forum available to the participants in their environment of choice. We therefore 'mirror' all postings on the discussion page to a mailing so that they can also appear in the electronic mailbox of the participants. Similarly participants can make responses to postings through their normal mail program thereby making it unnecessary to log on to the web site to take part in discussions. This is a particularly important feature during the initial trial period when there are relatively few users, but discussion should still be kept alive while the extranet is being established as a source of useful information for the participants.

Interaction and **information exchange** among users. The *discussion forum* mentioned above is one important way to foster interaction between the participants. It is worth noting that (as expected) participants must be actively encouraged to take part in discussions, preferably using carrots ("you are automatically included on the list of participants who receive copies of discussion postings in your mail box", "look at the discussion forum often because it will contain very useful information" or "for each contribution you make in a discussion you will receive some sort of bonus point"), but possibly also using sticks ("if you do not use the discussion forum you will miss important announcements which are vital to your business" or "participants who do not contribute to discussions will be excluded from the extranet after a period").

The extranet also has a permanently visible frame showing recent *footprints* from visitors to the site. The time of the last access by the most recent visitors are shown. A complete list of the pages visited by a given participant is also available. The purpose of this facility is to give a limited impression of 'togetherness' between the participants without compromising their need for privacy. Information shown on the page is based on real time processing of the server log. Participants are aware that others can see their movement. So far we've had no negative reactions regarding privacy.

Easy navigation. We produced a *shallow page structure* with a permanently available menu on the left which gives direct access to all pages on the site. We also implemented a *search engine* which can be activated from the permanently visible navigation bar.

Fast download. The prototype has no 'heavy' multimedia content. The only pictures so far are banners and small gif files used in the navigation buttons. We chose a *frames-based design* to minimise the amount of extra downloading required for each new page.

Attractive but yet 'sober' visual impact. We chose a visual design based *on consistent use of a few colours* for backgrounds, buttons, bullets etc. The design was made more attractive with 'rollover' *highlighting buttons*. This was implemented through JavaScripts embedded in the web pages which are executed in the client browser. These features require that participants use Netscape or Microsoft browser version 3.x or higher.

The extranet is designed using NetFusion3.0, Perl5 server-side scripts and JavaScript client-side scripts. The discussion facility also uses the standard Unix 'mail' program to implement the mailing list. The next version of the prototype will be modified according to the results of the evaluation period. We also plan to integrate the web server with our Oracle database through Java Servlets which communicate with the database through JDBC. This will allow us to *archive* all the web content in a database. The footprint facility may also be extended to include a *chat facility* through which participants can make on-the-fly contacts with each other.

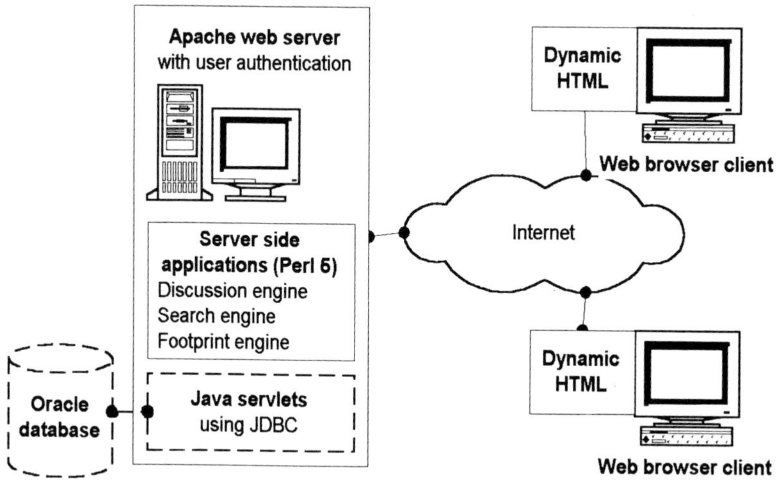

Figure X. Architecture overview for the extranet.

Figure X shows an architecture overview of the extranet. The dotted lines are components planned in the second development phase.

3 The partners and the test group - how the project is anchored in the tourism industry

The development of a good extranet, (technically and functionally), requires considerable care and effort in design and implementation. A separate and equally challenging task is to get the professionals within the tourism industry to use it. As mentioned previously, the extranet is part of an ongoing network project. Parts of the tourism industry, with NORTRA [2] in the forefront, has been involved in this project during the last two to three years. In this context it has not been difficult to get the

[2] 'Nor Travel Marketing' - the state funded tourist board in Norway

initial support for the extranet project. However, there is another important reason which also should be mentioned. It has become very common to a have a computer with Internet connection in Norway. Moreover, several of the organisations representing different parts of the industry have decided to increase the use of Internet as a communication medium with their members. A good example is the Norwegian Hospitality Association (RBL) which is part of The Confederation of Norwegian Business and Industry. Most hotels and restaurants are members of RBL, and the extranet project was very much in accordance with the long-term plans of RBL. The timing of the project was good, and with the support of NORTRA and RBL it was easy to recruit more partners and test-participants.
The partners, the organisations responsible for the extranet project together with NR, are; NORTRA, RBL, SND, and 'Landbruksbanken'.[3] NR is leading the project in the test-period.

Test participants were selected from different business areas in order to reflect the diversity in the industry in general and among the project partners in particular. Another criterion we used when selecting the participants was their level of knowledge of the Norwegian tourism industry. It is likely that knowledgeable users will better be able to provide relevant feedback regarding the content and functionality on the site. Finally, we tried to select users who had some experience with using the web.

The tourism industry consists of a conglomerate of businesses and organisations. A large proportion of these are SMEs who, in general, have not progressed as far as the larger organisations in adopting the emerging Internet technologies. The extranet must aim to include the SMEs in order to become a contender as an important information source and exchange in the industry. Hence, people from SMEs were preferred in the test group.

The test group, (23 individuals) consists of representatives from

- Privately owned businesses
- tourism organisation
- destination companies
- the university and research sector
- consultants including a representative from Statistics Norway

4 Test results

The test is organised in the following way. From September to January 1999 the extranet is run by NR in co-operation with the partners. Approximately every second

[3] The national bank for the farming industry. It is involved in a number of tourism projects in rural areas.

week the test-participants receive a message with 3 - 4 questions about the content on the extranet and related issues. The test started in September 1998, and 22 out of 23 responded to the e-mail questionnaire. The test participants confirmed that they will answer the mails and they were informed that it is OK not to answer the questions once. The second time they will change status from being a test-participant to an observer not receiving any emails. Even though there might be a number of good reasons for not answering a mail, the number falling off the list is interesting. One explanation is that the extranet is not that very useful to them.

The 22 answers to the first email-questionnaire were;

Table 1

To what extent do you think the extra-net is going to be useful to you in your job?
To a high extent: 7 To a medium high extent: 11 Neither - nor: 3 To a medium low extent: 1 To a low extent: 0

Table 2

The extranet has a 'table of contents' on the left-hand side; topics which show what kind of content the extranet is going to have. Which two are most useful to you? (Please rank the two you choose)	
As number one: The Press page: 9 The Statistics page: 6 The Market age: 5 The Search function: 1 The Norwegian Links page: 1	As number two: The Statistics page: 10 The Press page: 5 The Market page: 2 The Address page: 1 The Conference page: 1 The Discussion page: 1 The Foreign Links page: 2

Table 3

How often do you use the WWW on the Internet?
Daily: 13 Several times per week: 6 Approximately once a week: 1 Several times per month: 2

Table 4

When did you start using the WWW?
The first half of 98: 5 The second half of 97: 3 The first half of 97: 3 The second half of 96: 1 The first half of 96: none The second half of 95: 3 The first half of 95: 5 In 1994: 2

Of the test participants, approximately half of them started to use the web in 1994 or 95. These can be called experienced web-users. The other half started in 1997 or 98 and are less experienced. The purpose of the test is not to study differences (if any) with these two groups, but to gauge the web-literacy of the target audience for the extranet. However, when (if) the extranet is put into operation, it is likely that some of the users will have little experience with the web. The fact that two of the respondent seems to use the web less than once a week has to do with their job situation. One of them is not going to his or her office every week, and the other does not have Internet access on his or her computer.

The answers to the first question, the usefulness of the extranet, was not very surprising. The test-participants were positive to the project and this one of the main reasons for take part in the test. However, it will be more interesting to see their answer to this question in the last part of the test period.

The question about the content of the extranet is interesting. It is not unusual developing and put into operation a product or service without asking the users directly about their priorities. However, an advantage of using a test group from the industry in the development process is the possibility to get feedback directly from members of the target group. The response to the question 2 shows that news and statistics are important topics for the extranet to cover. The question will be repeated in the end of the test period to see if this still is the case, or if their views have changed.

5 Concluding remarks.

The test period will last for five months so only after one month it is still too early to draw any definitive conclusions. In the end the test group might recommend that the extranet should be launched as a permanent service. However, it is important to keep in mind that the test is in one sense artificial; the project is partly funded by research money (not from the tourism industry) and the participants are invited to use the extranet. Moreover, they receive emails that remind them about the extranet, and questions to answer. Still, the feedback they give should be taken seriously - they do represent potential users of an industry-net.

There are some important issues not covered in this paper. For instance, how should the extranet be financed? Should the participating organisations pay a fee or should the site be financed through advertisements? This question also has a political side since it can be argued that advertisers might eventually get undue influence over the site. Moreover, should the site maintainers (the partners in this project) collaborate with industry journals present on the web today in order to improve the site content? What form should this collaboration have? This has implications with regard to the editorial structure; should the editorial responsibility be held by a central 'neutral' agency or should various parts of the industry control their own parts of the content? This is a political issue as well as a technical and organisational one. In this project, answer to all these questions will not be given. However, recommendations will be made, and the tourism industry will then have to decide what to do with the extranet.

References

1. Tjostheim, I. (1997). The New Network in the Norwegian Tourism Industry - Marketing and Organisational theories as Perspectives for a Study. In A. M. Tjoa (Ed.), *Information and Communication Technologies in Tourism 1997* pp. 110-118. Springer Verlag.
2. Tjostheim, I. & Aanonsen, K (1997) Internet-marketing and the Norwegian tourism industry. A national coordinated marketing effort on the Internet. In *Proceedings for INET'97*, Kuala Lumpur, (http://www.isoc.org/inet97/proceedings/ C6/INDEX.HTM)
3. Marcussen, C. (1998) 'Extranets of national tourism organisations:'. In A. M. Tjoa (Ed.), *Information and Communication Technologies in Tourism 1998*, pp.103-119, Springer - Verlag
4. Baker, Richard H. (1997) From Intranet to Extranet, *The Complete Sourcebook MacGraw Hill's Beta Books*. ISBN: 0070063028 http://www.intranetjournal.com/expert4.html #fie

The Use of Internet and Intranet In American Convention and Visitors Bureaus

Y.Y. Yuan[1], D. R. Fesenmaier[1], L. Xia[2], and M. Gratzer[3]

[1]Leisure Research Institute, Department of Leisure Studies
University of Illinois at Champaign-Urbana

[2]College of Business Administration
University of Illinois at Champaign-Urbana

[3]Department of Computer Sciences
University of Vienna

Abstract.

The emergence of the Internet/Intranet offers new promise to American Convention and Visitors Bureaus (CVBs) to enhance destination marketing. This study examined the extent of the various capabilities of the Internet/Intranet are used by CVBs to augment marketing efforts and to improve their performance across all facets of their business. The results of this benchmark study show that CVBs directors have not recognized the potential of Internet/Intranet and point the direction to areas of development whereby information technology may more easily integrated into current marketing and management efforts.

1 Introduction

American Convention and Visitor Bureaus (CVBs) perform a wide range of activities to facilitate tourism development The general goals of CVBs are: (1) to manage and provide destination attractions (e.g. conventions, events/festivals, and outdoor recreations), (2) to manage and plan infrastructure on which tourism depends, and (3) to facilitate tourism promotion and marketing research [5]. In order to fulfill these goals, CVBs rely heavily on a variety of formal and informal information systems capable of assisting the implementation and facilitation of activities necessary to meet these goals. Current Internet/Intranet technology provides important capabilities which enable CVBs to act beyond the organizational hierarchy and to function better as a cohesive organization. The Internet/Intranet also can be used to enhance customer satisfaction and CVBs' service abilities. The use and adoption of Internet/Intranet technology, therefore, may enable CVBs to cope with the dynamic and rapidly changing business environment and continue to lead the industry.

2 Convention and Visitors Bureaus

The Convention and Visitor Bureau is one of the most pivotal type of destination marketing organization. Its primary mission is to promote tourism businesses and attract visitors by coordinating the variety aspects which comprise the local tourism industry. According to Gartrell [5] the convention and visitor bureau is defined as "a distinctive organization, which represent and market their communities in a very competitive market place that involves meeting and conventions, group tours, and visitors." Following from Buhalis [1,2], the activities of bureaus involve four distinct dimensions: activities within bureau, activities with bureaus' customers, activities with bureaus' members, and activities with other bureaus (see Table 1).

Table 1 Dimensions of Bureaus' Activities (adapted from Buhalis [1])

Intra-organization activities	*Inter-organization activities*
Within a Bureau	**Activities with Members**
Strategic planning	Provide general information
Marketing research	Support marketing activities
Marketing strategy/Implementation	Coordination of members and services
Pricing decision and tactics	Membership database management
Networking and information exchange	Communications
Coordination of staff/Volunteers	Publication/Newsletter
Finance/Administration	Convention/Event management
Event scheduling	Scheduling/Meeting
Resource management	Legal consultant
Publication/Press	Lobbying
Communications	
Management and storage information	
Activities with Customers	**Activities with Other Bureaus**
Information providing	Networking and information exchange
Itinerary planning	Conference/Meeting
Reservation and confirmation	Lobbying
Marketing research/Survey	
Publication/Press	
Feedback/complaints	
Convention/Registration	
Fulfillment	

In the information era, the rapid changes of external and internal environments bring tremendous pressures on bureaus. Being "information brokers," bureaus have been confronted with a series of challenging issues including:

Political issues and relationships. The successful tasks and activities of bureaus depend on the quality of infrastructure (e.g. road, highway system, information infrastructure, etc.) of destinations, the support and understanding from different levels of governmental sections, and the contribution and involvement of local communities [5].

Financial issues. One of general missions of bureaus is to contribute substantially to the viability of the local economy by increasing visitor expenditures.
Partnerships. Successful destination marketing is based on healthy partnerships between public and private sectors. To effectively fulfill their marketing responsibilities, bureaus build reliable partnerships with all the critical elements of a growing travel and tourism industry.

Bureau management and professional development. Bureaus are asked to provide leadership, to direct future vision, to identify additional sources, to motivate communities, and to coach partners in order to reach their goals. All of these tasks required different types of skills and supporting equipment. Furthermore, turnover is continually disrupting the professional or political experience to be passed-on. Therefore, bureaus often encourage/support training and education program to equip staff and executives with the tools to cope with the changes in this multi-faceted industry.

Time. Time is key to success in this competitive industry. Not only the amount of information appears in a myriad of ways, but also how information can be useful and meaningful to assist decision-making and marketing plan in a timely manner. Information technologies enable bureaus to "cope with the growth of information, makes it imperative that new techniques and strategies be developed upon which bureau marketing effort can be predicted." [5].

Types of services, service quality, and service attitude. Providing quality services is the key to retain customers and to keep long-tem partnerships. The question is how does an individual bureau know whether the services they provide are matched with the needs of their partners and customers. Although service quality is strongly related to service attitude held by a bureau's personnel, but a good infrastructure will augment the service quality and expand types of services.

3 The Strategic Influences of Information Technology

Regardless of the complexity of a bureau's organizational structure and scope of responsibilities, the flow of information crosses the four dimensions of a CVB (identified above) and interconnects primary and support activities. That is, information is the integrative element in CVB activities and can be represented as data, flows of service, and payment [8,9]. Each activity uses information technology to combine inputs and human resources to produce output. Bureaus provide information to tourists, exchange information with its members and other CVBs and collects information from tourists and other segments [3,4,6,7,10]. The value-added process of information begins at data collection, data management, interpreted information (data) and ends at strategy implementation and evalatuon. Collected information/data need proper IT structures to transform it into useful forms (i.e., knowledge). Information/data will be useless without IT to manage it. In

addition, IT enables bureaus to structure information/data in a rational database for supporting decision-making. Information/data are only valuable to the extent they support decision making. Furthermore, the extent to which IT will have an impact on bureaus will depend upon its effect on information. The implementation of Internet technology can influence a bureau's value chain in a number of ways including:
Inbound logistics. Activities, which are associated with the receiving and storing of information, are influenced by Internet technology. The Internet/Intranet changes the economics of information by providing the factors richness (interactivity bandwidth) and reach (connectivity). E-mail, for example, can exchange information across four dimensions of bureaus' activities. The emerging new applications will promote new forms of information processing and possibilities to rationalize the internal work.

Operations. The most popular applications such as electronic Mail (E-mail), World Wide Web (WWW), web-based reservation system [1, 6] have been reported to improve the efficiency and effectiveness of communication and extend business opportunities. The emerging new applications such as videoconference, co-text editor, workflow management system, bring new form of collaboration and new ways of competition into the tourism industry. For example, videoconferencing facilitates communication among discussions. Time and facilities will get better management by using scheduling tools to get right people/resources to the right place limited conflicts. On the other hand, the customer can, by using the Internet technology, create his/her own dynamic products by simply customizing the posted information for his/her needs. Additionally, bureaus can expand its information services by becoming more integrative and providing additional services on its homepage.

Outbound logistics. The Internet/Intranet offers bureaus a new distribution channel for products and services. Over the Internet/Intranet, bureaus can reach more people and by easier overcoming geographical boundaries they can attract new visitor from several market segments.

Marketing and sales. The Internet/Intranet enables bureaus to develop and implement new strategies in a timely manner by accessing and providing rich information. Compared with traditional tourism marketing channels, the Internet/Intranet is faster, less expensive and offers wider and deeper material and richer advertisement contents [6]. It also can be used as the basis for developing an effective direct marketing program.

Services. The Internet/Intranet improves responsiveness and effectiveness. It also is an instrument to outsource customer service functions to the customer. By building an interface into the bureaus' information sources customers can navigate though this information themselves. It also allows the creation of individual customer profiles; thus, bureaus can interact on a very personal level with its customers.

Following Tapscott and others [3,11,12] the Internet/Intranet can also have substantial impact of the nature of the workforce in the organization which, in turn, effects the nature

and structure of the organization in four stages (or levels). The first stage or basic impact of information technology is characterized as moving "from individual worker to workgoup computing." In this stage, all staff will be supported by the variety of Internet/Intranet applications. Self-educating tutorials and on-line learning programs can help bureau staff to learn and renew skills as well as update their knowledge over time. Horizontal and vertical communications within the bureau also could be greatly enhanced. Therefore, people who come from different areas (i.e., marketing, finance, etc.) are able to team up together to meet task requirements regardless of time and space.
The second stage or level of impact is described as "From Systems Islands to Integrated Systems." It is necessary to integrate separated categories of value activities to avoid data redundancy, overlapping of tasks, and miscommunication. Eventually, all of information technologies (e.g. telephone, fax, data management, etc.) will converge via the Internet/Intranet. The integrated network will enable CVBs to bridge the gap between the sources of information and the people actually who use it. Besides streamlining organizational processes, the boundaries will be blurred between each division/department within the bureau. Thus, the same sources of information can be shared and reused. Not only bureaus will be able to access the information, but also bureaus' partners. In addition, a basis can be established for quickly reacting to changing customer demands and business development.

Following is Stage three, "From Internal to External Cooperation." No single company succeeds alone in the network game. Public expectations regarding bureaus' service quality continue to rise. People will want more and better information. Bureaus that once serves regionally have to expand into vertically cooperate with other organizations in order to copy with the influences of globalization. The Internet/Intranet enables bureaus to reach out and develop new relationships with their members and to cooperate with other bureaus. The Internet/Intranet enables bureaus to overcome the barriers of time and distance to perform their activities and provide services. Therefore, the business orientation will shift from internal performance improvement toward external cooperation.

The last stage is "From One Effort to Collaboration Networked System." The diffusion of the Internet/Intranet compresses the world into a "Global Village". The barriers that separated economic and vertical market sectors and the companies that operated within them are quickly falling [12]. Competition can arise unexpectedly from anywhere. A bureau not only needs to operate locally, but also has to think globally. To survive, bureaus and other destination marketing organizations become inter-networked businesses. The promise of collaborative networked systems can be achieved through the empowerment of individual workers and collaboration through teams within a bureau which reach into the community and become part of an integrated regional, national, and international information network.

4 Methods

The goal of this study was to assess the nature, extent and impact of use of information technology (i.e., Internet/intranet) on American convention and visitor bureaus. The sample consisted of American convention and visitor bureaus that are members of either the National Union of City Tourism Organizations (NUCTO) or the International Convention and Visitors Bureau (ICVB). The survey effort included a telephone interview of bureau directors or marketing directors and a follow-up mail survey to the respondent. In total, 226 bureaus were identified and were contacted by telephone. Of these, 147 bureau representatives indicated they had a computer and were willing to participate in a follow-up mail survey. The telephone interview process was conducted over a two-week period during May 1998. The mail survey was conducted over a two month period (from May 11, 1998 to June 16, 1998) and followed a four step process (e.g., initial mailout, postcard follow-up, second and third mailouts to nonrespondents) designed to maximize the return rate. This effort resulted in 98 complete responses for a 69.1% percent response rate.

The telephone interview included eight questions used to identify those bureaus having computers and to invite them to participate in the mail survey. The follow-up mail survey was divided into three basic sections: (1) characteristics of bureaus; (2) use and implementation of computer Interent/intranet applications; and (3) evaluation and future use.

5 Analysis and Results

The majority of bureau representatives were directors or marketing directors and are relatively young, well educated and female. More than half (58%) of the participating bureaus are independent organizations where tourism is the primary marketing focus (51.6%). The majority of CVBs have 1-9 full time staff (54.3%) and 1-9 part time staff (64.2%). Almost half (45.8%) have an annual budget exceeding $1,000,000.

5.1 Computer Use

All bureaus surveyed own at least one computer. Most bureaus have 6-10 computers and almost all (96.9%) are connected to the Internet. More than 80 percent of the bureau representatives perceive themselves as having a reasonable knowledge/skill level of computers; few bureaus, however, have staff with an expert knowledge of IT.

5.2 Information Distribution and Access on World Wide Web

Over 95 percent of the bureaus indicated they have a Web site. All of participants indicated that they consider the World Wide Web (WWW) an important information/marketing delivery vehicle. Information provided on the Internet by bureaus varies substantially (see Table 2); 45.3 percent of the bureaus currently provide between 6 and 10 different categories of information on their web sites. The three most frequently provided categories of consumer-oriented information are attraction information (96.8%), calendar of events (87.4%), and maps/images (82.6%). The three least frequently provided categories of information are discussion forums (0.0%), classified advertising (5.7%), an on-line reservation services (8.7%). In the group of bureau-oriented information, the top three of the most frequently provided information are meeting/conference information (55.6%), mission statement (32.6%), and press releases (25.3%), while the three least frequently provided categories of information are training materials (2.4%), job bank (2.4%), and on-line conferencing (2.4%).

Many bureaus are planning to expand the amount and nature of consumer-oriented information provided via WWW. Attraction information (100%), hyper-linked to other site (89.5%), calendar of event and festivals (83.3%) are the most popular areas to expand in the near future. On-line vacation guide/planner and search engines will be provided in the future. However, there is only a small proportion of bureaus considering providing more bureau-oriented information. Overall, the results indicate that bureaus will use WWW to promote their attractions and have much less interest in using the Internet/Intranet to provide bureau-related information.

Table 2. Information provision provided via Web

Consumer-Oriented	**Provided**	**Plan**	**Bureau Oriented**	**Provide**	**Plan**
Calendar of events	89.7%	9.2%	Meeting/conference info.	59.8%	22.0%
Classified advertising	6.2%	13.6%	Mission statement	34.2%	16.5%
Attractions information	97.7%	2.3%	Press releases	27.5%	31.3%
Discussion forums	0.0%	13.8%	Affair updates	24.7%	14.3%
Feedback capability	71.1%	15.7%	Research and statistics	15.2%	24.1%
Frequently asked questions	26.8%	25.6%	Surveys	12.7%	24.1%
Hyper-links to other sites	82.1%	15.5%	Information on other Bureaus	10.1%	12.7%
Education materials	38.3%	19.8%	Job Bank	2.6%	1.3%
Maps/Images	83.5%	16.5%	Training materials	2.6%	10.3%
On-line reservation services	8.2%	35.3%	On-line conference	1.3%	13.0%
On-line vacation guide/planner	46.4%	31.0%			
Publication/Videos ordering	40.7%	29.6%			
Trip routing	11.0%	26.8%			
Weather information	54.8%	23.8%			

5.3 The Use of the Internet/Intranet Applications

Analyses were conducted to examine the number of applications used by bureaus, length of use, and perceived usefulness within the three different categories (i.e., communication, collaboration and coordination/management). Overall, bureaus used between 8 to 10 different types of Internet/intranet applications (see Table 3). All bureaus surveyed use the WWW and Email to enhance and improve communications. Broadcast fax and voice mail are also widely used by bureaus. The majority of respondents perceive E-mail, broadcast fax, voice mail, WWW, and Listservs the most useful. Talk/chat, Electric Bulletin Boards and Newsgroups were the applications least used by bureaus.

In the area of collaboration, applications to support shared document-editing tools were used most. Video conference (2.2%) is a relatively new innovation along with audio conference (6.6%), and electronic meeting systems (4.4%) that haven't received much attention. On average, respondents perceived these applications less useful than those applications supporting collaboration.

Table 3. Level of Use of the Internet/Intranet Applications in three major categories

Communication	%	Collaboration	%	Coordination/Management	%
Broadcast fax	48.2%	Audio conference	7.2%	Database management	60.0%
E-mail	100.0%	Electronic meeting systems	4.8%	Document management	46.3%
Electric Bulletin Boards	6.0%	Shared document editing tools	37.9%	Calendaring and scheduling	50.0%
Internet Phone	14.7%	Shared graphoic/Image tools	31.3%	Project management	30.5%
Listservs/Mail lists	17.1%	Video conference	2.4%	Search engine	58.3%
Newsgroups	4.9%			Workflow management	10.8%
Talk/Chat	6.1%			Reservation/Booking	10.8%
Voice mail	46.4%			Statistical analysis/Data mining	19.6%
World Wide Web	100.0%				

All of the coordination/management applications listed have been available for more than 4 years. Reservation/Booking was cited most often. It appears that many respondents have started using search engines (58.2%), electronic calendars and scheduling (40.9%), and workflow management (40.0%) to support their business-related activities.

5.4 Activities and Applications

The primary activities performed within bureaus include communication, networking and information exchange, publication/press, management and storage information, marketing strategy/implementation, and marketing research (64.9%). Almost 63% of the respondents perceived the listed applications that are useful to facilitate activities within bureaus, especially to publication/press, networking and information exchange, management and storage information, and marketing research. The main interactions between a bureau and its customer are information providing, fulfillment, and feedback/complaints. Fewer bureaus provide convention/registration and reservation/confirmation. The listed applications were widely perceived useful in terms of information providing, fulfillment, and itinerary planning. Fewer users perceived reservation and confirmation and convention/registration are useful. Feedback/complaints, publication/press, and marketing research/survey were activities cited a number of times by respondents. It appears that bureaus do not network and information exchange with other bureaus over 80% of respondents don't apply the listed applications on lobbying and conference/meeting.

More than half of bureaus provide general information, support marketing activities, membership database management, and coordination of members and services with their members (see Table 4). A number of respondents perceive the listed applications useful to supporting these activities. Less than 10 percent of respondents perceived the listed applications for lobbying and legal consultant as useful. In comparison, there is higher amount of attention paid on activities that are within the bureau and with bureaus' customers. Bureaus activities are heavily consumer-oriented and information-driven and it reflect on the perceived usefulness of the listed applications.

Table 4. Activities of Bureaus for Four Business Dimensions

1) Within your Bureau		**3) With the Bureau's Members**	
Strategic planning	29.2%	Provide general information	48.9%
Marketing research	42.9%	Support marketing activities	45.5%
Marketing strategy/Implementation	37.4%	Coordination of members and services	31.8%
Pricing decision and tactics	14.3%	Membership database management	40.9%
Networking and information exchange	48.9%	Communications	47.1%
Coordination of staff/Volunteers	25.6%	Publication/Newsletter	29.5%
Finance/Administration	34.1%	Convention/Event management	19.8%
Event Scheduling	35.2%	Scheduling/Meeting	25.0%
Resource management	30.0%	Legal consultant	4.6%
Publication/Press	44.0%	Lobbying	8.0%
Communications	63.0%		
Management and storage information	47.3%		
2) Within the Bureau's Customers		**4) With other Bureaus**	
Information providing	81.8%	Networking and information exchange	34.8%
Itinerary planning	42.3%	Conference/Meeting	17.7%
Reservation and confirmation	22.0%	Lobbying	13.3%
Marketing research/Survey	30.4%		
Publication/Press	34.8%		
Feedback/Complaints	37.0%		
Convention/Registration	20.9%		
Fulfillment	57.2%		

5.5 Impacts, Measurement Criteria, and Constraints

Respondents indicated that the use of the Internet/Intranet will improve: (1) access to information (85.4%), (2) customer service (71.9%), (3) communication (70.1%), (4) their ability to respond to customers (63.6%), (5) the sharing of knowledge (60.9%), and (6) their competitiveness (53.3%). Responses indicate they consider technology will have the least impact on reengineering work process, facilitating organizational change, shifting in human capital requirement, and organizational bonding.

The number of visits to the site is the most frequently used criteria to measure the effectiveness of the Internet/Intranet. The efficiency of distributing/collecting information and the ability to access new information are also considered as important criteria for measuring effectiveness. However, a high percentage of bureaus do not measure the effectiveness of their investment in the Internet/Intranet. They either do not know how to measure its impact or they do not perceive the necessity of its measurement.

Respondents were asked to indicate the factors which they consider to be constraints that limit their use of the Internet/Intranet: The need for in-house expertise (47.4%), the cost of equipment (38.9%), and the lack of knowledge (37.0%) were the top concerns constraining use.

6 Conclusion

The diffusion and adoption of the Internet/Intranet is industry-wide. The results of this study indicate American convention and visitor bureaus are active users of the Internet. Information provided via WWW is consumer-oriented, focusing on external aspects of the bureaus' functions. The "paradigm shift" described in the literature has not yet been realized and therefore the role of the bureau has not changed. It appears well understood that the Internet/Intranet enables bureaus to reach visitors in every corner of the world. However, bureau directors appear not to consider the Internet/Intranet useful tool to enhance their relationship among other constituencies. An important issue clearly identified is the ability/interest and/or desire for bureaus to prepare for the future. Are the bureaus as they are currently structured capable of satisfying their functions as defined by their local constituencies within the context of regional, national, and international market forces?

7 References

1. Buhalis, D. (1996). Information and telecommunication technologies as a strategic tool for tourism enhancement at destination regions. Paper presented at the ENTER '96 Conference, Innsbruck.
2. Buhalis, D. (1997). Catalysts in introducing information technology in small and medium sized hospitality organizations. Paper presented at the ENTER '97 Conference, Edinburgh.
3. Davenport, T. H. Prusak, L. & Prusak, L. Working Knowledge : How Organizations Manage What They Know. Harvard Business School Press.
4. Evans, P. B., Wurster, Thomas S. (1997). Strategy and the new economics of information. Harvard Business Review. 75(5), 70 - 82.

5. Gartrell, R.B. (1988). *Destination Marketing for Convention and Visitor Bureaus*. Iowa. Kendall/Hunt Publishing Company.
6. Morgan, R.F. (1996). An Internet Marketing Framework for the World Wide Web (WWW). *Journal of Marketing Management*. 12:757-775.
7. Poon, A. (1993). *Tourism, Technology and competitive strategies*. Wallingford: CAB Internetaional.
8. Porter, M. (1985a). Competitive Advantage. New York: The Free Press.
9. Porter, M. M. (1985b). How information gives you competitive advantage. *Harvard Business Review*, 149-160.
10. Schertler, W. (1994). Impact of new information technologies on tourism industry and businesses. *The Tourist Review*, 2:2-8.
11. Tapscott, D. & Caston, A. 1993. Paradigm Shift: The New Promise of Information Technology. New York: McGraw Hill.
12. Tapscott, D. (1996). The digital economy: Promise and peril in the age of networked intelligence. New York: McGraw Hill.

Networking for Growth and Digital Business: Local Urban Tourism SMTEs and ICT

Professor Graeme Evans, Centre for Leisure and Tourism Studies,
University of North London, England
g.evans@unl.ac.uk

Introduction

The paper is based on a three year action research project – *Networking for Growth* - which developed a network of tourism (SMTEs) and emerging multimedia firms in a local area ("borough" of Islington) of North London. This enabled collaboration between ICT/web designers, tourism information (TIC) and tourism suppliers, supported by local education and enterprise agencies. This action research project was initiated as a partnership between the University of North London; *Discover Islington* – the tourist information agency for this borough - with funding support from the area Training and Enterprise Council (TEC) and the UK government's Urban Programme.

The local area selected for this study is significant in both urban tourism and strategic development terms as the first Tourist Development Action Project (TDAP) selected by the English Tourist Board in London, as part of a national initiative to promote and develop tourism in lesser developed locations and widen the distribution of tourism activity – physical (e.g. hotel location) and economic (Evans 1994). This was an aspect of national tourism policy which sought to spread tourism activity away from tourism honeypots and areas of overcrowding, not least in the capital city, London, where tourism activity is highly concentrated with 75% of all bed spaces based in 3 out of 33 London boroughs, and the majority of visitor attractions clustered round the 'islands of culture' and heritage sites of central and west London. The promotion of urban tourism and associated alternative cultural tourism also formed part of regional strategies which sought to promote "unknown" areas of London and to utilise tourism activity as part of local economic development and regeneration policies.

Urban Tourism Destinations

The consideration and measurement of urban tourism in this case also raises particular research issues, due to the complexity of isolating tourism activity from within the general visitor and other economic activity in highly dense urban areas. As several authors have commented (*cf.* Page, 1993): *"urban tourism is almost certainly among the most misunderstood and underestimated of all tourist types. It suffers from underestimation - sometimes even unrecognition"* (Blank and Petkovich, 1987: 166), and as Inskeep also observed: *"There is surprisingly little literature on planning for tourism in urban areas - the characteristics of urban tourism and it planning have been studied less than resort and outdoor recreation development"* (1991: 236): this was echoed a year later by Law (1992: 599). Planning for tourism in the urban environment is therefore problematic, lacking adequate models and consideration, and in consequence requiring a sophisticated and integrated approach to the complex flows and impacts which prevail in the "dual" historic and contemporary city (Evans 1995). Whilst increasing attention has been given to city and urban tourism (Page 1993, Law 1993), local areas within larger cities or urban areas also present difficulties in terms of the measurement of tourism activity and the separation (and inter-relationship) of such activity from local and other trade and movement. It is at this level however, that local tourism development occurs through local government, local trade associations and town centre revitalisation strategies (Evans, 1994). The role of ICT in linking the local with the global in terms of tourist and other markets and in terms of cross-trading locally, is a particular opportunity which this action research explored in practice.

In terms of tourist and visitor activity in this area, and this is a feature of developed urban and city tourism, there is a diverse range of segments - from business tourists (including conference/exhibition trade); student and education visitors (including a University and several tertiary colleges) and VFR (including a high proportion of second and third generation immigrant and refugee communities) - from the UK, elsewhere in London (day visitors) as well as from overseas. Approximately 20% of visitors to the local area are domestic and overseas tourists, the latter 6% of the total. A wide temporal profile encompasses leisure shopping (street and crafts/antiques markets), exhibition and sports attendance (a major exhibition centre and Premier League football club, Arsenal F.C. are located in the area) during the day time and weekends (i.e. 'Sunday trading'), and a night-time economy based on late-night shopping and arts and entertainment - from cinema, performing arts and a host of fringe venues such as pub theatres, music and comedy clubs. Cultural tourism and speciality shopping are therefore high attractions to both tourists and locals alike.

Tourism SMEs

Another factor in developing both destination marketing and adoption of ICT by local tourism firms, is the nature and scale of the firms in this sector, which are primarily SMEs or more accurately micro-enterprises employing less than 10 staff (including sole traders). As Buhalis and Cooper report (1998: 325) such micro-enterprises within the European Union as a whole (14.5 million firms in 1993) represent over 93% of all firms, but only 30% of jobs and 22% of total turnover. Understanding and engaging SMEs within a particular sector is also particularly limited in terms of shortage of time, capital and investment in infrastructure, both 'hard' (e.g. I.T.) and 'soft' (e.g. training, marketing/research). This is further complicated by the fact that few of the firms actually identified themselves as 'tourism-based', or part of the visitor

economy. This reflects the hybrid and often fragmented nature of tourism activity, particularly outside of the more discrete resort or honeypot zones. Even hotels consider themselves part of hospitality, but not necessarily 'tourism' services, depending on their customer base (e.g. business hotels, conference centres), whilst shops identify with other retail trades; museums are curatorial or education-led, likewise arts venues; and transport operators cater for a mixed user, only identifiable in terms of peak and off-peak (including leisure tourist) markets.
At the same time, much research and analysis of the impact of ICT in tourism is dominated by global reservation (CRS) and integrated systems developed by the transnational travel, hospitality and tour operator sectors, where vertical and horizontal integration and economies of scale are established (Buhalis 1994). This places SMTEs at a distinct disadvantage at the outset. Whilst *"Tourism destinations are dominated by such small enterprises"* (Buhalis and Cooper 1998: 324) they are generally marginal in terms of the economic and market share of the package holiday total price, with over 75% distributed to transport carrier, travel and tour commissions, and contracted hotel and local transfer companies, prior to arrivals. This percentage is even higher where international operators integrate through local car rental and hotel ownership or franchise, squeezing out local suppliers even further (or all together in the extreme case of all-inclusive resorts). As Ebner (1994) points out, local SMEs lack the advantage of the advanced support systems of the airlines and tour operators who act on a worldwide basis with global information technology (see Mutch 1995 and Main 1995 on SME hotels and I.T.). Ebner argues therefore that comparable information technology infrastructure ('transfer') would increase the willingness of the potential customer to purchase the products of the smaller supplier.

Another factor in the analysis of SMTEs and destination management systems (DMS) is the relationship between the hybrid SMTE network and the large national and transnational operators and (generator) markets. This is particularly under-researched generally (Stanworth and Stanworth 1995) and particularly in the case of tourism destination economies where there is little transparency in cost and contractual relationships between tourism suppliers, intermediaries and generator markets and operators ('Fair Trade in Tourism' - Evans and Cleverdon 1998). In other services sectors for instance (Stanworth et al 1998), the contribution to the turnover of SMEs in the UK represented by one main client is 55%, and 82% from the two largest clients. The dependance of SMEs is therefore significant in terms of a small number of powerful large companies, and in tourism this is evident in the case of outsourcing and franchising of bar and catering, entertainment, tour guide and other support services such as cleaning, by larger hotel chains and resorts. Given the more extensive research into SMEs generally and the approaches to network development, (which are still little researched within tourism), this area has particularly been drawn upon and considered in terms of its transferability in this case of local area SMTEs.

Strategy and Response

Against this scenario, the remainder of this paper therefore presents an analysis of the network development process and the enterprise and development needs as expressed by this group of 30 tourism SMTEs (Small and Medium-Sized Tourism Enterprises, Buhalis and Cooper 1998), including their approach to I.T. development and marketing opportunities. The inter-action with ICT/multimedia firms also provides a link to a parallel SME group of web designers – the Web Creators Network - which was also initiated by the above partnership during the 3 year programme (see Fig. 2).

Faced with the twin challenges of a diverse urban tourism market and environment and SME base, the formation of a network of local area tourism firms adopted strategies of economies of scale and joint working and exchange, which were required in order engage what were predominantly small companies and sole traders, employing less than 10 and often less than 5 employees. As noted, the typology of tourism suppliers in the urban setting also reflects the nature of the visitor economy, which included not only traditional tourism services such as accommodation (mostly Bed & Breakfast), tourist information and visitor attractions (museums, galleries, theatres), but a high number of speciality retailing, crafts and street markets, as well as conference/exhibition venues. The first stage in developing a destination marketing and visitor-focus, therefore required the creation of a network of SMTEs with common markets and shared interests and needs.

Networking SMEs

The concept of networking is commonly applied in analysing how SMEs connect with their environment and overcome some of the comparative disadvantages of economies of scale, specialisation and training, available to the larger firm. Most research in this field has concentrated on a quantitative assessment of the extent of networks (e.g. counting the contacts owners-managers have with external agencies other than direct customers and suppliers themselves). These mapping exercises have not generally measured the quality or impact of the networking experience on SMEs and Blackburn *et al* question the idea of a SME network as some definable entity comprising a finite identifiable set of individuals (1990). Instead a conceptual network is seen simply as *"a particular type of interaction which may occur between the owner-manager or other organisational representative and the external environment of the enterprise"* (Blackburn and Curran, 1994). The motivations of SMEs in initiating or seeking external contacts are more obvious where material and information exchange is required and where a lack of business expertise might cause the owner to seek outside advice (e.g. on I.T.). Joining a network may provide an avenue for obtaining information (eg. market intelligence, legislation, financing) at critical points in the survival or development of any business, or in gaining further customers (see Bennett and McCoshan, 1993).

Research and case studies on SME networks have also focused on the local economic community, stressing the 'village', 'industrial quarter' (or destination area - Buhalis and Cooper, 1998) concept and the local production chain and cross-trading activity. Whilst examples within certain sectors - crafts and small scale production, high-tech, producer services - demonstrate this relationship, generally the extent of local networks in terms of sustained local trading in urban areas has been refuted by Blackburn and Curran and others. The particular relationship between small and larger firms (contracting-out/out-sourcing) has not stood up to scrutiny in terms of either network links or local economic trading - the post-Fordist services economy militates against this scenario (late payment by larger firms is often cited by SMEs). This also extends to the role of support agencies generally, whereas the most frequent external contact for SMEs is accountants (74%), solicitors (68%) and bank managers (36%), advice sought from more discretionary sources is much lower - Enterprise Agencies (19%), Small Firm Services (20%) and Educational bodies only 13%. This reflects the compulsory and voluntary continuum of networking activities (below), as well other barriers and a mismatch between supply and demand of support services:

Figure 1. Continuum of SME Network Relationships

Compulsory--Voluntary

Sales to customers	Purchase of resources	Government: Central (tax), Local (rates, planning)	Banks, Accountants, Solicitors	Marketing Research/ Strategies	Advice: Consultants, Agencies, Education	Membership of Trade Orgs. and *Networks*

Whilst educational institutions (higher and further education) have been found to be less well used than enterprise agencies in other studies (Blackburn et al 1990), service sector firms gave a higher rating to the advice actually received by HE colleges. This suggests that there are barriers to linking and gaining access to universities, but once contact is established the relationship and benefits are positive. The research capability is one resource that educational institutions bring to the local economic community, including market research and strategic planning, another is the I.T. resource that is otherwise outside of the reach of SMEs – mainframe computing, programming, R & D and networking facilities. The barriers to SME participation in networks have also been put down to, one the one hand, cultural factors (Bevan, 1989) and on the other, the practical one of time (lack of/opportunity cost/lack of staff cover). This is particularly the case in terms of training and meetings. The membership of groups may be antithetic to the stress that owner-managers place on autonomy and independence - the main reason they went into business on their own in the first place. Networks can be incompatible with such values and personalities if reliance on advice from others, sharing ideas and joint working is involved. One of the findings of the project has been the extent to which these barriers can be overcome and otherwise competitive and independent firms can come together for mutual benefit, particularly around shared needs and opportunities - marketing, product development, information/research, ICT and training. The project also demonstrates how operating through networks enables support agencies to reach and support SMEs more effectively.

The development of the networks

The Islington *Networking for Growth* project started in 1994 with the support of Central Government Urban Programme funding (75:25 central:local government). The aim of the project was to establish networks of businesses in two local sectors identified as having potential for growth and to use these networks as a means of identifying common training needs and delivering training which would facilitate growth. Most previous SME research including work on networks and linkages, has tended to focus on small-scale manufacturing and local services. By contrast the sectors identified for this project were all in the post-industrial services economy.

1. tourism and cultural services (visitor attractions/venues, arts organisations, specialist retailers, conference/accommodation and restaurants);
2. multi-media (design, information technology and services)

The strategy for developing each network involved setting up a core group of interested members using existing contacts and/or accessing potential members through other existing business networks. The availability of other networks such as Discover Islington (the local Tourist Information and Promotion agency) and BIMA - the British Multi-Media Association (the main trade association working for the industry) and the Chamber of Commerce, all proved an invaluable source of entry to network members and support. The co-ordinator's role was then very much one of facilitator encouraging the networks to identify their own agenda for action and providing the support needed to make it happen. The main concern of the networks was, not surprisingly, marketing. The activities therefore focused initially on one-to-one marketing "clinics" offering marketing and business planning advice and then evening seminars and short half day or evening training sessions on areas of concern including Finance & Fundraising, I.T./Internet applications, Marketing, Conference Market/Research, Forecasting and Analysis. Tourism trainees were also placed by the University within local firms, undertaking research, marketing and other project work. Businesses also participated in a number of joint promotions, including developing a web site of accommodation, retailing and attractions in the borough (below). Over 30 firms participated in network activities and made up the Discover Islington Network (DIN), a putative destination area tourism network (see Figure 2.).

Networks and Marketing

The greatest interest in using the networks for developing joint marketing initiatives came from those businesses who had the strongest links to the local economy i.e. tourism and cultural services firms and certain groups within the professional (advanced producer) services, who saw the potential of developing a stronger local customer base. Businesses in the Tourism Services network realised that their fortunes were closely linked to those of the area as a whole and were therefore willing to engage in activities designed to promote the borough as major destination for residents (including workers), domestic and overseas visitors. The advantages of joint promotions undertaken by the TIC and members as part of "Visit Islington" and “Hidden London” campaigns, were apparent and numerous joint marketing brochures, cultural trails and environmental improvements (e.g. street signage) were developed. The creation of an annual International Islington Festival in 1995 also provided a new focus for the locality in the summer. SMTEs soon saw the potential of using the networks as a means of promoting their business to other firms both within their own network and other networks within London. There were at least five known instances of inter-trading within the network during the duration of the project. The networking and collaborative measures employed during the project included the following:

- Joint-promotion (e.g. at the annual *Multimedia* trade exhibition, publicity materials and maps/guides)
- Seminars - EU funding, practical skills (management), using I.T./Net (marketing) and design (web)
- Business Planning Advice (one-to-one, e.g. marketing, financing, funding, personnel)
- Seminar presentations and showcases to wider group/sectors (demonstrations, using Web/Net/Design and Intranet applications)
- Local economy research into I.T./Telematics usage and awareness

The project also demonstrated the benefits of the partnership/networking approach adopted by the local co-ordinating agencies and the strategy of working though their existing network of contacts, be it other support agencies or existing business networks. Each partner in the *Networking for Growth* project was able to bring different expertise and their own network of contacts to the partnership, so that an extensive pool of skills, knowledge and linkages were available to the project as a whole. Thus the University with its research capacity, I.T. facilities and access to market research reports was able to provide details of market intelligence sources and an overview of developments, including in ICT and tourism markets. Figure 2. summarises the networking and support structures which developed within this local economic and destination area, including jointly-created ICT applications.

Figure 2. Local Area Tourism & Support Network and ICT Relationships

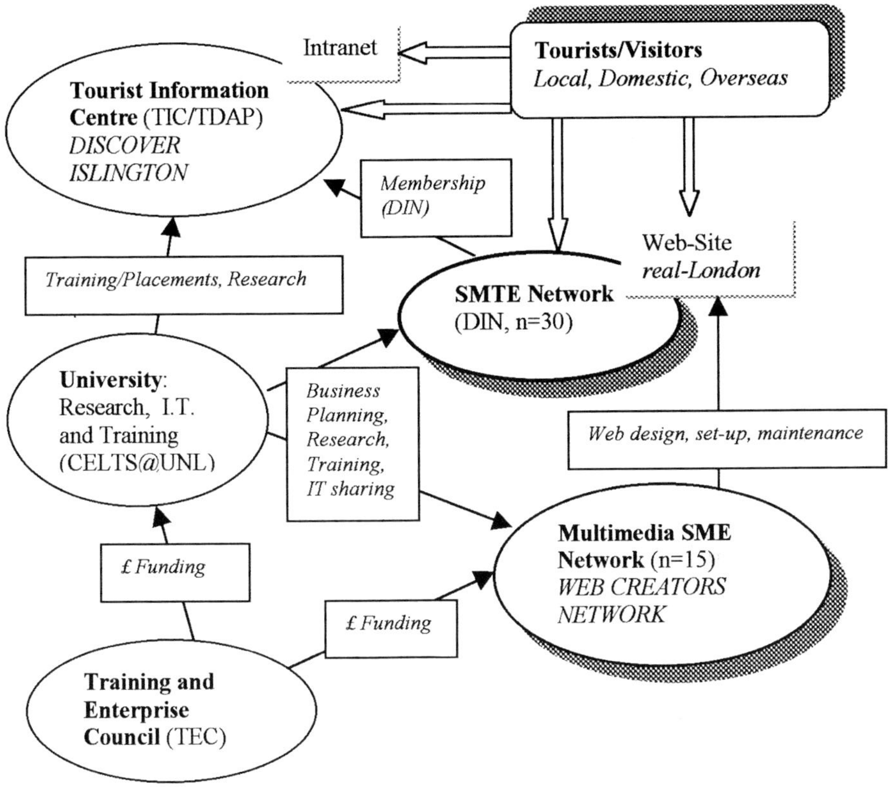

Vickerstaff and Parker (1995) suggest that government Training Enterprise Councils (TECs) with a range of connections to existing local, regional and industry networks may be maximizing their chances of reaching SMEs. The existing connections of the support agencies in the *Networking for Growth* project certainly facilitated their access to the firms who became involved. Previous research (Hughes, 1996) has highlighted the benefits to SMEs of joining networks and Hughes suggests that, *"Firms which are more likely to survive are those which have built up a network of collaborative relationships with suppliers and* higher education *establishments...and an infrastructure in which smaller firms can help themselves by pooling resources and learning from each other"*. The network and support structure which the project developed (Figure 2) highlights the ICT applications which also emerged between the Tourism and I.T/multimedia network SMEs, and the tourism information and support agencies. The extent of inter-relationships also indicates the scope for enterprise and

I.T. support which can develop in a local (destination) area and the experience of the *Networking for Growth* project suggests that working through sectoral or common-market networks may offer a more effective strategy for intervention.

ICT and Digital Business

The first phase of the pilot project naturally focused on the grouping and identification of development needs (expressed and perceived) of the tourism SMEs, based on the establishment of a clear common mission - that of a Visitor and Destination strategy and market. This also drew on city imaging, place and destination marketing strategies which have been successfully developed in former industrial cities and urban areas in North America, Continental Europe (Bianchini and Parkinson, 1993) and particularly in the industrial heartlands of midland and northern Britain. Significantly many of these regional cities have developed major Visitor and Convention Bureaux linked to inward investment agencies and more integrated CRS and I.T-based marketing facilities (e.g. Manchester, Leeds, Glasgow, Sheffield - see Evans and Taylor, 1997). The combination of inward investment and visitor-based promotional strategies were therefore adopted, in recognition of the linkage between other services-based economic activity and investment and 'quality of life' indicators. These increasingly require a lively and diverse range of visitor attractions, amenities and animation of retail and public realm areas (e.g. cultural and tourist quarters, waterfronts etc.). Tourism and related retail and cultural attractions therefore provide an economic development option in their own right, and help attract and retain other forms of economic activity and trade.

In terms of technology applications however, the SMTEs in this local destination area had relatively undeveloped knowledge or access to ICT. Participating firms were asked whether they currently used the following in their business and operations, and their related development needs (Table 1). The second column gives a comparison from a UK national survey (DTI, 1996) of medium-sized firms (100-199 employees). This finding contrasts the poor awareness and usage of I.T. communications by SMTEs compared with larger firms. This was also confirmed by a recent DTI study (1997) which found that 57% of smaller firms (< 10 employees) maintained that the contribution of communications and I.T. was not important to their competitiveness.

Table 1. I.T. Usage by local SMTEs

Used now	Local area SMTEs	Medium-sized (DTI, 1996)
Email	20%	40%
InterNet	3%	6%
CD-ROM	6%	14%
Access to Web	25%	29%

In a similar study of 100 SMEs in the North East of England, whilst firms appreciated the importance of telematics, many did not fully recognise the special benefits that its use could bring to their companies. Here, I.T. networks were found to benefit local economies, but only where all sectors - including SMEs - recognize the potential and possess the required staff skills and equipment (Tyneside TEC 1996). This divergence is also evident in the UK hotel sector. Main (1995) for instance found that smaller hotels with less than 20 rooms were less likely than their counterparts (50+ rooms) to use I.T. and such small hotels tended to have older managers and relatively unqualified staff, whilst those that were more I.T.-proficient employed younger and well-educated managers. Mutch (1995) similarly found that 66% of small hotels had not used I.T. due to 'lack of resources and computing experience'. Conversely, larger hotels in the USA perceived that I.T. plays an important role in improving operational effectiveness and customer satisfaction (Hoof et al 1995).

A key element in the operation of the network was therefore expanding the use of Email as the prime communication and means of exchange between SMTEs and the support agencies, which reduced meeting and reporting time (above) - a 'virtual network' - despite the close proximity of the firms themselves (in some cases social exchange substituted for formal meetings). The use of the web as a promotional tool (under the joint marketing vehicle of 'Digital Business') also enabled detailed monitoring of usage and enquiries by customers (through digital analysis and Email responses/follow-up surveys). Once Net-based exchange was established and self-managed by the SMTE network itself, ICT applications were introduced firstly as a tool for network promotion and training and then as a marketing tool in itself, both in promoting the destination area, and individual SMTEs (through web-page links). This was manifested in a web site designed by network members and the TIC: www.real-London and the piloting of an Intranet system located at the Tourist Information Centre – *Discover Islington*. The latter sought to integrate the local area destination 'offer' and suppliers with city-wide (LTB) and national (BTA) marketing and reservation systems. The latter was also facilitated by the development of the British Tourist Authority's 'Britain on the Web' project which enabled customer enquiries at pre-trip and on-trip stages to link to the local area 'DMS' and reservation system and for local visitors to the TIC to make ongoing reservations and enquiries elsewhere in the country.

Conclusion

Micro-firms make up a large element of the growing SME economy in the UK and particularly in southern Europe (Stanworth, 1998), but generally have a high staff turnover and also a high failure rate. This is not the case in this urban SMTE sector which had high levels of motivation, proprietor enthusiasm and specialism, although the next growth phase will be a challenge as larger companies move in and existing markets are saturated (e.g. retail, visitor attractions, ICT and DMS 'overload'). This success to date is largely due to their innovative nature and skills, including the application of ICT itself in maintaining networks, product development and marketing: *"Firms which innovate either in processes or products are more likely to survive than those that do not, as do businesses which have built up a network of collaborative relationships with suppliers and HE establishments"* (IPPR, 1997).

The project also highlighted the differences between and within the SME sectors, in terms of the level of interest shown in joining networks and the nature of the networking activities engaged in. It is important therefore to guard against treating SMEs as a homogenous group (*viz* "tourism": hospitality, retail, cultural, transport et al). Curran & Blackburn (1994) argue that a sector-based approach is more likely to reach owner-managers than a locally based one-stop shop approach (i.e. the usual enterprise agency approach promoting generic 'business support' and advice). Key to the establishment and retention of SMTEs in this case was a Destination Marketing focus, through which ICT and other joint product and marketing efforts were justified. Acting through intermediaries also helped overcome the access and cultural barriers that traditionally exist between SMEs and educational establishments and TECs, and enabled them to play a more active role in supporting the local business community.

The development of a joint Web site promoting their services and the application of the internet as means of exchange and marketing has proved to be an attractive one in securing new business and gaining the attention of enterprise agencies in the area. The ease of monitoring ICT usage and the development of customer feedback via the Net has also provided a rare market research opportunity for this group. This has extended to the development of a local interactive network focusing on the local area and economy, and targeting visitor information and venues and retail sectors. The role of intermediary support organisations has also been key in providing I.T. and training services, and maintaining the momentum which individual firms naturally lack given their size and priorities: *"Firms should be encouraged to win new business via the Internet and e-mail and the Government could do this by offering more online information and encouraging academic institutions to support electronic networking between businesses"* (op.cit.). This suggests that in order for SMTEs to genuinely benefit from ICT, rather than suffer from yet another form of competitive advantage from major tourism suppliers (and 'technical determinism' from I.T. suppliers), a support infrastructure and networking approach is needed and recognition of this given by intervention agencies (local, national, EU) who currently pursue, perhaps over-optimistically, vigorous SME-based economic, regional development and employment policies.

References

- Bennett, R.J. and McCoshan, A. (1993) *Enterprise and HRD*, London: Paul Chapman
- Bevan, J., et al (1989) *Barriers to Business Start-Up, A Study of the Flow Into and Out of Self Employment*, DE Research paper No.71, London: DE
- Bianchini, F. and Parkinson, M. (1993) *Cultural Policy and Urban Regeneration: Western European Experiences*, Manchester: MUP

- Blackburn, R., Curran, J. Jarvis, R. (1990) *Small Firms and Local Networks: Some Theoretical and Conceptual Explorations*, National Small Firms Research Conference, Harrogate
- Blank, U., Petkovich, M. (1987) *Research on urban tourism destinations*, in Ritchie,J.B. and Goeldner, R. *Travel, Tourism and Hospitality Research* New York: Wiley: 165-77
- Buhalis, D. (1994) *ICT as a StrategicTool for Small and Medium Tourism Enterprises'*, in A.V.Seaton et al, *Tourism: The State of the Art*, West Sussex: Wiley: 254-274
- Buhalis, D. and Cooper, C. (1998) *Competition or Co-operation? Small and medium-sized tourism enterprises at the destination*, in *Embracing and Managing Change in Tourism'* (Laws, E. et al, eds.), London: Routledge
- Curran, J. and Blackburn, R. (1994) *Small Firms and Local Economic Networks, The Death of the Local Economy*, London: Paul Chapman
- DTI (1996) *Survey of IT Usage in the UK*, Department of Trade & Industry
- Ebner, A. (1994) *TIS - Tourist Information System for the Tyrol*. In Schertler, W., et al (eds), ICT in Tourism: 35-42, ENTER '94, Innsbruck, Springer-Verlag, Wein
- Evans, G.L. (1994) *Urban Tourism and Local Economic Development - the TDAP model*, 2nd Global Conference on Sustainable Tourism, IIPT, Montreal
- Evans, G.L. (1995) *Planning for Tourism in London: World City-Whose City*, Urban Environment: Tourism Conference, South Bank University: 55-62
- Evans, G.L. (1998) *Fair Trade in Tourism'* in *Tourism and Sustainable Community Development* (Richards, G. and Hall, D. – eds.), London: Routledge
- Evans, G.L. and Taylor, M. (1997) *Destination Marketing Strategy for East London*, LDDC
- Hoof, H.B.et al (1995) Technology Needs and Perceptions: An Assessment of the US Lodging Industry, *Cornell Hotel and Restaurant Administration Quarterly*, 36(5): 64-69
- Hughes, A (1996) *The Changing State of British Enterprise*, Cambridge University
- Inkpen, G. (1998) *Information Technology for Travel and Tourism* (2nd ed), Harlow: Longman
- IPPR (1996) *Small Firms On-Line*, London: Institute for Public Policy Research
- Law, C.M. (1992) Urban Tourism and Economic Regeneration, *Urban Studies* 29: 599-618
- Law, C.M. (1993) *Urban Tourism: Attracting Visitors to large Cities*, London: Mansell
- Main, H. (1995) IT and the Independent Hotel – Failing to make the Connection, *International Journal of Contemporary Hospitality Management* 7(6): 30-32
- Mutch, A. (1995) IT and Small Tourism Enterprises: A Case Study of Cottage-Letting Agencies, *Tourism Management*, 16(7): 533-539
- Page, S. (1995) *Urban Tourism*, London: Routledge
- Rimmington, M. and Kozak, M. (1997) Developments in Information Technology: Implications for the Tourism Industry and Tourism marketing, *Anatolia* 8(3): 59-80
- Stanworth, J., Purdy, D and Kirby, D. (1992), *The Managment of Success in 'Growth Corridors'*
- Small Business Research Trust, Open University, Milton Keynes
- Stanworth, J., Purdy, D., Stanworth, C. and Rieple, A. (1998) *The Role of Small Business in the U.K.*, Research Report No.1, May, London: University of Westminster
- Sussman, S., Baker, M. (1996) Responding to the electronic marketplace: Lessons from Destination Management Systems, *Int. Journal of Hospitality Man.* 15(2): 99-112
- Tyneside TEC (1996) *Telematics and SMEs in the North-East*, Gateshead
- Vickerstaff, S. and Parker K.T., (1995) Helping Small Firms: the Contribution of TECs and LECs, *International Small Business Journal* 13(4)

Publishing tourism statistics and market intelligence on the Internet

Ann. Hartl-Nielsen
Research Centre of Bornholm
hartl@rcb.dk

1 Introduction

So far National Tourism Organisations (NTO's) have mainly focused on using the Internet/World Wide Web solely for disseminating tourism information and for marketing purposes towards the customer. However, the Internet seems an optimal tool for dissemination of tourism statistics and market intelligence information from the NTO's to the tourism businesses and other users of this type of information.

This paper describes the results from a project carried out by the British Tourist Authority/English Tourist Board (BTA/ETB) in order to formulate a strategy for web-publishing for the above-mentioned type of information. It analyses users' needs and expectations as well as considerations for pricing of the information versus supplying it free of charge. The paper also describes implications of electronic publishing as against in print publishing.

In the following the findings from the case study will be given, at the same time the intentions and recommendations for a future strategy will be described.

To take the analysis further, other web-sites currently offering tourism statistics and market intelligence will be briefly presented and related to the ongoing work at the BTA/ETB.

The paper will be concluded by some general remarks on aspects of publishing market intelligence and tourism statistics on the Internet.

2 Case study findings

The case study was carried out in March - May 1998 in order to provide the Research Department of the BTA/ETB together with the co-operating tourist board's equivalents (Northern Ireland Tourist Board (NITB), Scottish Tourist Board (STB) and Wales Tourist Board (WTB)) with a basis for decision for their future publishing strategy with specific reference to web-publishing.
In the following the case will be described from the BTA/ETB's viewpoint.

2.1 Methodology

As resources were limited most of the research was carried out as desk research relying on secondary sources and information available through the Internet.

The project had a very practical oriented connotation and therefore also involved semi-structured interviews with parties/people involved in the publication process, i.e. members of staff of the various research departments at the tourist boards. The publications available at present, mainly from the BTA/ETB research department were surveyed as well.

In order to provide a view from current and/or future users an e-mail survey was conducted amongst the approximately 250, mainly UK based, chiefly academic subscribers to the *e-mail discussion list* of *tourism mailbase* (http://www.mailbase.ac.uk/lists-p-t/tourism/). "This discussion group is aimed at academics and researchers working in all areas of tourism. This includes issues involved with the teaching of tourism at undergraduate and/or postgraduate level, and research into tourism and its related areas." At the above-mentioned web-site one can find an introduction as well as a list of members. Anybody can become a member and post a message to the list, which automatically will be received by e-mail by all active subscribers.
The survey was carried out by sending a message to all subscribers with a short description of the project to be undertaken and asking for expressions of interest to participate in the survey. The questionnaire was then mailed to those who wished to partake in the survey.
In return to this the response rate was 81%. The intention was not to create a statistically valid output of data, but to create an impression of attitude towards the possible future web-site.

2.2 Current situation

The BTA/ETB has some 17 research publications which are published on a regular basis, most of these come out once a year, whereas two are published quarterly and bi-monthly respectively. The data for the publications is retrieved from various sources, e.g. the International Passenger Survey (IPS), the UK tourism survey (UKTS), the attractions survey etc. Thus some of the data is collected and owned by the BTA/ETB and other is held by the Office of National Statistics (ONS).

The BTA/ETB research department employs a staff of eight to produce the above-mentioned publications, also there is a staff of five in the library, who amongst other tasks provide a brokerage service.

During interviews with the research staff some expressed the view that they currently spent most of their time on preparing the collated data for standardised output (i.e. printed publications).

2.3 Users' needs in general

Current users of publications. A previously carried out in-house investigation as well as the current investigation, indicated that educational establishments and academics were the main user-group for the majority of publications, followed by private individuals. As the investigation was based on subscription data, the other national and regional tourist boards as well as governmental bodies appeared to be less important. However, it was confirmed by the staff of the research departments of the tourist boards that these were also a main user-group of the current output.

E-mail survey. As mentioned previously an e-mail survey was carried out in order to receive some qualitative feed-back from one of the main user-groups of the current publications. The survey consisted of nine questions, covering the following aspects: respondents institutional connection, knowledge and usage of as well as access to BTA/ETB publications, interest in electronic availability of the information, expectations to the intended Internet-site, current Internet access and the opportunity to make further comments.

Findings: Quite strikingly all respondents said that they would like to be able to access the contents of the publications electronically. However, this outcome was not totally unexpected, bearing in mind that this survey was conducted by e-mail, and thus all respondents were accustomed to using electronic means of communication. Nevertheless, there were several interesting other aspects that were mentioned by the respondents.

Firstly, there was one librarian who mentioned that she had observed 'a phobia for paper' amongst the academics. Secondly, there was an officer working for the Countryside Council of Wales, who said they currently did not use any of the BTA/ETB publications, but that they probably would use them, if they could access the same information via the Internet. There were also several who mentioned an expectation that one in this way could access more recent data in a more direct way. Finally there was one respondent who pointed out that it was very important not to expect only to make available electronically what currently was available in print, but to make a broader and more interactive approach than printed publications could offer.

Respondents were asked to give their expectations to the intended Internet site. 79% expected to be able to search the publications by key word. 55% wanted to be able to view output data and 24% expressed interest in producing their own output from data available. Clearly a search facility was the most important issue. This might

also increase the knowledge dissemination of the contents of the available publications.
It was also mentioned as desirable to be able to display output data, created by the BTA/ETB and other researchers.
Creating own output is another, somewhat more difficult, issue. Depending on the level of complexity of the output, this would mean that the user would need to have certain knowledge of both statistical methods and the programme used in order to produce a correct output. However, it seems important that the first two options are available, creating output from the data should be given further consideration.

2.4 Pricing

The question of pricing the information both today and in future is critical. Currently a high level of revenue is obtained from both sales of publications and brokerage services. If the data was to be put on the Internet there would have to be access restrictions in order to obtain payment for the data.
Various pricing structures were considered, but the final decision has to be taken by the BTA/ETB in regard to which structure to choose. In section 3. the other examples include two web-sites that currently charge for their services.

Options. The following options were reviewed:
1. to provide abstracts and samples free of charge as well as an area with restricted access for which the user would have to acquire a password and user-id against payment. This payment could be in two ways:
a. payment per datacell,
b. a general annual subscription to access all the available data as often as necessary.

2. to provide free access to all data.

3. to provide on-line ordering information for the printed publications only.

The third opiton is today available for some of the BTA/ETB's research publications at www.visitbritain.com (consumer web-site).
Options 2 and 3 were soon dismissed as long-term solutions, whereas option 1 was considered the most feasible. Cf. below (section 3) for further considerations.

2.5 Electronic vs. in print publication

The question arose whether it would be possible to move from in-print publishing to solely publishing electronically. While this might be an option in a few years time, it is currently not possible to omit conventional publishing completely, as there are too many hardcopy users who do not have access to the Internet.

Another question that had to be considered was whether the information to be made available on the Internet should be the same made available through today's publications. It was considered that this would be an interesting solution as to those publications that would be easy to convert to a web-document from its current form, as all reports were produced in some kind of electronic form today. However, the possibility of offering a greater variety of services and various outputs through the Internet was considered. Thus it was suggested that a subscriber might gain access to the database material in order to create individual output. This might on the one hand relief the staff of the research department and leave more time for more in-depth research, on the other hand this would, as mentioned above, require a certain expertise from subscribers in order how to operate the system.

2.6 Future strategy

Consideration should be given as to where the research department's priorities lie with regard to its publications. Is it envisaged that the priority will be given to making them available as web-pages or will the priorities be given to hardcopy? If the priority is to have them as web-pages, then it is easier to design the document so that it is user-friendly and aesthetically pleasing as a web-page. If not, then compromises have to be made, or work will be duplicated.

Alternative strategy. An alternative strategy to having the documents as HTML, it would be possible to place a copy of the source on the server and create a hyperlink to it from a web-page. The user could then download the document or open the document within the web-browser.

Other strategic recommendations. *Partners:* Contacts with the regional tourist boards for more close co-operation should be explored. It has also to be decided whether to go forward in one joint operation or to co-ordinate individual web-sites for each of the currently involved partners. Another approach could be the involvement of relevant universities and determination of their possible interest in participation in the project.

Copyright implications. An agreement with the ONS and probably other copyright holders has to be reached regarding the usage of their data for web-publication.

Technological implications. A security level has to be determined. Also format and style for web-publication in co-operation with partners has to be agreed.

Financial implications. It has to be determined who should have free access. Fees should be set according to the current level of subscription prices.

3 Web-sites currently offering tourism statistics on the Internet

There exist today already several web-sites offering tourism statistics and market intelligence on the Internet at various levels of detail. Some of these are very comprehensive, others are rather limited. The list below is far from comprehensive as new web-sites come out all the time. However, all the web-sites mentioned below were consulted during the case study period.

3.1 List of web-sites of National or Regional Tourist Boards incl. statistics and market intelligence

Austria National Tourist Office and Austrian Society of Applied Research in Tourism: http://tourmis.wu-wien.ac.at
Australian Tourism Commission: http://www.atc.net.au/
Office of National Tourism – Facts and Figures – Australia:
http://www.dist.gov.au/tourism/new/ifa_home.html
Canadian Tourism Commission (CTC): http://206.191.33.50/tourism/
CTC – Info for tourism businesses: http://206.191.33.50/tourism/tindu.html
Finnish Tourist Board: http://www.mek.fi
Hawaii Tourism Office: http://www.hawaii.gov/tourism/index.html
Singapore Tourism: http://www.mfasia.com.sg/mfasia/tourism/html/sing.html
US Tourism Industries network: http://www.tinet.ita.doc.gov/
Wales Tourist Board: http://www.i.visitwales.com
World Tourism Organization: http://www.world-tourism.org

In the following a short description of web-sites currently offering access to tourism statistics and market intelligence will be given. Finally, there will be a section giving an assessment of the sites and relating them to the case study.

3.2 TourMIS

This service was designed by the Institute for Tourism and Leisure Studies at the University of Vienna, Austria for the Austrian National Tourism Organisation (NTO). The Institute is also responsible for the maintenance of the TourMIS system. TourMIS is short for *Tourismus Marketing Information System*, and the system has been used for research and consultancy for more than 10 years. Originally the system was exclusively for the Austrian NTO, but in 1993 it was decided to transfer TourMIS into an on-line system, available through the Internet. Thus today the system is used by regional and local tourism organisations, government bodies working with tourism, schools and universities and consultants in tourism, additionally to the employees of the NTO.

The system includes data from some nine sources, which normally are also available in a hard copy version. Agreements with the copyright holders exist or were assumed unnecessary.

Whereas the system in the beginning only provided prepared tables and records, it is now possible to access the data interactively, thus creating own output on the basis of data available in the system.

The users have the choice of 12 different options for access rights and accordingly different prices for each option, varying from approximately GBP 100 up to GBP 2,200[1] respectively for data provided by the Austrian Statistical Office only and a campus license of a complete data set accessible for the general public. It is possible to view free samples of the data provided in the databases.
It is stated in the information available on the Internet that these fees only cover the costs involved in converting the material for Internet use and no charges for the data itself is made.

3.3 WTO

The World Tourism Organization (WTO) provides a tourism statistics service on their Internet web-site. The material is based on the publications, reports, brochures and other statistical material produced by the Statistics and Market Research Department of the WTO and includes data from 1985 to the most recently compiled data. The data available through the Internet is the same data as in the printed publication of the WTO. However, the data on the Internet is constantly up-dated.

One has the choice of two different options of data access, this is access to the database or the regional tourism reports. Using the database one is charged by data cell, i.e. requesting a table with five entries you pay for each entry. The price per data cell is approximately GBP 0.06. Access to the tourism reports is on an annual basis, i.e. the WTO charges an annual fee of approximately GBP 30[2] and the users are then free to access the data as often as they wish. The price for tourism reports is the same as the hardcopy price.

Whereas the WTO does not offer any samples of what can be obtained from the web-site's restricted area, there is a comprehensive section of FAQ's giving information on the statistics services.

---

[1] Prices converted from ATS/ECU.
[2] Both prices stated here are applicable to a discount for WTO members. The prices are converted from US$.

The WTO could not supply information on who the users of the statistics service are, but stated that all people in principle could access the service once they had registered, and thus could be charged for their usage of the available data.

3.4 Finnish Tourist Board

The Finnish Tourist Board supplies a free service called *Tourism Dataline*, where information on tourism statistics, strategy, publications, libraries, educational establishments as well as projects and reports can be obtained. The information is maintained by the tourist board in co-operation with other information providers.

Amongst other things, the pages present statistics prepared by the board and categorised by year as well as an overview over publications by publisher and year giving bibliographic information. Together with the statistics information there are two full-text reports available on tourism in Finland. Also, there is a list of projects that are currently being undertaken, which can either be sorted by name, English or Finnish key word, on the next level one can then obtain information on the project mainly consisting of the name of the person in charge of the project and contact details.

The way the information is presented is confusing at times, for example, there is no sub-division of the statistics other than the year of publication, and the projects by title are listed by both English and Finnish titles at the same time (for a non-Finnish speaker this makes it rather difficult to obtain a clear overview).
The site also has a search facility, which can be used to find various statistical information, and which to some extent makes up for the above-mentioned drawback.

3.5 Wales Tourist Board

The WTB is the only of the partners in the BTA/ETB co-operation who already has a web-site containing statistical information. However, these are, as in the Finnish NTO's web-site, statistics listed by year and giving under each year a number of tables and graphs taken from the board's publications.
The information is supplied free of charge through the trade section of the WTB's web-site (www.i.visitwales.com).

3.6 Lessons to be learned

It is obvious from sections 3.2. to 3.5. that there are different approaches to setting up a web-site containing statistics and market information. It appears that the approach chosen for the TourMIS is the one that is tested the most and has had the chance to develop over the years into a useful tool for similar target groups as for the intended BTA/ETB web-site. Also the chosen pricing strategy seems to be the most cost-effective as it appears to involve as little administration as possible, and the price is kept at the lowest level possible as there is no profit calculated. This, however, does not correspond with the wishes expressed by the BTA/ETB.

The web-site maintained by the WTO offers an interesting perspective, with a combination of an interactive section (the database) and a 'pre-fabricated' section with the reports section. Also the pricing structure is adapted to these two different approaches, with one being 'pay as you use' and the other giving unlimited access at the same price as the printed publications.

This is very much in line with what the BTA/ETB would like for their web-site and it might be an interesting challenge to start by offering some of the existing publications on-line for the same price as the printed version and later adding an interactive section.

As described earlier the BTA/ETB was not really interested in offering free services as described in the other two examples. These sites are interesting, but might need some more refining in terms of user-friendliness, i.e. the listings should be more narrow and give time series or the possibility to create an overview with annual data from several years at the same time.

The search facility available at the Finnish NTO site was rather useful, and might be a good idea to copy.

4 Conclusion

It became evident from the BTA/ETB project that web-publishing is a good supplement to the current hard-copy publications, but no substitute at present. In order to be able to launch a web-site of this type many technical implications have to be solved, and existing publications have to be re-structured.

With the explosion of the Internet in terms of new web-sites, its effectiveness as a marketing tool has been doubted by many experts (e.g. Marcussen, 1997 and 1998), whereas it is undoubtedly an extremely useful tool for distribution of information. This is particularly the case where there is an existing relationship with users who also are potential users of the intended web-site.

No doubt NTO's and other major tourism organisations will turn more and more to the use of the Internet in their provision of information services targeted at the tourism industry, as the Internet becomes more and more common.

Here is the best opportunity for NTO's to leap into information society by providing market intelligence to their partners and the tourism industry, information that is highly relevant and maintained at the highest level of topicality and providing an interactive means whenever the information is requested.

5 References

1. Hartl-Nielsen, A.: National Tourism Statistics and Market Intelligence Website - Analysis, unpublished report to the BTA/ETB (1998)
2. Marcussen, C.H.: Turistinformations- og bookingsystemer - en casesamling, Bornholms Forskningscenter (1996)
3. Marcussen, C.H.: Distribution af danske turismeprodukter i Europa - status, trends og udviklingsmuligheder, Bornholms Forskningscenter (1998)
4. Austria National Tourist Office, Austrian Society of Applied Research in Tourism: http://tourmis.wu-wien.ac.at
5. Australian Tourism Commission: http://www.atc.net.au/
6. Australian Office of National Tourism: http://www.dist.gov.au/tourism/new/ifa_home.html
7. Canadian Tourism Commission: http://206.191.33.50/tourism/ and http://206.191.33.50/tourism/tindu.html
8. Finnish Tourist Board: http://www.mek.fi
9. Hawaii Tourism Office: http://www.hawaii.gov/tourism/index.html
10. Singapore Tourism: http://www.mfasia.com.sg/mfasia/tourism/html/sing.html
11. Tourism Mailbase: http://www.mailbase.ac.uk/lists-p-t/tourism/
12. US Tourism Industries network: http://www.tinet.ita.doc.gov/
13. Wales Tourist Board: http://www.i.visitwales.com
14. World Tourism Organization: http://www.world-tourism.org
15. Information kindly supplied by: Lorenzo, Cintia, World Tourism Organization
    Wöber, Karl, Institute for Tourism and Leisure Studies at Vienna University of Economics and Business Administration

Destination Marketing System Strategies: Refining and Extending an Assessment Framework

Dr Andrew J Frew
Napier University, Edinburgh
a.frew@napier.ac.uk

Peter O'Connor
Groupe ESSEC, IMHI, Paris
oconnor@edu.essec.fr

Abstract

The paper describes an approach to assessing the success of Destination Management System strategies and a range of critical success factors have been extended and modulated through iterative feedback from a variety of systems experts; system developers and operators as well as those involved in academic research and in consultancy work in the area. Key system attributes are examined from the perspectives of database, distribution, operation and management issues and the final format has been ranked and appropriately weighted. This range of factors has then been applied to systems representing Austria, England, Ireland and Scotland with a tentative score being generated for each factor and for each overall system. The results provide a means of rating each system as at presently configured and additionally a similarly rated comparison was generated based on the DMS operator's own future projections. The paper concludes by proposing a broader validation and an extension of the scope of the work.

1 Introduction

The authors have previously examined destination marketing system (DMS) implementation strategies [1] by drawing some broad lessons from a variety of published accounts of strategies and implementations and an assessment framework was developed and tentatively applied to two destinations, Scotland and Ireland. This preliminary investigation was largely based on secondary research, including published literature, in-house documentation and was supplemented by one-to-one interviewing. However, the response to this work, suggested that further primary research was merited and given the provisional nature of the framework it seemed appropriate to reconfigure and validate a more comprehensive approach. In relation to the scope of the systems previously covered, there had been significant activity in each and, it was felt that, with the growing importance of the destination perspective on the field of global electronic distribution, it would be of interest to encompass additional DMS implementation approaches. To this end both England and Austria were included in this new study.

2 First Approach

A series of key issues were identified as being important attributes of any approach and in the previous work this framework was tentatively applied to both the Scottish and Irish situations as shown in table.

Table 1 DMS Implementation Comparison

Implementation Characteristics	Scotland		Ireland	
	Now	Future	Now	Future
Comprehensive Accommodation Database	?	√	√	√
Comprehensive Tourism Supplier Database	x	?	√	√
Data Quality Control Procedures	x	?	√	√
Official Web-site	√	√	√	√
Official Web-site + full supplier representation	x	√	√	√
Official Web-site + on-line booking	x	√	x	√
On-line (national) destination information at TIC, etc.	x	?	√	√
On-line (national) reservations at TIC, etc.	x	?	√	√
Central reservations function	x	x	√	√
Cost-effective supplier data maintenance	x	?	√	√
Property Management Systems interface	x	x	√	√
Global Distributions Systems link	x	?	x	?
Start-up and implementation finance in place	√	?	√	√
Inter-organisational collaboration arrangements in place	?	?	√	?
Private sector migration strategy in place	x	x	√	√
Ongoing stakeholder protection	?	?	√	√
Clear link to promotion/marketing strategy	x	?	√	√
Strategy and resource allocation conflicts resolved	x	?	√	√
Clear project management structure	x	?	√	√
Settled software ownership (IPR) issues	x	?	√	√

This was a crude but useful means of assessment although the initial analysis suffered from a variety of limitations such as excluding consideration of the absolute or relative importance of the attributes. Furthermore, since the application to both the Irish and the Scottish situations was consciously based primarily on published data, it necessarily excluded more recent developments and thus may have presented a somewhat false picture. It was decided to continue the study to address these issues while also broadening the scope to identify other key attributes that should be included in the framework.

Each of the countries chosen for inclusion in this study has been a pioneer in the development of DMS and each is from an economic perspective, highly dependent on tourism with a high percentage of small and medium sized tourism enterprises. These tend not to be members of a chain or group, and thus tend to be less well represented on "traditional" electronic distribution systems.

3 Destinations

3.1 Austria

The Tyrol Information System (TIS) was developed by the Tyrolean Regional Tourist Board with the dual aims of supplying tourist information to the marketplace, and information on trends and markets to local suppliers. The initial system was limited to the Tyrol region, and concentrated on distribution information about accommodation, prices, resort accessibility and leisure amenities, with reservation facilities deliberately not being included. Data was collected and maintained by a large number of local tourist boards, consolidated centrally and then redistributed to each of the users. Distribution channels used included the TICs located throughout the region, through videotext and teletext systems in each of the Tyrol's major markets and over the Web. In 1996, the system was renamed TIScover, and refocused on providing more comprehensive DMS services [2]. The data architecture was changed to Internet based technology, the geographical scope extended to include the other regions of Austria and online booking facilities were developed. Suppliers and tourist boards are now able to update their information using an Extranet, and users may access information and make bookings over the Internet. Overall TIScover http://www.tiscover.com has positioned itself as a core system for marketing and distributing Austria tourism products.

3.2 England

One of the earliest studies on DMS was in England, when in 1968 it was proposed to use surplus capacity on the National Coal Boards mainframe computer to distribute tourism information to tourism centres and travel agents. The general operating principles were virtually the same as many "new" proposals being made over twenty years later [3]. England was again a pioneer with the BRAVO project, which in 1986 tried to bring telecommunications companies, technical suppliers and the travel sector together into a co-operative venture that would allow the tourism sector as a whole to benefit from developments in electronic distribution. The initial BRAVO was envisaged to be a truly national operation, owned and controlled by the industry itself that would act as a facilitator and provide a range of essential technical facilities including access to the major GDS networks. However, although the project was privatised and its scope broadened to include maintaining a database of accommodation suppliers and the processing of reservations, investment and support were inadequate and the company was wound up in 1991. Contemporaneously, the English Tourist Board (ETB) was also working on the development of another related project – the Tourism Resource Information Processing System (TRIPS). This was developed jointly by the British Tourist Authority (BTA), ETB and the regional tourist boards, and was designed to be internally focused [4]. The central database is comprehensive, and is maintained by the ATBs who update it based on information collected manually from tourism suppliers. The system deliberately does not hold availability or process reservations, but does maintain a client database that can be used for database marketing purposes.

Another project, English Tourism Network Automation (ETNA) commenced in 1988 and was collectively developed by the ETB and various Regional Tourist Boards within England to distribute TRIPS information to Tourism Information Centres (TIC). Diffusion of the system has been hindered by the structure of the tourism sector in England, where, with few exceptions, TIC are funded by their respective local authorities and neither managed nor owned by the tourist boards. This "division" has made it difficult to introduce a consistent approach to DMS across the entire region, and inter-organisational difficulties have been cited as one of the major reasons behind DMS failure [5] The current position sees English suppliers having a major representation on the Internet http://www.visitbritain.com via the TRIPS database but as yet this is more of a destination database than a DMS.

3.3 Ireland

DMS development in Ireland began in 1990 with the conception of a system that was to become "the main channel of distribution for information and reservations on all major aspects of tourism in Ireland" [6]. The system was a key part of increased co-operation between Bord Failte - the Irish Tourist Board and the Northern Ireland Tourist Board to market the entire island as a tourism destination. Funding came from a variety of sources, including the national tourist boards, the European union and the International Fund for Ireland. The system maintained a comprehensive database of tourism data, including information on accommodation, events, places of interest, transportation, entertainment and attractions. However, rather than simply being seen as a distribution system, the development of Gulliver was regarded as improving the infrastructure of tourism, making it easier for tourist to book Ireland both at home and abroad. As such, it was seen as being a critical part of the Irish government's plan to increase tourist numbers and also as a key component of the "Tourism Brand Ireland" campaign.

Although the system initially suffered technical difficulties, mainly arising from its mainframe-based hardware configuration, Gulliver was successfully re-engineered into a client server based system in 1993. The resulting increases in performance allowed Gulliver to broaden its range of distribution channels, including the development of its award winning Web site www.ireland.travel.ie. Gulliver has recently been privatised which has allowed the system to begin processing reservations for accommodation and other tourism services. Continued expansion of the system is planned, particularly through the Web, with online booking facilities to be shortly introduced and a variety of product / regional focused web sites being developed, all driven by the Gulliver information and reservations engine.

3.4 Scotland

The first attempt to implement a DMS strategy was in January 1984 with the introduction of Hi-Line. This ran into procedural and technical problems at an early stage as it was under-resourced and the initial platform of dial-up service from dumb terminals proved troublesome. Despite re-structuring, re-financing, a positive response from users and a proposed, but doomed, link to BRAVO, Hi-Line failed in 1992. A wide range of causes was suggested from economic recession to political and inter-organisational difficulties [7]. A brief flirtation with a local system from Orkney (ORKID) came to nothing but in due course led to the next effort - the Area Tourist Board Computerisation Project. This was intended to improve the quality of service to tourists, enhance the effectiveness of the ATB/TIC operation, improve the quality of management information and improve the marketing of tourism. In 1992, the ITIS system from Integra Ltd was proposed for nation-wide adoption as "*the preferred supplier of a proven back and front office TIC system*" [8]. Despite deployment in about half of all ATB, the effort, however, became fragmented, amid claims of project management difficulties, of technological challenges and of concerns over 'proprietary' systems and despite a far from complete implementation of the ITIS in Scotland, another new 'vision' was proposed. The © IDMS (Intelligent Destination Management Systems) based upon an Open Systems approach promised full integration across tourism management functions with an explicit statement that the proposed system would maximise utility from the "*customer's viewpoint first*".

Before development work was even complete, a re-think took place and a new, ambitious DMS programme emerged - the Ossian project. Unlike previous projects, the signs are that Ossian has substantial political and financial support and the system proposes to "*provide an information dissemination system that will be accessible world-wide. It will accommodate access stratification to create virtual communities within the one physical system*" [9]. The core customer is seen as the tourist and the infrastructure designed to "*optimise performance for incoming tourist enquiries*". The system will feature permanent scaleable connections to the Internet with an infrastructure comprising a federation of Area Tourist Board servers. The Ossian architecture and its implications are addressed elsewhere [10], while Scotland's current site is available at http://www.holiday.scotland.net

4 Research Method

The initial step in refining and validating the assessment framework was to enlist an expert panel comprising system developers, owners, managers, operators, academics and consultants. A detailed questionnaire containing a wide range of potential key attributes was presented along with an explanation of the purpose of the study and, for consistency, a definition of terms. Each recipient was asked to comment on each question and to rate the importance of each attribute for the success of a DMS on a five-point scale. An opportunity was also presented to add to the question range or provide other comment on the process. The questionnaire was administered electronically to all recipients except the destination representatives where it was personally administered and supplemented by a one to one structured interviews. Taking due account of non-response factors, and omitting extreme outlier data, the scores for each factor were consolidated and an average calculated. The results produced through the structured interviews could then be treated by passing them through this weighted framework. These interviews provided substantial qualitative data, the treatment of which lies beyond the scope of the present paper. For each core question however, there was in almost all cases a straightforward positive or negative response which was represented by scoring 1 or 0 respectively and for the few cases where the response lay somewhere between, it was allocated the nearest score.

5 Results

5.1 A clear picture?

The weighted ranking of the key characteristics applied to the reponses elicited from the system principals is displayed in Table 2. This data was used to generate a sub-total score for each of the four dimensions examined and a total used to gauge overall DMS success. These are presented in the first section of Table 3. As an exercise to examine the effect of stripping out some of the lowest priority characteristics, all weightings below 3.5 were omitted and the results presented in the second section of Table 3. Finally, all characteristics with a weighting of less than 4.0 were omitted and the outcome presented in the third section of Table 3. It should be emphasised that each respondent was given the opportunity of adding to the list of questions, but no additional characteristics were suggested. This was explored more fully during the structured interview with the DMS representatives and the feedback received was that while some questions could benefit from further refinement, all the core questions were being asked.

The overall picture to emerge on first analysis is readily apparent with Austria and Ireland displaying the characteristics of successfully implemented systems whilst England and Scotland lag some way behind. This accords with the general view of Gulliver and TIScover being well-regarded systems. Removing the characteristics with a weighting below 3.5. does not in fact affect this overall ranking although England and Scotland appear to rate more strongly. This is a consequence of neither destination having scored on any of the four characteristics that were removed and this still places Austria and Ireland at the forefront of current DMS implementation. Interestingly enough, even when the characteristics weighted at less than 4.0 were removed, the relative ranking of each destination remained unchanged.

Table 2 Extended DMS Implementation Comparison

Implementation Characteristics	weighting	Austria	England	Ireland	Scotland
DATABASE ISSUES					
A comprehensive accommodation database?	4.90	1	1	1	1
A comprehensive database of tourism suppliers?	4.30	1	1	1	0
Explicit data quality control procedures in place for the database(s)?	4.40	1	1	1	1
Cost-effective data maintenance procedures in place?	4.10	1	1	1	0
DISTRIBUTION ISSUES					
Destination database information available at the destination?	4.67	1	1	1	1
On-line booking available at the destination?	4.70	1	0	1	1
An official destination web-site?	4.60	1	1	1	1
An official destination web-site with full accommodation data?	4.50	1	1	1	1
An official destination web-site with full tourism supplier data?	4.10	1	1	1	0
An official destination web-site with on-line availability?	4.50	1	0	0	0
An official destination web-site with on-line booking?	3.80	1	0	0	0
MANAGEMENT ISSUES					
Are the development IPR issues clearly resolved?	3.86	1	1	1	1
A clear project management structure?	4.13	1	1	1	1
Resource provision and strategy conflicts resolved?	3.75	1	0	1	0
Issues regarding ongoing stakeholder protection resolved?	3.38	1	0	1	0
A private sector migration strategy under consideration or in place?	3.43	1	0	1	0
Inter-organisational collaboration arrangements been put in place?	3.71	1	0	1	1
Start-up and implementation finance been secured?	4.00	1	0	1	1
OPERATIONAL ISSUES					
A single central reservations function at the destination?	4.25	1	0	1	1
An automated availability update for all suppliers?	4.50	0	0	1	1
Does the DMS offer PMS interfacing?	3.13	0	0	1	0
A link between the DMS and any GDS, uni or bi-directional?	3.38	1	0	0	0
Monitoring and evaluation procedures in place for systems?	4.00	1	0	1	1
Monitoring and evaluation procedures in place for assessing impact?	3.75	0	1	1	1
Are there training programmes in place for operators?	4.38	1	1	1	1
Statistics gathered to inform the overall tourism impact picture?	4.00	0	1	1	0

Taking the views and plans of the DMS representatives into consideration and treating these through the assessment framework allowed some forward projection. If these anticipated developments unfold as envisaged, the position changes significantly with the relative position of the Scottish DMS improving to the front rank and, while Ireland also shows a projected absolute improvement, neither the Austrian nor the English situations have changed. If the Ossian project indeed develops as indicated, then it appears that Scotland could well produce a successful DMS after 15 years of effort.

Table 3 Current and Projected Cross-Comparison of DMS Approaches

Implementation Characteristics (weighted scores)	Austria	England	Ireland	Scotland
Database issues	17.70	17.70	17.70	9.30
Distribution issues	30.87	17.87	22.57	18.47
Management issues	26.25	7.98	26.25	15.70
Operational issues	16.00	12.13	28.00	20.88
Overall system score	**90.82**	**55.67**	**94.52**	**64.34**
Projected system score 1999	90.82	55.67	102.82	103.07
Re-weighted total scores 3.5+				
Overall system score	**80.64**	**55.67**	**84.59**	**64.34**
Projected system score 1999	80.64	55.67	92.89	92.89
Re-weighted total scores 4.0+				
Overall system score	**65.52**	**48.07**	**69.52**	**53.02**
Projected system score 1999	65.52	48.07	74.02	74.02

5.2 What is wrong with this picture?

In some regards very little since the proposed core characteristics do indeed seem to provide results which reflect informed opinion, removing two tiers of those less heavily weighted revealed the strength of this core. However, there remains a difficult underlying issue referred to in the earlier work, that of DMS definition [1]. There may be substantial agreement amongst experts on DMS characteristics but this does not mean we are examining the same model in each destination. This fact becomes especially important since in presenting a measure of DMS success, the mission and intentions of those charged with DMS implementation should be kept firmly in view. An approach to assessing DMS success is offered *not* a means of measuring each project's success against its aims and objectives.

A consequence of this may be seen on closer examination of the results. The gap separating each destination's performance narrows significantly when only the most heavily weighted characteristics are considered and furthermore, in projection, Austria and England appear to remain static. This should not be taken to imply complacency, in fact research revealed that each was highly active. The truth is that many development plans fall outwith the core characteristics, reflecting these individual models and strategies. For example, among other things, England are pursuing links to third party reservations providers while Austria are actively developing broadcast and interactive TV possibilities, neither of which will affect their rating.

6 Conclusions and Future Work

Although it is clear that we are beginning to see defining features of DMS, two aspects of the current methodology require development. Firstly, the questionnaire addressing core characteristics, despite some iteration, is a largely passive response tool and the authors feel that confidence in the weighting would benefit from being challenged by adding a more interactive element such as a focus group workshop. And secondly, the questions addressed through personal interview while providing a sound foundation, would yield a more subtle differentiation if modified to give a more detailed measure than a simple dipolar response. Following from this, degrees, or levels of implementation, standards and so forth would provide a finer insight into the characteristics. Nevertheless it is felt that the above framework does indeed provide a good first measure of DMS implementation success. In terms of extending the scope of the work, the intention is to address the methodology issues above by reiterating the overall process and the research constituency will again be enlarged to encompass additional destinations. As a final observation, which will also guide future work in this area, it is evident that while DMS strategies vary across destinations, a central feature is their application is in support of the destination marketing effort. It is further apparent that their web presence is of increasing importance and this raises the key question of effectiveness. Thus, Gulliver may be widely regarded as successful at offering and managing information but is it successful in conversion terms? The authors have begun to examine means of closing this loop and in particular have adapted some recent work on measuring web effectiveness [11] for application to DMS endeavours. Future work should therefore lead to the prospect of not only demonstrating the *implementation* success of a range of DMS but also assessing impact performance.

References

1. Frew A.J, and O'Connor, P., "A Comparative Examination of the Implementation of Destination Marketing System Strategies: Scotland and Ireland, " Information and Communication Technologies in Tourism, Springer-Verlag (1998).
2. Proll, B, Retschitzegger, W, Kroi, P & Wagner, R "Online Booking On The Net – Problems, Issues and Solutions", Information and Communications Technologies In Tourism, Proceedings of the ENTER Conference, Istanbul, Springer, New York (1998)
3. Archdale, G, Stanton, R & Jones, C "Destination Databases: Issues and Priorities", Pacific Asia Travel Association, San Francisco. (1992)
4. Scarfe, D "The role of NTO's in Advancing Technology, Information for Travel & Tourism Marketing: a Tool for Profit", A Conference held in Vancouver, British Columbia, February, Pacific Asia Travel Association, p 88 – 94. (1994)
5. Mutch, A., "The English Tourist Network Automation project: a case study in inter-organisational system failure", Tourism Management, Vol. 17, No 8, 603-609 (1996)
6. O'Connor, P., and Rafferty, J., "Gulliver – Distributing Irish Tourism Electronically", Electronic Markets, Volume 7 No 2. (1996)
7. Pringle, S.M., "International Reservations Systems - Their Strategic and Operational Implications for the UK Hotel Industry", PhD Thesis, Napier University.(1995)
8. Pollock, A., "Planning for the Digital Economy - An implementation plan for Scotland's tourism industry", The Strategy Group, a report to Scottish Tourist Board and Area Tourist Boards, Nov.(1996)
9. Wallum, B., Project Ossian Outline Plan, STB Internal Document, 1998.
10. Frew, A.J., "Ossian, Destination Distribution and Global Networks", Proceedings of the Hospitality Information Technology Association Conference, Los Angeles, June 1998.
11. Pitt L, Berthon, P and Watson, R, "Marketing on the World Wide Web", Journal of General Management, vol22 No1, Autumn 1996, pp1